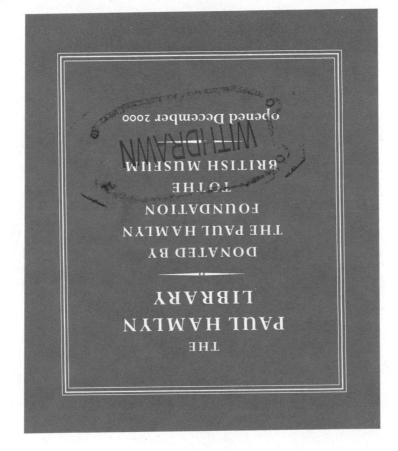

THE COLLECTED LETTERS OF
KATHERINE MANSFIELD

VOLUME FOUR

1920–1921

Photograph of Katherine Mansfield taken in Menton, France in 1921

THE COLLECTED
LETTERS OF

KATHERINE MANSFIELD

EDITED BY

VINCENT O'SULLIVAN

AND

MARGARET SCOTT

VOLUME FOUR

1920–1921

CLARENDON PRESS · OXFORD

1996

Oxford University Press, Walton Street, Oxford OX2 6DP

Oxford New York

Athens Auckland Bangkok Bombay
Calcutta Cape Town Dar es Salaam Delhi
Florence Hong Kong Istanbul Karachi
Kuala Lumpur Madras Madrid Melbourne
Mexico City Nairobi Paris Singapore
Taipei Tokyo Toronto

and associated companies in
Berlin Ibadan

Oxford is a trade mark of Oxford University Press

Published in the United States
by Oxford University Press Inc., New York

British Library Cataloguing in Publication Data
Data available

Library of Congress Cataloging in Publication Data
(Revised for vol. 4)
Mansfield, Katherine, 1888–1923.
The collected letters of Katherine Mansfield.
Vol. 4: Oxford [Oxfordshire]: Clarendon Press;
New York: Oxford University Press.
Includes bibliographical references and indexes.
Contents: v. 1. 1903–1917—v. 2. 1918–1919.
1. Mansfield, Katherine, 1888–1923—Correspondence.
2. Authors, New Zealand—20th century—Correspondence.
I. O'Sullivan, Vincent.   II. Scott, Margaret, 1928– .
III. Title.
PR9639.3.M258Z48   1984   823'.912   83–12189
ISBN 0–19–818532–4

1 3 5 7 9 10 8 6 4 2

Typeset by Hope Services (Abingdon) Ltd
Printed in Great Britain
on acid-free paper by
Biddles Ltd.,
Guildford & King's Lynn

CONTENTS

The eighteen months of Mansfield's life taken in by this volume—from her return from France to England in the spring of 1920, to her impending decision in the Swiss Alps at the end of the next year to go it alone, to 'risk everything' both medically and emotionally—cover as well the most important time in her life as a writer. Most of the stories she is known for were written in the Villa Isola Bella at Menton or the Chalet des Sapins, near Sierre. From 'The Daughters of the Late Colonel' and 'Miss Brill' to 'At the Bay' and 'The Garden Party', these two distressing but sustained periods of work brought her to maturity as one of the shapers of modern fiction.

Yet in her own insistent reservations about her work, in her confession that 'As I write I falsify slightly' (to Murry, 31 October 1920), there is her increasing conviction that there is an intimacy between the business of writing and the business of shedding what she thought of as 'false selves'. To examine things closely, to push through to a necessary honesty, to do justice to her craft, converge as the dominant theme of this volume, whether her immediate concern is what writing should achieve, or what living and thinking as a woman should mean. It is a troublesome and currently unfashionable stance, this running of aesthetics and morality so deliberately along the same tracks. Yet *not* to do so would have struck Mansfield as a kind of intellectual evasiveness. Lawrence, at least, would have understood that. At a time when she had good reason to resent him, and held strong reservations about his recent fiction, she believed that 'What makes Lawrence a *real* writer is his passion' (to Dorothy Brett, 29 August 1921). Much of the passion of these letters, the fascination beyond their engaging flair, is the almost daily drama of Mansfield's determination to reshape and refine herself as much as her prose, in her belief that these are not matters to be engaged in separately. The reader who arrives from the three earlier volumes of Mansfield's correspondence may be struck by a certain sense of *déjà vu*. As English spring moves into summer, and plans are made to move to the south of France as autumn approaches, there emerges what by now is not a repetition so much as a hardened pattern. Her health lapses from assumed improvement into a new turn for the worse. There is the familiar track of her responses to where she is. That first novelty of being back home, the pleasures of her own room and her own possessions, yet the pleasure too in leaving them again within months, in the raised hopes that accompany her departures. This will flare again as she leaves Menton the next May, and prepares to leave Sierre at the end of 1921. By then, however, a subtle change has taken place in her expectations. A physical cure is now only part of what she looks for. There is a new 'spiritual' insistence that is both elusive and resolute.

Ill as Mansfield was during the period of this volume—Dr Bouchage's medical report in May 1921 and her own letter to Dr Sorapure soon after make very clear what she endured—and however much immediacy seems to let her down, the charm of personality does not diminish in these letters. It is a charm touched often enough with the feeling that personal relations are a knife-edge affair. Hasn't it been heard so often, this delight at being back with her husband, the anticipations of their time together, yet her refusal to concede to anyone else just how important he is to her? And so again those broad hints of discontent, the tart condescensions, as she speaks of him to her latest friends from the Riviera, the wealthy man-of-letters and novelist 'Stephen Hudson' and his wife Violet Schiff. That tendency to undermine, that fear, as it seems, to 'let on' how much others matter to her, gathers as the volume proceeds. It is as if whoever is brought into the circle of her intimacy must inevitably come in for a drubbing to someone else's confiding ear. Well before the year is out, the Schiffs, so flattered for their Proustian sensitivity to the artistic life, will be scorned for self-importance, for presuming to tell *her*, Mrs Middleton Murry, that T. S. Eliot is the up-and-coming critic. Once back in France, she will encourage her cousin Sydney Waterlow to confide as much as he feels inclined—isn't friendship, after all, so rich and precious a thing? Yet to Ottoline Morrell there will be the casually dropped aside that Waterlow, surely, presumes an intimacy to which he has no right, just as there will be impatience with Dorothy Brett for her insensitivity, for assuming a jaunty matiness, even though some of Mansfield's warmest and most buoyant letters are in fact to Brett. Having received such confidences, Ottoline—as often before— is regretted for her trying ways. Virginia Woolf is quietly dropped.

Although she writes with affection to Murry's younger brother, Richard, the few letters to her own sisters never move far beyond fey pieces of sibling manœuvring or claims that only with *them* is there so much to remember; and remembering, she reminds them, is Katherine's especial game. But those letters are shot through with the small boasts, the dashes of envy, that are set more intricately in Mansfield's projection of herself as Kezia in 'At the Bay' or 'The Doll's House'. There it is she who is indisputably the perceptive one among the sisters, the unsnobbish one, the child to whom readers naturally respond. If only Father could be won round so easily. The long letter of apology and fear and ingratiation that she wrote him in November 1921 moves in the psychological patterns of the child who still believes that he is the centre of the world. As she had told Murry seven years before, 'I feel towards my Pa man like a little girl. I want to jump and stand on his chest and say "you've *got* to love me". When he does, I feel quite confident that God is on my side' (May 1913). The Stanley Burnell of her stories is a deft yoking of homage and revenge. So pompous and secretly fearful, so demanding of a filial devotion he never quite receives, he stands squarely in the shoes of Harold Beauchamp, whose parental love was never given in the quantity his daughter craved.

Only with Ida Baker, perhaps, is there ever total directness, although that directness by no means precludes manipulation. In ties going so much further back than those with Murry, there is the play of a complex dependence. Mansfield frequently puzzled in her notebooks at how this friendship, at times apparently so repellent, could also be so necessary and indeed rewarding. Now, as much as ten years before, Mansfield found Ida gauche, cumbersome, infuriating. At times it may seem almost pathological, this desire of one woman to serve to the point of abasement and the irritation of the other that such service must be accepted. Yet from the comparatively few letters between the two that survive— Ida obediently destroyed a huge number when Mansfield gave the command—it is clear that no other shared the daily details of her life as did her old schoolfriend and minder. There was no one else she confided in, with such glee, on Murry's behaviour and weaknesses, no one so dependable. And when the chips were down, Mansfield would make it very clear how she valued that awkward friendship, and on what terms. When the 32-year-old spinster makes a mild bid for independence, she is reprimanded for being a flirt, and her services again corralled. But there is no reason to question the affection behind the seductive play, any more than the power.

I am not going to flirt back, Miss & say how I want you as part of my life and cant really imagine being without you. The ties that bind us! Heavens, they are so strong that youd bleed to death if you really cut away. But *don't*. Oh please dont make me have to protest. Accept! Take your place! Be my friend! Don't pay me out for what has been. (20 August 1921)

But how straightforward any of Mansfield's other correspondence seems when placed against the bulk of her letters to Murry. It is there that one traces the rapid currents and veerings, that web of entanglements and misunderstandings, as well as confidences and affection, within the encompassing and sustained seriousness of their love. 'Bogey and I have chosen each other for lovers in this world, and I believe absolutely in our choice' (6 October 1920). A few weeks later, she writes of 'the final realisation that Life for me was intimacy with you. Other things attend this' (31 October 1920). However genuine her individual declarations may be, and her pleas for utter honesty between Murry and herself, there is also a manipulative calling of shots.

Another point of view might insist that it is hardly our brief to sit in judgement on relationships that fortuitously survive on paper, but are themselves long since buried. Isn't it the text, after all, rather than any putative claim on 'reality', that ought now to concern us? The fact is, of course, that few readers approach published letters in that way, or are convinced that they should. Whether with Byron or Virginia Woolf or Philip Larkin, the moment their correspondence is embarked on, so too is their emotional as much as their intellectual milieu, their particular network of tastes and approvals, preferences and errors. The moral dilemmas of that fact may be various, but readers do not suspend the values brought to bear on the rest of their lives.

A related and touchier problem confronted Murry when he prepared his wife's letters to himself for publication, and ran into the awkwardness of warning old friends that what she said of them was not always kind. Yet how to say that she remained, none the less, a 'friend'? His explanation is simple and humane. As he wrote to Violet Schiff:

The truth (as I see it now, when I am old and fairly detached) is that K. had an inveterate tendency to extremes. When she was disappointed in me, she worked herself into a slightly extravagant enthusiasm for others, which she would subsequently (and as extravagantly) disown. Though I think the phthisis greatly increased this tendency, it was there in her from the beginning: and she was fairly well aware of it. But not until she took the final 'leap in the dark' of going to Fontainebleau, did she make a determined effort to conquer it.

. . . I came across a tiny, almost venial example – but a striking one, in its way, of this 'variation' of Katherine's. At the end of April 1921 she wrote to you and Sydney: 'I hope you'll read my story in the Mercury. It's not pride that makes me say that. It's only that you and Sydney are my true readers in such a *special* sense. I don't care a farthing for what the others may think.' . . . On May 9 she wrote to me, 'Tell me if anyone says they like it, will you? That's not vanity . . .. Tommy [H. M. Tomlinson] and De La Mare are the people I'd *like* to please.' I don't pretend entirely to understand this trait in her. But it's ineluctably true that she tended to assume a personality to please her correspondent. I suppose we all do, to some degree. But in her it was very pronounced: and because it was very pronounced, her reaction from it was equally pronounced. (21 December 1948, BL)

Murry's explanation may not be the whole story, but what it suggests is convincing. He was right too in noting that Mansfield was aware of this in herself, and that she came to regard flaws in her personality as spiritual impediments. It did not, though, take until Fontainebleau for her to tackle these head on. Several of the letters in this volume, as well as notebook entries made during the same period, reveal that along with her health, her writing, and her relationship with Murry, she was preoccupied with this need to 'reshape' herself.

Mansfield seldom spoke of her stories except in passing, in occasional exchanges with Dorothy Brett and young Richard Murry, who was hoping to be a painter, or in an almost offhand way with other friends. T. S. Eliot could detect in them no critical method, no considered stance.[1] Certainly one will not glean from her letters anything approach-

---

[1] See T. O. Beachcroft, *A Survey of the Short Story in English* (1968), p. 174.

ing what Eliot so missed. She may explain that she chooses each sentence with an ear to its rhythmic effect, or mention that she 'identifies' with her characters. More common are her reservations about her own work. As she waits for *Bliss, and Other Stories* to go through the press, she judges a 'great part' of that collection 'trivial' (to Murry, 25 September 1920). When she speaks directly of her writing, there is none of the arch celebration of artists that she indulges in with the Schiffs, none of that slightly fluttering 'joy in life' that Ottoline Morrell is treated to. In that same disclaiming letter to Murry, she draws together her declining health, her writing, and her sense of moral imperative, as she states her simple conviction with a pointed reference to her Russian master: 'You see its too late to beat about the bush any longer. They are cutting down the cherry trees; the orchard is sold—that is really the atmosphere I want.'

'The Young Girl', the first of the stories she wrote after her return to Menton, immediately attempted that. Set in the drifting, comfortable ambience of tourists in Monte Carlo, it also moves where Mansfield was already at ease, in the superficially confident 'poise' of a young girl on the verge of maturity: 'her white throat—all her soft young body in the blue dress—was like a flower that is just emerging from its dark bud.' But adult life is already challenged by a hovering apprehension which shadows that apparent promise. 'The Singing Lesson', the story which follows it, offers apprehension writ large, and in details so much closer to home— the dependence of a woman's emotions on a man's letters and telegrams. In 'The Stranger', the Wellington businessman and *pater familias* of so many of her stories, is brushed by jealousy and death, inseparably linked; the 'flicker and fall' of a fire in a hotel bedroom is both echo and parallel to how intimacies flare and falter. By contrast, in that mangy fox-fur stuffed back in its box at the end of 'Miss Brill' with its imagined faint cry, there is the furthest remove of a woman's life from that of the young girl, waiting and expectant, on the steps of the casino. Between those stories there is the sharp narrative of 'Poison', which Murry disliked so much that he discouraged his wife from publishing it. On the Riviera, in a house which shares the features of the Villa Isola Bella, a woman and her younger lover play out the subtle moves towards separation. Written in November 1920, during those months when Mansfield's letters carry such an undercurrent of disquiet in her own marriage, her character Beatrice speaks of a crime that fascinates the public:

'Guilt' she cried, 'Guilt! . . . They're fascinated like sick people are fascinated by anything – any scrap of news about their own case. The man in the dock may be innocent enough, but the people in the court are nearly all of them poisoners. Haven't you ever thought' – she was pale with excitement – 'of the amount of poisoning that goes on. It's the exception to find married people who don't poison each other – married people and lovers.'

Mansfield's stories are too sophisticated, too intricate in their relationships, to be read as one-to-one commentaries on her own states of mind or the tides of her own feelings. But what might reasonably be called their Chekhovian note of evening coming on, of plangency and indecisiveness and impending loss—the selling of the cherry trees—inescapably edges fiction and biography towards obviously shared concerns.

There is a paradoxical turn to Manfield's thinking, once she is settled back in Menton, and pushing on with these and other stories. There is the insistence that one needs to live immediately, an existential drive to locate one's being, to derive one's values, from the present and its contingencies. 'There is only TODAY' (to Murry, 1 October 1920). On the other hand, she saw her writing as the means to circumvent the *Angst* of too vivid an attention to the present. 'The only way to exist is to go on—and try and lose oneself—to get as far as possible away from *this* moment. . . . So its stories or nothing' (to Murry, 28 September 1920). Either way—the demand for total immersion or the use of fiction as the evasion of time—the hoped-for result was much the same: contingency became less pressing, the disparate was brought under control. Her bid was for something larger, something less debilitating, than those swings of mood she ascribed variously to her temper, her health, her opium-based medication, or the strains of Ida's presence or Murry's absence. '*Whatever* my feelings are I am *not* justified in giving way to them before you or in letting you see even the shadow of the border of that shadowy country that we exiles from health inhabit' (to Murry, 4 October 1920).

Conrad Aiken, writing fiction but with the intention of catching Mansfield as directly as he could, picked up what seemed so defining and febrile to those who met her at about this time:

There was something gingerly about her self-control; and also something profoundly terrifying. It seemed to me that I had never met anyone whose hold on life was so terribly *conscious.* . . . And to sit with her, to watch the intense restraint of all her gestures and expressions, and above all to listen to the feverish controlledness with which she spoke, was at once to share in this curious attitude to life. (See n. 3, letter to Aiken, 24 October 1921)

That effort toward austere control rapidly broke down when Mansfield had to face Murry's interest in other women. Although she insisted on his freedom, she was distressed by his decent if bumbling attempt to be straight with her in December 1920. But the entries in her notebook are charged with a larger fear and a broader concern than her husband's mild admissions. Her own long self-styled 'confession' on 19 December (quoted in full in n. 1, telegram of 15 December) pushes beyond the distress of her suspicions towards an 'attitude' to life. Her new insistence on submission—on not fighting circumstances but absorbing them, on locating victory in acceptance—may draw on the Eastern mysticism she had recently discussed with a friend in England, on her revered Chekhov's refusal to hold out conventional expectations, or even on a vein of quietism that she may have picked up first in her schooldays, in Wilde's debt to Tchuang Tzu, or have come upon more recently in Arthur Waley's translations from the Chinese, which she very much admired. Certainly she was influenced, as well as moved, by R. O. Prowse's novel *A Gift of the Dusk*, which she reviewed under the title 'The Silence is Broken' soon after she returned to Menton. She responded at once to this account of a tubercular patient in a Swiss sanatorium, although biographers have not followed up how she took into her own vocabulary and her own way of thinking about her illness notions she encountered in Prowse. As she wrote in her review, 'It is not easy to be heroic in such circumstances; it is infinitely harder to remain true to one's secret self—to one's vision, or dream. But Stephen succeeds; he discovers how to bear the "silence"'; it is to surrender to it.' And in speaking of Prowse's central character, she raises a question prompted as much by experience as by the book under review: 'What is the present when the future is removed, when life is haunted, not by Death in the fullness of time, but by Death's fast-encroaching shadow?' (*Athenaeum*, 29 October 1920).

She copied a related sentence from the novel into her notebook—'That constant taking of leave which has haunted my secret thought' (*Journal* 1954, 244). Early in the New Year she copied sections from Keats's last letters. Although she insisted on a compact with Murry not to discuss her health when it could be avoided—the stoicism of her letters is one of their qualities—her private jottings reflect no such inhibitions. 'Why am I haunted every single day of my life by the nearness of death and its inevitability?' I am really diseased on that point?' (*Journal* 1954, 271–2). Her long, previously unpublished letter to Dr Sorapure in May 1921 makes clear what physical rigours her daily life entailed.

The recurrence of the thought of death, the importance of being straight with herself in what time there was, brings a new tone to Mansfield's notebooks, a kind of laicized spiritual exercise as she sets herself new ideals, and records her falling short of them. 'My temper is bad; my personal habits are not above reproach; I am ungracious—mentally untidy.' Ten months later she finds herself 'dissipated, vague, not *positive*, and above all, above everything, not working as I should be working—wasting time (*Journal* 1954, 240, 270). Almost as if she is undergoing a stringent novitiate, she thanks Koteliansky for pointing out her faults and agrees with Conrad Aiken that some of her stories, indeed, are mercuricious. In an enigmatic unposted letter to an unnamed correspondent early in 1921 (see p. 170), she quite specifically imposes this urge to moral regeneration on the stories she would like to write. 'You see—to me—life and work are two things indivisible. It's only by being true to life that I can be true to art. And to be true to life is to be good, sincere, simple, honest.'

As Antony Alpers suggests, it may have been Mansfield's reading of *Women in Love*, and what she took to be its falsifications, that was part of her drive to write about family love in 'At the Bay'. This was her major work in the eight months she spent in Switzerland after leaving Menton in May 1921. Some of her stories during this intensive period of fiction writing were tailored to the specific editorial demands of the *Sphere*. She was not satisfied even with the best of them. But she was paid ten guineas for each, and already she had in mind the expensive, and medically useless, treatment she would take in Paris the following year. At least in 'At the Bay' she was writing at what she knew was her best, shaping a testament to values she admired, to the childhood memories of Wellington she was strongly drawn back to, a past where simplicity and sincerity were demonstrably rooted. (Her other major biographer, Claire Tomalin, reads that story as continuing the motif of *unhappy* families, however much Mansfield herself thought it a celebration.) Other stories from Switzerland variously ring the changes on those configurations so evident in what she wrote at Menton—the 'beautiful flying wheel' of immediate experience, as she calls it in 'Her First Ball', with the brilliance of the colours, the 'melting, ravishing tune' counterpointed by that other sombre note of impending loss, the presence even of death, which as the end of 'The Garden Party' puts it, is both 'awful' and 'simply marvellous'. And in 'Six Years After' she takes up a favourite image, with its implication of life as performance, and the theatricality of any termination: 'But softly without a sound the dark curtain has rolled down. There is no more to come. That is the end of the play. But it can't end like that—so suddenly.' A few months earlier, she had remarked to Ottoline Morrell, 'How strange talking is—what mists rise and fall—how one loses the other & then thinks to have found the other—then down comes another soft final curtain . . . But it is incredible, don't you feel, how mysterious and isolated we each of us are—at the last' (24 July 1921). Written at much the same time as 'At the Bay', the enigmatic and unfinished 'A Married Man's Story' returns to the motif of domestic poisoning with a kind of hallucinatory wilfulness, a bitter reversal of so much that is proposed in the more famous story.

If often in the stories, as in so many of the letters, there are traces of a dread subdued only with difficulty, it is in those moves Mansfield makes towards balance and control, towards redemptive memory and unflinching honesty, that one looks for its containment. The larger interest of her correspondence of this period, one that goes beyond its sustained intelligence and constant vivacity, is that increasing sense of *effort* to get things straight, to arrive at some stance that is not expected to improve anything, but makes sense of the inevitable. To confront directly is to absorb; it is to accept that what is happening is actually oneself, and not simply what is being done to one. Mansfield's increasing talk of simplicity and acceptance, control and freedom, tends towards that point. A few days after her thirty-second birthday, she finds a vivid image for what later in the century will be known as 'existential dread': 'The little boat enters the dark fearful gulf and our only cry is to escape—"put me on land again". But its useless. Nobody listens. The shadowy figure rows on. One ought to sit still and uncover ones eyes (to Murry, 18 October 1920).

It is a pity that Murry's later version of his wife's last years became such a mawkish fabrication. He set her up as a kind of secular Thérèse of Lisieux—an attempt, as Lytton Strachey delighted in pointing out, so obviously undone by a rather too nasty tongue. That constructed spiritual savante, burning ever more purely towards the end, is much less interesting than the woman these letters reveal. The story—now that these often daily missives can be read with something like complete-ness—is one of emotional distress and confusion, a record of disappointments working against small successes, and the sheer persistence of hard work and artistic effort. Long, difficult habits of personality are being directly confronted, and there is a temperament sharply acknowl-edging its own fastidiousness, its limiting commitment to nuance and the fleeting glimpse. It is a story of very considerable courage, against increasingly adverse odds. But despite all this, in a prose of such preci-sion and directness, intelligence and wit, observation and actual fun, that delight remains the letters' final effect. By the volume's end, this is insep-arable from Mansfield's largest claim: 'I am afraid of NOTHING. I mean that' (c. 10 December 1920).

VINCENT O'SULLIVAN

TEXTUAL NOTE

The text attempts to reproduce what Mansfield wrote as accurately as possible. There has been occasional editorial intervention in providing full stops when this omission was clearly inadvertent; in regularizing single and double inverted commas when these were omitted or mismatched; and in silently emending the very few obvious slips of the pen. When a word or phrase finally resisted attempts to read it, the word 'illegible' appears in italics, within square brackets. When a phrase has been crossed out, the deleted words are enclosed in angle brackets. Any words supplied by way of clarification are in square brackets.

Mansfield's emphases have been rendered in the conventional manner, with words underlined once printed in italics, those underlined twice in small capitals, and further underlinings printed as in the manuscript. The sketches with which she occasionally adorned her letters have been reproduced as they occur in the manuscripts. When these were too small to reproduce, or the originals were not available, they have been briefly described.

When Mansfield did not herself date a letter or provide an address, the date supplied is enclosed in square brackets; where the date is uncertain or approximate it is preceded by a query or the conventional '*c.*' for *circa*. Complimentary closures have been standardized, with vertical rules indicating line breaks. Where Mansfield sometimes drew a line between paragraphs or sections of a letter a printed rule has been used.

Because of the difficulty of KM's handwriting the typed transcriptions in the Huntington Library of her letters to Elizabeth, Countess Russell, which do not otherwise survive, contain many gaps and misreadings. However, half a dozen of these letters had already been transcribed, in part at least, by Murry for inclusion in *LKM* II, and from these versions it has been possible to fill some of the gaps and correct some of the errors of the Huntington transcripts. This has been done with the Huntington Library's permission, and each word so supplied or altered is marked with an asterisk.

Important literary figures and personal friends already identified and noted in volumes I–III have not been annotated again in this volume.

ACKNOWLEDGEMENTS

The editors are obliged to the various institutions and private owners listed under 'Manuscript Sources', who have allowed the use of original letters or transcriptions of letters in their possession.

All unpublished material by Katherine Mansfield and John Middleton Murry is copyright by the respective Estates of Katherine Mansfield and John Middleton Murry, and appears here by permission of the copyright owners. Thanks are due to the Murry family, especially Mr Colin Middleton Murry, for their kind support of this edition, and to Messrs Constable and Co. for allowing quotations from C. A. Hankin's selection, *The Letters of John Middleton Murry to Katherine Mansfield* (1983). Published material (such as the text of the *Journal of Katherine Mansfield*) has been corrected against the manuscripts.

Once again, the editors are indebted to Mansfield's senior biographer, Antony Alpers, and her bibliographer, Brownlee Kirkpatrick, for unstinted generosity. They are grateful also to Gillian Boddy, Paul Millar, Elizabeth Marsden, Irene Zohrab and Roger Robinson, and to Dunstan Ward, in Paris, for medical as well as literary information.

In this volume, as in previous volumes, the transcriptions of the letters were made by Margaret Scott. Vincent O'Sullivan is responsible for all annotations, dating, and other editorial aspects of the edition.

The reader is referred to Volume I for a Chronology of Mansfield's life (1888–1923).

VINCENT O'SULLIVAN
MARGARET SCOTT

Wellington
April 1995

LIST OF ABBREVIATIONS AND MANUSCRIPT SOURCES

KM = Katherine Mansfield

The following abbreviations and short forms are used in the description and provenance given at the foot of each letter:

MS	autograph original
TS	typescript original
draft	autograph draft
MSC	handwritten copy of original
PC	photocopy
TC	typed copy

MANUSCRIPT SOURCES

Institutions

ATL	Alexander Turnbull Library, Wellington
Berg	The Henry W. and Albert A. Berg Collection, New York Public Library, Astor, Lenox and Tilden Foundation
Birmingham	Birmingham University
BL	British Library
Huntington	The Huntington Library, Pasadena, California
Menton	Municipality of Menton
Newberry	The Newberry Library, Chicago
Stanford	Stanford University, Stanford, California
Sussex	University of Sussex, Brighton
Texas	The Humanities Research Centre, University of Texas at Austin
Witwatersrand	University of Witwatersrand, South Africa

Private owners

Bell	Andrew Bell Estate
Cains	Mr Geoffrey Cains, Mittagong, Australia
C. Murry	Colin Middleton Murry
R. Murry	Richard Murry Estate
Parker	Mrs Henry McBurney Parker
Spiro	Mr and Mrs H. Spiro
Targ	Mr W. Targ

SOURCES OF PREVIOUS PUBLICATION
and short forms used in the annotation

Adam 300	*Adam International Review*, no. 300 (1963–5)
Adam 370–5	*Adam International Review*, nos. 370–375 (1972–3)

Alpers 1980	*The Life of Katherine Mansfield* (1980)
Bibliography	*A Bibliography of Katherine Mansfield*, by B. J. Kirkpatrick (1989)
CLKM I	*The Collected Letters of Katherine Mansfield*, ed. Vincent O'Sullivan and Margaret Scott, vol. I (Oxford, 1984)
CLKM II	*The Collected Letters of Katherine Mansfield*, ed. Vincent O'Sullivan and Margaret Scott, vol. II (Oxford, 1987)
CLKM III	*The Collected Letters of Katherine Mansfield*, ed. Vincent O'Sullivan and Margaret Scott, vol. III (Oxford, 1992)
Dickinson	John W. Dickinson, 'Katherine Mansfield and S. S. Koteliansky: Some Unpublished Letters', *Revue de littérature comparée*, no. 45 (1971), 79-99
Exhibition	*Katherine Mansfield: An Exhibition*, Humanities Research Center, University of Texas (Austin, Texas, 1973)
Journal 1954	*Journal of Katherine Mansfield*, Definitive Edition, ed. John Middleton Murry (1954)
LJMM	*Katherine Mansfield's Letters to John Middleton Murry, 1913-1922*, ed. John Middleton Murry (1951)
LKM	*The Letters of Katherine Mansfield*, 2 vols., ed. John Middleton Murry (1928)
Mairet	Philip Mairet, *A. R. Orage, a Memoir* (1936)
Meyers	Jeffrey Meyers, *Katherine Mansfield, a Biography* (1978)
MLM	Ida Baker, *Katherine Mansfield: The Memories of LM* (1971)
Murry	*The Letters of John Middleton Murry to Katherine Mansfield*, ed. C. A. Hankin (1983)
Poems	*Poems of Katherine Mansfield*, ed. Vincent O'Sullivan (Oxford, 1988)
Scrapbook	*The Scrapbook of Katherine Mansfield*, ed. J. M. M. (1939)
Selected	*The Selected Letters of Katherine Mansfield*, ed. Vincent O'Sullivan (Oxford, 1990)
Stories	*The Stories of Katherine Mansfield*, Definitive Edition, ed. Antony Alpers (1984)
Usborne	Karen Usborne, *'Elizabeth': the Author of Elizabeth and her German Garden* (1986)

The place of publication is London unless otherwise noted.

I

ENGLAND – LONDON:
MAY–AUGUST 1920

When she returned to Hampstead at the end of April, KM had spent eight months in Italy and France – five at Ospedaletti, three in Menton – longing, as she told Murry, 'for the time when we shall be together,' all the year round.' (*CLKM* III, 277). As so often before, she hoped that when they were together in their own home, her health would improve almost as a matter of course. She was realistic enough, however, to accept that she would have to leave England at the end of the summer, and so arranged to rent the *Villa Isola Bella* for later in the year.

Once back at Portland Villas, KM threw herself into work for the *Athenaeum*, kept a close eye on its editing, renewed old friendships, and grew closer to Sydney and Violet Schiff, whom she had recently met in France. She enjoyed what social life she could until, by August, she was again bed-ridden and ailing. But, as she told Dorothy Brett, perhaps a little too insistently, just before she left England, 'don't think I am unhappy or desperate or lonely. I am not. I am simply a woman with a craving to work – who longs to get away to her own tiny house and indulge the craving. My one regret is – health.' (29 August 1920).

To Sydney and Violet Schiff,[1] *[2 May 1920]*

2 Portland Villas | East Heath Road | Hampstead N.W.3
Sunday.

My dear friends,

At last the writing table is in perfect order and I have put a notice round the neck of the small angelic creature who is 'knock man' to my door: "Engaged". At last I'm free to sit down and think of last Sunday and wish it were this. This is cold, reluctant, uneasy. Now and again a handful of rain is dashed against the window. The church bells have stopped ringing and I know that there is a leg of something with 'nice' spring greens, rhubarb tart and custard in every house in Hampstead but mine. Its very cold, very grey; the smoke spins out of the chimney. But thank God there *is* a far-away piano, rocking, plunging, broken into long quivering phrases – it sounds as though it were being played under the sea.

How glad I am – how deeply glad – that we stopped the car on the other side of the tunnel and got out & leaned against the wall – with the broken village behind and then the falling terraces of green – Will you ever forget how those mountains were heaped and folded together? And the fat comfortable man taking a cigarette at his ease in the lap of the world and the small impudent children watching us while we enjoyed our timeless moment? I shall go on reliving that day down to the very last drop – But so I shall with all the time we spent together. Life is so much the richer for knowing you both and rejoicing in you. Are you my friends as much as I am your friend? There you *are* in my life, part of all I do and think. Let us meet very soon after you come back.

I have been thinking about your new work. Have you done any more? Its *very* good. Delicate perception is not enough; one must find the exact way in which to convey the delicate perception. One must inhabit the other mind and know more of the other mind and your secret knowledge is the light in which all is steeped. I think you have done this – *Do more.* Tell me, if you can, what you are writing.

Violet, I have nearly finished the story I wrote for you.[2] I shall type it out and send it to you.

Murry is desperately pessimistic about – everything – more especially he feels that the wicked writers are triumphing to such an extent that its nearly impossible ever to beat them. Things have gone too far. I don't feel that at all. I think our duty lies in ignoring them – all except those whose faults are important – and in working ourselves, with all our might and main. It is waste of time to discuss them – and waste of energy. Its a kind of treachery to all that we intend to do. I am sure the 'day will come'. . . .

It is joy to have one's room again. Everything is in its place. The black & gold scarf lies across a little couch. I am meeting [T. S.] Elliot next week.

Goodbye. This is not the letter I wanted to write – its only the fringe of it.

K.M.

MS BL. *LKM* II. 33–4.

1 KM had met Sydney Schiff, a wealthy patron of the arts and a novelist under the name 'Stephen Hudson', and his wife Violet on the Riviera the previous April. (See *CLKM* III, 268 n. 1.) She formed an immediate, warm, and at times duplicitous friendship with them. As she wrote to Murry on 11 Apr. 1920: 'It makes another great joy in my coming back here this winter to know III have the Schiffs at Roquebrune. Do I take violent fancies? . . . I must say at present, I love Violet Schiff. I think you would too. [You] would certainly find her very beautiful, as I do . . . Shes extremely sympathetic' (*CLKM* III, 278).

2 'Revelations', published in the *Athenaeum*, 11 June 1920.

To Sydney and Violet Schiff [4 May 1920]

[2 Portland Villas, East Heath Road, Hampstead]

My dear friends,

Art and Letters[1] came today reminding me of the day we talked it over. It *looks* very well.

Still the sun lingers. Still, one walks up and down and down wait-ing, staring out of the windows – waiting for that moment – that mar-vellous moment – when you step out of the shadow into the embrace which is like a blessing. It is very cold; do not come back too soon.

Yesterday I drove down to the city to my Bank. It is almost terrifying to see such blank, strained faces moving in the fog. I drove to the office of the Athenaeum & thought there at least there would be men I knew who responded who – were alive and cared about life and the paper and work and – 'The untidiness of John's desk (laugh, Violet dear!) was my first crushing blow. There was over all the office a smell of stone and dust. Unthinkable disorder and ugliness. Old Massingham[2] like a cat dipped in dough blinking in the doorway & asking whether the French were furious with [Lloyd] 'George' – Huxley wavering like a candle who expected to go out with the next open door, poor silly old men with pins in their coat lapels, Tomlinson harking back to the mud in Flanders, Sullivan and E. M. Forster? very vague, very frightened. I heard myself speaking of lemon trees & then I said that in one valley I knew there was a torrent. Nobody cared, nobody wanted to know. I ran downstairs back into the car with Murry (we were going to buy a coffee pot because it was the anniversary of our wedding.) He was sure the shop would be shut because I'd talked instead of coming away so he looked out of his window and I looked out of mine and I listened to that lovely swift rushing sound & remembered how blue the lavender was the day we sat in that part of the garden.

One must live alone and work & put away one's passion – ones passion for Life. It must all go into work. Queer – isn't it – how one realises it and yet there persists this longing not to take part in, but to see, to feel, to absorb, to find out. But perhaps, by accident, it will be fed occasionally – and for the rest – travailler – travailler – – –

Goodbye

K.M.

MS BL. *Adam* 300, 96–7.

[1] The Spring issue of *Art and Letters*, a journal financed by Sydney Schiff, ran KM's story 'The Man Without a Temperament', which she had written in Ospedaletti at the beginning of the year.

[2] Henry William Massingham (1860–1924), editor of the *Nation*, for which Murry frequently wrote, and KM occasionally. The *Athenaeum* and the *Nation* both had offices in the same building at 10 Adelphi.

[3] Aldous Huxley was then, with J. W. N. Sullivan, one of Murry's two assistant editors on the *Athenaeum*. Henry Major Tomlinson (1894–1963) was a close friend of Murry's and a journalist with the *Nation*. E. M. Forster wrote frequently for the *Athenaeum*.

To Violet Schiff, 4 May 1920

2 Portland Villas | East Heath Road, | Hampstead N.W.3
4.v.1920.

Violet dear,

If Camellia hasn't closed her doors, if you *should* happen to pass them would you order another silk jumper for me – a small size with long sleeves, yellow or beige or something approaching the strawberry. I will pay you when we meet. But my green one and even my adorable shawl only make me long for more in this sober sober weather. I am going to hear the Spanish singer[1] next week. When Murry *speaks* of her she sounds wonderful.

Yours ever,
K.M.

If this is the least trouble of course you will just ignore it. But it need not necessarily be Camellia – any shop that sells them will serve. Here is a female commission! I feel I should send you at the same time my pattern for a 'body' which hooks up from left to right and right to left.

MS BL.

To Ottoline Morrell, [early May 1920]

2 Portland Villas, | East Heath Road, | Hampstead N.W.3.

Dearest Ottoline,[1]

A thousand thanks for the lovely Basket of Flowers. They were more than welcome in this cold and sad country after the South.

Yes I am home again but only until September. Then I go back into the small mountains until November and then to a flat near Monte for the winter. I had to come back; there were so many things to see to and M. had found his domestic worries more than he could bear. It is dreadful to be in England again. I had had a perfect time since January and am determined never to *live* in England again. There – in the South – one regains all one's love of life and people and one 'walks in Beauty'[2] – unimaginable beauty this spring. It is simply tragic to meet this reluctant painful England again. I thank Heaven that September is so soon. What ungracious words! But you know how one has always longed to find one's country, one's few friends, climate, way of Life and having found all this and more I feel rather lost at present. I do hope we shall meet when you are in town. Brett came in to tea yesterday. She and M. are grown fast friends.

I suppose you have heard the Spanish singer Raquel Meller. I wish we could go to to hear her together[3] – I *long* to.

Yours *ever* with love
Katherine

MS Stanford.

[1] As with several of her earlier friendships, KM's feeling for Lady Ottoline had diminished since she left England in autumn of 1919, and she had answered only one of several letters she received from her—a long, evasive apology on 20 Jan. (see *CLKM* III, 182–4).

[2]
> She walks in beauty, like the night
> Of cloudless climes and starry skies;
> And all that's best in dark and bright
> Meet in her aspect and her eyes.

(opening of Byron's 'She Walks in Beauty' (1815))

[3] KM and Lady Ottoline particularly enjoyed going together to music-hall and minstrel shows.

To Sarah Gertrude Millin[1] [c.9 May 1920]

10 Adelphi Terrace | London W.C.2.

Dear Mrs Millin,

I am just returned from abroad and the editor has handed me your letter. Please forgive me for not replying to it sooner. It gave me such very great pleasure.

I wished I had said more about your book. I have felt ever since the notice appeared that I didn't really do it justice – didn't express as I should like to have expressed, how 'original' it was – how different from the many novels, how anxious it made the reader feel to know more of this author's work. It had some wonderfully good moments – I kept feeling: if she can keep this up – if she *does* keep this up in her next book – if she goes on 'freeing' herself and exploring *her own gift* this woman is going to be a rare writer!

Im very interested to hear you write short stories. I want to ask you, on behalf of the editor, if you would send us some to see – would you? We are going to publish one short story a week in the Athenaeum, starting in June. And I shall look out for your new novel – all success to it.

Your delightful letter makes me so happy. I like to think of us writers, scattered far, and making a gesture of friendship towards each other.

Yours sincerely

'K.M.'

MS Witwatersrand.

[1] Sarah Gertrude Millin (1888–1968), a South African novelist and historian. KM had reviewed her novel *The Dark River* in the *Athenaeum*, 20 Feb. 1920, finding it 'fascinating, tantalizing'. KM decided to print Millin's short story, 'A Pair of Button Boots', in the *Athenaeum*, 3 Sept. 1920.

To Sydney and Violet Schiff, [10 May 1920]

[2 Portland Villas, East Heath Road, Hampstead]
Monday.

This morning brought me the joy of letters from you. I look forward, with how much eagerness, to seeing you again. My story (don't please expect too much) I'll send to Cambridge Place [Kensington]. Last week here I hadn't time to write a word; this week is already covered under manuscripts to be read, poems, essays to choose 'finally', novels to review, schemes to draft, an article to write on *why we intend to publish short stories*,[1] and then there's a special smashing review to be written for the Nation[2] . . . I shall get these things into order presently; I'll find their each his separate place. Last week, really, it was like having Murry a

wistful shepherd leading his troop of sheep into the room and I was ill
and in dreadful pain, physical and mental pain, that could not be spoken of.

But *Work*, real work – the longing and the desire to work is all that
matters. Why does one rebel so at isolation. It must be. Why can't one
accept it at once and for all, and put all that other side of oneself into work
– all the desire to love, to share, to be someone's *first thought*, to have
someone who talks to you endlessly and to whom you talk endlessly, to
give – to receive – tenderness, and all that quick, ardent interchange. I
should like *all* this *and* work. I should like to live in this atmosphere –
sympathy, happiness abounding, every moment lived, and then shut the
door and sit down at the table and write. But here's a woman who has
been ill for over two years, who instead of 'looking after' the other has
made demands upon a man who confesses he has very little vitality to
spare and doesn't ultimately care for people except as symbols. Who
finds that after all, he doesn't in the least desire her kind of Life, but
wants to be a scholar and live quietly, remotely, writing poetic drama,
growing learned, and feeling – that she is by and sympathetic but does
not interfere . . .

Oh how well I understand this jealous passionate love of himself, this
absorption and tenderness which comes from his wretched childhood
and poor stifled youth. Then, it seems to him now, he was engulfed,
swept away . . . Someone tried to make him other than he was, to fit
him with qualities he had not got, to look after him, to 'give him things'
. . . Now he's managed to get quite apart, to possess wholly this his critical, intellectual self. And people take him seriously, they make no
demands, they ask nothing and never oppose him. I understand him
beyond words. I have been living in a dream but it's been a long
intensely vivid dream. As we drove down to Sospel, Violet, I still believed
what I said and thought – when my illness was over the queer cloud
would sail out of the sky. . . .

Does it seem revolting to you that *however* deeply one is shaken Art
remains, and yes, one goes on finding out that it is all. If one could only
say what it means to have you two to write for . . .

I remember that house, Violet, I should like it *all* for the season if
they'd take 3000 frcs. for it. I wish I could make them rent it to me for
that. I would decide *immediately*. The Hotel doesn't sound quite mon
affaire, but that solid house is extremely intriguing. Shall I write to them?
I shall try and read Madame Bovary again before you come back. Here's
a small letter I had from Eliot.[3] He and Murry meet very often. I have
asked them both here for Thursday or Friday evening. What will they
be like, I wonder? The grey door of my room keeps on opening and
opening in my mind and Mrs Eliot and Eliot enter. I can't see her at all
– only something slightly conscious and over confident . . . Jones is in a

hovering mood – very unsure. She brings one flowers that simply droop and hang their heads with soft sentiment. And I say I only like hard bright round flowers with straight stems. I can't bear those curving languid creatures. So they go into her room. Poor Jones. I am *so horrid*.

Men come up in the evenings – immense men about 7 or 8 foot high. They sprawl on the sommier, lounge on the little couch, take chance shots with the cigarette ash and never reach the inside of the fender. They boom: 'It's impossible to write now a days. For there is nothing to write about. The artist must be at one with his times. There must be, as there was in the 18th century, a rich, leisured, cultivated public who understood the artist. You can't pretend that anything *happens* now a days. It's impossible. An artist can't cut himself off from his times and what has he got to hang on to now a days? The short story is either over or it's not going to be written in our time . . .' One has the impression that each gentleman has a large loaf of household bread and is cutting you off and handing you large chunks on the tip of – such a dreadfully blunt knife.

On Wednesday I am going to hear the Spanish singer I mentioned to you – *Raquel Meller*.

Is the paper arriving regularly now? Please let me know if it is not . . .

It is very exciting that you have written another sketch. I so want to read the first one again. Oh, there are so many things to be done. We start the short stories in the paper in the month of June. You *will* send one? They are to begin with my story about your tree.[4]

It is a pale English day – more silver than white. The cook has brought me in a bunch of bluebells. How lovely they are, these flowers of the wood. They have a sweet smell and like all these early spring flowers as one touches them one thinks of water.

Yours ever,
K.M.

Yes, the grey jersey was a parting gift from ces dames à la Villa Flora. It's much too big for me.

MS BL. *Adam* 300, 97–9.

---

[1] No article appeared to argue the editorial decision to publish short stories, merely a paragraph under 'Literary Gossip' on 18 June declaring 'It is the intention of the *Athenaeum* to devote a portion of its space henceforward to prose fiction', and setting the limit at 2,000 words.

[2] Nothing of KM's appeared in the *Nation*.

[3] Eliot's letter does not survive. Although KM's earlier dismissive opinion of Eliot had altered, and she now regarded him as a friend, his view of her was suspicious and slighting. (See his letter to Ezra Pound, just before her return to England, quoted *CLKM* III, 292 n. 1.)

[4] K.M.'s 'Revelations' (see n. 2, p. 5) concluded with a quasi-mystical 'epiphany' as the protagonist observes a remarkable tree. The Schiffs' home at Roquebrune was called 'Big Tree Villa'.

To Sydney and Violet Schiff [*11 May 1920*]

[2 Portland Villas, East Heath Road, Hampstead]

Tuesday night.

My dear Friends,

I feel I have done wrong in speaking to you as I did about Murry. Yes, that was wrong. But I can't recall the words, or the mood or anything. I can only ask you to forget them if you will.

We look forward to seeing you on Thursday – *very* much.

Yours ever
K.M.

MS BL.

To Sydney and Violet Schiff [*14 May 1920*]

[2 Portland Villas, East Heath Road, Hampstead]

Friday.

I have had your note; I have had your postcard and am wondering every day if you are home. The Elliots have dined with us tonight.[1] They are just gone – and the whole room is *quivering*. John has gone downstairs to see them off. Mrs E's voice rises "Oh dont commiserate Tom; he's *quite* happy." I know its extravagant, I know, Violet, I ought to have seen more – but I dislike her so *immensely*. She really repels me. She makes me shiver with apprehension . . . I don't dare to think of what she is 'seeing'. From the moment that John dropped a spoon & she cried: "I say you are noisy tonight – whats wrong" – to the moment when she came into my room & lay on the sofa offering idly: "This room's changed since the last time I was here." To think she had been here *before*. I handed her the cigarettes saying to myself: "well you won't find it changed again". Isn't that extravagant. And Elliot, leaning towards her, admiring, listening, making the most of her – really minding whether she disliked the country or not . . .

I am so fond of Elliot and as he talked of you both tonight I felt a deep sympathy with him. You are *in* his life like you are in mine. Don't think that is impertinent. Oh, I could explain and explain that. But this teashop creature.

M. comes up after they are gone, and he defends her. He tells me of a party he gave here & how she came & was friends with him & how he drank to get over the state of nerves she had thrown him into. "I like her; I would do the same again." I feel as tho' I've been stabbed.

Now its dead still – except for the far-off noise of the trains drumming round the hollow world.

Where are you both? You are *somewhere*. I am in the middle of a long

long new story. I must push further out to sea.

Let us meet soon.

Yours ever

K.M.

MS BL. *Adam* 300, 99–100.

[1] T. S. Eliot had married Vivienne Haigh-Wood in 1915, but by now she was increasingly affected by mental illness.

To Dorothy Brett, [20 May 1920]

2 Portland Villas | Hampstead | London

My dearest Brett

The STOVE is come, installed, burning, giving out the most blessed benificent heat imaginable! I *cannot* tell you how good it is to be in this room – in a whole warm room with no smoke, no making up fires, just a silent, discreet, never failing heat. If I were a savage I should pray to it & offer it the bodies of infants. Thank you a billion times for your dear thought. And now a belated thank you for the yellow roses – which are perfection. Now stop being generous or Ill have to lead a baby elephant[1] washed in rose soap, hung with lily buds & marigolds, carrying a flamingo in a cage made of mutton-fat jade on its back to your doorstep as a return for past favours.

You dine here on Saturday – don't you?

Love from

Tig

MS Newberry. *LKM* II. 34.

[1] The Murrys' nickname for their house in Portland Villas was 'The Elephant', because of its height and colour.

To Violet Schiff [c. 20 May 1920]

[2 Portland Villas, East Heath Road, Hampstead]

Violet, my dear woman,

Your letter makes me happy; it has your fragrance about it. I read and read – and my heart is warm. Do you know, tho' – a thousand devils are sending Elizabeth without her German Garden[1] to tea here tomorrow – her last time before she goes abroad into her Swiss chalet. I expect she will stay, at longest half an hour. She will be Oh, such a little bundle of artificialities – but I cant put her off. I want both of you – I dont want – I hate to give you up. Will you come & stay after she has gone? Stay as long as you like? Come when you like. But if you feel you could not bear her – there is the Flower Show.[2] You were going there, weren't you?

If you are inclined – come any time. If not I shall understand absolutely. Im 'free' on Wednesday & on Thursday – at any hour.

I rejoice to think of you. Be happy. Youre so beautiful –

Murry is out. He shall phone you tomorrow. I think he will love to come. I want him to very much.

My love – In haste

K.M.

MS BL.

1 KM's cousin Elizabeth, Countess Russell, whose autobiographical *Elizabeth and her German Garden* (1898) had been an enormous success. She was now an established novelist. (See p. 250, n. 1.)

2 The eighth Royal Horticultural Society's Chelsea Flower Show.

To Anne Drey, [c. 22 May 1920]

2 Portland Villas | East Heath Road, | Hampstead N.W.3

My darling Anne,

Yes, Im back until the end of August – just looking back, as it were. I have been longing to see you. But chère the bother is Im not up to coming to tea and dinner. I cant go anywhere except by car – & I simply can't afford cars for long times. So, as a rule, Im stranded on my hill top & have to ask people to come to me. This is a *great curse* – but there you are. Im much better but no good at all at walking or taking public conveyances. In that case would you and Drey come & see me? As for that blessed infant I can't expect him – the darling. What would be too lovely for words would be if you'd come to tea with me & Drey come onto dine on May 31st. Or if you'd rather just come to dinner or if you would come to tea. Whatever suits you. I should love to see you, my darling Anne. And I want to ask you if you & your baby wouldn't care to come out to me the next winter in the South for a while. I was always

thinking it over. Theres so much I'd like to talk about & to hear about.
Tell the precious one how sorry I am I cant come & see him in his bye.
And fondest, tenderest love.

Ever your
Katherine

MS ATL. *Adam* 300, 91.

To Virginia Woolf [25 May 1920]

2 Portland Villas | East Heath Road | Hampstead N.W.3

Dear Virginia,[1]

Its very kind of you to have sent me a card. Yes, Im back in England
until August. I would be delighted if you'd care to come & see me one
afternoon, but I am grown *very* dull.

Yours ever,
K.M.

MS Sussex. *Adam* 370–5, 24.

[1] Woolf wrote to KM in mid-May, but received no reply until, as her diary records on 26 May:
'This morning Katherine writes a stiff & formal note thanking me for my kind postcard and saying
she will be delighted to see me, though "grown *very* dull". What does this mean – *she* hurt with *me*?
Anyhow I go on Friday to find out, unless stopped as is always possible. I praised her story ['The
Man Without a Temperament'] warmly; sincerely too.' When Woolf did visit her on 31 May, she
recorded: 'A steady discomposing formality & coldness at first. . . . No pleasure or excitement at
seeing me. It struck me that she is of the cat kind: alien, composed, always solitary & observant.
And then she talked about solitude, & I found her expressing my feelings as I never heard them
expressed. Whereupon we fell into step, & as usual, talked as easily as though 8 months were minutes' (*The Diary of Virginia Woolf, 1920–24*, II, ed. Anne Oliver Bell, assisted by Andrew McNeillie
(1978) 43).

To Mark Gertler,[1] [c.26 May 1920]

[2 Portland Villas, East Heath Road, Hampstead]

My dear Gertler,

Will you please accept my assurance that I did not mean what I told
Murry to go any further – *ever*. A friend of mine told me the silly, stupid
'gossip' & talking CONFIDENTIALLY to John I repeated it – Of course I fully
and absolutely accept your statement. It was a typical, idiotic London
rumour. As such I told it John – I never dreamed he'd retell it or Id

rather have done anything than start a grimy snowball. My fault – for not making him realise it was for his ear alone.

But let's stop it – *please*. The odious affairs are too horrid. Will you come and have tea with me one afternoon & tell me what you told them about Cezannes pictures – Could you come next Wednesday – you needn't talk about Cezanne if you don't want to.

Kamerad! Kamerad!

Dont lets pay any attention to rumours. Id never have breathed a word except to John.

Yours
Katherine.

MS BL.

1 Mark Gertler (1892–1939), the London Jewish painter who had trained at the Slade School of Fine Art, had been part of Lady Ottoline's Garsington circle, and was in love with Dora Carrington (see p. 255, n. 1) both before and after her involvement with Lytton Strachey. KM had known him since 1914, and provoked something of a crisis at a Christmas party that year when, with the Lawrences and the Cannans, she acted out 'leaving' Murry for Gertler in an impromptu play. (See CLKM I, 146 n. 1 and a full account in Alpers 1980, 172–3.) Their friendship had cooled over the last couple of years, and the precise nature of what she now told Murry, and Murry relayed to Brett, is not clear. As her later letter to Murry, 10 Oct. 1920, makes clear, she had been hurt when she was 'just back from the South' by Gertler's callous joking about her disease. (See p. 64.)

To Dorothy Brett [26 May 1920]

[2 Portland Villas, East Heath Road, Hampstead]

My dear Brett,

What I told John about a report that had been spread I told him in confidence, as it had been told me. I would not have breathed a word to *anybody* except John. This he didn't understand when he repeated it to you.

But Id be so immensely grateful if you forget it. I detest such affairs and cannot bear to think I have been the unconscious creator of one.

Yours ever
Katherine

MS Newberry.

*To J. M. Murry, [June 1920]*1

2 Portland Villas | East Heath Road | [Hampstead]

Dear Darling,

Forgive me. I believe I always *do* 'start it'. It's become a half-conscious habit with me to exaggerate my opinions whenever I speak to you just to *provoke* your attention – to stir you, rouse you. It is simply horrid. I never talk in that extreme dogmatic way to others, you know. I hear myself even *lying* to you to bring you out of your cave. Of course I'm not as anti-Sorley[2] as 'all that'. What I have said to you isn't my opinion at all.

It all narrows down to the old evil. No time to talk anything *out* or to think or to be gently poised. No time for that long breath. So we are both unjust to each other very often, and sometimes *I know* I am unjust in my criticism.

It's so difficult to explain: we have to take things on trust. A whole book wouldn't explain it fully. But let's try and get free and write – live and write. Anything else isn't worth living. You see we are both abnormal: I have too much vitality and you not enough. Your

Wig.

MS ATL. *LJMM*, 532.

[1] Murry's note (*LJMM* 532) says that this 'was a note written to me while we were both at Hampstead'. A notebook entry includes a draft that reads 'Yes, there is more to be said for Sorley than I admitted to you, but until I began to talk about him to my enemy I wasn't *anti*-Sorley as you thought. Really, really not. That's the curse: you're not' (Newberry).

[2] Charles Sorley (1895–1915), educated at Marlborough and then briefly in Germany, joined the Army soon after the declaration of the First World War. Already an 'anti-war' poet by 1915, his verse emphasized the fratricidal pointlessness of the conflict. He was killed in action in Oct. 1915. Murry had reviewed *The Letters of Charles Sorley* in the *Athenaeum*, 30 Jan. 1920, admiring Sorley's philosophy and writing in a way that KM obviously did not.

To Anne Drey, [10 June 1920]

[2 Portland Villas, East Heath Road, Hampstead]

Anne Darling,

Will you come Tuesday of next week to tea and then to dinner and Drey at 7 p.m. that will be very perfect. I expect I will meet David in a railway carriage when he is about 20 and too beau for words and I am 53. At any rate I shall always carry a gay umbrella from this day. I shall have un ombrelle vert fait exprès avec des petits harpes d'or. Heaven keep us until Tuesday.

MS ATL. *Adam* 300, 92.

To Anne Drey, [18 June 1920]

[2 Portland Villas, East Heath Road, Hampstead]

Anne darling,

After you had gone I really found your small South Sea Island or Pacific Summer on the blue chair in the fish basket. What an ungrateful creature I must have appeared. And Ive been living on the contents ever since. At this very moment my lunch tray has just appeared crowned with the pineapple. Thank you mille mille fois, darling, generous woman. If you will let me know your address I will post the basket; they are so useful especially at the bord du mer.

I cant tell you what joy it was to see you again – and I loved your dress, your hat and the big comb in your hair, and the baby's photographs and our conversations and I wished more than ever that we lived within more frequent hailing distance – in France – Perhaps one year we shall.

> Toujours, toujours
> ton devouée
> Katherine

Mille baisers pour le petit.

MS ATL. *Adam* 300, 92.

To Dorothy Brett [20 June 1920]

[2 Portland Villas, East Heath Road, Hampstead]

Brett,

I must work like a Trooper tomorrow. Ive promised an article by Friday & I can't fail. So would you come on Thursday instead if you are free. I am so sorry about tomorrow but may the horn blow & the worm come for me this very night if I am not too busy for *anything*.

> K.M.

Picture postcard[1] ATL.

¹ The postcard is of William Blake's engraving of Mirth and her Companions from Milton's 'Allegro'.

To Violet Schiff [28 June 1920]

[2 Portland Villas, East Heath Road, Hampstead]

Monday

Violet dear,

I must reply to your card. I would love to lunch with you this week but my only free day is your engaged day: that is Wednesday. Today & tomorrow I am buried alive under the Athenaeum; on Thursday I must attend the first of the lunches[1] & we are going away for a weekend on Friday afternoon. This is perfectly devilish. Wednesday Im free all day – but its just Wednesday that won't do. You would not care to come & see us on Thursday evening? Its so far for you to come – I feel that – while I propose it. Otherwise – might I come to lunch with you tomorrow (Tuesday) week? That is years away.

I do hope you will be able to come to the lunches – both of you. I wish you could have been there for the first: it might have been rather fun.

Please don't think about my health. Folkestone or Margate (dread places!) wouldn't give it me back again. No, I shall go away in September – somewhere. I don't know where – preferably – and here one wants to throw down ones pen (no, to lay it down, *carefully* & *gently*) and to dream of some place where nobody says: "But, one moment, if you have fish for lunch you won't want it for dinner will you and I *had* thought of it for breakfast tomorrow . . . I'm not interrupting seriously. You've not really started work yet, have you?'

Violet: "You know I think K.M. is rather ungrateful & exasperating."

Oh, don't think that. Its only impatience. There is so much to write & there is so little time.

Your loving

K.M.

Will you give this little photograph to Stephen Hudson?

MS BL. *LKM* II. 36–7.

----

[1] Murry initiated *Athenaeum* literary lunches on 1 July. Virginia Woolf recorded a scathing account of the occasion: 'We were at the first Athenaeum lunch. – a long single file of insignificant brain workers eating bad courses. Katherine was opposite and I heard her enthusiastically praising [Joseph Conrad's *The Rescue*]. At last, appealed to, I confessed my perversity, whereupon she hedged – so did I. . . . This lunch was a little dingy and professional, a glimpse into the scullery where the Sullivans & Pounds & Murrys & Huxleys stand stripped to their arms in wash tubs' (*Diary of Virginia Woolf*, ed. Anne Olivier Bell and Andrew McNeillie, II (1978), 52).

To Sydney Schiff, 1 July 1920

[2 Portland Villas, East Heath Road, London]
1 vii 1920

My dear Sydney,

The idea that we might possibly get that house in your village[1] for August is very exciting. Jack is awfully keen. I shall be much beholden to you if you do find time to inquire.

MS draft Newberry.

----

[1] The Schiffs owned a house close to Eastbourne.

To Virginia Woolf [10 July 1920]

[2 Portland Villas, East Heath Road, Hampstead]

My dear Virginia,

This afternoon was such a terrific storm that I can hardly recover. The play was so wonderful — so bad — it triumphed — it failed — a little of everything seemed to happen and all round one there were these strange human beings — I don't know — they seem to me, I think, *too* strange. They frighten me beyond words at moments. I feel the only thing to do is to run away, crossing oneself — or doing whatever one would do if one was terrified. And I feel, too, that the only person who did understand The Cherry Orchard1 as Tchekhov meant it to be understood was – – –

Would you come & see me one day next week: Ill keep all next week free until I hear from you. Or I could meet you in town. There's so much to say & I am going away the first week in September.

May I have 2 copies of 'Prelude'?2

I want to send you my love & admiration dear Virginia.

Katherine.

MS Sussex. *Adam* 370–5, 21.

1 KM has seen the Art Theatre production of *The Cherry Orchard*. An unsigned review in the *Athenaeum*, 16 July 1920, was reprinted by Murry as by KM in the *Adelphi*, Aug. 1923, but the marked file of the *Athenaeum* identifies Murry as the reviewer. See B. J. Kirkpatrick, *A Bibliography of Katherine Mansfield* (1989), 150.

2 The Woolfs' Hogarth Press had published KM's *Prelude* in July 1918.

To Dorothy Brett. [12 July 1920]

[2 Portland Villas, East Heath Road, Hampstead]
Wednesday

Brett,

I would be delighted to see you on Friday but we have the little tiny Blundens1 coming to dinner and as Arthur is here as well we are full up inside. If you would come after it would be delightful – or dine here on Sunday evening – come early so that we can talk. On Saturday evening I am taking le jeune Peintre2 to see the Rushing Ballet.3 My mornings are all spent *on* the typewriter: I am simply fiendishly busy with journal-ism and the Higher Walks . . . But what price Blazing July!! Every stove in the house is red. Do come soon and tell me of your discovery if its undiscoverable.

Come button your boots with a Tiger's Tail
And let down your golden hair
And live for a Week on Bubble and Squeak
At the foot of the Winding Stair
And when you feel like a conger eel
Or as Tough as an old Split pea
Lift up the lid as the hedgehog did
And come and listen to me
FOR
To be Kontinued.[4]

MS Newberry.

[1] Edmund Blunden (1896–1974) had married Mary Davies in 1918. Murry began publishing him in the *Athenaeum* a few months before, when KM had warned against being 'over generous' because Blunden had attended Christ's Hospital, Murry's own school. (See *CLKM* III, 236.)
[2] Her 17-year-old brother-in-law, Richard (Arthur) Murry.
[3] The Russian Ballet had opened a season at the Royal Opera, Covent Garden. One of the pieces KM saw was Igor Stravinsky's new ballet *Le Chant du rossignol.*
[4] A favourite children's rhyme of KM's.

To Violet Schiff, [?16 July 1920]

[2 Portland Villas, East Heath Road, Hampstead]
Friday

I was on the point of writing to you about tomorrow evening. Conrad Aitken[1] cannot come. Instead, Max Bodenheim[2] a new American just fresh from New York, having come over steerage with Minna[3] his wife to 'look around and see if he can start roots anyway . . . say, Mrs Murry, I've got the goods to hand over if you've got the window space for them' will be here, and Tom Moult and his Bessie. Tom Moult is the editor of Voices,[4] a little, rather childish naive creature who writes poems and has a novel just coming out and Bessie is a smaller quieter creature who is everything that is good and kind but will talk to me about Madame Montessori[5] and persist in telling me it's not so important to attract the child's attention as to guide it. This, because I am bad and wicked, bores me. I do not see why you should have to endure such people. *If* you did come we should be *very* happy, but I shrink from boring you, while I long to see you.

We both enjoyed immensely our evening. The play began so splendidly and, even though it did not keep it up, I for my part was so happy to be there . . . We discussed, all the way home, a new Athenaeum – the idea of throwing overboard all the learned societies and ancient men and reviews of Dull old Tomes, and opening the windows to the hurrying sounds outside, and throwing all the old gang into the river. After all, is it good enough to be *half way* between what we really want to do and what we don't care a pin for. What will the Bishops and the Antiquarians say to the short stories?[6] And just supposing we really told the truth abut everything, *confidently*. The car rushed through St. John's Wood and we decided to do it, but not to use violence. I wonder if it is possible . . .

I wish you could see my roses. They are so exquisite that yesterday I made Jones photograph them so that I should be able to show you how they looked.

Oh, the *devastating* cold. I cannot keep warm & all day long people walk up and down the stairs & just don't knock at my door. Do you ever want to *hide*, Violet, to be completely hidden so that nobody knows where you are. Sometimes one has a dreadful feeling of *exposure* – its intolerable. I mustn't say these things.

With love to you both: I think of you constantly.

K.M.

MS BL, *LKM* II. 35–6.

1 The American poet Conrad Aiken, who was now a contributor to the *Athenaeum*. (See letter, p. 304.)

2 Max Bodenheim (1892–1954), educated in Chicago, was a poet and later a novelist given to severe psychological disturbance, as recorded in his novel *New York Madness* (1933). Ending up a derelict and murdered, at this time he was known for his acerbity and promise.

3 Minna Schein, whom Bodenheim married in 1918, the year of his first volume of poetry, *Minna and Myself*.

4 KM's friends Thomas and Bessie Moult. Primarily a journalist, Thomas Moult edited the short-lived magazine of poetry and prose, *Voices*, Jan. 1919–Autumn 1921.

5 Maria Montessori (1870–1952), an Italian physician and the originator of the 'Montessori method' of education, which emphasizes children's initiative and sensory development.

6 Clearly KM believed that the weekly publication of short stories altered the general direction of the *Athenaeum*, and disconcerted the more staid part of its readership.

To Sydney Schiff [25 July 1920]

[2 Portland Villas, East Heath Road, Hampstead]
Sunday.
I wish I had not given you that book; it is too old and too bad. However, the mischief is done.[1]
Jones has taken rooms for us at a place called Hampton Park. It is three miles distant from Eastbourne – three minutes by train. There's a taxi at the hotel, too, what is at ones disposition. It was the best she could do. There's nothing to be had in Eastbourne itself. I *do* hope we shall meet often. There is a telephone at the hotel too.
We go on Wednesday week.

I am still 'with you' after our last meeting. Really one could talk for days – for far longer.
With my love

Katherine.

MS BL. *Adam* 300, 103.

---

¹ KM had loaned Schiff a copy of *In a German Pension*.

To Sydney Schiff, [? July 1920]

[2 Portland Villas, East Heath Road, Hampstead]

I have just read your letter. I want to reply. But it must be at leisure. Jones shall take a reply tomorrow and some work if she can find some. I have read and read your story. It is great happiness that you should be writing – today. I should like to greet you – a special greeting as a fellow writer. Its raining. No, Ill write tomorrow. I hope you will see M. on Wednesday. If you choose the flowers tomorrow they will be wonderful. I hope they will make you happy. Your rose is perfect – so strange – so white – without perfume – without thorns. I see it.
Goodnight

MS BL.

To Violet Schiff, [?July–August 1920]

[2 Portland Villas, East Heath Road, Hampstead]

Violet dear,

Forgive me for not answering before. I had asked some people for next Sunday: I was hoping they would refuse. But no, this morning they will be 'so pleased' to come. So Murry and I regretfully cannot. I do want to see you both soon – and really *talk*. It seems – I suppose it isn't, really – so long since we have had time to talk. What I always want to do with you both is to share the event and then to share the impressions of it – the 'afterwards'. If only there were more time but it seems to go faster and faster. One is so conscious of it sometimes. I feel as though we were trying to talk against the noise and the speed of the train – trying to hear each other – trying to convey by a look, by a gesture, what we long to talk about for hours – days. What a story one could write about a train journey – *not* a trip to X with the Times on ones lap "in a crisp square" but a real journey across strange country. A 'party' of people with the carriage to themselves, travelling together, and two of them who have something they must say to each other. Can you imagine it? The impatience, the excitement, the extraordinary nearness of them all to one another, the meals in the restaurant car "the new warm plates seem to come flying through the air" – & then preparing for the night – those who *do* sleep – those who don't. My God! Theres such a novel to be written there. Will there be *time* to write it?

Yours ever with love
K.M.

MS BL. *LKM* II. 36.

To Violet Schiff, 7 August 1920

[2 Portland Villas, East Heath Road, Hampstead]
7.VIII.1920.

My dear Violet

I would have written before but Ive not been well. The weather has been so terrible. On the day we should have come to Hampden Park I felt I couldn't face an hotel especially as Jones was not to have come too. So we are both staying here instead. Murry spends his time playing tennis, playing 'games' and I spend mine – in my room. Im simply longing to go away and WRITE. The only reason I mind leaving London is that I shall miss you and Sydney. But – there it is. And you understand. Heavens! How dear you both are to me – Don't forget our last afternoon together.

With my love
Yours ever
Katherine.

MS BL. *Adam* 300, 104.

To Violet Schiff, [9 August 1920]

[2 Portland Villas, East Heath Road, Hampstead]
Monday.

I am writing to say that to our great disappointment we shall not be able to come on Wednesday. It is my fault. I am in bed with a very loud-beating and hateful heart for company. And I can't walk for the present. I must just keep still . . . Is there any way of removing the wrath of the Lord? It has pursued me for nearly *three years*. Oh, how I should love to have come! But you know, when I am better perhaps we can go out together again.

I wonder what you felt about our talk here. It made Murry *very happy.* I wish you could know him better. Do not wait for me. Its so useless to ever count on me. At the last moment I begin to cough and Ive no breath. But I do so immensely wish you could know him – or would ask him to come & see you. Am I impertinent? Please forgive me if I am. I am writing in a little top room. The sun shines, faint, reluctant. But its pleasant here – so still. If only one can get ones stories written – if only one is allowed time enough!

I hope you will be happy on Wednesday.

With love to you both.

Yours ever

K.M.

MS BL.

To Violet Schiff, [10 August 1920]

[2 Portland Villas, East Heath Road, Hampstead]

My dear Violet,

Yes, our letters crossed. It was a joy to hear from you and you are too generous in your criticism of my work for the paper. Nevertheless, its immensely stimulating to know that I give you pleasure – I often say things *expressly* for you both – Im sure you know I do.

This week I had happened to read a really typical article in an imbecile 'womans paper' and I threw my three silly novels away and wrote about it instead.[1] I am afraid the greater number of readers will think I have gone mad. But oh, they are such DULL dogs sometimes and I am ill – I *must* be gay. My heart and my cough,[2] my dear woman, won't let me walk up and down stairs, even, at present. Im afraid I cannot come to you. You know how much I would like to. And Im not sure when I can get away to France; Im not 'up' to the journey – as they say, at present. It is very cursed; I try not to mind: I mind *terribly.*

But forgive me. You have a right to be disgusted with me for being ill, I know. If I ever am well and strong again Ill try and make up for this unsatisfactory

K.M.

MS BL. *LKM* II. 37.

---

[1] In the *Athenaeum*, 13 Aug. 1920, KM's usual reviews were replaced by 'A Holiday Novel' claiming to discuss 'X X X By X. X. X. (X. X. 7s 6d net)', an essay in mock-journalese on holiday reading.

[2] In mid-Aug. KM was struck with severe illness, which coincided with bitter feelings towards Murry. On 12 Aug. she wrote in a notebook:

I cough and cough and at each breath a dragging, boiling, bubbling sound is heard. I feel that my whole chest is boiling. I sip water, spit, sip, spit. I feel I must break my heart. And I can't expand my chest; it's as though the chest had collapsed. Life is – getting a new breath: nothing else counts. And Murry is silent, hangs his head, hides his face with his fingers *as though* it were unendurable. 'This is what she is doing to me! Every fresh sound makes *my* nerves wince.' I know he can't help these feelings. But, oh God! how wrong they are. If he could only for a minute, serve me, help me, give *himself* up. I can so imagine an account by him of a '*calamity*'. 'I could do nothing all day, *my* hands trembled. I had a sensation of *utter* cold. At times I felt the strain would be unbearable, at others a *merciful numbness* . . .' and so on. What a fate to be self-imprisoned!! What a ghastly fate! At such times I feel I never could get well with him. It's like having a cannon-ball tied to one's feet when one is trying not to drown. It is just like that. (*Journal* 1934, 207)

To Violet Schiff [c.15 August 1920]

[2 Portland Villas, East Heath Road, Hampstead]
Tel 1277 HAM

My dearest Violet,

Forgive my silence. I have been in bed ever since I last wrote to you and having an odious time. But today I am better and shall get up at the end of the week. Down in my writing room there is your last letter unanswered. I have kept thinking about it, thinking about you both, and seeing you out in this marvellous weather (at last). Is Sydney writing? I simply long to know. Hail! my Brother-artist! And Violet, let me clasp you warmly one little moment . . .

I shall not be able to leave London until I go away. That will be, I hope, the second week in September. May I know your plans? When do you return to London? I long to go, but I do want to [see] you both first. Lying here in my little top room at night I hear the trains go thrumming round the hollow world and the old longing comes back.

Oh what is the use of a letter. I cant write letters. Let us sit together in some corner of a warm quiet café, let us talk endlessly. I could talk about *Tolstoy* for hours. I burn to talk about Tolstoy. And then – and then –

But – one thing. The story for the English Review – is it to be published?[1] Today is my first day free from pain – and just to be washed up on the shore and allowed to think about this '*writing*' is almost too much. I will write when I am, as they say, more sensible. My love to you both

Katherine.

MS BL. *Adam* 300, 102–3.

[1] A story Sydney Schiff sent to the *English Review*, which was not accepted.

To Violet Schiff [c.15 August 1920]

[2 Portland Villas, East Heath Road, Hampstead]

Dearest Violet,

I shall be delighted to keep Tuesday afternoon free. Im much better. The 'trouble' has been Ive had an overdose of vaccine and it laid me low. Ten million – oh twenty million – *hosts* of streptococci attacked and fought one another. I have done with vaccine. The English Review is become so degraded that one can expect nothing better of it. All the same it is disgusting; one *longs* to see such work in print.

Weren't those Tchekhov sketches[1] absolute *parings*. But M. was not responsible that time. It was the staff's choice. My Catholic cousins (the Villa Flora ones) have bought a new huge villa in Garavan – the other bay. It has, at its gates, a dolls house with a verandah, garden, everything complete. And this I have taken from them. I shall be in touch with them, still, & they are getting me a maid and so on, but at the same time Im *free*. Can you imagine the delight of writing to the villa Violet of telephoning to them (my Isola Bella has a telephone) and asking them if they will come over? Don't you envy me? By the time you come my garden will be full of flowers – Heavens! What a joy that will be. And we shall ignore Time – trick the wretch just for a little –

Yours ever
Katherine.

MS BL. *Adam* 300, 100.

[1] 'Two Sketches' by Chekhov, 'At the Cemetary' and 'At the Post Office', the *Athenaeum*, 13 Aug. 1920.

To Dorothy Brett, [19 August 1920]

[2 Portland Villas, East Heath Road, Hampstead]

My dear Brett,

If you really *do* feel any friendship for me – it is a rare feeling, terribly rare – will you send me any letters you have of mine to you.[1] I am the most unfortunate of women – There were one or two or even three times when I committed to paper what I never ought to have let out of my heart. Grant my prayer for the sake of any good moments we may have had and let me have the chance of destroying what ought never to have been sent. I felt (very queerly) that you were in a specially confidential 'position' because you had been a witness at that Registry

Office.[2] But that was great nonsense – such ceremonies are no more binding than tea parties. But please send the letters.

Yours
Katherine

MS Newberry.

[1] Brett did return or destroy some of the more intimate letters.
[2] Brett, with the Scottish painter J. D. Ferguson ('Johnny') had been a witness at the Murrys' marriage at the South Kensington Registry Office on 3 May 1918.

To Sydney and Violet Schiff [c.22 August 1920]

[2 Portland Villas, East Heath Road, Hampstead]

Tuesday night

Are we to meet again soon? I have been thinking of you both so much today. We loved the evening when you came; Mr Trench[1] is delightful. My private feeling is that the last story in the paper[2] – which reminded me of nothing so much as a galosh or an unclaimed umbrella has disgusted you both. It's useless to pretend I can control what stories we do print. I can up to a certain point (that, of course, makes it ridiculous) but after that Murry says I am "too precious in my taste". However, I shall go on until I *do*. I have been out today for a little walk on the Heath. It was so wonderful to feel the summer wind.

I hope you are happy. *Be* happy. Thats my great constant wish for you. *You* are the people to whom happiness should come – I love you both.

K.M.

MS BL, *Adam* 300, 100.

[1] Herbert Trench (1865–1923), minor poet and playwright. (See *CLKM*, II, 345.)
[2] H. M. Tomlinson's 'Illusion', the *Athenaeum*, 20 Aug. 1920.

To Charlotte Beauchamp Perkins, [23 August 1920]

[2 Portland Villas, East Heath Road, Hampstead]

Tel: 1277 Hampstead
Monday

My precious Marie

I am up today and lying on the sofa in my room. Its such a joy to feel dry land under one's feet once more instead of the heaving bed.

Have you ever known anything to equal this weather? It is winter in Hampstead – a pale red sun, deep misty mornings and china asters in the vases. I think this is the *final summer* England will ever have. Its been just a lick and a promise. Next year it will be a promise only. Why not bow down to it & all dress in rabbit skins and not attempt anything less substantial than long sleeves and high necks. The gooseberries at Woodhay[1] and the raspberries and the beautiful springing bunches of sweet peas & those lovely lilies in the corner were (in spite of the rain) my real summer this year.

We have taken tickets for September 7th subject to my *teeth, feet* etc. And I have really rented Jinnies small villa the Isola Bella which she is having made ready – The darling woman came in the other day & we had a pow-wow about our plans. I hope to be able to help her about things until she can get out there – give an eye to her villa & its arrangements. It will be perfect joy to be 'over there' just in time to put in all the Christmas flowers – Menton is real *home* to me: I love the little town – and the idea of pottering in it – making my Isola Bella really as pretty as I can, buying little spotted curtains for its windows and cups with lemons painted on them for its breakfast is very delightful *after* cold London. I shant come back here next year. Its useless. Ive lost 5lbs of very valuable flesh – stolen – nipped away – so I shall stick to furrin parts until I am really mended. Do remind me of this when I write wicked letters wailing to you about Hampstead darling.

How are you? How is everything going? Are your plans advanced? Are you happy? I wish I could pop in & find out these and many other things. I am always thinking about you – as you know.

Jack is so full of fire and health that I feel I have married a prize fighter. He plays tennis every day for hours – and even started at 7 A.M. one morning! I never seem to see him except in a white woolly sweater, *clean* white flannel trousers & wet hair after a cold bath. Men whose names Ive never heard of – names like Mr Funnel and Mr Nutt ring up & ask if he will be "at the Courts this morning" as though he were in a perpetual state of being taken before a magistrate. Its very good for him – I feel just like his Mother – sitting up in bed and saying "run along dear & put on your jacket if you get over heated . . ." I am so sorry I have not sent the paper this week. I am sending it today. Did you see your dear sister was mentioned in The Times last week? It was funny to hear the solemn old Times call me 'K.M.', *tout court*.[2] Better than 'Kassie', tho.

Well, dearest here comes lunch – grilled sole, cream cheese & grapes. Its borne by the faithful Violet[3] who came back from her wedding last night. I have had to admire the photographs today – can't you see them – Pa, Ma, and relations so complicated that ones brain whirls. "Thats

Roger's sister's niece-by-marriage with her step brother by her Father's first wife." "Oh, yes, Violet – I see!"

Goodbye darling. Give the Little un my best love. Do let me hear from you.

Your own
K.

MS Newberry.

---

[1] The comfortable home in the New Forest that Harold Beauchamp bought for his daughters Chaddie (Marie) and Jean, an act of generosity that KM rather resented.

[2] KM is playing up the reference. In fact it was part of an advertisement placed by the publisher Grant Richards, that reads: 'The *Athenaeum* declared the other day that "no first novel of literary merit can hope to sell more than a thousand." I assure the *Athenaeum* that it is unduly pessimistic. Take for instance James Agate's "Responsibility" (7s). It was a first novel; it had literary merit (I do not think that even "K. M." denies it this quality); and it did sell – oh! very many more than a thousand.' The KM reference is to her review of *Responsibility* in the *Athenaeum*, 16 Jan. 1920, where under the heading 'Words – Words – Words', she had found the novel's 'passion for display . . . so ungoverned that we cannot see the stars for the fireworks'. Grant Richards presumably had not forgotten either that KM turned him down when he had approached her for a volume of short stories in late 1919.

[3] Violet, the maid at Portland Villas, had married 'Roger' less than a year previously, so presumably had been to some other family wedding.

To Dorothy Brett, [29 August 1920]

[2 Portland Villas, East Heath Road, Hampstead]

My dear Brett

Thank you for letting me see the book. I've read it. But it wouldn't be fair for me to say to you just what I think about it. After all the blood bond between sisters is very very strong; I'd hurt you. The little children Laurette and Elissa say some nice things – don't they?[1] I didn't really hope to get that letter back. One never does, neither on the stage, nor in novels nor in real Life. This is a rule. One might as well try to lure the moving finger back to cancel half a line.[2] However, I *did* ask for it: I *have* repudiated it. That puts me right with posterity . . . But don't think I am unhappy or desperate or lonely. I am not. I am simply a woman with a craving to work – who longs to get away to her own tiny house and indulge the craving. My one regret is – health. And that doesn't *remind* me – but gives me the chance to say to you how much, how deeply I feel for you in your deafness. Perhaps you think people "accept" it, forget it. I never do and I never could. I think you are wonderfully courageous to accept it as you do and I am constantly realising what it must mean to you.

I hope you have a happy time.

Katherine

MS Newberry.

---

[1] Brett's sister Sylvia married Vyner Brooke, the last white Rajah of Sarawak, and published several romantic novels, as well as her autobiography, *Sylvia of Sarawak* (1936). Brett had sent KM her new novel, *Toys* (1921).

[2]
> The moving finger writes; and, having writ,
> Moves on; nor all thy piety nor wit
> Shall lure it back to cancel half a line,
> Nor all thy tears wash out a word of it.

(Edward Fitzgerald, *The Rubaiyat of Omer Khayyam* (1859), stanza 51)

To Violet Schiff, [29 August 1920]

[2 Portland Villas, East Heath Road, Hampstead]
Sunday Evening.

Dearest Violet

I look forward tremendously to seeing you on Tuesday week: it will be great happiness. But I DO hope you are not coming up 'specially' as they say.

I suppose you know – but can you really know – what delight it gives me to feel that you like my work a little. But never *bother* to acknowledge any. Im sending you one with this – just in case you feel inclined to read it. Its a perfect night. Ive spent the day preparing for flight – sorting papers, burning papers. Now there is nothing to do but look at the moon – I wonder what you and S. are doing: I wish you were *here* or I *there*.

Yours with love

Katherine.

MS BL. *Adam* 300, 104–5.

To Violet Schiff, [30 August 1920]

[2 Portland Villas, East Heath Road, Hampstead]

Dearest Violet,

It is now decided that we leave on Thursday week. So that if you come on Wednesday it will do just as beautifully well as Tuesday.

That 'Pickle'[1] comes in my book; I wrote it in 1917. But there's a much longer story to be written about those two – the man and woman – when they *were* together.

S. made me feel in his letter how vital it was to have the *full* free courage of one's ideas. Its time [we] told, as Tolstoi says, "everything, everything".²

I look forward to seeing you both – immensely.

With love

Yours ever

K.M.

MS BL, *Adam* 300, 104.

---

¹ 'A Dill Pickle' was published in the *New Age*, 4 Oct. 1917, and revised for *Bliss and Other Stories*. It had drawn on KM's love-affair in 1910 with Francis Heinemann, a young man whose family disapproved of his associating with a separated married woman. Ida Baker (*MLM*, 63) believed he was the father of a child conceived during KM's time at Cheyne Walk and lost during a visit to the Continent.

² A phrase variously used by Tolstoy in several works.

II

FRANCE – MENTON

SEPTEMBER 1920–MAY 1921

KM left for Menton in the middle of September, again with Ida Baker as companion and aide. In her renewed enthusiasm for the south of France, in a house she found congenial, and without the strains that London had assumed before she left, KM was eager to begin work on a new set of stories. Although 'weak as a butterfly and *thin* as a match' (to Murry, 16 September 1920) when she first arrived, by the end of the year she had completed, among others, 'The Stranger', 'Miss Brill', and 'The Daughters of the Late Colonel'. The publication of *Bliss, and Other Stories* towards the end of the year established her place among important contemporary writers. Yet the months until Christmas were also painful ones. She fretted at Murry's interest in other – and as she realized, healthier – women, and by mid-December wrote in a notebook how 'There is no limit to human suffering. When one thinks: "now I have touched the bottom of the sea – now I can go no deeper," one goes deeper' (*Journal* 1954, 228).

Murry, perplexed but considerate, came to Menton earlier than he intended, and threw in his editorship of the *Athenaeum*. Although she was happy that they were again living together, KM's health continued to decline. She was now troubled by glandular infection as well as by her lungs. Her customary restlessness again took over, even as she was evolving a personal existential response to the vagaries of her life. 'One must *submit*. Do not resist. Take it. Be overwhelmed. Make it *part of life*' (*Journal* 1954, 228).

To J. M. Murry, [14 September 1920]

Isola Bella | Garavan | Menton.
Tuesday.

Darling Bogey,

What shall I tell you first? I have thought of you often & wondered if the beau temps est chez vous aussi, now that Ive gone away. We had a good journey but a slight contretemps in Paris. Ida disappeared with the porter to find a taxi, and she forgot the door she'd gone out – rushed off to another & lost me. After about ½ an hour I appealed to the police but they were helpless. The poor creature lost her head & when we *did* meet finally it was only because I saw her in the distance & simply *shouted*. This tired me & made my nose bleed and I had a v. bad night & had to do my review in bed next day, being fanned & bathed with eau de cologne. Its of no importance *to me* but I felt *all the time* I was betraying you and the paper. Forgive me once again. We arrived here yesterday at 4.50 after a day of terrific heat. Menton felt like home. It was really bliss to sit in the voiture and drive through those familiar streets & then up a queer little leafy 'way' and then another at right angles to a gate all hidden by green where la bonne Annette stood waving her apron and the peke leapt at her heels. This villa is – so far – perfect. It has been prepared inside and out to such an extent that I don't think it will ever need a hand's turn again. The path from the gate to the two doors has a big silver mimosa showering across it. The garden is twice as big as I imagined. One can live in it all day. The hall is black & white marble. The salon is on your right as you enter – a real little salon with velvet covered furniture and an immense dead clock and a gilt mirror & two *very* handsome crimson vases which remind me of fountains filled with blood. It has 2 windows: one looks over the garden gate, the others open on to the terrace & look over the sea. I mustnt forget to mention the carpet with a design of small beetles which covers the whole floor. The dining room is equally charming in its way – & has french windows, too. It abounds in cupboards full of wessels & has a vrai buffet with silver teapot, coffee & milk jug which catch the flashing eye. All is delightful. There are even very lovely blue glass finger bowls . . . On the other side of the passage is the garde-linge big enough for all our boxes as well. The linen is overwhelming. It is all in dozens – even to maid's aprons . . . The kitchen premises are quite shut off with a heavy pair of doors. The kitchen gleams with copper. Its a charming room & there's a big larder & a scullery big enough for a workshop and outside there's a garden and three large caves & the lapinière. Upstairs are four bedrooms – the maid's on the entresol. The others have balconies & again are carpeted all over & sumptuous in a doll's house way.

Annette had prepared everything possible. The copper kettle boiled. Tea was laid. In the larder were eggs in a bowl & a cut of cheese on a leaf & butter swimming & milk, & on the table coffee, a long bread, jam, and so on. On the buffet a dish heaped with grapes & figs lying in the lap of fig leaves. She had thought of everything & moreover everything had a kind of chic – and she in her blue check dress & white apron sitting down telling the news was a most delightful spectacle.

The heat is almost as great as when we arrived last year.[1] One can wear nothing but a wisp of silk, two bows of pink ribbon & a robe de mousseline. Moustiques and moucherons are in full blast; we are both bitten to death already. They are frightful. But so far I can accept them without a reproach. The compensations are so great.

I must tell you a very big date palm grows outside my bedroom balcony window. At the end of the garden wall (a yellow crumbling wall) there is a vast magnolia full of rich buds. There is a tap in the garden. In the vegetable garden the french artichokes are ready to eat and minute yellow and green marrows. A tangerine tree is covered in green balls.

I hope all this description doesn't bore you darling. But I content myself with thinking you are going to see it yourself one day & so my description is only "in advance".

The view is *surpassingly* beautiful. Late last night on the balcony I stood listening to the tiny cicadas & to the frogs and to someone playing a little chain of notes on a flute.

I do not know *what* it is about this place. But it is enough just to be here for everything to change. I think already of the poetry you would write if you lived such a life. I wish you were not tied. I have always at the bottom of my deep cup of happiness that dark spot which is that you are not living as you would wish to live . . .

Here is Annette with a big dish of fresh lemons – broken off with the leaves remaining. And its lunch time. The heat!

Goodbye darling. Take care of yourself. I hope you have good tennis & that all goes well. Yours ever

Wig.

MS ATL. *LKM* II. 37–9.

[1] When KM, Murry, and Ida Baker had first arrived in Ospedaletti, at the beginning of Oct. 1919.

To J. M. Murry, [15 September 1920]

[Villa Isola Bella, Garavan, Menton]

My darling Bogey

Your letter and card this morning were so perfect that (only you will understand this) I felt you'd brought up a little kitten *by* Wingley and put it on our bed & we were looking at it together. But it was a very kitten of Very Kittens . . . with wings. I must answer it just this once & risk breaking the agreement *not* to write. But my letter to you was so inferior to yours to me.

Yes, that suddenness of parting – that last moment. But this last time I had a deep, strange *confidence* – a feeling so different to that other desperate parting when I went to France.[1] We are both so much stronger & we *do* see our way and we do know what the future is to be. That doesn't make me miss you less, though.

Dont ask my parding humbly. Open any letter you like. You know you can; I only pretend to mind. I like you to open them, for some queer reason. Ill reply to Methuen[2] tomorrow. Ive got the 2 novels for this week, thank you. Ill write to old Sorapure[3] about that vaccine. You were right. It was a case of moral cowardice.

Im in bed – not very O.K. The moustiques have bitten me & Ive had pains & fever & dysentery. Poisoned, I suppose. It was almost bound to happen. But don't worry, my dear love. Annette is in the kitchen & her soups & rice climb up the stairs.

I think Ive got a maid, too, Mme Reveilly, 5 bis Rue des Poilus. Shes a police inspector's *sister* and she looks indeed as though she had sprung out of a nest of comic policeman. Fat, dark, sitting on the sofa edge, grasping, *strangling* indeed a small black bead bag. 'Si vous cherchez *une personne de confiance* Madame *et pas une imbecile . . .*' she began. I felt that was a poor compliment to my appearance. Did I look like a person who wantonly cherched imbeciles to do the housework? But, of course all the time she recounted her virtues I saw the most charming imbecile with woolly shoes like rabbits and a great broad beaming smile . . . which I couldn't help dismissing rather regretfully.

The villa is even lovelier than it was. Once I am up again and out again I feel it will be almost *too* fair. I do miss you tho, my darling. I have (Ive told you a thousand times) always such a longing to share all that is good with you and you alone. *Remember that.* Events move so awfully strangely – we live & talk & tear our Daily News up together and all the while there is a growth going on – gorgeous deep glories like bougainvilleas twine from your window to mine.

Tell me all you can but don't worry to tell me. I only want just what comes into your head. After today I shall begin sending a card a day (for 40 cents pay). Yes, you'll have a photograph when the moustiques are less like mousquetaires. Ive begun my journal book. I want to offer it to Methuen – to be ready this Xmas. Do you think thats too long to wait? It ought to be rather special, *dead* true – and by dead true I mean like one takes a sounding (yet gay withal). Oh, its hard to describe. What do you advise? The novels, dear love, won't bear rehashing – not *really*. I can imagine what a difficulty your Harris is.[4] The idea of it excites me awfully – your exquisite writing!

Yours for ever

Wig.

MS ATL. *LKM* II. 40–1.

1 When KM travelled alone to Bandol in early Jan. 1918.

2 KM had agreed to write a literary journal for the publishers Methuen. She began on a few entries, but the plan for a book was not carried through.

3 Victor Sorapure, a doctor KM had been consulting since she first moved to Hampstead in the summer of 1919.

4 Murry reviewed Frank Harris's *Oscar Wilde: His Life and Confessions*, in the *Athenaeum*, 24 Sept. 1920. Harris had been something of a hero for the young Murry when KM first knew him in 1912, and one of her uncollected stories, 'The House', was published in Harris's magazine *Hearth and Home* in Nov. 1912.

To J. M. Murry, [16 September 1920]

[Villa Isola Bella, Garavan, Menton]

Darling Bogey

Re Floryan[1] – the letter is of course for you to read.

It is imbecile and odious that you should be so troubled. What F. refers to as the Chelsea period[2] and good received beats me. But it is true that he does possess letters written during my acquaintance with him which I would give any money to recover. And it is true that especially if he is married he'll never cease threatening. What I propose is this. I talked it over with Ida. She agreed to give me £40. I want you to go with F. to a solicitor receive the letters get his sworn statement and hand him my cheque for the amount. Its *not* a waste of £40. I couldn't ask it or get it from Ida on another pretext but I don't hesitate now – will you wire me if you agree? And that ends *all communication with him*. As to the letters, needless to say they are yours. I'd like them destroyed as they are, but thats for you to say, darling.

Im better today, fever gone, but weak as a butterfly and *thin* as a match. All well except I can't bear you should be troubled with all this. Tig.

MS ATL. *LJMM*, 536.

¹ Floryan Sobienowski (1881–1964) was an opportunistic Polish translator and littérateur when he met KM in Wörishofen, Bavaria, soon after her pregnancy in 1909. It is likely that they were lovers briefly. He had encouraged her interest in Russian literature, and lent her translations of Polish poetry and drama, after which she had written her poem, 'To Stanislaw Wyspiansky' (*Poems*, 30–1). Sobienowski contributed to *Rhythm* as its Polish correspondent, but had become a tiresome scrounger by the end of 1912, when KM and Murry lived near Chichester. He had seen her again in 1917, and pressed her to attempt a translation of Wyspiansky, which remains incomplete and unpublished. Now working at the Polish Embassy in London, he had got in touch with Murry, asking £40 payment for the return of letters KM had written him ten years before. As this and following letters make clear, KM regarded him as a considerable nuisance, and wanted her letters back; but there is no evidence that she feared the possible results of 'blackmail'.

² KM had lived in Chelsea, at 131 Cheyne Walk, for several months at the end of 1910, and again between Feb. 1917 to early 1918 at 141A Church Street.

To J. M. Murry, [16 September 1920]

[Villa Isola Bella, Garavan, Menton]
Thursday.

The clock goes perfectly but it has a surprised look and an interrogatory tick.

Hullo, darling. These are going to be my cards. They are more private. Do you see the good advice written on the sides? What else would you do with it? But you know the kind of people who use these cards in France . . . people who have *one pen* a generation.

Let's see – what's the news. (1) Where is my Daily News? I haven't seen one since Saturday. This is V. great treachery on your part, darling Boge. I shall miss all that Eastbourne case¹ – which really *was* interesting.

N.P. The heat is terrific. It beats Italy and the insetti are beyond imagination. Does the moustique roar *before* or *after*: this question beats the lion one. But Ive a note on moustiques in my journal.² (Let me hold your ears very softly, my dog and kiss your lovely eyes.)

N.P. Ive got a maid. Theres matter for song in it. Not the black one. A grey one about 55, a real expert servant who does everything & is installed today because Vendredi is a mauvais jour. Her name is Marie. I believe she has real gaieté de coeur. I pay her 160 par mois. But I dont grudge it. Those old wages were *shameless*.

N.P. Im still in bed, precious in awful spasmodic pain. Tomorrow Ill call in another doctor to consult with me. I *wish* it would go away and let me begin mending.

N.P. – A bouquet of plumbago – no theres only room for LOVE

Tig.

MS ATL. *LJMM*, 536.

1 There was wide publicity surrounding the discovery on 20 Aug. of the body of a young woman beaten to death and buried in sand near Pevensey Bay, Eastbourne. Two men were arrested a fort-night later, and their trial in December concluded with their being sentenced to death.

2 The 'journal' for Methuen that she soon abandoned.

To J. M. Murry, [17 September 1920]

[Villa Isola Bella, Garavan, Menton]

Dear Darling,

Thank G. for Milne![1] Hold fast to him. He's so nice and she's not a bit nice. She's like an unripe banana.[2] Im longing to see your 'Wilde-Harris'. I am *sure* O.W. was negligible but he *is* an astonishing figure. His letters, his mockeries and thefts – he's a Judas who betrays himself. Which is the more tragic figure – the master without a disciple or the disciple without a master?' . . . Thats by the way.

Can I have the Times Lit. Sup. I freeze I burn for the printed word. You touch me so with what you say about my bouquets. I put them there expressly for you. I said to them: Please last as long as you can for him – and you understood.

Do kiss the cats noses for me. I thought I heard Wing crying the first night I was here. Which reminds me – there's a little kid tethered below and it "kyes and kyes so so defful."

Saturday. I sent my review last night. I do hope it arrives in time. Dearest Im better. Temperature normal – pain gone – up & lying in the salon. I am eating again too and now really *will* mend. But I have *never* been so thin – not even in Paris.[3] Im simply melted like a candle with that fever. I rock when I stand. But – Hurrah! Its over. These cards are no good today. I will send a cleaner one tomorrow. Your own

Wig.

MS ATL. *LKM* II. 41.

1 Murry's friend Herbert Milne, a classics scholar who worked in the manuscript room at the British Museum, had moved into Portland Villas.

2 Presumably Ida Baker's sister May. See letter to Murry, 21 Sept. 1920, n. 2.

3 KM lost weight during her three weeks in Paris between 22 March and 9 April 1918, when the city was under intensive German bombardment, and there was severe food rationing. Two months later, in a telegram to Murry from Looe, Cornwall, she mentioned that she was now seven stone, twelve pounds (see *CLKM* II. 216).

To Richard Murry, [c.19 September 1920]

[Villa Isola Bella, Garavan, Menton]

My dear Richard,[1]

I was very glad to hear from you. The drawing of the Flight into Menton was really superb; Athy was the spit of himself.

Yes, I think you'd find the South of France was good country. I could be content to stay here for years. In fact I love it as Ive never loved any place but my home. The life, too, is so easy there is no division between ones work and one's eternal existence – both are of a part. And you know what that means. My small, pale yellow house with a mimosa tree growing in front of it – just a bit deeper yellow – the garden, full of plants, the terrace with crumbling yellow pillars covered with green (lurking-place for lizards) all belong to a picture or a story – I mean they are not remote from one's ideal – one's dream. The house faces the sea, but to the right there is the Old Town with a small harbour, a little quai planted with pepper and plane trees. This Old Town, which is built flat against a hill – a solid wall, as it were, of shapes & colours is the finest thing Ive seen. Every time I drive towards it it is different.

And then, there's no doubt that the people here – I mean the working people make no end of a difference. My servant Marie is a masterpiece in her way. Shes the widow of a coachman – just a woman of the people, as we say, but her feeling for Life is a constant surprise to me. Her kitchen is a series of Still Lives; the copper pans wink on the walls. When she produces a fish for lunch it lies in a whole, tufted green seascape with a large tragic mouthful of 'persil' still in its jaws. And last night, talking of her desire to buy bananas she explained it wasn't so much that they should be eaten but they gave 'effect' to the fruit dish. "A fine bunch of grapes, deux poires rouges, une ou deux belles pommes avec des bananas et des feuilles" she thought worth looking at.

You know to live with such people is an awful help. Yesterday, par exemple, I had a sack of charcoal & some pine cones delivered. And passing the kitchen I saw the woodman, in a blue overall & yellow trousers, sitting at the table with Marie taking a glass of wine. The wine bottle was one of those wicker affairs. One doesnt (God forbid) want to make a song about these things, but I didn't realise they *went on* naturally and simply until I came here. In England one gets the feeling that *all is over*. Do you know what I mean? And there's never time for more than a rough sketch of what one wants to do, or what one feels. I hope you don't think Im running down your country. Its not that. Its Life in any city.

How is your work getting on? Let me know whenever you feel inclined. I have such a vivid mental picture of your picture – on the mantelpiece in the studio propped against the clock. I wish you'd send me a small sketch for my walls one day. It can be a Loan Exhibit if you like.

Jack told me of the putting to its winter sleep of the lawn-mower, and how Wing looked on.

Goodbye dear Richard

    With love from your other Brother

Katherine.

Will you tell me what procedure to follow in addressing your envelopes? Editor: What is your name? Infant: R or A.

MS R. Murry. *LKM* II. 44–5.

1 Although christened Arthur, Murry's younger brother Richard adopted Richard as his permanent name on KM's recommendation.

To J. M. Murry, 19 and 21 September 1920

Villa Isola Bella.

Sunday afternoon | September 19th 1920

My darling little Follower,

It is true – isn't it – that we are going to walk out together every single Sunday? All through the week we are hard at work – you, in that horrible black town that I hate, me, on my beautiful island but when Sunday comes (it was my first thought this morning) we adorn ourselves and soon after midi I hear that longed for but rather peculiar, rather funny whistle. I run to the window and there below is a lovely vision in a faded very much-washed creamy linen shirt, linen trousers, a scarlet bellyband – a wide silver-grey hat just a little on one side. I kiss my hand to it, spin down the stairs, and away we go. But for this week at least we'll not go far – only out of sight of the world – that's far enough. For your Wig is still so weak that she can't walk straight – sometimes I fling myself at the doors or take a great high step in the air. But I *am* really on the mend, dear darling and as to my cough – fancy – I've been here five days & I cough hardly at all. This morning in fact I didn't cough *at all* and cant remember if I have until now 6 *p.m.* I only have to get my strength back after this 'attack'. That is all about me, dear darling.

(There is so much to tell you. I tell you in my mind and then the effort of writing is too much. Forgive for this week an infernally dull girl.)

My feeling for this little house is that somehow it ought to be ours. It is I think a perfect house in its way and just our size. The position – up a side road *off* a side road – standing high – all alone – the chief rooms facing South & West – the garden, the terrace all South is ideal. You

could do all the garden. Theres a small vegetable plot outside the kitchen
& scullery – there is a largish piece in the front – *full* of plants & trees –
with a garden tap and at the side another bed – a walk – a stone terrace overlooking the sea – a great magnolia tree – a palm that looks as
tho dates must ripen. You shall have photographs of all this. And then
its so solid inside and so somehow – spacious. And all on two floors and
as well all the kitchen premises away – shut away and again perfectly
equipped. I shall of course keep the strictest accounts and see exactly
what it would cost us to live here.

Marie, the maid, is an excellent cook – as good as Annette was. She
does all the marketing, and as far as I can discover she's a very good
manager. A *marvel* really. Of course she cooks with butter but then one
doesn't eat butter with ones meals so it comes to the same thing. The
food is far better than any possible house we go to in England. I don't
know to whom to compare it – and all her simple dishes like vegetables
or salads are so good. Its a great pleasure to go into the kitchen for my
morning milk & see this blithe soul back from market in the spotless
kitchen with a bunch of lemon leaves drying for tisane & a bunch of
camomile hanging for the same. All is in exquisite order. There are pots
on the stove, cooking away – mysterious pots – the vegetables are in a
great crock – in bundles – and she tells me of her marvellous bargains
as I sip the milk. She is the kind of cook Anatole France[1] might have.

As to the weather it is really heavenly weather. It is too hot for any
exertion, but a breeze lifts at night – and I can't tell you what scents it
brings – the smell of a full summer sea and the bay tree in the garden
and the smell of lemons. After lunch today we had a sudden tremendous
thunder storm, the drops of rain were as big as marguerite daisies – the
whole sky was violet. I went out the very moment it was over – the sky
was all glittering with broken light – the sun a huge splash of silver. The
drops were like silver *fishes* hanging from the trees. I drank the rain from
the peach leaves & then pulled a shower bath over my head. Every violet leaf was full. I thought of you – these are the things I want you to
have. Already one is conscious of the whole sky again & the light on the
water. Already one listens for the grasshoppers' fiddle, one looks for the
tiny frogs on the path – one watches the lizards . . . I feel so strangely
as though I were the one who is home & you are away. I long for you
here.

Tuesday. I dropped this letter and only today I pick it up again. Your
cards came & your treasure of a letter, *my own boy* and I long to answer
– I keep on answering, as it were. There is so much to tell you & apart
from that there's the paper – your Stendhal,[2] so *first chop* – the books
you've sent me. And I still haven't told you about this house or the life
or the view or what your room is like. It all waits. Will you – my wise
comprehending boy – just take me and it for granted for about a week?

In a week Ill be a giant refreshed — but Ive simply got to get back my strength after the last blow.

But you know how soon I come to the surface. It did pull me down. Its only a few days. Its over. Im on the *up grade* but there you are — just for the moment. Each day the house finds its order more fixed and just made so that I can lie out all day. The weather is absolute exquisite radiance — day after day just variegated by these vivid storms. Its *very* hot & the insects are a trouble — but its perfect weather for you & me here. Im doing all wise things.

Dear Darling. I'll just have to ask you to take a wave of a lily white hand to mean *all* for the moment. Yes, Im sending a review this week. I note the novels are coming across quickly. Im going to do three together. Can you bring Wing at Xmas? If not Ida says she will go across & fetch them both when you give up the house. They'd be happy here. I *wish* I were stronger. Im so *much* better. My cough is nearly gone. Its nothing but de la faiblesse & I know it will pass. But not to be able to give you all this when I so want to — that's hard to bear. The papers come, thank you dearest.
Your own loving
Wig.

MS ATL, *LKM* II. 41–4.

1 Anatole France (1844–1924), French novelist, poet, editor, and critic.
2 Murry had reviewed Stendhal's *Rome, Paris et Florence* and *La Jeunesse de Stendhal* by Paul Arbolet in the *Athenaeum*, 17 Sept. 1920.

To J. M. Murry, [21 September 1920]

[Villa Isola Bella, Garavan, Menton]

Shaw seems a pure dotty in that review,[1] and what a shameless piece of work. Its disgraceful lack of form its impertinent ½ padding & then when padding failed 'quote'. I *constantly* dream of the English Critic who'll (Hurrah for Bogey!) set all these at nought.
I feel convinced by the way that Eliot is no good. Hes a dead horse at the races. Wish Id seen that football match.

My precious Bogey
I must answer your Sunday letter. Now DONT bother to answer this. But it sends waves & waves of love beating through me — even tho' the

storm that raises them is you as a landlord or the cuticura unguent. I had too my best night here and the day is surpassingly lovely. It rained all night. You know that freshness of early morning in the South. The palm swings, rocks, the sky is in great broad bands of white & deep blue; there's a sound of someone sawing wood & a sound of hens cackling. FIRST: About your poem. Devil take it – I am plagued in exactly the same way. I cant begin a thing yet. Ive put it down to my fatigue & then Im so *troubled* – just as if, beneath all my other feelings, someone stirred the pool with a stick & all is muddy. The someone is L.M. Ill get over it but my weakness has given her a chance she hasn't failed to take advantage of. Ill get over this, and perhaps its not that at all.

Truth to tell, I miss you, too, more than I'd imagined. Together, we seem to make something: we seem to be *building* something & I don't like to think of anything stopping those building operations. Time is too short. I wonder if you know what I mean? Do you? Its hard to explain. But even while we lie in bed & the eiderdown slips to the floor its going on. And now its not going on. The bricks & mortar & heavy planks are all tumbled in the long grass. Well, it can't be helped. I am going to astonish you at Xmas if I can by then. Ill have broken through.

It DELIGHTS me that Milne has ousted May. What infernal cheek! Oh, I DO rejoice. Im so glad you were firm. I shiver to think of her in possession – with her earrings tinkling triumphantly. "We've got the Murry's house for the winter!" My Vord, what an escape.[2]

Re book box. I burn for it. No, there's nothing more to come, love, in it. What I miss here terribly is *odd* things, *ornaments*, scraps of stuff for little tablecloths, all nice things for the table, but especially little personal 'bits'. But those you can't provide. WHEN we live here we'll have them.

I must get up. Marie has gone to market. She bought a superb carpet sweeper yesterday acting on my orders. It cost 50 francs (£1!).

The invisible worm[3] has got into my Founting Pen – alas!

Yours truly & faithfully

Wig.

I'm DEAD OFF Schiffs. Had a card from them which for some reason finished them. This I tell you in case they invite you there. Don't *bother* to go if you don't care to. They wrote me a kind of rhapsody on Eliot – *idiocy*. I've had enough. Finito. Now Id run 10 miles to escape them!!

MS ATL. *LJMM*, 540–1.

---

[1] George Bernard Shaw, the *Nation*, 18 Sept. 1920, reviewed at length *Satan the Waster. A Philosophical War Trilogy* by Vernon Lee. The book, which Shaw found 'of first-rate workmanship from beginning to end', and whose author he saluted as 'the noblest Briton of them all', praised Lenin at the expense of Lloyd George.

[2] KM's mocking of the South African accent suggests that Ida Baker's Rhodesian-born sister May had approached Murry about sharing Portland Villas.

The invisible worm
That flies in the night,
In the howling storm.

(William Blake, 'The Sick Rose', in *Songs of Experience* (1794))

To Sydney Schiff, [21 September 1920]

Villa Isola Bella | Caravan | Menton
Tuesday

Very many thanks for your card. I will write as soon as I can. All goes well, but I am tired after that journey. I can't lift a pen for the moment. But I can let it go about T.S.E. For my money is on JMM as THE English Critic. I agree, he makes mistakes sometimes; he's rash, he's not steady yet, he leaps before he looks. But there is a sign – a something in what he writes which the opaque frigidity of Eliot *never* has. Thats my opinion. Hurra for JMM.

Murry with all thy faults I love thee still.[1] And I mean as a *critic* please. Hes the man of the future, Im sure. He risks himself. T.S.E. never.

My love to you both

K.

MS BL, *Adam* 300, 105.

[1] 'Jesu! with all thy faults I love thee still', quoted from Samuel Butler, *Notebooks* (1912), in H. F. Jones, *Samuel Butler, Author of Erewhon (1835–1902): A Memoir* (1919), i.183, which Murry had reviewed in the *Athenaeum*, 24 Oct. 1919. Butler in turn was adapting a line from William Cowper, 'England with all thy faults I love thee still' (*The Task* (1785), bk. 2, i. 206).

To J. M. Murry, [23 September 1920]

[Villa Isola Bella, Caravan, Menton]
Thursday

Yesterday a man came up & measured for an awning – a top & three sides – a kind of *tent* to be fixed in a corner of the 'Terrace' – where one can sit the whole day. And I also bought a chaise longue and a green chair which is (privately) yours.

Dearest Dear
DONT worry about me; I beg you not to. I am certainly on the mend. All that remains is for me to get back my strength. And I SHALL in no time now. I haven't worried an atom bit about Floryan except in so far as it worried you and affects us. I won't have that Pole outside our door. Burn all he gives you – won't you? A bonfire . . .

Im sending my reviews tomorrow. Wish I was a trump. Its most fright-fully nice to be called one. Tommy (Ill send you his letter on Sunday. It was a masterpiece) sent me Arnold Bennett's new book to do for the Nation.[1] I must do it & at once. Its a chance for me. But I wish you could melt me down some iron nails or better make some iron tea in a jug in our backyard where we played when we were tinies, first. *Wanted*: Old or New *Iron*. Good Price Given.

I thought on the spot *Roger* when you mentioned Violet. I had thought it before. My literary watchdog bayed at that marriage & always called it a tragedy. I hope its not. The Newspapers arrive every day. But look here!! What a trick to play on your little pal. There was I reading away about Miners Ultimatums and Darker Prospecks per usual & suddenly – *plop* I went through the bed – just my toes waving au secours. 'Mr J.M.M., Editor of the Athenaeum, writes . . .' Can you imagine it??? You, with your absurd little coal shovel talking about Blood Money & International Coal Scuttles.[2] I see you with your hands behind your back at the Miners' Congress singing: 'My pay was 40 cents a day, twing!' Oh my Preposterous Darling –

Wig.

MS ATL. *LJMM*, 541–2.

[1] Two new books were published by Arnold Bennett in September: *A Man from the North* and *The Roll Call*, but neither was reviewed by KM.

[2] Murry's letter to the *Daily News*, 20 Sept. 1920, called for an international perspective to the miners' strike. He pointed out that the profits from coal came from selling to a starving Europe, and proposed:

1. It is not equitable that these profits should go either to the mine owners, or the miners, or the English nation. They are blood money.
2. It is equitable that these profits should be considered as a trust, and used to give loans on easy terms to the European nations who must urgently need credit.

.   .   .   .

4. It is reasonable that a proportion of the interest on these loans should be applied to ameliorating housing and other conditions in the mining districts.

To J. M. Murry, [24 September 1920]

[Villa Isola Bella, Garavan, Menton]
Friday.

I am 'getting on' darling – theres no doubt about that – but its a stiff climb pour le moment.

My own Bogey

A clap of Thunder and the long arm of Jove thrust through the shutters with your precious telegram upon a silver fork of lightning. That is what happened last night. You are *too* thoughtful; it bouleverses me. There the matter ends I hope about F. Ill keep the letters till you come at Xmas. Your card with the cutting re tuberculosis came today. What a splendid letter it was – 'advanced stage' & now 'splendid health' – what that means to read!

I want very much to know about your dinner with Kay.[1] My theory is *drunk*. Did I tell you I had another letter from Beatrice H?[2] A hateful sniggering letter – a hiccup of thing. People are rather dreadful, Boge. Bogey, love, *Wingley* is on my heart awfully. I keep seeing him & remembering how he sat – a teapot cat – so serene in my room & how he touched my hand at meals with his gentil paw. You must love him tenderly – as you alone know how & whisper him our secrets. *No* one else understands him. He's very like us, really. Im writing my reviews today. It has been raining – torrents of warm heavy rain & now it is marvellously fine & warm again & one can hear the buds uncurling. WHEN you come – I am making preparations even now – not to hurry my dearest dear but –

Your own

Wig.

MS ATL, *LJMM* 542.

1 Alexander Kay, manager of the London branch, Victoria Street, of the Bank of New Zealand, had acted as financial advisor and avuncular friend since KM returned to London in 1908.

2 An intense friendship with Beatrice Hastings, a South African-born journalist and A. R. Orage's mistress during the early years of KM's association with the *New Age*, had turned into bitter enmity, mainly because of Hastings' inveterate jealousy. When in Mar. 1920 she wrote to Murry asking for work, KM had told him, 'Yes, it is true, I *did* love B. H. but you have utterly forgotten what I told you of her behaviour in Paris – of the last time I saw her and because I refused to stay the night with her she bawled at me and called me a femme publique in front of those filthy frenchmen' (*CLKM* III. 258; see also *CLKM* I. 97).

To J. M. Murry, [25 September 1920]

[Villa Isola Bella, Garavan, Menton]

Photographs included. Ill try to send some every Sunday. They are not good but – you'll see.

PLEASE } Tell me your small worries & big worries.
Tell me what annoys you & what you'd like changed and what plagues you.

Samedi soir.

My own precious Bogey

I am beginning my Sunday letter.[1] I can't resist the hour. Its 6.30 just on sunset – the sea a deep hyacinth blue – silver clouds floating by like sails and the air smells of the pine and the bay and of charcoal fires. Divine evening! Heavenly fair place! The great RAIN has brought a thousand green spears up in every corner of the garden. Oh, you'll be met by such Flowers on Parade at Christmas Time. There's a winey

smell at the corner of the terrace where a huge fig tree drops its great
purple fruits. At the other the magnolia flashes leaves; it has great buds
brushed over with pink. Marie has just brought in my chaise longue &
the green chair which is yours to escape l'humidité du soir . . . Do these
details bore my darling in London? Oh, I could go on for ever. But I do
think this place, villa, climate, maid, all are as perfect as can be. Marie's
cooking infuriates me. Why don't I help you to her escaloppes aux
tomates, with *real* purée de p. de terre, deux feuilles de salade and des
oeufs en neige. And her Black Coffee!!

Sharing her return from market tho' is my delight. I go into the
kitchen & am given my glass of milk & then she suddenly rushes into the
scullery comes back with the *laden* basket and (privately exulting over her
purchases) 'Ah cet-te vie, cet-te vie. Comme tout ça est chère, Madame!
Avant la guerre notre jolie France, c'était un jardin de Paradis et main-
tenant c'est que le Président même n'a pas la tête sur les épaules. Allez!
allez! Douze sous pour les haricots! C'est vrai qu'ils sont frais – qu'ils sont
jolis, qu'ils sont enfin – enfin – des haricots pour un petit Prince – mais
douze sous, douze sous . . .' etc.etc. This at a great pace of course. Does
it come over? Does it seem to you the way a cook ought to talk? Theres
a mouse in the cupboard. When she brought my bregchick this morning . . . 'le p'tit Monsieur nous a visité pendant la nuit, Madame. Il a
mangé presque toute une serviette. Mais pensez-vous – quelles dents.
Allez-allez! C'est un *maitre*!!' I don't know. I wont bore you with any
more of her – but it seems to me that this is the way people like her *ought*
to talk.

I heard again from Methuen today. They now say they'd like 2 books
for next spring. I think there must have been some trunk work, some
back stair work[2] in this on the part of Bogey. But Ill see what I can do
without promising in my fatal way what I can't perform. I wish I could
begin real creative work. I haven't yet. Its the atmosphere, the . . . tone
which is hard to get. And without it nothing is worth doing. I have such
a horror of *triviality* – a great part of my Constable book is *trivial*.[3] Its not
good enough. You see its too late to beat about the bush any longer.
They are cutting down the cherry trees; the orchard is sold[4] – that is
really the atmosphere I want. Yes, the dancing and the dawn of the
Englishman in the train who said 'jump!', all these, with the background.
I feel – this is *jet* sincere – that you and I are the only 2 persons who
realise this really. Thats our likeness and thats what makes us, too, the
creatures of our time.

Speaking of something else, which is nevertheless connected – it is an
awful temptation in face of all these novels to cry 'woe – woe!' I cannot
conceive how writers who have lived through our times can *drop* these
last ten years & revert to why Edward didn't understand Vi's reluctance
to be seduced or (see Bennett) why a dinner of twelve covers needs

remodelling.[5] If I did not review novels I'd never read them. The writ-ers (practically all of them) seem to have no idea of what one means by continuity. It is a difficult thing to explain. Take the old Tartar waiter in Anna who serves Levin & Stepan.[6] Now, Tolstoy only has to touch him and he gives out a note and this note is somehow important, per-sists, is a part of the whole book. But all these other men – they intro-duce their cooks, aunts, strange gentlemen, and so on, and once the pen is off them they are *gone* – dropped down a hole. Can one explain this by what you might call a *covering* atmosphere. Isn't that a bit too vague? Come down O youth from yonder Mountain height? & give your worm a staff of reason to assist her. What it *boils down to* is 'either the man can make his people live & keep em alive or he can't'. But Criticks better that . . . (Dont bother to answer if it bores you, my darling.)

Reams came from Brett. She ruffled my feathers. She is keeping you at your tennis because of the good it does you. Your Mind can think of Nothing/'Except the Flying Ball. You are not to be allowed to work too hard but she means to be wily & in the future you and I and she & Gertler are all going to live in some huge untidy chateau with Arthur 'for a tornado' upsetting my exquisite ways & eating all the jam. This made me – all the heathen in me – rage so furiously together.[8] Sunday afternoon.

Really today is the Best Day. Its hot – yet theres a breeze. Im much better. I went into Jinnies garden & lay all the morning under the pine trees. To have all that over grown half run wild garden has simply *intox-icated* me. I found it this morning. It was like a better Karori.[9] There's not a soul there – the great shuttered villa so white in the sunlight, so serene – & she went voyages of discovery. At the end of an avenue of bamboos there was a small round bamboo parlour. Is it really there? For another time? I doubt very much. But I want & I want my play mate. Please don't mind me saying that – it leaves you as free as Ariel,[10] love. You can go up half a hundred Amazons tomorrow or live in a tower on wheels. I don't want my cry to follow you even as a plaintive cry or a pleading cry.[11] But just suppose there's a small gold cloud and a bird hidden behind it – its note is a kind of hoch celestial 'Bogey'. No more than that. I kiss you. I am proud of you. I love you for ever. I am at your side. Darling please take care of yourself Wig.

MS ATL. *LKM* II. 45–7; *LJMM* 543–5.

1 That is, she is beginning her usual Sunday letter on the Saturday evening.
2 Cf. 'Some trunk-work, some behind-door-work': *The Winter's Tale*, III. iii. 75.
3 *Bliss and Other Stories*, which was now with the publishers, and would be released in early Dec.
4 KM is thinking of the last act of Chekhov's *The Cherry Orchard*, when the family home has been sold and the axes are already heard felling the cherry trees.
5 KM is vaguely recalling a point in Arnold Bennett's essay 'The Social Intercourse Business', which appeared in *Cassell's Magazine of Fiction*, Aug. 1920, and as ch. 7 in *Our Women: Chapters on the*

Sex Discord (1920). Bennett begins a section on pp. 181–2: 'We will pass from the vocabulary to the dinner itself. Take a dinner. Let it be of medium size, say a dozen covers.'

⁶ Levin and Stepan Oblonsky are dining in a restaurant in Moscow, and are served by a Tartar waiter, in *Anna Karenina*, pt. I, ch. 10, 11.

⁷ Cf. 'Come down O maid from yonder mountain height!': Tennyson, *The Princess*, vii, l. 177.

⁸ 'Why do the nations so furiously rage together', from the bass lines in Handel's *Messiah*, drawn from "Why do the nations rage": Ps. 2:1.

⁹ The small village, 6 miles from Wellington, where KM had lived between the ages of 5 and 10, and the setting of several stories.

¹⁰ The spirit of intelligence and freedom in Shakespeare's *The Tempest*.

¹¹ KM was more expansive in a notebook entry in Aug., written after she learned of the flirtation between Murry and Brett, and the fact that he had considered taking a room in her house while KM was in the south of France: 'I suppose one always thinks the latest shock is the worst shock. This is quite unlike any other I have suffered. The lack of sensitiveness as far as I am concerned – the *selfishness* of this staggers me. This is what I must remember when I am away. J. thinks no more of me than of anybody else. . . . To plan all this at such a time, and then on my return *the first words*: I must be nice to D. How disgustingly indecent!' (*Journal*, 1954, 208.)

To J. M. Murry, [27 September 1920]

[Villa Isola Bella, Garavan, Menton]

Dearest Bogey

I want to go through the paper with you and a card wont do. Before I begin – I am thrilled about Shaw of course.¹ All is forgiven. In fancy I slipped down to the town & sent him a straw basket of tangerines – with an inscription which rolled and rolled and rolled to small golden perfection like the ripest & the fairest in the bastick. Aren't we a pair if people smile on us? But Ill be silent. Ill not exist. *You* are the one who climbs the stairs & sitting in a delightful room with some quite peculiarly delicious tea you and cette belle barbe have it out. Oh, I DO envy you. And what are you going to reply to Methuen?

'Dear Sir A.²

Ah – there you have me I'm afraid.'

To business.

Your Wilde, Bogey, was extremely good. You put him in his place without for a moment pronouncing a judgment which was not strictly *critical*. What I mean is its so very difficult with a man like Wilde to get him & keep him inside that strange sort of ring through which one gazes at ones 'specimens' at the moment of writing. Know what I mean? Its a kind of expanding & contracting ring – you can pull your specimen up very near, so near that you can count the hairs of his spiritual eyebrows – or you can send him far far – a speck on the horizon. Wilde – the immense temptation is to take your eye away and see him *there* without its aid. You haven't. I note, tho', darling, the last sentence and it makes me smile a little . . . Instead of 'a great biography' you can't resist poor old Frankie's dreadfully battered hat & his: 'I knew you as a boy, Sir.'³ I understand . . .

May Sinclair's finished – good. Its a flabby dabby babby.[4] But it will go down no doubt. Oh, it *is* bad, isn't it.

I thought Duprée too missish.[5] It read like one essay one handed in on Monday and got back on Wednesday. No style, no attack, no *reason* for it. God forbid he writes the same number of lines on Shakespeare – or Hamlet. Mad or Sane?

Blunden is in danger of writing stunt prose. His Sussex (is it he?) is good but he bangs the drum too hard himself.[6]

I thought Aldous v. good on Thomas – didn't you? And Old Sullivan was excellent. He has got a good firm touch with him – nowadays.

D.L.M. is excellent.[7]

410–411 look very dull, don't they?[8] But it can't be helped, I realise. I think our Library Table is – no, its not dull. At the same time its not interesting – is it? I feel the paper *lacks* something, *lacks* a column – on the lines we suggested for Delamare.[9] Do you feel it a bit scrappy? I don't bite in to it.

About the leaders – there again.[10] I think they ought to be more pronouncedly the work of one hand. They ought to be just a touch *caustic* or (appalling word) *bright*. They can't *compel* in such a little space ∴ they ought to *attract*. If that can't be done I think real good pars. would be better. Talk it over with me – will you?

I wish & I wish & I wish – Why aren't you here? Even tho I am as poor as a mouse don't publish Sun & Moon.[11] I'll send you a story this week. *Do* publish it if you can. Of course don't if you're full up – but alas! for my £25 a month – its gone.

This however is sheer waiting & nothing to do with my blessed little editore. I embrace you.

Yours *ever*

K.M.

Just a line more.

The lizards here *abound*. There is one big fellow, a perfect miniature crocodile who lurks under the leaves that climb over a corner of the terrace. I watched him come forth today – *very* slithy – and eat an ant. You should have seen the little jaws – the flick flick of the tongue, the queer rippling pulse just below the shoulder. His eyes, too. He listened with them – and when he couldn't find another ant he stamped his front paw and then seeing that I was watching *deliberately* winked, and slithered away.

There is also a wasps nest in the garden. Two infant wasps came out this morning & each caught hold of a side of a *leaf* & began to tug. It was a brown leaf *outside* the size of three tea leaves. They became furious – they whimpered – whiney-pined – snatched at each other – wouldn't give way & finally one *rolled* over & couldn't roll back again – just lay there – kicking. I never saw such a thing. His twin then couldn't move the leaf at all. I pointed out the hideous moral to my invisible play-mate.

Fabretta[12]

MS ATL. *LKM* II. 47–8; *LJMM*, 545–7.

[1] George Bernard Shaw, who lived above the *Athenaeum* office at 10 The Adelphi, had flattered Murry on his achievements as editor.

[2] Sir Algernon Methuen (1856–1924), founder of the large publishing house.

[3] Murry's review of Frank Harris's *Oscar Wilde* on 24 Sept. concluded with 'gratitude for what is, take it all in all, one of the most masterly biographies in the English Language'. KM's own view of Harris as mentor had not been so different from Murry's when they were first together. She had written to him herself in 1912: 'You are our hero and our master – always' (*CLKM* I.113).

[4] The novelist May Sinclair, whose *Mary Olivet: A Life* KM reviewed in the *Athenaeum*, 20 June 1919, had contributed a short story, 'The Bambino', to the paper on 24 Sept.

[5] Bonamy Dobrée's essay on John Ford, the Elizabethan playwright.

[6] Edmund Blunden had reviewed *Life in a Sussex Windmill*, by Edward A. Martin, and *The Book of Sussex Verse*, ed. C. F. Cook.

[7] Aldous Huxley had written on Edward Thomas's *Collected Poems*; J. W. N. Sullivan on Hilaire Belloc's *Europe and the Faith*; D. L. Murray, under 'Schopenhauer and Realism', reviewed Desmond Skillingford's *Daisy* at the Kingsway Theatre.

[8] What KM found dull were pages of four unbroken columns in 8-point type.

[9] 'Our Literary Table' was a page of brief entries on miscellaneous book matters; Walter de la Mare did not take up the possibility of his own column.

[10] The unsigned leader for that week, 'St Mathew's Day', was on the Lord Mayor's visit to Murry's old school, Christ's Hospital. Often there were several discrete editorial notes.

[11] It was too late for Murry to follow KM's request. 'Sun and Moon' appeared in the *Athenaeum* the next week, 1 Oct. 1920.

[12] KM is recalling Jean Henri Fabre (1823–1915), the Provençal naturalist whose studies of insects were highly regarded as both literature and science.

To J. M. Murry, [28 September 1920]

[Villa Isola Bella, Garavan, Menton]

Dear darling,

Ive just got your further notes about the A. I agree absolutely. (Oh, Bogey, if you knew what a *bridge* such a piece of paper is to me. You fling it across and it holds – and I seem to somehow emerge and cross over to your bank for a minute. Its *miraculous*.) However – revenons: Im for *pars* instead of leaders. They are a grind and I don't think the grind worth it. Yes A.L.H. this last week struck me so much that I sent him a p.c.[1] Hes enormously improved. YOU mustn't do a stroke more. I agree with Shaw. You write too well to be a really good editore. You can't take your ease at the job: you can't write without your nerves being in the job. Nor neither in my wormhigh way can I.

I burn to see a chunk of your poem. I am not in the least settled down to anything yet. The journal – I have absolutely given up. I dare not keep a journal – I should always be trying to tell the truth. As a matter of fact I dare not tell the truth – I feel I *must* not. The only way to exist is to go on – and try and lose oneself – to get as far as possible away from *this* moment. Once I can do that all will be well. So its stories or nothing. I expect I shall kick off soon – perhaps today – who knows? In the meantime I peg away too, darling, in my fashion.

Stick things into envelopes & send them over when you can – will you? Any old thing becomes a treasure on the way. Remember that, old boy. I must get up and take my first cure d'air. Its a fine day – very fine, very blue –

Ive still *never* had that packet of letters – never had the document. I heard from Cooks today that the box has left. What an excitement it will be – unpacking it! Dont forget what *news* means – a magazine, the L.M. [London Mercury], anything that keeps one in touch. Kiss our sweet cats for me.

Farewell my precious Boge and be happy.

Wig.

MS ATL. *LKM* II. 51; *LJMM* 551–2.

1 Aldous Huxley's review of Edward Thomas's *Collected Poems*, which she had praised in her previous letter.

To J. M. Murry, [29 September 1920]

[Villa Isola Bella, Garavan, Menton]

Darling

Your letter came today. I had looked forward to it so tremendously – and it told me what I wanted to know – it brought you close to me for a little moment.

Im rather upset. Ive never got over that first illness – and I keep having fever. That's the truth. Fever & headache & nightmare pursue me. I should not have walked in that garden – it was too much & it has laid me low again. I must just keep dead quiet & pin my flag a small and trembling banner on to some less high mountain top for the present.

I *tell* you because its all of me for the moment. Disappointment – to be so weak and so queer. It will pass. Ill be glad when Jinnie & Connie[1] come. I feel Id like barricades. One feels so alone when one is cast down again. Isn't it the irony of fate that just when it would be (so it seems) so much easier to get well if one were with ones darling – its denied. Well, we must just *bear* it – thats all! But the awful sense of insecurity. One puts out ones hand & theres nothing there. (Are these three years a dream?)

Now Ive taken your hankyberchief & cried on your shoulder & you've kissed me – we'll wave it away. We'll get up & go on. Can you *bear* me to do that? Ah dearest – *ought* I to? Not to make *you* sad – never that – just to hear from you: *I know* Worm. I too am nearer you than ever before in *spirit* more.

Your Wig,

MS ATL. *LJMM*, 547–8.

---

[1] KM's cousin Connie Beauchamp and her companion Jinnie Fullerton had not yet come from London to their recently acquired Villa Louise, immediately behind the Isola Bella.

To Richard Murry, [? September 1920]

VILLA ISOLA BELLA | GARAVAN | MENTON A/M.

Dear Richard,
    The painting has come. I like it tremendously. I think there is very fine feeling in that landscape seen across water; the house, the trees, the grassy levels all seem to partake of the watery element. Do you know what I mean? . . . It seems to me that not only the water reflects the house and trees but they reflect the water. I'm not trying to be literary . . . It's in your painting. I think, too, the 'balance' of water and land is very nicely adjusted. It's awfully good, Richard. It's full of colour. I can look long at it.[1]
Merci de tout coeur. I'm very happy and proud to own a 'Richard Murry'.

Katherine.

MS R. Murry.

---

[1] Richard Murry noted: 'I think this must have been one of my very first paintings: of Hurlingham House seen from Wandsworth Park.'

To J. M. Murry, [1 October 1920]

[Villa Isola Bella, Garavan, Menton]
Friday.

V. warm – overclouded with a vague, dark wind.
Dearest Bogey
    I repent of having sent you that depressed card.[1] I ought not to have, I suppose. Really, its rather a nice point of conduct. I cant decide it for myself. Knowing you – should I refrain? But the falsity – Oh, Blow. Yes,

How is the house going, darling? Does it go smoothly? Are you left untroubled? Please let me know this. And do take great care of getting hot at tennis & then not putting on a thick enough coat after. Do be careful of your colds.

You've so precious little money (2d less than £1!) that I don't dare suggest the dentist – yet you ought to go. You ought to keep as fit as you can in every way to withstand the winter cold. Dont save. Spend it on (getting) keeping healthy. What in Heaven's name is there to equal HEALTH. There's no future if youre not well, no solid substantial Xmas with £50 in the pudding. There is only TODAY. That reminds me of your buying the Hardy.[2] How fantastic it seemed when I was just holding on to the hour and the minute in Ospedaletti. But this feeling (which is making me simply reckless at present) would be very difficult to imagine if one had not been ill. Really if one is healthy one can live on next to nothing still – of course one can – OR once one is well one can make money – easy as winking. Why not? But if ones ill – well – there one is with a grey gown and a rattle coughing in the wake of the chariots.

Dear little Wing would make a sweet acolyte at a ½d a week. I see him. He is a precious little cat. Whisper my name in his ear. Im afraid tho', he wont smile. He'll more likely sneeze.

Oh, Bogey that packet of letters never fetched up, nor did the signed declaration. Were they sent? The letters have been 9 days on the way, so they *must* be lost.

I shall be more than thankful for my books. It was v. silly not to have brought Shakespeare.

Suppose you didn't glance at a novel by a man called *Prowse.* 'A Gift of the Dusk.'[3] A simply terrible book – awful – ghastly! And about as good as it could be. Its just a kind of . . . journal the man kept while he was at a sanatorium in Switzerland. It is the goods if you like! But he must be a wonderful man. I wish I knew if he is dead. Will you PLEASE ask Beresford[4] if you see him (Collins is the publisher). I wish very much I could hear of him. One's heart goes out to anyone who has *faced* an experience as he has done. "One must tell everything – everything." That is more and more real to me each day. It is, after all, the only treasure heirloom we have to leave – our own little grain of truth. As I write I am deeply loving you. Do you feel that? Sitting opposite to you – talking – very quietly. You *are* there? You *do* reply? Tell me about yourself, my darling, whenever you can.

Your own
Wig.

MS ATL. *LKM* II. 48; *LJMM*, 548–9.

¹ Her letter on 29 Sept.
² In Jan. 1920 Murry had bought some volumes of Thomas Hardy 'when we could not afford them' (Murry, 246).
³ Under 'The Silence is Broken', KM reviewed *A Gift of the Dusk* by R. D. Prowse in the *Athenaeum*, 29 Oct. 1920. His last work, *Proud Ashes*, was published in 1934.
⁴ Their friend the novelist J. D. Beresford (1873–1947), also a journalist and reviewer with the *Westminster Gazette*.

To J. M. Murry, [3 October 1920]

[Menton]

RECEIVED PAPER EXCELLENT DONT LET ME DEPRESS YOU FIGHTING HARD LOVE

TIG

Telegram ATL.

To J. M. Murry, [4 October 1920]

[Villa Isola Bella, Garavan, Menton]

My darling Bogey

Its Monday – and the sun has come back – its fine and warm. I had 2 cards from you today – but you didn't tell me how your cold was. Does that mean it is better?

Yesterday the paper came. *I* thought it a very good number. You felt rather 'faint' about it didn't you & Miss Brett found it 'dull'. But I thought it was full of meat, somehow. I read it, and I thought of you and of what an amount of work it means and of how you labour at it – and I sent you that wire. *Whatever* my feelings are I am *not* justified in giving way to them before you or in letting you see even the shadow of the border of that shadowy country that we exiles from health inhabit. It is not fair. So Im resolute that you shant be plagued again, my dearest darling and determined to keep my resolution. Help me to.

Im sending you and Milne a dozen kāhki (I don't know how to spell it thats phonetic) to eat for your breakfasts. They are very good & very healthy. I send them unripe. You must wait until they are soft, then cut off the top, squeeze a *lot* of lemon juice inside & eat with a teaspoon. Perhaps they won't be a treat, after all. I always long to *send* you things. Please give my love to Milne. He sounds so nice in the house. I wonder what Wing thinks of the clarinet.

Walpoles novel¹ which I mean to do for next week (1 col.) ought to

be a very good prop to hang those very good ideas on that I tried to communicate to you. I want to take it seriously and really say why it fails –
for of course it does fail. But his 'intention' was serious. I hope Ill be able
to say what I do mean. I am *no* critic of the homely kind. "If you would
only explain quietly in simple language" as L.M. said to me yesterday.
Good Heavens that is out of my power.

The garden menagerie includes snakes – a big chap as thick as my
wrist, as long as my arm, slithered along the path this morning and
melted into the bushes. It wasn't horrid or fearful, however. As to the
mice – Marie's piège seems to snap in the most revolting way. A fat one
was offered to a marauding cat at the back door yesterday – but it *refused*
it. "Polisson! Tu veux un morceau de sucre avec?" I heard Marie scold.
She is very down on the cats here; she says they are malgracieux. Yes,
she is a most *remarkable* type. Yesterday afternoon – it was terribly gloomy
& triste outside & she came in for the coffee tray – & said how she *hated*
Menton. She had lived here 8 years with her pauvre mari and then
they'd lived 2 years in Nice where he died & was buried. She said she
could *bear* Nice because il se repose la bas mais ici – Madame – il se
promenait avec moi – partout partout – and then she beat her little black
crepe bodice & cried "trop de souvenirs – Madame – trop de souvenirs".
Oh, how I love people who feel deeply. How restful it is to live with them
even in their 'excitement'. I think for writers, people like you and me, it
is right to be with them – but the feeling must be true – not a hair
breadth assumed – or I hate it as much as I love the other. As I write
that I don't believe it any more. I could live with you and not care 2
pins if people 'felt' anything at all – in fact I could draw away and be
very aloof and cold if they did. *I* don't know. Its too difficult.

More reams from Brett. Tennis and Gertler's threatened tuberculosis[2]
are the themes. How he mustn't be told and will crumple up if he *is* told
and Dr Sorapure says and she dreams tennis. But I wish she would keep
her pen off tuberculosis – she doesn't know what she is writing about &
its desperately tactless to 'tee-hee' at the idea of it. Heavens what irony!
I have no doubt Gertler's friends will subscribe £1000 and send him to
Egypt for the winter. Oh, Brett does make me loathe London. She seems
to sweep a gutterful of it into an envelope and then she *goads* me – on
purpose. *She's* not ill *she* can run, *she* can play tennis with Murry. No, I
can't write to her. "You must get better & you & I & Murry will go
streaming away." Oh BOGEY!! But people with spots on their lungs are
not subjects for merriment.

I feel this letter is cold and poor; the fruit is not good to eat. Its rather
like that withered fig tree.[3] Do you know there is a kind of fig tree which
is supposed to be of the family of that unfortunate one – it is dark
stemmed and its leaves are black. They flap on the blackened boughs –
they are like leaves that a flame has passed over. *Terrible.* I saw one once

in a valley, a beautiful valley with a river flowing through it. There was
linen drying on the banks and the women were beating the water and
calling to one another – gaily. And there was this *sad* tree. L.M. who was
with me said "of course the *explanation* is that one must never cease from
giving." The fig tree had no figs – so Christ cursed it. *Did you ever*! There's
such a story buried under the whole thing – isn't there if only one could
dig it out.

Well darling Im going back to my chaise longue. I spend all day either
lying on the terrace or in this salon with both windows open and I go to
bed at 8 p.m. & get up at 10 a.m. Each day is the same.

How are you? Your poem? You – the very you? Do you feel we are
near each other? I love you. I think of you at the yellow table. I miss
you at night & in the early morning & when I am awake at night I think
of you – lying asleep. I wonder what suit you are wearing. I see you in
your jersey. "Don't be afraid". I do not ask you, my darling own, to
come under my umbulella.[4]

But I have a deep, *pure* love for you in my heart.
Your Wig.

MS ATL. *LKM* II. 48–50; *LJMM*, 549–51.

---

[1] KM reviewed Hugh Walpole's *The Captives* under 'Observation Only' in the *Athenaeum*, 15 Oct.
1920.
[2] Mark Gertler did in fact contract the disease, which was at an advanced stage when he committed suicide in 1939.
[3] See Matt. 24: 32, Luke 21: 29.
[4] KM several times quoted from a favourite rhyme:

> Come along Isabella
> Under my umbulella
> Don't be afraid
> There's a good maid
> Come along Isabella.

To J. M. Murry, [6 October 1920]

[Villa Isola Bella, Garavan, Menton]

Your Saturday night letter.
Darling,
Forgive my unworthiness and my failure these last days.

Your letter – surely the most wonderful letter a man ever wrote a
woman, or a Boge ever wrote a Wig almost made me cry out: "Forgive
me, forgive me".

It is what my suffering has given to me, this letter, the reward of it. I seem to have just a glimpse of something Ive never known before as I sit here thinking of you and me and our love . . . Its as though, looking across the plains, what I had thought was cloud dissolves, lifts and behind it there are mountains. Always a new silence, a new mystery.

My precious love.

You HAVE come here. I mean – the ache of desolation is over. Im not alone. Of course I long for you here, sharing my daily life, but I do not say 'come'. Its not only on account of the money, Bogey. If I believed at this moment that I was going to die of course I would say 'come' because it would be unbearable not . . . to have you to see me off on the journey where you know the train drops into a great black hole.

(No, I believe even then I couldnt say 'come'.)

But what is it? I feel our 'salvation', our 'future' depends on our doing nothing desperate – but on holding on, keeping calm (this from *me*!) and leaving nothing in disorder, nothing undone. The 'paper' isnt really the paper, I suppose. Its a kind of battle that the Knight has to wage and the Knight is you and me – he's our spirit. Also, my darling I have got the queer feeling that 'holding on' we declare our faith in the future – our power to win through. *This* year is the important year for us. You ought, for your future freedom, to be where you are. You ought for *THE FUTURE* to keep the paper going one more year.

And there's this, too. But here I am speaking to myself. If I am to be what I wish to be I must not be rescued. Thats *dead true*. Bogey and I have chosen each other for lovers in this world, and I believe absolutely in our choice. But I believe the reason beyond all other reasons why we chose each other is because we feel FREE together. I know that, at the last, I do not put the lightest chain on him – nor he on me. I feel, if he were here now, if I gave up and said 'come' there might be a danger – in fact the very cry is a denial of what I really really believe.

But its all mysterious, it all seems to belong to another country. This speech will not explain it. There are signs, silences, a kind of flowing from light to shadow. I can only say – my love, we shall stay as we are. I live for you. I will prepare myself for our life. Look into my heart. Believe in me. *Would I sooner have Bogey here now. NO.* (What a funny looking no – a little bit gothic!) Oh dear oh dear, put your arms round me. Come at Christmas with candles in your hair – I want to hold you very tightly. I want to make you smile. I feel we are deathless when you write to me so. You HAVE come, Bogey; I say it again. You are here and now Im going to get up and work.

Let me not fail again. It is my dream to be here alone until Christmas and to do my work – to have a book ready by then. I shall begin my book today. Its just as though the ship had sailed into harbour . . . Now, get off my pilot, until next Christmas. I can manage rocks and shoals and storms – anything. (But even now your letter is unanswered. It is a

GIFT. Time will show how I will use it.) My darling love – you are happy? You understand?

I am your Wig.

MS ATL. *LJMM*, 552–4.

To J. M .Murry, [7 October 1920]

[Villa Isola Bella, Garavan, Menton]
Thursday.

My beloved darling

Your Sunday and Monday letters are come. With them I feel more convinced than ever that we do right to keep our promises: you know how I love you. Truly, I can't get over having troubled you like this: it seems impossible and yet – now that I know you *do* understand I cant regret it. I called upon you in my time of trouble and you heard me – that is enough. My dearest own, don't feel you must keep on holding me or that you must keep listening for another cry. I have a perfect *horror* of demanding help, of asking you to – hold my hand. Youre as free as can be again. Youve wonderfully responded. The miracle that I couldn't have believed could happen HAS happened. If I could love you more absolutely (it seems I always can) I do. But – do you understand? I want to put my arms round you – hold you – let you hear my inmost heart say thank you thank you my Boge and then *let you go*. Be undisturbed; be free of me now. Think of me as here & working and getting better so that all we intend to do we shall do. I feel immensely glad we have Broomies.[1] Its somehow so important that it should be there. I feel we shall return one day – not too far off and *it* will be our home. I feel nearer you than ever. There is *you* and *work*.

Dont write me any more letters now except on Sundays. Oh, my own precious little mate, do you see Wig imploring you to smile & be calm and wear a bow tie & sit at my yellow table with our teapot cat & save pennies and talk to your friends and keep warm.

As for me I am in the open air day and night. I never am in a room with the windows shut. By great good fortune Ive got Marie who every day looks after me better. And she is so sympathetic that all she cooks tastes especially good. She looks after me and anxiously asks if "la viande etait assez saignante" but *sanely* – in the way one not only can stand, but one loves, and when I go into the kitchen & say Marie je tremble de faim her 'tant mieux' as she butters you a tartine is just absolutely right. So you see I *do* count my blessings; this house – this climate and this good soul.

It will be perfeck if you can come for Xmas, but there again you must feel free. Dont think of me as too disappointed if you cant. Just feel free. If you do come L.M. is going to England to spend the 3 weeks with her sister so we'd be quite alone in the little house . . .

It happened just as I thought it would. I began on my own work yesterday & did a big chunk. I think its alright. But today Im reviewing Walpole as I feel you may want an extra novel or two in the paper just now as its 'the season'. Walpole is a *real case*.

Tom Moult's letter was a most pathetic document, Boge. Poor little chap. He would sweep the very office. I have an idea that Bessie leads him a devil of a life. What *was* her operation. I feel she had – no, it sounds indelicate. Ill not write it. But shes just the kind of woman who would have that operation & then trade on poor old T.'s sympathies for ever after. By the way *Maggie*,² Walpoles heroine had the Kosmos behind her, too. Its blowing guns today – a choppy sea – my favourite sea – brilliant blue with the white lifting – lifting as far as one can see – rather big unbroken waves near the shore. Butterflies love a day like this. They love to fling themselves up in the air & then be caught by the wind and rocked and flung and lightly *fluttered*. They pretend to be frightened. They cling as long as they can to a leaf and then – take a butterfly long breath – up they go – away they sail – quivering with joy and delight. It must be a kind of surf bathing for them – flinging themselves down the wind.

You know how when one woman carries the newborn baby the other woman approaches & lifts the handkerchief from the tiny face & bends over & says "Bless it". But Im always wanting to lift the handkerchief off lizards faces & pansies faces & the house by moonlight. Im always want-ing to *put a blessing* on what I see. Its a queer feeling.

Am I near you? I feel we are so near each other. I feel that our love *has* changed: it seems to have grown in grace.

Here are three little photographs, darling. Do you like them? L.M. always seems to take the same, and then she has (cant you see it) *wash-basins* full of prints – dozens of *one* kind.

Goodbye for now my darling

Wig.

MS ATL. *LKM* II. 50–1; *LJMM* 554–5.

¹ The cottage that Murry bought on Marsh Common, Chailey, Sussex, in 1920, which was let to tenants.
² The heroine of Walpole's recent novel, *The Captives*.

To J. M. Murry, [10 October 1920]

[Villa Isola Bella, Garavan, Menton]

I think it was too sweet of the cats to have gone to the bathroom. Pathetic! Wonderful cat psychology, really. You ought to have a minute one installé with a mouse's tail for a plug.

My darling Bogey

Its Sunday and after awful storms fine again. My darling I cant understand why my letters don't arrive. I know they are safely posted; I am sure they are stolen your end. My mind says Sydney egged on by Marge.[1] But it is simply more than maddening to know the letters dont come. It makes me feel so helpless. And I know the feeling TOO well when they don't arrive.

Thank you, my precious, for sending me Bretts to you. As a matter of fact I do resent it most deeply – the peeping into your shirt and the threat to be severe with you. I cant say how hateful that was to me. I felt violently physically sick. And the *sickly barbed* letters she sends me. "MURRY & I pick the bone fairly clean about so and so and so and so" . . . "WE seem to do nothing but play tennis, dream tennis, eat the balls and chew the racquet strings" . . . I cant reply. I 'frissonne'. But Bogey don't let her come near. Forgive me – dont let her touch you. Ive no earthly right to interfere and yet – there it is . . . Is Gertler really *ill*? Do tell me. I always remember him swaggering up to me when I was just back from the South: "Well Katherine, I hear you've got it. Do you spit blood and so on? Do all the things in the books? Do they think youll get over it." And then he laughed out. Its like all Brett's friends having *spotty lungs*. I am very sorry, but I can't forgive these things. They may be ignorance and so on but I not only can't forgive – I *do* condemn them. Theres a kind of agitation in Brett's atmosphere that repels me.

Oh, if you knew what a joy your Shakespeare was. I straightway dipped in the Tempest and discovered Ariel riding on *curlèd clouds*.[2] Isn't that adjective perfect? Id missed it before. I do think The Tempest is the most radiant, delicate exquisite play. The atmosphere is exactly the atmosphere of an island after a storm – an island reborn out of the sea with Caliban tossed up for sea wrack and Ariel blowing in a shell. Oh my divine Shakespeare!! Oh most blessed genius. Again I read of the love of Ferdinand and Miranda, how they met & *recognised* each other and their hearts spake.[3] Everything – everything is newborn and golden. God knows there are desert islands enough to go round – the difficulty is to sail *away* from them – but dream islands . . . they are rare, rare.

Yet, if I had not loved you I should never have understood Shakespeare as I do. His 'magic' is the same magic as our love. "Where the bee sucks there lurk I: in a cowslip's bell I lie"[4] – I believe this all sounds quite quite different to us than to all the rest of the world. I feel,

if I lived with you where the climate was delicate the air most sweet fertile the isle[5] — we should end by talking in a kind of blank verse. (Im
smiling as I write this, my true love, and yet I mean it). Looking back at
our time in the Villa Pauline[6] when the almond tree was in flower
remembering how I saw you come out of the cave in your soft leather
boots carrying logs of wood . . . it is all a dream.

Oh, Bogey I dont like the world. Its a horrid place. When I think of
the Schiffs — Sunday lunch — Osbert Sitwell[7] & Cie — I feel there is no
place for us except Beyond the Blue Mountains. I want to wander
through valleys with you drink out of leaves for cups, sit on warm hillsides & listen to bees in the heather. I want a house as small as possible
and there to live & watch the clouds and mark the seasons — with you.
There to work and live — no servants. Friends sometimes to see us, but
all *just simple* . . . (I came to the back door then with a bowl of crumbs for
some migratory birds that had come to rest on our hill top after a storm
and were still too weak to fly. They were quite tame — hopping about —
rather large slender grey birds with silver breasts. You came walking
from the field with a pail of milk. Our lovely little fawn cow was just
wandering away. The pail glittered — you *strolled* along. I looked at the
cow & the birds & thought all are enchanted.)

Yes I do understand how you must hate the idea of *dinners*. Carry me
in your pocket. No, that won't do any good. Id give my eyes to watch
you dress. Youll look so lovely in your evening clothes & Ive never seen
you in them. But your *best dress* is that Jaeger jersey. Thats the very
Bogfication of you — — —

Im hoping for the paper tomorrow. The D.N. [*Daily News*] for October
1st came today (October 10th) Could I have the Mercury please?

Now I want if I can to finish a story today for you. Ill write it out here.
Ive got a HUGE umbrella lashed to the Terrace in place of that tente
which was too expensive, of course — The umbrella does just as well. Oh
that you were here, just at this moment, sharing this sky and this gentle
breeze!

Your own Wig.

Just as I folded that I had *callers*. A. M. et Madame showed on to the
Terrace. Very gracious but oh DEAR! What a ghastly idea it is. What
can one say? I cant play 'ladies' unless I know the children I'm playing with.

Now theres an asp come out of a hole — a slender creature, red, about
12 inches long. It lies moving its quick head. It is very evil looking but
how much nicer than a caller. I was warned yesterday against attempting to kill them. (Do you see me trying to kill them, Boge?) But they
spring at you, if you do. However darling, Ill catch this one for you at
the risk of my life & put it in your Shakespeare for a marker at the
scene where the old man carries in the basket of figs.[8] You will have

to hold your Shakespeare *very firmly* to prevent it wriggling, Anthony darling.

Lovingly yours

MS ATL. *LKM* II. 51–2; *LJMM*, 556–8.

¹ KM is unfairly accusing her relative Sydney Waterlow, who was staying with Murry at Portland Villas. Marge was Sydney's sister.
² 'To dive into the fire, to ride | On the curl'd clouds': *The Tempest*, I. ii. 192.
³ Ibid., I. ii. 418–50.
⁴ KM is slightly misquoting Ariel's song, 'Where the bee sucks, there suck I', ibid., v. i. 88.
⁵ 'The climate's delicate, the air most sweet, | Fertile the isle': *The Winter's Tale*, III. i. 1.
⁶ KM and Murry were together at the Villa Pauline, Bandol, for 3 months at the beginning of 1916.
⁷ Osbert Sitwell (1892–1969), first known for his satirical war poems, was a prolific writer of fiction and autobiography, and, like the Schiffs, an ardent advocate of Modernism.
⁸ *Antony and Cleopatra*, v. ii, where the clown brings in an asp concealed in a basket of figs.

To J. M. Murry, 11 October 1920

[Villa Isola Bella, Garavan, Menton]
11.X.1920

Darling Bogey,

I send the story.¹ As usual I am in a foolish panic about it. But I know I can trust you. You know how I *choose* my words; they can't be changed. And if you don't like it or think its wrong *just as it is* Id rather you didn't print it. Ill try & do another.

Will you tell me, if you've time, what you think of it. Again (as usual) I burn to know & you see there's NO-ONE here.

It was one of my queer hallucinations; I wrote it straight off. And Ive no copy.

Wig.

I hope you like my little boy. His name is HENNIE. May I use that address?

MS ATL. *LKM* II. 52.

¹ 'The Young Girl', which Murry ran in the *Athenaeum*, 29 Oct. 1920.

To J. M. Murry, [12 October 1920]

[Villa Isola Bella, Garavan, Menton]

My darling Own Bogey

It is such a Heavenly Day that I hardly know how to celebrate it – or rather I keep on celebrating it – having a kind of glorified mass with full

Choir (but *à bas* the Roman Catholics!). Its just blue and gold. In the valley two workmen are singing – their voices come *pressing* up, *expanding,*
scattering in the light – you know those Italian voices! I think from the
sound they are building a house. I am sure the walls will hold this singing
for ever & on every fine day your hand there on that curve or that
arch and there'll be a warmth a faint vibration . . . The sun woke me at
7 oclock – sitting sur mes pieds comme un chat d'or mais c'était moi qui
a fait ron-ron. And at 7.30 Marie brought dejeuner – petits pains with
miel des Alpes & hot coffee on a fringèd tray. Her old bones were fairly
singing too. I said vous allez au marche Marie. She said, rather aggrieved,
mais comme vous voyez, Madame. Je suis en train d'y aller. And then I
noticed she was 'dressed' for the occasion. i.e. She had hung on her shoulders a most minute black shawl with a tiny bobble fringe. This she always
holds over her mouth to guard against le frais du matin when she scuttles off with her panier and filet. She really *is* a superb type.

Good God! There are two lizards rushing up the palm tree! A Boge
& a Wig. Lizards *glister* Heaven bless them. In the trunk of the palm high
up some tiny sweet peas are growing & some frail dandelions. I love to
see them. As I wrote that *one* lizard fell – simply fell with a *crash* (about
5000 feet) on to the terrace – and the other *looked* over one of those palm
chunks – really it did. Ive never seen such an affair. It was Wig that fell
– of course. Now shes picked herself up & is flying back. She seems as
good as new – But its a mad thing to do.

I have a hundred things – oh a million things I want to talk about but
the sun seems to draw them away from my heart into a heaven where
they are little clouds with seraphim on them singing of her love of Bogey.
The papers have come dearest love, likewise books. Im going to do 4
females this week.[1] You were *excellent* on Delamare.[2] Since I was here
those two lines But beauty vanishes Beauty passes, However rare rare it
be have sounded so often in my mind[3] – – I love Delamare love the
man who came to tea – with his wife sitting there by the fire and dark,
young, lovely Florence.[4] The memory of that afternoon is so precious.
For one thing I feel that Delamare *recognised you*. I mean a certain you –
I almost mean 'us' – but that he couldn't have known . . . And that
brings with it always a sense of Peace that endures –

Ida has come for this letter & cant wait. I will write again.

You *feel* my love?

I *am* you

Wig.

MS ATL, *LKM* II. 52–3; *LJMM,* 558–9.

[1] 'Under "Ask No Questions", the *Athenaeum*, 22 Oct. 1920, she reviewed *The Romantic* by May
Sinclair, *The Last Fortnight* by Mary Agnes Hamilton, *The Headland* by C. A. Dawson-Scott, and *The
Passionate Spectator* by Jane Burr.

² Murry's article 'The Poetry of Mr De La Mare', the *Athenaeum*, 8 Oct. 1920, reviewing *Poems 1901 to 1908* and *Peacocks Pie*.
³ From de la Mare's poem 'An Epitaph':

> Here lies a most beautiful lady,
> Light of step and heart was she;
> I think she was the most beautiful lady
> That ever was in the West Country.
> But beauty vanishes; beauty passes,
> However rare − rare it be;
>   And when I crumble who will remember
> This lady of the West Country?

⁴ De la Mare had married Constantia Ingpen in 1899. Florence was the younger of their two daughters.

To J. M. Murry, [13 October 1920]

[Villa Isola Bella, Garavan, Menton]

Last day of *my* old year.

Dearest love,

I want to make something clear. When I say and have said in my letters I shall not say 'come' you must understand very very deeply that I only mean − not on my account − not because of my illness. What I mean is: I would give up the world, the sea and all the tiddimies in a blink of the eye if you *felt* it was the thing to do. Im not in the very slightest frightened of being poor. I am sure we shall sell our *real work*. Im confident of that, tho' it may take time. So if you arrange it to be for next Easter my darling − O BLISS − is my signature to the agreement. We'll talk it out at Christmas shall we? As a matter of fact now speaking dead true I think its a waste of time for me to do journalism. I think Id *make more* with stories only. Truth is I *detest novels* and think theyre simply rubbish − on the whole. But in saying that I dont mean I couldn't mean that I want to give up my work for the A. *I could not live here without it.* But I just *tell* you that − see? darling? Because it *is* la vraie verité.

I think at Easter L.M. had better go off to London, meet you there, & take over the affair of settling up. Then you'll come here or hereabouts & we'll live on − love and work.

Youre not to speak about yourself as a silent Boge, an irritating Boge. It makes me hang my head.

This is the last letter I shall ever write to you at 31, the very last. An end and a Beginning. Oh God, how deeply and truly I love you. I am so divinely happy − somewhere − in some still place.

Henry[1] has your note and is replying to the Yinkum people today. I just took it in to him. He was sitting on his windowsill smoking. He intends going off to Annunciata for the day.

I DESPISE and shrink from that vulgar Bennet.[2] C-B,[3] too, with his

Wordsworth complex! This queer half-hinting, half-suggesting · · · and yet what he *does* say doesn't help one in the very slightest to understand Wordsworth better. I am amazed at the sudden 'mushroom growth' of cheap psycho analysis everywhere. *Five* novels one after the other are based on it: its in everything. And I want to prove it wont do – its turn-ing Life into a *case*. And yet, of course, I do believe one ought to be able to – not ought – ones novel if its a good one will be capable of being *proved* scientifically to be correct. Here – the thing thats happening now is the impulse to write is a different impulse. With an artist – one has to allow – oh tremendously for the subconscious element in his work. He writes when he's *inspired* – as a sort of divine flower to all his terrific hard gar-dening there comes this subconscious · · · wisdom. Now these people who are nuts on analysis seem to me to have *no* subconscious at all. They write to *prove* – not to tell the truth. Oh, I am so dull aren't I darling. I'll stop. I wish they'd stop, tho' Its such gross impertinence.

Later.

Ive just been to the Louise⁴ – stolen three whopping lemons & had a talk to their jardinier who comes here le vendredi to plant flowers autour de la palmier. This man drew a design of the flower bed on the gravel, & then after telling me the names of the flowers he described them. You know Bogey it was *terrific* in trying to describe the scent – c'est – un – parr-rum – & then he threw back his head put his thumb & forefinger to his nose – took a *long* breath & suddenly exploded it in a kind of AAAHHH, almost staggering backwards – overcome – almost fainting. & then in telling me of des paquerettes "ce sont des tous petits fleurs qui se regardent comme ils disent: c'est moi qui est plus jolie que toi!" Now Bogey – oh dear me – I wonder if it *is* so wonderful. I sat down on a bench & felt as though waves of health went flowing through me. To think the man *cares* like that – *responds* – laughs like he does and snips off a rosebud for you while he talks. Then I think of poor busmen & tube men and the ugliness of wet dark London. Its wrong. People who are at all sensitive ought not to live there. Ill tell you (as its my birthday tomorrow) a tale about this man. He came to see me. I had to engage him. First he passed me in the garden & went to Marie to ask for Madame Murry. Marie said – but you've seen her already. He said – No, theres only une petite personne, une fillette de quinze ans, enfin, sur la terrasse. Marie thought this is a very great joke. Bit steep, wasn't it. I expect Ill be about 5 by Xmas time – just old enough for a tree · · ·

Doctor Mee – who was Mother's doctor too – cant get over my improvement in the last fortnight. He's *staggered*. But he says he does wish you would go to Gamage & buy her a pair of *shoulder straps*. You know the things I mean. Theyre to keep me from stooping. I stoop mainly from habit. I feel so much better that I almost have to tie myself to my chaise longue. But I know now is the moment to go slow. Alas Im so infernally wise in these things. Oh Heavenly day. I wish you'd shared my boisson — that fresh lemon with a lump of sugar & Saint Galmier —

Every morning I have a seawater bath in a saucer & today after it, still wet, I stood in the full sun to dry — both windows wide open. One cant help walking about naked in the mornings — one almost *wades* in the air. As for my old feet — Ive never felt them since the first days I was here — never dream of wearing that awful strapping or anything. Im writing facing Italy — great mountains, grey gold with tufts of dark green against a sheer blue sky. Yes, I confess its very hard work to wait for you. Can we hope for more than — how many? springs & summers. I don't want to miss one.

Such a strange feeling. I seem to *be* you — not two persons but one person. You must feel my love. Do you? Precious Bogey . . . dearest dear.

I am your true love

Wig.

MS ATL. *LKM* II. 53–5; *LJMM*, 559–62.

---

[1] Murry's note (*LJMM*, 560) identifies Henry as a banker in Menton, who wrote on KM's behalf to the Income Tax Department.

[2] The novelist Arnold Bennett (1867–1931).

[3] Alan Clutton-Brock (1868–1924), whose *Essays in Books* Murry would review in the *Athenaeum* on 3 Dec. 1920.

[4] Her cousin's large villa next door.

To J. M. Murry, [14 October 1920]

[Menton]

WIRE RECEIVED BUT LOOK HERE ITS MY BIRTHDAY

TIG

Telegram ATL.

To J. M. Murry, [15 October 1920]

[Villa Isola Bella, Garavan, Menton]

Thank you for the answer to my telegram, love.

My own darling,

I confess it *was* a bit of a jar yesterday to have no birthday. You know how silly I am about them. Of course I didn't expect to hear from anybody but you this year as the children are in N.Z.[1] but I waited & waited

for the post in my room & then when he did come & the envelope was
rather fat it was a terrific relief. I thought youd sent me a handkerchief
or praps a han made poem. Oh – it was only enclosures after all. I was
very glad to get them of course but all the same. It was a misty old day
and nobody said many happy returns but when the telegraph man came
I was so relieved I gave him 50 centimes. *Then* I found you really had
forgotten. First time since we've been together – and I *did* give you a nice
one – didn't I with that almond paste and all? I felt so desolé that I sent
a wire after that myself.

How perfectly awful about your income tax. It sounds incredible –
£198! I think one would have *more* money if one had less . . . I love your
little notes. They are much nicer than cards.

This AWFUL photograph L.M. took on the orchard path the day I
went lemon stealing. She does seem to be bad at cameras. Does she *make*
me look like that?

Im going to see Bouchage[2] today – just to know how much I can do.
One cant tell. One is so immensely better & then one has a fit of coughing which – isn't better at all. One hears, out of the depths of it the old
wolf howling as loud as ever[3] when one thought he'd been driven off &
never would dare to attack again – But one couldn't be as hungry as I
am and not be getting better. I am sending my review today – its *done*
& ready to go. Now Im going to make another effort to write four during the week & catch up. This time I must because Im so much older.
Ida has gone for a voiture. I must put on my chapeau.

Goodbye, my precious Boge – 'Tell Wing I bet he didn't remember
either.
Your
Wig.

MS. ATL. *LJMM* 562–3.

1 KM's sisters were on a visit to their father in Wellington.

2 The doctor she had first consulted early in the year, before returning to England. Ambroise
Bouchage was born in Savoie in 1885, trained as an externe des Hôpitaux de Lyon, and in 1912
defended his *Essai sur glycosuries dans leurs rapports avec le joie* at the Faculté de Médicine de Paris. He
was awarded the Croix de Guerre in the First World War. (See Appendix for his full report on KM
in May 1921.)

3 An image KM returned to, drawn from her translation of Alphonse Daudet's 'La Chèvre de
M. Séguin' in the *New Age*, 6 Sept. 1917. In the story an adventurous but reckless goat leaves the
safety of her farm, is overtaken by darkness on the hillside, and at dawn, 'all spotted with blood',
is devoured by a wolf.

To J. M. Murry, [16 October 1920]

[Villa Isola Bella, Garavan, Menton]

URGENT

May I have the money for the novels I left at home & for those Ive sent over?[1] I really badly want it. Had I better send the novels direct? If so, please send me the address. I dont want to complain of my partner but my expenses are very heavy & every little counts no end. It would mean ever so much to me to have it – and its MINE – isn't it, Bogey? It is a bit cool of you just to pocket it – the female in me rebels. You wouldn't dare to if I could fight you.

Darling,

Ive just got back from Bouchage. I expect you'd like to know what he's like. He seems to me a very decent intelligent soul – quite as good as any other doctor. He approved absolutely of my life & conditions of life here & is going to keep an eye on me. The result of his examination was the eternal same. Of course one can see that the disease is long standing but there is no reason why – provided – subject to – if – and so on and so on. Not in the least depressing, yet the foolish creature always does expect the doctor to put down his stethoscope, to turn to her & say – with quiet confidence: *I can cure you Mrs Murry.*

He has the same disease himself. I *recognised* his smile – just the least shade too bright and his strange joyousness as he came to meet me – just the least too pronounced – his air of being a touch more vividly alive than other people – the gleam – the faint glitter on a plant that the frost has laid a finger on – – – Hes only about 33 – and I feel that his experiences at the war had changed him. In fact he seemed to me awfully like what a young Duhamel[2] might be. Im to go on just as Im going until he sees me again i.e. ½ an hour's walk, the rest of the time in my chaise longue. There's really nothing to tell. He had such a charming little old fashioned photograph in a round frame on his mantelpiece – faded – but so delightful – a girl with her curls pinned back & a velvet ribbon round her throat. His mother I suppose. This seemed to me more important than all else –

Your

Wig.

MS ATL. *LKM* II. 55–6; *LJMM*, 563–4.

---

[1] KM sent back the novels she reviewed to be sold at a second-hand bookshop.

[2] KM and Murry were both admirers of Georges Duhumel (1884–1966), French poet and nov-

elist and author of *Vie de martyrs* (1917), a realistic account of his experiences as an army surgeon. They considered him a kindred spirit, particularly in his 'La Recherche de la grâce.' (See *CLKM* II. 228.)

To J. M. Murry, [17 October 1920]

[Villa Isola Bella, Garavan, Menton]

Darling Bogey

Its 3.30, Sunday afternoon. Marie is out and L.M. has gone off to tea with some cronies & a french poodle. So I have the house to myself. Its a cloudy, windless day. There is such a great stretch of sky to be seen from my terrasse that one's always conscious of the clouds. One forgets what clouds *are* in London and here they are – how shall I put it – they are a changing background to the *silence.* Extraordinary how many planes one can see – one cloud & behind it another and then a lake and on the far side of the lake a mountain. I wonder if you would feed on the visible world as I do. I was looking at some leaves only yesterday – idly looking & suddenly I became conscious of them – of the amazing 'freedom' with which they were 'drawn' – of the life in each curve, but not as something *outside oneself* – but as part of one, as though like a magi-cian I could put forth my hand & shake a green branch into my fingers from . . .? And I felt as though one received – accepted – absorbed the beauty of the leaves even into ones physical being. Do you feel like that about things? Ah, but you would have loved the golden moth that flew in here last night. It had a head like a tiny owl, a body covered with down, wings divided into minute feathers and powdered with gold. I felt it belonged to a poem of yours.

The paper has come – I think the paragraphs are an extraordinary improvement.[1] They 'catch hold' of the reader, they draw him in. The frigidity which was a danger in the leader is gone. There's somehow a welcome touch in them as old Moult would say. Seriously Im sure they are right. I always *miss* a long review by you. I hunt down your initials first. Tomlinson's story was *very* good.[2] It just missed it, though, at the end – I mean judging from the Tchekhov standpoint. The thing I prize admire and respect in his stories is his knowledge. They are true. I trust him. This is becoming most awfully important to me – a writer *must have* knowledge – he must make one feel the ground is firm beneath his feet. The vapourings I read – the gush – wind – Mrs Dawson Scott – give me a perfect sehnsucht for something hard to bite on. Darling, you know Im bouleversé by the papers nowadays. I mean the Times Lit Sup. Their reviewing is a filthy scandal. Theres no other word. I mean they gave for instance Mrs D.S. a long review & talked of her 'wisdom' took her seriously – didn't say a word about her real *disgustingness* & absurdity &

then again – to find a firm like Duckworth publishing Jane Burr.[3] Its a
book for a rubber shop (mes excuses). Its a book about what she calls
'bedroom talk'. Its not downright lewd of course, not decent bawdy but
its a defence of female promiscuity by an hysterical underbred creature.
I don't know whether its I that have 'fallen behind' in this procession but
truly the books I read nowadays astound me. Female writers discovering
a freedom a frankness a licence to speak their hearts reveal themselves
as – – sex maniacs. There's not a relationship between a man & woman
that isn't the one sexual relationship – at its lowest. *Intimacy* is the sexual
act. I am terribly ashamed to tell the truth; its a very horrible exposure.
Ill do Prowse, Adam of Dublin, the Cobden-Sanderson novel[4] (an exception) & another this week & take them seriously – good ones after last
week's bad ones.

How is the paper doing? How is our circulation? It ought to be high.
Heavens – its a topnotcher – isn't it compared to any other.

Bogey I loved Susannah Burns' letter. I am glad you gave the children
the racquets;[5] Chummie would have liked them to have them, too. I
always connect them with him. I like to think little children play with
them.

Connie & Jinnie & entourage have arrived – Its pleasant to feel all the
life there – to let ones thoughts play with the party sometimes. Its a large
open book near enough but not too near – stimulating. The maids & old
Hill the gardener arrived at 11.30 last night. I heard the voiture clatter-
ing up the dark lane & then presently Jinnie's *whistle* to them. She must
have come on to a balcony. There was a shrill piping . . . & I saw her
in my mind, greyhaired in her camel dressing gown. For a woman of 64
– NOT BAD!!

Im working a great deal. Ill send another story this week. I ought to
write a story a day. I would I believe if you were here & L.M. wasn't.
But she is my curse, my cross that for some reason I just *have* to bear.
Now that she has nothing on earth to do – she does – absolutely nothing but make *french knots* in her bedroom & ask questions like: "Can you
tell me a book that will explain what makes the sea that funny yellow
colour so far out. What is the *Authority*."

Goodbye my darling Boy
Your

                                                                    Wig.

MS ATL. *LKM* II. 56–7; *LJMM*, 564–6.

[1] Instead of its customary editorial, the *Athenaeum* now opened with 'Notes and Comments'.

[2] H. M. Tomlinson's short story 'In a Coffee Shop', the *Athenaeum*, 15 Oct. 1920.

[3] *The Headland* by C. A. Dawson-Scott, which KM would review the next week, as she would
Jane Burr's *The Passionate Spectator*, a novel 'out to explain love. . . . But Miss Jane Burr and her
explanation disgust us.' The *Times Literary Supplement*, 14 Oct. 1920, reservedly commended *The
Headland*, but complimented the author for the 'truth and wisdom' finally evident.

To J. M. Murry, [18 October 1920]

[Villa Isola Bella, Garavan, Menton]

My darling Bogue (yes that is right. Its your other name, you know)

I return DelaMare's letter. I long to hear of your time with him. Its very queer; he haunts me here – not a persistent or substantial ghost but as one who shares my (our) joy in the *silent world*. Joy is not the word: I only used it because it conveys a stillness – a remoteness – because there is a faraway sound in it.

You know, darling, I have felt very often lately as though the silence had some meaning beyond these signs these intimations. Isn't it possible that if one yielded there is a whole world into which one is received? It is so near and yet I am conscious that I hold back from giving myself up to it. What is this something mysterious that waits – that beckons?

And then suffering – bodily suffering such as Ive known for three years. It has changed forever everything – even the *appearance* of the world is not the same – there is something added. *Everything has its shadow.* Is it right to resist such suffering? Do you know I feel it has been an immense privilege. Yes, in spite of all. How blind we little creatures are! Darling, its only the fairy tales we *really* live by. If we set out upon a jour-ney the more wonderful the treasure the greater the temptations and perils to be overcome. And if someone rebels and says Life isn't good enough on those terms one can only say: 'It *is*'. Dont misunderstand me. I don't mean a "thorn in the flesh,' my dear" – its a million times more mysterious. It has taken me three years to understand this – to come to see this. We resist – we are terribly frightened. The little boat enters the dark fearful gulf and our only cry is to escape – "put me on land again". But its useless. Nobody listens. The shadowy figure rows on. One ought to sit still and uncover ones eyes.

I believe the greatest failing of all is *to be frightened.* Perfect Love casteth out Fear.² When I look back on my life all my mistakes have been because I was afraid . . . Was that why I had to look on death. Would nothing less cure me? You know, one can't help wondering, sometimes . . . No, not a personal God or any such nonsense. Much more likely – the soul's desperate choice . . .

Am I right in thinking that you too have been ridden by Fear (of quite a different kind). And now its gone from you – and you are whole. I feel that only now you have *all* your strength – a kind of *release.*

---

⁴ In the *Athenaeum*, 29 Oct., KM reviewed R. O. Prowse's *A Gift of the Dusk*, and on 12 Nov. Conal O'Riordan's *Adam of Dublin*.

⁵ Murry had passed on to friends the tennis racquets belonging to KM's brother Chummie (Leslie), killed in Oct. 1915. (See *CLKM* I. 198 n. 1.)

We are as different as can be but I do believe we have the same devils as well as the same gods.

Here are your letters back again, love. They interested me deeply. Your Stendhal article . . . seemed to fetch the french ducks off the water . . . didn't it? Im sorry about Knopf and the Yazpegs[3] – but cant be helped.

Take care of yourself – my beloved child with all these wild men about throwing stones and striking. Make yourself small – fold yourself up. Im (privately – it doesn't do to tell you these things) terrified that in your lunch hour you'll take your bisticks into the street & get caught in a crowd & march away. *Eat*, don't catch cold whatever you do. I want to put my hands on you – to touch you – anxiously & lovingly. I *miss* you. Do you miss me? I miss your voice and your presence and all your darling ways.

Your　　　Wig.

Could you bring Ribni[4] at Xmas? There is a shop in Nice which cures poupées cassées. When I read of it I almost telegraphed for Ribni. I want him to be made good as new again. He haunts me. Ah, I can see a story in this idea . . .

MS ATL. *LKM* II. 57–8. *LJMM*, 566–7.

---

[1] 'There was given to me a thorn in the flesh . . . lest I should be exalted above measure': 2 Cor. 12:7.

[2] John 4: 18.

[3] KM's jokey spelling of 'aspects'. Murry's *Aspects of Literature*, published in England in 1920, had been turned down by the New York publisher Knopf.

[4] One of her favourite dolls, named after Colonel Ribnikov, in a story with that title by Aleksandr Kuprin (1870–1938).

To J. M. Murry, [21 October 1920]

[Villa Isola Bella, Garavan, Menton]

(Did the fruit ever arrive?)

Later. Yes. Ive just heard it did. Please nota bene my nota beenies.

Darling Heart

I have your Sunday letter about your finances. I am properly horrified at the whacks – the huge whacks that tout le monde takes out of your £1000. Poor little boy with the pudding! Everybody seems to have a spoon except the child with the plate.

There is no doubt in my mind that you would fare better with £300 abroad. There is also the chance that by next Avrilo we shant want any money at all; we shall be living in caves & minding what flocks & what herds are left a leg to stand on. Even so, if you can, come out to me

then, my darling. Life is so terribly short. I know that, on my death bed,
I shall regret the time we didn't have together.

As regards my own situation — I feel I ought to and could make a fair
amount of money by my writing. Its not really health that keeps me back
but the peculiarity of my relations with L.M. But dont misunderstand
me: I can and am determined to stick it until April. The 'trouble' is that
while it endures don't expect a terrific flowering de la part de ta femme.
No, that's not quite what I mean. It suggests that Im not making every
effort to adjust the relationship and escape into my own kingdom and
write, I am. But it is not an easy task. Jinnie and Connie have been in
several times. They are very tamed OR they are offended with me for
not giving in about the Church.[1] That's it. Its in their eyes every time
they look at me. Very uncomfortable. Every pause in the conversation,
I hear Jinnie silently saying: 'Dont you think dearest you would like to
see Father X?" And I have in consequence a kind of No Popery manner. What a bother!

To be free — to be free! Thats all I ask. There's nine oclock striking
gently, beautifully from a steeple in the old town. The sound floats across
the water. I wish you were here and we were alone . . .

Did I tell you I have a little bookcase made by a carpenter *wot* lives
on the hill? He made it most rarely: dovetailed the corners — isn't that
right — and cut a little ornament on the top shelves and then painted it
pale yellow. 24 francs. His wife sent with it a bouquet of zinnias the like
of which Ive never seen. These people with their only child a lovely
little boy of about five in their *own* house with their *own* garden. He
seems to work for his own pleasure. Where do they get the money? The
little boy who's like an infant St. John wears little white overalls, pink
socks and sandals. "Dis bonjour à Madame! Où est ton chapeau! Vite!
Ote-le!" And this hissed in a *terrible* voice with rolling eyes by the father.
The little boy slowly looks up at his father and gives a very slow ravishing smile.

Its really queer about these people. Marie was saying the mimosa tree
leans — its got a list on it — and of course, prophesying that ("esperons
toujours que *non* Madame *mais*") it will fall and crush us all. When she
described how the tree leant she took the posture — she became a
mimosa tree — little black dress trimmed with crepe white apron, grey
hair, changed into a tree. And this was so *intensely* beautiful that it made
me almost weep. It was Art, you know. The day is still. I *must* get up. The day is still
unbroken. One can hear a soft roaring from the sea and that's all.
Goodbye for now my darling Heart.
Wig.
I think that Love is glorified childhood. Except ye become as little children ye cannot enter . . .[2]
Later.

Your Monday letter has just come. My own, forget that you forgot: I give you my pure wool guaranteed warmest Blessing. So wrap yourself up in it & dont even let your (gentlemans size) nose show. Suffice it to say that she adores him . . .

About the DelaMares – its mutual. I feel just the same about that afternoon. I love them, too. Its really cold today – a winter day, but lovely all the same – charged with beauty & white radiance.

Your own

Souris.

X X X

N.B. Ive just got the milk book to pay. Its a minute pink carnet de – appartenant à . . . commencé le . . . You know the kind with *broad* lines inside and on the back the Table de Multiplication – but only up to 6 fois 1 font 6. Doesnt that make you see its *real* owner?

MS ATL *LKM* II. 59–60; *LJMM*, 567–9.

---

[1] Before she returned to London the previous May, KM had been strongly drawn to Roman Catholicism, but then turned against her cousin's pietistic narrowness and her misunderstanding of art. (See her letter to Ida Baker, *CLKM* III. 240, and to Murry, ibid. 271.)

[2] 'Except ye be converted and become as little children, ye shall not enter into the kingdom of heaven': Matt. 18: 3.

To J. M. Murry, [22 October 1920]

[Villa Isola Bella, Garavan, Menton]

Dear Love

I had your letter with the enclosures today: all interesting indeed to me. I feel Knopf is Knopf very friendly, tho', don't you? Id like to send him the sheets of a book that he DID consider an absolute korker. Its very cold here. I have a fire & a rug & a screen. But of course the cold is not London cold – its pure – and its somehow *exciting*. In fact the cold here is *intoxicating* – its as marvellous as the heat. The leaves shake in the garden – the rosebuds are very tight shut – there's a kind of whiteness in the sky over the sea. I loved such days when I was a child – I love them here. In fact I think Menton must be awfully like N.Z. – but ever so much better. The little milk girl comes in at a run, letting the gate swing; she has a red stocking tied round her neck. Marie predicts a strike, snow, no food, no fuel and only la volonté de Dieu will save us. But while she drees her weird she begins to laugh & then forgets. A *poor* little cat, terrified with pink eyes looked in & begged, & then slunk away. To my joy I hear it dashed into the dining room, seized a poisson on the console & made off with it. Hooray!

What silly little things to tell you – but they make a kind of Life – they are part of a Life that – Bogey – I LOVE. If you were here you'd know what I mean. Its a kind of freedom – a sense of *living* – not enduring – not existing – but being alive. I feel I could have children here for about a farthing each & dress them in little bits cut off ones own clothes. It would't *matter* as long as they had feathers in their hats. Its all so EASY. Would we really be so happy, so blissfully happy as I imagine? Could you delight in a little town? In this country? In burning the dry rose-mary? In tying up the very headstrong and dashing periwinkle? I could spend at least 2 years at it. Working & reading & living like this. But there must be *you*. You are always part of it.

Dunning's[1] letter was a *very* nice letter. Dents[2] was typical & delight-ful. The par. from the Weekly Dispatch amused me. Did you get the full flavour of the title. *Double Harness*.[3] Oh, darling, fancy that in cold print about Bogue and Souris. (Do you like my new name. *Its very important* to know.)

Well I must finish my reviews. Be careful of stones & bottls flying in the air. Dont shout 'hooray' whatever happens. Oh, I must say – I *long* for you, here. But April isn't far & I am better – and Bouchage begins to remind me of Tchekhov. But you'd like this room so. You'd love this villa so. I actually, in bed this morning, saw that there were 2 cans of hot water for your bath when you arrive . . . You *had* a bath & put on a jersey. Supper was ready. We sat down. Marie brought the potage . . .
Oh *dear!* Yours for ever.

MS ATL. *LKM* II. 60–1; *LJMM* 569–71.

1 Miller Dunning, a friend of Murry's interested in Eastern religions and meditation. There is an undated notebook entry, made during her months in England before the return to Menton: 'After the talk with Dunning there *is* a change. I believe that D. has the secret of my recovery and J's awakening. All that he spoke of yesterday . . . the terms were strange, but what he *said* was what she had known for a long time' (*Journal* 1954, 211.) Soon after KM's death, Bill Dunning, the wife of Miller, claimed to have spiritualistic communion with her, and fell in love with Murry.
2 Edward Joseph Dent (1876–1957), a friend of KM's since he wrote for the *Blue Review*, regu-larly contributed music criticism to the *Athenaeum*.
3 In the 'Books and Writers' column, *Weekly Dispatch*, 17 Oct. 1920, the paragraph 'In Double Harness' began: 'Not everyone who reads the brilliant (and often scathing) criticisms in the *Athenaeum* appearing over the initials "K.M." recognizes them as the work of Katherine Mansfield.' The note goes on to mention the forthcoming publication of *Bliss* and Murry's *Aspects of Literature*.

To J. M. Murry, [23 October 1920]

[Villa Isola Bella, Garavan, Menton]

Darling Bogie
You should see the colour of the sea today. Royal blue with (as Pa would say) *crests* on every wave! I've got your lunch with O. [Ottoline]

letter. Roquebrune isn't really near.[1] Its near Menton but then Garavan is another bay and my villa is about 5 minutes from the pont which carries you over to Italy. Its at the extreme end & hard to find. However I bet she wont come. I dont care one way or another. Shes such un feuille mort to me. I am very interested in what you say about Gertler. I wish you'd tell me more if you can. Is Sorapure his doctor? *What is his state?* Its not really morbidity that makes me ask.

Precious, please don't feel pangs at my notes. I cant send them if you do. And if a thing is important I *have* to put ⌐☐⫤ a hand pointing to it because I know how sleepy you are in the morning & I *imagine* these devilish devices wake you or terrify you (*pleasantly*).

Yes, really the papers are disgusting. Rebecca West gave Jane Burr a whole column with '*Sorel*' & 'syndicalism' & 'any-fresh-light-on-the-problem-of-marriage-is-to-be-welcomed' etc.[2] She makes *me* feel a very old fashioned creature. I feel if I met her I should have to say: 'And are you one of these *New Women?*'

Did you see that Connie Ediss[3] has had the thyroid gland treatment (shes 50) and is now become 18 and climbs trees. I should just think *she did* climb trees. That seemed to me terribly significant. I remember her singing "It seemed a bit of alright" years ago. Poor old Schiff will become a *great climber*, I expect! Well dearest Love I seem a bit silly today. Its the wind. I feel inclined to sing:

> "When I was young & had no sense
> I bought a Fiddle for eighteen pence"[4]

Perhaps it was Maries lunch. A good cook is an amazing thing. And we have *never* had one. Heavens! It is a relief to me to do the housekeeping (I dont, Marie does) but to not have L.M. doing it. All that awful invalid rookery and then her anxiety. Here things just appear, though at a price. Faux filet – a piece for 3 is 11 francs!

Im interrupted by the electrician who comes to mend a wire. He is a boy of certainly not more than 14 in a blue overall. Just a child standing on the table & fixing wires & turning over tools (rattling them) in a box. I don't know – the world is changing. Hes a *very* nice little boy. He asked Marie pour une échelle. We haven't one. Donnez-moi une chaise. She brought one. C'est trop *bas*. Vous avez une table *solide* (as tho none of your fandangles here). But *she* scorns him & made him stand on a newspaper – nearly tied a bib round him.

Also spricht Doctor Mee: If your functions trouble you *dont* take drugs. Take an ounce of paraffin in a *glass of soda* water at night – get 2 siphons from the chemist. This is really good for you – it is you see a lubricant which is what you need in cold weather. If you want anything more drastic take ONLY *cascara evacuant* (Parke Davis preparation) for that is a bowel tonic. It improves the action & doesn't weaken it. How is your general health and condition? Will post reply in plain sealed envelope.

Mee
M.D.[5]
Your own
Souris.

MS ATL. *LKM* II. 61–2; *LJMM* 570–72.

1 Roquebrune is a few miles to the west of Garavan, past Menton.
2 Rebecca West wrote a long review of *The Passionate Spectator* by Jane Burr in the *Daily News*, 16 Oct. 1920. Although she found it 'a barbaric yawp of a book', she considered seriously its case for polygamy. In passing, she referred to Georges Sorel (1847–1922), the French socialist who elaborated the theory of syndicalism, the movement for transferring the means of production and distribution from owners to workers, principally through the use of strikes.
3 Connie Ediss (1871–1934), a popular music-hall performer, a report of whose rejuvenating treatment was in the *Daily News*, 16 Oct. 1920.
4 A traditional playground rhyme.
5 A large circle is drawn around 'Mee/M.D.'

To J. M. Murry, [24 October 1920]   [Villa Isola Bella, Garavan, Menton]

Darling.
The writing in this letter goes off. But I do awfully want you to read it, if you've time.

Wig.

La dimanche.
My darling Bogue,
I got a letter from you today written on Thursday. I must answer a point or two. Schiff *entirely* mistook my intentions when I (most deliberately) lent him In a G.P. [German Pension]. What impertinence. I suppose he is angry with me (I know he is) because I didn't answer his last letter. Somehow I could not. He spoke of Couperus[1] and himself as being co-equal and altogether his letter was unpleasant. It seemed too hectic and arrogant. It frightened me. I mean I wanted to *sheer off*. His hour had struck. You know the feeling? And *hers* struck in London when in saying goodbye to me she very nicely, a touch playfully, put her hand on my hair. *Finito*. These things are mysteries, but I can't help it. They now become to me a trifle grotesque, especially Schiff – overheated and (it seems now) overpoweringly *deaf* – deaf to every thing! Still I must write politely & get that book back. Will they make me pay £0000 for it. Hm! . . . The paper has come. Your Baudelaire is *excellent*. I could not help

comparing Eliot and you as I read.[2] Your patient never dies under the operation – his are always dead before he makes an incision. To be serious I thought it really remarkable because of the way in which you conveyed the *quality* of Baudelaire. I mean you produced Baudelaire, as it were. Thats where Mat Arnold failed so lamentably.[3] One never feels that Shelley or Keats or whoever it was sat on his bosom's throne, & though I dont mean that your subject should occupy that position when you write about him he's got to have been there – – –

I am exceedingly glad you joined hands with the Oxford Professors.[4] The Daily Mail *foamed* today on the subject.[5] It almost went so far as to say the library at Liege and such acts of burning were by Professors only. It – but let it pass! In the Times I noted a book by a Doctor Schinz[5] – not a good book but the Times noticed it as though Schinz were kneeling on Podsnap's[7] doormat. Faugh!

How long *can* it go on! You know whenever I go away I realise that it has happened. The change has *come*. Nothing *is* the same. I positively feel one has no right to run a paper without preaching a gospel. (I know you do but I mean with all the force of ones soul). I get an evangelist feeling when I read Fashion News in the D.N. [Daily News] and then Strike News & Irish News and so many thousands out of work. But above & beyond that when I realise the 'spiritual temper' of the world I feel as though the step *has* been taken – we *are* over the edge. Is it fantastic? Who is going to *pull us up*? I certainly had no end of an admiration for L.G. but then he's capable of that speech on reprisals – which really was a vile speech from a 'statesman'.[8] It was perfectly obvious he had no intention of saying what he did when he got up to speak – he was carried away. It *is* all over really. Thats why I shall be so thankful when you pack your rucksack & come over here. The only sort of paper for the time is an out and out *personal dead true, dead sincere* paper in which we spoke our HEARTS and MINDS.

I want to say I was wrong about your book The Intellectual.[9] I was right about the spirit (or so I think). I was wrong about the aim.

You know there are moments when I want to make an appeal to all our generation who do believe that the war has changed everything to come forward and lets start a crusade. But I know darling I am not a crusader & its my job to dwell apart & write my best for those that come after.

It *is* Sunday. Don't turn away if I talk. I have no one to speak to here – and I don't only want you to listen, Bogue. I want you to reply.

Does your *soul* trouble you? Mine does. I feel that only now (October 1920) do I really desire to be saved. I realise what salvation means and I long for it. Of course I am not speaking as a Christian or about a personal God. But the feeling is . . . I believe (and VERY MUCH) Help thou my unbelief.[10] But its to myself I cry – to the spirit, the essence of me –

that which lives in Beauty. Oh, these *words*. And yet I should be able to explain. But I'm impatient with you. I always "know you understand & take it for granted". But just very lately I seem to have seen my whole past – to have gone through it, to have emerged – very weak and very new. The soil (which wasn't at all fragrant) has at last produced something which isn't a weed but which I do believe (after Heaven knows how many false alarms) is from the seed which was sown. But Bogue its taken 32 years in the dark . . . Without our *love* it would never have come through at all. And I *long* for goodness – to live by what is permanent in the soul.

It all sounds vague. You may wonder what induces me to write this. But as I walked up & down outside the house this evening the clouds heaped on the horizon – noble, shining clouds, the deep blue waves – they set me thinking again. I never felt the longing for you as I do this time – but for such other reasons.

Take care of yourself, my Beloved Boy.
Ever your
Wig.

MS ATL. *LKM* II. 64–5; *LJMM* 572–4.

1 The Dutch novelist Louis Couperus (1863-1923), whose novel *Old People and the Things that Pass* KM had reviewed in the *Athenaeum*, 12 Dec. 1919, finding it 'one of those rare novels which, we feel, enlarge our experience of life'. Also in the *Athenaeum*, 18 June 1920, she discussed Teixeira de Mattos's translations of *The Later Life*, *The Twilight of the Souls*, and *Doctor Adriaan* praising them as 'delicate and profound'.

2 Murry's 'Baudelaire', the *Athenaeum*, 22 Oct. and 29 Oct. 1920, was a review essay on A. van Bever's critical edition of *Les Fleurs du mal*, *Le Spleen de Paris*, and *Journaux intimes*. KM is not making a specific comparison, as T. S. Eliot had not yet published on Baudelaire.

3 She is speaking generally of her view of Matthew Arnold's critical essays.

4 The opening 'Notes and Comments', the *Athenaeum*, 22 Oct. 1922, read: 'We rejoice to learn that no fewer than fifty-seven professors and doctors of Oxford University have sent a message of reconciliation and goodwill to the professors of the arts and sciences and to members of the universities and learned societies in Germany and Austria.'

5 The *Daily Mail*, 21 Oct., ran a quotation from the *New York Times* of the same day: 'Pardon is earned by reformation, and reformation is more than a willingness for renewed behaviour on the old terms.'

6 A condescendingly pompous review of *French Literature of the Great War*, by Albert Schinz, appeared in the *Times Literary Supplement*, 21 Oct. 1920.

7 Charles Dickens's character in *Our Mutual Friend* (1865), who became a synonym for inflated self-importance.

8 Lloyd George, the Prime Minister, had made a strong speech at Caernarvon on 9 Oct., justifying reprisals against the Sinn Fein republicans in Ireland.

9 *The Evolution of an Intellectual* (1920).

10 'And straightway the father of the child cried out, and said with tears, Lord, I believe; help thou mine unbelief.' Mark 9: 24.

To Sydney and Violet Schiff, 24 October 1920

[Villa Isola Bella, Garavan, Menton]
Sunday October 24th

I did not answer your letter at the time because I was ill, and I become so utterly weary of confessing it. Especially as its the kind of thing one does so hate to hear, one can't really sympathise with. People who are continually crying out are exasperating. And they (or at any rate *I*) am dreadfully conscious of it.

But now that I have been let out on ticket of leave at least – I long to write to you. You are never far from my thoughts. Some afternoons I feel positive that the voiture down below there is come from Roquebrune and that in another moment or two you will be here on the terrace. But there is too much to talk about. In London there never seems time. One is always just beginning when one is whirled away again. Here, one is so uninterrupted, it is like one immensely long night and one immensely long day.

But it takes long before the tunes cease revolving in one's head, before the sound of the clapping and the sensation of the crowd forsakes one. One cannot hail solitude as one can hail a dark cab. To disentangle one-self completely takes long . . . Nevertheless, I believe one must do it – and no less – if one wants to work.

I feel I *never* shall see the story you sent to The English Review, about the boy.[1] Have you been writing.

Violet – do you remember the afternoon you sang just before we all came away. The shadow of the green leaves trembled in the dark piano.

Forgive my long silence,
With love to you both

K.M.

Would you send my ancient book to JMM before you come abroad. I forgot to ask you if you would on that last afternoon. Thank you.

MS BL. *LKM* II. 58–9.

[1] The story was not accepted.

To J. M. Murry, [25 October 1920]

[Villa Isola Bella, Garavan, Menton]

As far as I can see from a months full accounts we can live here EASILY as I live now on £300 each. That is saving £100 a year, as we must do – I mean saving £50 each. But that's real luxurious living, mind you. I mean such living as weve never had before. The best of everything. It could be done cheaper. Of course I have L.M. to pay for now but she won't be here when you come.

My silly little Trot

Monday

You are a nuisance to me. I cant mention money without you putting your hand in your sailor pocket, bringing out your handkerchief with a knot in it – and oh! wringing my heart by untying the knot & showing me the penny. I dont even want to borrow it from you. Take back your old cheque. I am very hard up but not to that extent. But the sooner you leave there the better. If it isn't rates its taxes. And now you can't chew – on your left or right side. This put me in a panic & ∴ I sent a wire. Chew you *must* at whatever cost or you'll ruin your health and strength. And NO dentist if you're in pain should keep you waiting. You cant bear six days toothache. Its terribly bad for you. I would tie a hand-kerchief in two rabbits ears on top of your head & march you off there in two winks.

Darling Precious Noble little Bogue I cant scold you without kissing you. You are wicked & awfully sweet. But I DO wish Avrilo would hurry. <By the way – would you like to give up the house at Xmas? Would it be possible? L.M. is going over for 3 weeks. She *could* stay longer – as long as necessary. I mean, if Roger & Violet don't mind – I don't know their plans, or if Mrs K.[1] would like them to stay on (she wouldn't). If youd like to go into rooms instead.> *No, its an absolutely mad idea.* Pay no heed to it. As long as you are there you'll do no cheaper than you do now & without any comfort. It would be a ghastly uprooting. I cant think what made me even consider it. Think of the worry & upset for 3 months. Lordy! Who took hold of my pen!

No, its April I must live for. But Xmas is near even. The station at Caravan will be open by then. This villa is only a minute away. You'll arrive 5.15 p.m. As I write I see a fussy little engine bustling along I see Bogue sitting in a small kerridge. I see Wig trying not to let *everybody* see & Marie on the terrace here crying. Our 'separation' always moves her terribly. Our bedrooms are side by side. They communicate & have a mutual balcony as well. Yours has a live writing table & a pink velvet sofa – mine a rich saignant stickeback in plush. But they are lovely rooms. *Now as you read these words* you must feel how I love you. Put your arms round me & I will hold you.

You're everything, my dear blessing.

Wig.

MS ATL. *LJMM*, 574–5.

[1] The house in Portland Villas was to be taken by Mrs E. V. Knox, formerly Christina Hicks, who in 1912 married Edmund Valpy Knox (b. 1881), humourist and poet, who became editor of *Punch* in 1932.

To Hugh Walpole,¹ 27 October 1920

Isola Bella | Garavan-Menton | France
27.X.1920.

Dear Mr Walpole,

I must answer your letter immediately.² It has dropped into the most heavenly fair morning. I wish instead of writing, you were here on the terrace & you'd let me talk of your book which I FAR from detested. What an impression to convey! My trouble is I never have enough space to get going – to say what I mean to say – fully. That's no excuse, really. But to be called very unfair – that hurts, awfully, and I feel that by saying so you mean Im not as honest as I might be – Im prejudiced. Well, I think we're all of us more or less prejudiced, but cross my heart I don't take reviewing lightly & if I appear to its the fault of my unfortunate manner.

Now I shall be *dead frank*. And please don't answer. As one writer to another (tho' Im only a little beginner, and *fully realise* it):

"The Captives" impressed me as more like a first novel than any genuine first novel Ive come across. Of course there were signs enough that it wasn't one – but the movement of it was the movement of one trying his wings – finding out how they would bear him, how far he could afford to trust them. I felt you were continually risking yourself, that you had, for the first time, really committed yourself in a book. I wonder if this will seem to you extravagance & impertinence. I honoured you for it . . . You seemed to me determined to shirk nothing. You know that strange sense of insecurity *at the last* – the feeling: "I know all this. I know more. I know down to the minutest detail and *perhaps more still* but shall I – dare I trust myself to tell all?" It is really why we write, as I see it, that we may arrive at this moment and yet – it is stepping into the air to yield to it – a kind of anguish and rapture. I felt that you appreciated this, and that, seen in this light, your 'Captives' was almost a spiritual exercise in this kind of courage. But in fact your peculiar persistent consciousness of what you wanted to do was what seemed to me to prevent your book from being a creation. That is what I meant when I used the clumsy word 'task'. Perhaps 'experiment' was nearer my meaning. You seemed to lose in passion what you gained in sincerity and therefore "the miracle" didn't happen. I mean the moment when the act of creation takes place – the mysterious change when you are no longer writing the book – IT is writing, IT possesses you. Does that sound hopelessly vague?

But there it is. After reading 'The Captives' I laid it down thinking: having "broken with his past", as he has in this book, having "declared himself" I feel that Hugh Walpole's next novel will be the one to look for. Yes, curse me, I should have said it!

I sympathise more than I can say with your desire to escape from autobiography. Don't you feel that what English writers lack today is experience of Life. I don't mean that superficially. But they are self-imprisoned. I think there is a very profound distinction between any kind of *confession* and creative work – not that that rules out the first by any means.

About the parson and his sister. Yes, they *are* truly observed, but they wouldn't come in to my review because I didn't think they really came into the book! What was Maggie to them – or them to Maggie? What did they *matter* to Maggie – what was their true relation? I can't see it. I can't see the reason for those two. I can imagine Maggie forgetting them utterly the moment she set foot in London. That their religion was more foreign to her than the other one doesn't need to be told. The point is Maggie never was in Skeaton; she was somewhere else. As to her holiday in that place where everything was green – I never knew what happened on that holiday? The parson's sister – what a story you might have made of her and Paul! (I don't think that Paul's passion for Maggie would have lasted, either. He would have become frightened of her, physically – and terribly ashamed.[3]) Yes, I feel Skeaton could have had a book to itself with Paul's sister – getting old, you know – her descent into old age – her 'fears' increasing, and then something like the Uncle Matthew affair breaking into her life![4] . . .

And I stick to what I said about Caroline. Yes, you might have trusted Caroline,[5] but a young female wouldn't. If Caroline had come to her father's door Maggie would have *stiffened*, have been on her guard immediately. As to trusting her with a letter to Martin – never!

Some of their lovemaking was very beautiful – it had that tragic, youthful quality. . .

But enough. Forgive this long letter. Ill try & see more round the books. Ive no doubt at all Im a bad reviewer. Your letter makes me want to shake hands with you – across the vast.

I hope this isn't too illegible. But Im rather a feeble creature in a chaise longue.

Yours sincerely

Katherine Mansfield

MS Texas. *LKM* II. 62–4.

[1] Hugh Walpole (1884–1941) was, by chance, a countryman of KM's. His father was the incumbent of St Mary's Church, Parnell, Auckland, and the family returned to England when Hugh was five. A friend of significant Modernists such as Virginia Woolf and an intimate of Henry James, Walpole was an extremely popular novelist, but also regarded as 'old-fashioned'.

[2] Walpole had written to KM on 23 Oct. in response to her review of his novel *The Captives* in the *Athenaeum*, 15 Oct., taking issue with her reading of it, as well as her general approach to fiction: 'Is there only one kind of novel, only one method, only one school? Do let your influence, which is very great, extend more generously to work that is good, even though it is not *your* good' (ATL).

[3] The novel's heroine, Maggie Cardinal, daughter of a conventional clergyman, is drawn to

Martin Warlock, son of the leader of a millenialist sect, but marries the orthodox Revd Paul
Trenchard. She then lives with her husband and his sister Grace in his parish at Skeaton, until she
leaves him to nurse the declining Martin.
  [4] When Maggie's paternal uncle Matthew, a tippler and small-time businessman, is turned away
from Maggie's home by the puritanical Grace, he hangs himself in a boarding-house.
  [5] A pretty but flighty friend of Maggie's in London, who breaks confidence as a go-between with
Martin.

To J. M. Murry, [28 October 1920]

[Villa Isola Bella, Garavan, Menton]
Im sending 2 lots of reviews this week.
Dear Love
    The letters I have had – three from you! I expect the railway has
delayed them: I mean the shortage of traigins. (Thats a queer word of
ours isn't it!) I am glad to hear your tooth is better & very sorry you are
going to be patched by a tooth-tinker and more than sorry about my old
yinkum-tags. I ought to pay that moi-même. How much is it exactly? Let
me have the forms – will you, darling? Never a word more came about
H. King's form.[1] Yes, you're right to come in April – its too marvellous
to miss. I mean *Life* is and one is alive here. The weather is simply
enchantment. I am taking a sun bath cure – on Doctor Bouchages
advice & at 8 oclock the sun streams on my bed & nearly burns me. Its
a very wonderful treatment. I believe in it. Im also having those con-
founded iodine injections which make me an appalingly tired girl. But I
believe in them, too, so I must put up with the feeling. Doctor Bouchage
is of the same school as Doctor Sorapure; I have great confidence in him.
He helps me greatly – so far. But I am having the iodine every other day
– for a fortnight. By that time I shall have to hang like a bat when Im
not walking. Like the poor Lord who had no place to rest His head;[2] Ive
no place to rest my derrière.
    Hugh Walpoles letter was very nice, I thought. People *are* a bit sur-
prising, aren't they, Bogey? I heard from poor old Newte again – really
his name is awful. Horace W. C. . . . and then *Newte*,[3] & to write from
Wimbleton Hall!! It is the comble.
    I was very interested in what you said about Halle.[4] Queer chap. I
should think he was in a way uneasy with you. Has he any children? I
wish Id seen him and Rosy. And I would have enjoyed Goodyear pa-
man.[5] I remember giving F.G. my photo and he telling me his father
had said it was a *fine head*. I remember how he laughed and so did I –
and I said I shall have to grow a pair of horns and have it stuffed to hang
on Murry's door. When I recall Goodyear I can't believe he is – nowhere
– just as when I think about Chummie he comes before me, *warm*, laughing, saying "Oh, abso*lu*tely". What a darling boy he was. You were

always so beautifully generous in your thoughts of him. One – just one, my precious of the things I love in you is the way you speak of him some-times. Because, after all, you saw him so little –

I love this place more and more. One is conscious of it as I used to be conscious of New Zealand. I mean if I went for a walk there & lay down under a pine tree & looked up at the wispy clouds through the branches I came home plus the pine tree – don't you know? Here its just the same. I go for a walk & I watch the butterflies in the heliotrope & the young bees & some old humble ones and all these things are added unto me. Why I don't feel like this in England heaven knows. But my light goes out, in England, or its a very small & miserable shiner.

This isn't a letter, darling. Its just a note. Yes I shall provide small pink carnets for our accounts at Xmas. Slates, too, with holes burnt in them for the sponge string. Did you ever burn a hole in the frame? Thrilling deed. It was Barry Waters[6] specially with his initials burnt too – and a trimming. I can see it now.

Dearest most precious one

Wig.

MS ATL. LKM II. 66. LJMM 575-6.

1 Henry King, a name under which Murry published his own verse in the Athenaeum.
2 Matt. 8: 20.
3 In the Athenaeum, 24 Sept. 1920, KM had reviewed with both admiration and serious reserva-tions The Extra Lady, a novel of life in the theatre, by Horace W. C. Newte.
4 Not identified.
5 KM's close friend and admirer Frederick Goodyear had been killed near Arras in May 1917. In 1920 his father put together and published Frederick Goodyear, Letters and Remains, 1887–1917. (See CLKM I, 248–50.)
6 KM's first cousin, son of her maternal aunt Agnes, lived close to the Beauchamps in Karori from 1893 to 1898. He and his brother Eric were the source of Pip and Rags in Prelude and 'At the Bay'.

To J. M. Murry, [30 October 1920]

[Villa Isola Bella, Caravan, Menton]
Saturday.

New Block. Bought today, 7.50.
My own Love
Yesterday I was so busy I didn't send you a personal letter. Only the reviews went off. Your Tuesday letter came, telling me you intended to visit Achner[1] (wise boy) and that you were reading Mrs Asquith.[2] I read certain parts of her book and felt – just that – there was something decent. At the same time the whole book seems to me indecent. Perhaps

I feel more than anything that shes one of those people who have no past and no future. She's capable of her girlish pranks and follies today − in fact shes at the mercy of herself now & forever just as she was then. *And thats bad.* We only live by somehow absorbing the past − changing it − I mean really examining it & dividing what is important from what is not (for there IS waste) & transforming it so that it becomes part of the life of the spirit and we are *free of it.* Its no longer our personal past; its just in the highest possible sense, our servant. I mean in that it is no longer our master. That is the wrong image. I used to think this process was fairly *unconscious.* Now I feel just the contrary. With Mrs A. this process (by which the artist and the "living being" lives) never takes place. She is forever driven. Shes of the school of Ottoline, isn't she.
"I am the Cup that Thirsteth for the Wine"
These half-people are very queer − very tragic, really. They are neither simple − nor are they artists. They are between the two & yet they have the desires (no, appetites) of both. I believe their *secret whisper* is: "If only I had found THE MAN I might have been anything" − − − But the man isn't born and so they turn to life and parade & preen and confess and dare − and lavish themselves on what they call *Life.* "Come woo me − woo me". How often Ive *seen* that in Ottoline as her restless distracted glance swept the whole green countryside − −

Oh, God! God! As I write − I want to write. I see our work. Oh to be a writer!! What is there like it! (By the way, Heart dearest, I do love Sir Tobys saying to Viola "Come *taste your legs*, Sir. Put them in motion"[3] when he wanted her to leap & fly. I wish I had a little tiny boy to say that to.)

Todays letter says you have been to Achner & you do think he's good. Yes, isn't he? He is a change after poor old Lucas hooking his saliva carrier on to the arum lily jar.

Theres a violent N.W. wind today − a howling one. I had to go into town. The great immense waves were sweeping right up to the road & over. I wish youd seen them. Three brigs are in − the sailors pants hanging on lines & dancing hornpipes. Leaves are falling; its like autumn. But the shops are full of flowers & everywhere little girls, wrapped up to the eyes go by at a run carrying a bouquet of chrysanthemums in a paper. For tomorrow is La Toussaint.

When I got home − I found my BOX had arrived. The thrill was terrific. I wondered & wondered what little oddments you had found − whether Id find − − − Well − it didn't matter. I found in addition to the book the 2 Indian figures & the small tan cushion. Was that all? Will you tell me? In case anything was stolen. I really had a laugh over it. And the bookcase made to hold the book (one shelf half full!) It was my fault. Im NOT for a minute blaming you, my precious love.

Dont forget Mignonette to tell me your date of probable arrival at
Xmas time –

Goodbye for now, dearest Love

Yours for ever amen

Wig.

MS ATL. *LKM* II., 66–7; *LJMM* 576–8.

1 Murry's new dentist.
2 His review of *The Autobiography of Margot Asquith* appeared in the *Athenaeum*, 5 Nov. 1920.
3 'Taste your legs, sir; put them to motion': *Twelfth Night*, iii. i. 87.

To J. M. Murry, [31 October 1920]

[Villa Isola Bella, Garavan, Menton]
Sunday.

My dear Love

Your Thursday letter & Hardys letter[1] have arrived. I shall keep
Hardy's letter for you – unless you'd rather have it back. Ill put it in my
Spenser.

In reply to your letter: I don't doubt for one instant that your feelings
and mine have been alike: that we have been haunted again by our
strange correspondences. Your letter might *be* my letter – if you know
what I mean. You say just what I had meant to convey in my letter and
I too, feel that I don't *want* a God to appeal to – that I only appeal to
the spirit that is within me.

You say you "dearly love to know exactly what I feel". I thought I had
told you. But my writing is so bad, my expression so vague that I expect
I didn't make myself clear. Ill try to.

> "Between the acting of a dreadful thing
> And the first motion, all the interim is
> Like a phantasma or a dreadful dream;   *What a book*
> The genius and the mortal instruments   *is hidden*
> Are then in council; and the state of man   *here!*
> Like to a little Kingdom suffers then
> The nature of an insurrection."[2]

The "thing" was not always "dreadful" neither was the "dream", and
you must substitute "spirit" for genius. Otherwise there you have my life
as I see it up till now – complete with all the alarms, enthusiasms, terrors, excitements – in fact the nature of an insurrection. Ive been dimly
aware of it many times. Ive had moments when it has seemed to me that
this wasn't what my little Kingdom ought to be like – yes and longings

and regrets. But only since I came away this time have I *fully realised* it −
confronted myself as it were, looked squarely at the extraordinary "conditions" of my existence.

It wasn't flattering or pleasant or easy. I expect your sins are of the
subconscious; they are easier to forgive than mine. You are I *know* a far
nobler and stronger nature. Ive *acted* my sins, & then excused them or
put them away with "it doesn't do to think about these things" or (more
often) it was all experience. But it hasnt ALL been experience. There IS
waste − destruction, too. So, Bogey − and my inspiration was our Love
− I never should have done it otherwise − I confronted myself. As I write
I falsify slightly. I can't help it; its all so difficult. The whole thing was
so much *deeper* and more *difficult* than Ive described it − *subtler* − less conscious & more conscious if you know what I mean. I didn't walk up &
down the room & groan, you know, darling. As I am talking to you Ill
dare say it all took place on another plane, because then we can smile
at the description & yet mean something by it.

But as I say my inspiration was Love. It was the final realisation that
Life for me was intimacy with you. Other things attend this. But this *is*
my Life on this earth. I see the Fairy tale as our history really. Its a
tremendous symbol. The Prince & the Princess do wed in the end and
do live happy ever after as King & Queen in their own Kingdom. Thats
about as profound a Truth as any. But I want to talk to you rather than
write to you. I feel − only *now* can we talk.

And I dont want to imply that the Battle is over and here I am vic-
torious. Ive escaped from my enemies − emerged − that is as far as Ive
got. But it is a different state of being to any Ive known before & if I
were to 'sin' now − it would be mortal.

There. Forgive this rambling involved statement. But my treasure, my
life is ours. You know it.

A thousand thanks for managing the Constable affair.[3] I am of course
more than satisfied.

The papers have come. Ive not read the A. yet. The D.N. [*Daily News*]
astounds me. I believe they are making a dead set against us. Rose
Macaulay cracking up to the sky May Sinclair, Mary Hamilton & Mrs
Scott.[4] But really my quotations proved the idiocy of Mrs Scott, surely.[5]
Really − I CANT understand this world. Then did you see their carica-
ture of Prowse's novel?[6] Ill send it to you. Its almost *word for word*. But
Prowse wrote as seriously as Duhamel. *AND* the D.N. reviewed his novel
− gave it a 'good' review a week or two ago. Its like each time one picks
up a dish the crack seems more evident. Each time I read the paper I
get the same sharp little shock. But it will be funny to see how they'll
rend me.[7]

Its a very cold sea shell of a day. *But I am content.* That is what this climate makes me feel.

Ill write about the Athenaeum tomorrow.

Goodbye my own Love

Wig.

MS ATL. *LKM* II. 68–9. *LJMM* 578–80.

1 Thomas Hardy wrote Murry a brief letter on 26 Oct., saying he was looking forward to reading *Cinnamon and Angelica*, Murry's recently published verse play and that he was rereading Jane Austen. ('The Collected Letters of Thomas Hardy, ed. Richard Little Purdy and Michael Millgate, vi (1987), 42–3.

2 *Julius Caesar*, II. i. 63–9. KM has written 'dreadful' for 'hideous' in the third line.

3 The dealings with Constable over the publication of *Bliss*.

4 Rose Macaulay reviewed May Sinclair's *The Romantic* and Mary Agnes Hamilton's *The Last Fortnight*, describing them as 'these two interesting books' in the *Daily News*, 27 Oct. 1920.

5 In reviewing *The Headland* by C. A. Dawson-Scott in the *Athenaeum*, 22 Oct., KM observed: 'There are no hard words in this novel, and there are an immense number of dots; they are so many and so frequent that we believe they must mean more than we have understood.' She goes on to quote several sentences that taper off with three dots . . .

6 The *Daily News*, 18 Oct., ran a brief but favourable review by R. Ellis Roberts of R. O. Prowse's *A Gift of the Dusk*. On 27 Oct. 'A Swiss Cure', signed K. J. M., purported to be diary entries of a patient in a sanatorium, concluding 'I am utterly without hope now and forever. I am getting well.'

7 In fact it was her friend Sylvia Lynd who sympathetically reviewed *Bliss* in the *Daily News*, 29 Dec. 1920.

To J. M. Murry, [1 November 1920]

[Villa Isola Bella, Garavan, Menton]
Monday. Midi. Waiting for lunch. ''En tirant la langue comme un chien'' as they say here.

My Own Precious

Its simply heavenly here today – warm, still, with wisps of cloud just here & there & le ciel deep blue. Everything is expanding & growing after the rain; the buds on the tea roses are so exquisite that one feels quite faint regarding them. A pink rose – 'chinesy pink' in my mind – is out – there are multitudes of flowers and buds. And the freesias are up & the tangerines are turning. A painter whose ladder I see against the house across the valley has been singing ancient church music – awfully complicated stuff. But what a choice! How much more suited to the day and the hour than – and now, Im dished. For every song I wanted to find ridiculous seems somehow charming & appropriate & quite equally lovable.

I put more white wash on the old woman's face
Than I did on the gar-den wall!

For instance. That seems to me a thoroughly good song. You know the

first two lines are
Up an' down up an' down in an'out the window
I did no good at all.
Sam Mayo used to sing it.[1] Things werent so bad in those days. I really
believe everything was better. The tide of barbarism wasn't flowing in.

Oh, Bogey I want to ask you. Did you care about the Mayor of Cork?[2]
It was a most terrible shock to me. Id been reading about his appaling suffering in the Eclaireur and you know I never thought he *would* die.
I thought he simply couldnt. It was a ghastly tragedy. Again, I feel the
people ought to have rushed out of the prison and made Lloyd George or
whoever it was free him. My plan (this sounds heartless; yes, but I would
have done it, Im not laughing at the Lord Mayor – God forbid) was to
kidnap Megan Lloyd George[3] & inform the père that as long as the Lord
Mayor was imprisoned she went unfed. Why don't the Sinn Feiners do
things like this. Murder Carson[4] for instance, instead of hunger strike.

After lunch

Ive read your Baudelaire. I think its extremely fine – really *masterly*. It
made me thirst after a book of such critical portraits. Youve made a most
extraordinary leap forward in your *power of interpreting*. One used to feel
with you a certainty that the knowledge was there but a kind of difficulty
prevented you from sharing it. There was in spite of your desire to
express yourself *almost an involuntary* withholding of something. Thats very
difficult to explain. I felt it until quite recently, really. And now that its
gone not only have I the readers deep "relief" but I seem (am I fantastic) almost to rejoice in your consciousness of your liberation as well.

Goodbye dearest love. No letters today – as yet. NEXT month we meet!
Oh, *Bogey*.
Your

Wig.

I was all wrong about the house painter!! Hes just come back from lunch
– in a grey flannel suit, put on his white overall & started singing in
English! Elizabethan airs. He must be some sensible fellow who's taken
the little house and is doing the job himself. He makes me think of you
– but his singing is different – more difficult, darling.
'What is milk a *metre* now?' L.M.
Dream I.
I was living at home again in the room with the fire escape. It was night:
Father & Mother in bed. Vile people came into my room. They were
drunk. Beatrice Hastings led them. "You dont take me in old dear" said
she. "Youve played the Lady once too often, Miss – coming it over me."
And she shouted, screamed *Femme marqué* and banged the table. I rushed
away. I was going away next morning so I decided to spend the night in
the dark streets and went to a theatre in Piccadilly Circus. The play a
costume play of the Restoration had just begun. The theatre was small

and packed. Suddenly the people began to speak too slowly, to mumble: they looked at each other stupidly. One by one they *drifted* off the stage & very slowly a black iron curtain was lowered. The people in the audience *looked* at one another. Very slowly, silently, they got up and moved towards the doors — stole away.

An enormous crowd filled the Circus: it was black with people. They were not speaking — a low murmur came from it — that was all. They were still. A whitefaced man looked over his shoulder & *trying to smile* said: "The Heavens are changed already; there are six moons!"
Then I realised that *our* earth had come to an end. The sky was ashy-green; six livid quarters swam in it. A very fine soft ash began to fall. The crowd parted. A cart drawn by two small black horses appeared. Inside there were salvation army women doling tracts out of huge marked boxes. They gave me one. "Are you Corrupted?" It got very dark and quiet and the ash fell faster. Nobody moved.

Dream II
In a café. Gertler met me. "Katherine you must come to my table. Ive got Oscar Wilde there. Hes the most marvellous man I ever met. Hes splendid!" Gertler was flushed. When he spoke of Wilde he began to cry — tears hung on his lashes but he smiled.

Oscar Wilde was very shabby. He wore a green overcoat. He kept tossing & tossing back his long greasy hair with the whitest hand. When he met me he said: "Oh *Katherine*!" — very affected. But I did find him a fascinating talker. So much so I asked him to come to my home. He said would 12.30 tonight do? When I arrived home it seemed madness to have asked him. Father & Mother were in bed. What if Father came down & found that chap Wilde in one of the chintz armchairs? Too late now. I waited by the door. He came with Lady Ottoline. I saw he was disgustingly pleased to have brought her. Dear *Lady* Ottoline & Ottoline in a red hat on her rust hair *'hounyhyming'*[5] along. He said "Katherine's hand" — the same gentle hand!" as he took mine. But again when we sat down — I couldn't help it. He *was* attractive — as a curiosity. He was fatuous & brilliant!

"You know Katherine when I was *in that dreadful place*[6] I was haunted by the memory of a *cake*. It used to float in the air before me — a little delicate thing *stuffed* with cream and with the cream there was something *scarlet*. It was made of *pastry* and I used to call it my little Arabian Nights cake. But I couldn't remember the name. Oh, Katherine it was *torture*. It used to *hang* in the air and *smile* at me, and every time I resolved that next time *they let some one* come and see me I would ask them to tell me what it was but every time, Katherine, I was *ashamed*. Even now . . ." I said "mille feuilles à la crème?" At that he turned round in the armchair and began to sob, and Ottoline who carried a parasol opened it and put it over him . . .

MS ATL. *LKM* II. 69–71. *LJMM*, 580–3.

¹ Sam Mayo (1884–1938), a music-hall artist and composer, celebrated for his lugubrious delivery of comic songs.
² Terence MacSwiney, mayor of Cork, dramatist, member of the Irish Parliament, and commander of the First Cork Brigade of the Irish Republican Army, was court-martialled and charged with sedition. He refused to recognize the courts, began a hunger strike on 12 Aug., and died on 25 Oct.
³ The 18-year-old daughter of the British Prime Minister.
⁴ Sir Edward Carson (1854–1935), the eminent barrister and MP for Balcairn, Belfast, was the strongest Unionist voice against home rule in Ireland.
⁵ From the Houyhnhnms, the speaking horses in book 4 of Jonathan Swift's *Gulliver's Travels* (1726).
⁶ Oscar Wilde variously served his prison sentence at Pentonville, Wandsworth, and Reading gaols.

To J. M .Murry, [2 November 1920]

[Villa Isola Bella, Garavan, Menton]

My precious Bogey

Your Saturday & Sunday letters have come, and Ive read them twice. Ill expect you then on the 20th of next month – on or about – thats it, isn't it? Be sure to have your passport ready in time. I feel we have such a tremendous lot to settle. We shall be talking nearly all the time. But I expect it wont seem ½ so much once you are here. Things will go easy. Yes, my calculation included rent. I think its more or less just. About this little house – I don't *think* I shall be allowed to keep it after May. At any rate we ought not to stay the summer through here. I should like to have this little house by the year. Its extraordinarily satisfactory. In fact its almost ideal – quite ideal in its way. So small & yet not cramped – the position perfect – the garden perfect. I love the little place *deeply*. It will be a great wrench to get away. But Ive got my eye on another – quite near. At any rate we shall not have great difficulty I don't think. I should like to keep Marie if possible wherever we are in France. She saves enormously in time, worry, energy, everything & looks after all ones interests. But indeed Marie is such a jewel that I expect to lose her any day. She's much "too good to be true". Shes what one has always sought after. We'd better keep all our plans *dead secrets* until we have discussed them – hadn't we.

Im not up to much today. Yesterday was dark & stormy: today is too. And in spite of my feelings the weather affects me physically. I fly so high that when I go down – its a drop, Boge. Nothing serious; just a touch of cold, but with it to "bear it company" a black mood. Dont pay any attention to it. I expect it will have lifted utterly by the time this reaches you. And its really caused by a queer kind of *pressure* – which is work to be done. *I am writing*. Do you know the feeling & until this story is finished I am engulfed. Its not a tragic story either – but there you are. It seizes me – swallows me completely. I am Jonah in the whale & only you could charm that old whale to disgorge me.[1] Your letters did for a minute but now Im in again & we're thrashing through deep water. I fully realise it. Its the price we have to pay – we writers. Im lost – gone – possessed & everybody who comes near is my enemy.

The very queer thing is tho' that I feel if you were here this wouldn't happen. Work wouldn't be then the *abnormal* but the normal. Just the knowledge that you knew knew would be enough. Here's egoism!! But its to excuse a very faded old letter.

Its so *unfair* with these letters of yours. But you understand don't you love. Tomorrow I expect I shall be up up in the clouds again with the story finished.

And my deep love – my new love – no breath could ever touch it. It abides. I am *your*

Wig.

Floryan's letters came – thank you darling & a cheque for the books – 5/- too much. Take it off the next ones. Wig.

MS ATL. *LKM* II. 72; *LJMM*, 583–4.

1 Jonah 2: 10.

To J. M. Murry, [3 November 1920]

[Villa Isola Bella, Garavan, Menton]
8.35 Wednesday.

Darling Own,

Here it is under my hand – finished – another story about as long as The Man Without a Temperament! – praps longer. Its called *The Stranger*. Its a "New Zealand" story. My depression has gone, Boge, so it was just this. And now its here – thank God – & the fire burns and its warm and tho the wind is howling – it can howl. What a QUEER business writing is. I don't know. I dont believe other people are ever as fool-ishly excited as I am while Im working. How could they be? Writers would have to live in trees. Ive been this man *been* this woman. Ive stood for hours on the Auckland Wharf. Ive been out in the stream waiting to be berthed. Ive been a seagull hovering at the stern and a hotel porter whistling through his teeth. It isn't as though one sits and watches the spectacle. That would be thrilling enough, God knows. But one is the spectacle for the time. If one remained oneself all the time like some writ-ers can it would be a bit less exhausting. Its a lightning change affair, tho. But what does it matter. Ill keep this story for you to read at Xmas.

I only want to give it to you now. Accept my new story – my own Love. Give it your blessing. It is the best I can do and therefore it is yours. If it pleases you nobody else counts – not one.

   Your own

                                                                              Wig.

MS ATL. *LKM* II. 72–3.

---

¹ A story she wrote in Jan. 1920. Based on an incident in her parents' lives, 'The Stranger' was published in the *London Mercury*, Jan. 1921.

To J. M. Murry, [3 November 1920]

Darling Bogey

Will you have this typed for me? AT MY EXPENSE. Two copies. And what do you advise me to do with it. I mean – ought I to try & sell it?

   If you can just give me your opinion – – – Im not registering it so Im asking you just to wire me if it comes for I HAVEN'T ANOTHER COPY.

   I am for ever your own

                                                                              Wig.

You know my state of mind: (a) He'll not like it. (b) it will be lost.

MS ATL.

To Sydney Schiff, 3 November 1920

                                          Villa Isola Bella | Garavan-Menton.
                                                                    iii.XI.1920.

My dear Sydney

   I cannot tell you how distressed I am to hear of Violet's illness. My heart goes out to you both. I wish I could know how she was this very minute. Give her my tender love; tell her that my wishes join the wishes of all who know and love her that she'll be better soon – and soon her beautiful radiant self again.

   I sympathise with your anxiety, my dear friend. I do appreciate the relief it must be to you to know that she is recovering. Will you let me have – just a note as soon as you can, telling me how she is? I will look for it.

As soon [as] I can manage the journey I will go to Roquebrune. I think I'd better send Jones instead, and she shall report. Your mention-ing the verbena made me think of the lavender bushes last year – and the morning we sat in the garden for a little while. I always see *across our* conversation those lovely spikes of deep purplish blue, and the bees were busy in them. That and the sound of water and the flight of three swal-lows – all are 'important' to the moment.

Yes, there are weak spots in *A Gift from the Dusk* but compared to the unworthy, stupifying, *untruthful* rubbish of today it did not do, I felt, to comment on them. The worst of it is, nowadays, that the majority of novels is so bad one becomes almost fearful of the strength of one's feel-ing for a 'good' one. There were touches in that book that moved me tremendously. I felt that in the intimacy between Stephen and Mary, Prowse was, many times, speaking a language which I long in vain to hear spoken. The intimacy of two beings who are *essential* to each other – who is going to write that? And yet Love that is less than that – one wearies of hearing of it.

Im sure Ive read 20 novels this autumn by LADY writers that might all be called *How I lost my Virginity!* If that wasn't bad enough – they never tell the truth – they always tell *How I WISHED to lose my Virginity*, and in fact I don't believe they ever did lose it.

I wish there were 6 or 7 writers who wrote for themselves and let the world go hang. But where are they? As to critics – to have to print Herbert Read[1] is enough proof of their scarcity. I can't bear Herbert Read; he always sounds so puffed up and so dull.

What did you think of Lady O? Its difficult to imagine her in rooms at Roquebrune.[2] She's a queer study – she's early sixteenth century really & I think she suffers very much in trying to accommodate herself to today. At the same time (and EVER to be remembered) she is of the same school as Margot Asquith.

The weather these last few days is infernal, but my doctor is kind and *still* tells me I must have courage. It makes work rather a labour, though. How I look forward to seeing you both! Not a day passes but I think of you.

Yours ever

K.M.

MS BL. *LKM* II. 73.

---

1 Herbert Read (1893–1968), at that time primarily known for his war poems and his connec-tion with Imagism, had written for the *Athenaeum* on 'Boyle and Byron', 13 Aug. 1920, and on 'Jay criticism' and painting, 29 Oct.

2 In Nov. Lady Ottoline Morrell began a 7-month stay in Europe with her teenage daughter Julian. The Morrells were in straitened financial circumstances, and Lady Ottoine frequently trav-elled by bus, and stayed in modest rented rooms.

To J. M. Murry, [4 November 1920]

[Villa Isola Bella, Garavan, Menton]
Thursday.

I had about 1 inch of mouse's tail from you today but it was the gay and wavy end so it didn't matter. Twas writ on Monday. Good morning, my darling. Theres a debonaire wind blowing today and a very pale, faint, jonquil sun. I send you Hugh Walpole's letter. He seems to me most awfully nice and it is in reply to one which I sent him telling him what I really DID think of his book – I mean as man to man. I said: "Just for once Ill be *dead frank*" & you know what that means. But I felt nobody else ever *would* & it was an opportunity. Besides his letter somehow called for ones deep sincerity. And instead of sending mine back with 'this is outrageous' – he replies – so gently. Won't you see him? I feel (what a volte face!) hes almost a friend of ours.

Schiff wrote yesterday too – touched ones heart. Violet has been very ill. Shes had an operation and so on – & poor old Schiff is shattered – a kind of wrecked Luft-Schiff. His letter has actually "by the grace of God" and "D.V." in it! What old Death can't shake out of us! But its very touching to know how frail is ones hold on Picture Galleries and Editions de luxe.

If the Last Trump ever *did* sound – would it frighten US? I don't think it would in the least. If God didn't take us both into Heaven Id *rather* be in Hell and out of sight of anyone so stupid. (I told poor old L.M. yesterday that after I died to PROVE there was no immortality I would send her a coffin worm in a matchbox. She was gravely puzzled.)

I must write my review. Goodbye my precious. The sun has gone in again – he'll have to do better than this at Christmas.

Wig.

MS ATL. *LKM* II. 73–4.

To Hugh Walpole, 4 November 1920

Isola Bella | Garavan-Menton.
4.XI.1920.

Dear Hugh Walpole

Please do not praise me.[1] But – let me say how I look forward to that talk, one of these days. The fact that you care about writing as you do, that 'you are working' is such happiness that all my good wishes & my sympathy cannot repay you for letting me know.

Your from-this-time-forth '*constant reader*'

Katherine Mansfield.

MS Texas.

1 On 2 Nov. Walpole replied to KM's letter of 27 Oct, telling her 'It was a fine letter and I agree with so much of it' (ATL).

To J. M. Murry, [5 November 1920]

[Villa Isola Bella, Garavan, Menton]
Friday

My precious darling.

You've NOT done it again. Ill never mention a single thing again. I meant to be rather funny about the box with all the cardboard – the famous box – like our grands meubles at Paris which ended in two of the smallest tables in the world with the tiniest jugs & basins on them. *Send no more Basil*,[1] please, love. Re books Ill not have any more just now. Dont worry.

I am glad you are going to see Elizabeth.[2] I confess Ive a great tendre for her really, more than Id tell anybody. Perhaps its just sentimentality but I feel that in her "innermost she" – Oh p'raps thats too much. Id better wait and here what you dishcover. The Flat iron party (a VERY good joke) amused me awfully. I like Mrs Wells, too. But no, we never were bright & young like people are. Oh, by the way, I had my photo taken yesterday – for a surprise for you. Ill only get des epreuves on Monday tho. I should think it ought to be extraordinary. The photographer took off my head & then balanced it on my shoulders again at all kinds of angles as tho it were what Violet calls an art pot. "Ne bougez PAS en souriant leggerreMENT – Bouche CLOSE." A kind of drill. Those funny studios fascinate me – I must put a story in one one day. They are the most *temporary shelters* on earth. Why is there always a dead bicycle behind a velvet curtain? Why does one always sit on a faded piano stool? And then, the plaster pillar, the basket of paper flowers, the storm background – and the *smell*. I love such endroits.

MS C. Murry. *LJMM*, 585–6.

1 Murry's note (*LJMM*, 585) points out that this is probably a reference to the telegram in KM's story 'The Singing Lesson', which may have been written a short time before: 'Pay no attention to letter must have been mad bought hat stand today Basil.'
2 KM's cousin Elizabeth Russell.

To J. M. Murry, [6 November 1920]

[Villa Isola Bella, Garavan, Menton]

My precious darling

Your Friday letter has come & the new Tchekhov.[1] Ill do the column as quickly as I can. You wonder I am sure that I dont send more work; that I take so long. Its not my fault. As a matter of fact I ought not to do even what I do just now. Ive had the subject out several times with Bouchage. For some reason Im in such a queer state mentally – work excites me MADLY, and fatigues me, too. I can't take it calmly. It sounds perfectly absurd but its an immense effort to begin and when I do begin I begin to get into a fever. And I am suffering with pains in my head-box. Awful ones. Of course with our imagination I think it can only mean my brain's going up like a rocket one day soon or Ive got something pressing on it or a vine curling round it or a fox eating it. You know our pleasant fancies. But in fair moments I think its only the result of my long illness and coughing and nerves. But they were so severe (are) this evening that I thought Id write and tell you about them. Not to apologise or to frighten you but just to let you know because I think you ought to. Another reason may be that in my cough mixture that Ive been taking for 2 years there has been a certain amount of opium. Im trying to knock it off now but it has had a certain effect and I think accounts for my sensitiveness now – nervous sensitiveness. I simply have to tell you this tonight. Not because anything might *happen*. But I know you are my own and will understand why I tell you. Im a bit frightened (as we are) about these head pains and sensations of violent raging excitement.

Love don't let this make you sad or worry you or *anything* like that. Just put it aside for future reference (I hope you'll never need it) and never forget that living alone is the devil for me: it starts all my terrors to life. You know that from experience. Just as I am more sensitive than other people *to* other people so I am, I suppose to myself. I always notice that when I am *with* people these frights and premonitions die away – and I forget "whether I am going mad" or not (!) I suspect most writers of my kind share my nervousness, but in my case its immensely accentuated by illness.

What a perfectly horrid letter – and written on the divinest evening. Ive just seen all the anemones are up, too. Thats much nicer than talking about my old head.

I wish Fergie[2] would give us some little models. I always feel artists ought to give away their works more than they do – for some reason. Ill post you my photos on Wednesday. One is looking *bang* at you like you asked for and one half-bang.

You will understand this letter as I mean you [to] wont you darling?

If I feel you do it relieves me to have told someone: to have broken the silence about it. My head feels better already. What a wife!

Wig.

MS ATL. LJMM, 587-8.

1 KM did not write anything on Chekhov, although Murry reviewed *The Schoolmistress and Other Stories*, translated by Constance Garnet, in the *Athenaeum*, 7 Jan. 1921.
2 Their close friend, the Scottish painter J. D. Fergusson.

To J. M. Murry, [8 November 1920]

[Villa Isola Bella, Garavan, Menton]

Always examine *both sides*. In my house both sides is buttered.

Tuesday.

Darling

Re your Mrs A.[1] I thought it was *very good* but . . . your feeling was really contained in your words: "the type it reveals is not very intrigu-ing". She isn't your game. When all is said and done I feel that *you* havent time for her and you don't care a Farthing Taster[2] whether she made her horse walk upstairs or downstairs or in my lady's chamber[3] She would *weary* you. What is there really to get hold of? Theres – noth-ing – in the sense you mean. The direct method (no, I can't for the life of me 'see' the other) of examining the specimen isn't really much good except in so far as one can . . . make certain deductions – discover cer-tain main weaknesses and falsities. But its a bit like trying to operate on a diseased *mind* by cutting open a brain. The devil is – oh the very devil is that you may remove every trace of anything that shouldn't be there & make no end of a job of it & then in her case in the case of all such women, the light comes back into the patients eyes and with it the vaguest of vague elusive *maddening* smiles . . . Do you know what I mean. Here's I think the root of the matter. What IS Insensitiveness? We know or we could find out by examination what it is NOT but it seems to me the quality hasn't been discovered yet. I mean its X – its a subject for research. It most certainly isnt only the *lack* of certain qualities: its a kind of *positive unknown*. Does all this sound most awful nonsense to you? My vocabulary is awful but I mean well & I faint I thirst to talk. My land-scape is terribly exciting at present. I never knew it contained such fea-tures or such fauna (they are animals various, aren't they?) But I do want a gentleman prepared to pay his own exss to join me in my expedition. Oh, wont you come? No one else will do. But when you do its a bit sick-ening – all my wild beasts get a bit funny looking – they don't look such serious monsters any more. Instead of lions & tigers its apt to turn into an affair of

"The turkey ran pas' with a flag in his mas'
An' cried out: Whats the mattah?"[4]

NOT that I think for one minute, my precious that you don't treat me au GRAND serieux or would dare to question my intelligence. Of course not. All the same − there you are. Alone Im no end of a fillaseafer but once you join me in the middle of my seriousness − my deadly seriousness I see the piece of pink wool I have put on your hair (& that you don't know is there).

Queer isn't it! Now explain *that* for me. Do I intrigue you? I wonder. But don't misunderstand me & think I think you can afford to laugh at me because of your great mind & my little one. The laugh is a mutual affair, really.

"Oh, Wig these subtleties are too much for me."

I am sorry, sweetheart; I am just going. Farewell. Let thy garments be always white & thy head lack not ointment.[5]

Your own

Wig.

It came over me sudden. In having your passport renewed wouldn't it be worth it to remember your O.B.E.[6] These things are sometimes useful in foreign parts. If we wished to smuggle, steal, flay alive. If we have no money & only our poor faces for our fortunes your O.B.E. would go miles further than my − nose, say. An O.B.E. may move a 'blighter' to some kind of respeck.

Dont scorn

Wig.

MS ATL. *LKM* II. 77–8; *LJMM*, 589–91.

---

[1] Murry's review on 5 Nov. of Margot Asquith's autobiography, the main purpose of which was to demonstrate what the last sentence asserted: 'There is no sentiment so false as the sentiment of the insensitive.'

[2] A 'taster' was a portion of ice-cream served in a shallow glass.

[3]   Goosey, goosey gander
         Whither shall I wander?
    Upstairs and downstairs
         And in my lady's chamber.

(Children's rhyme, first recorded in 1784)

[4] Presumably lines she remembered from a minstrel show.

[5] Eccles. 9: 8.

[6] Murry had been awarded the Order of the British Empire in Jan. 1920 for his work in M17 during the War.

To J. M. Murry, [10 November 1920]

[Villa Isola Bella, Garavan, Menton]
Wednesday.

Darling little Fellow
Your long descriptive letter has come. Dont observe too much. I feel at the end you were GASPING. I dont want you to see more than its easy to see. Yes, I do admire your observations of course & I am ashamed to say a wave of pure disgusting female relief went over me at your description of Rose Macaulay.[1] I was lying on my bed, dressed in a peach coloured handkerberchief having my bang de soleil and I kicked up my toes at their dinner. Oh, how it does *bore* me – the Naomi type[2] & that kind of conversation. If I were there & you were there we should do something desperate. Youd make yourself a ladder & Id climb on to your head & turn there on one toe. (Perhaps). All that you said about Elizabeth is extremely interesting. And the queer thing is that she only wants a *male appearance*. Theres her essential falsity. Forgive my frankness: she has no use for a physical lover. I mean to go to bed with. Anything but that. That she cant stand – she'd be frightened of. Her very life, her very being, her gift, her vitality, all that makes her depends upon her *not surrendering*. I sometimes wonder whether the act of surrender is not one of the greatest of all – the highest. It is one of the [most] difficult of all. Can it be accomplished or even apprehended except by the *aristocrats* of this world? You see its so immensely complicated. It 'needs' real humility and at the same time an absolute belief in ones own essential freedom. It is an act of faith. At the last moments like all great acts it is *pure* risk. This is true for me as a human being and as a writer. Dear Heaven how hard it is to let go – to step into the blue. And yet ones creative life depends on it and one *desires* to do nothing else. I shouldn't have begun on this in the corner of a letter, darling. Its not the place. Forgive
Wig.

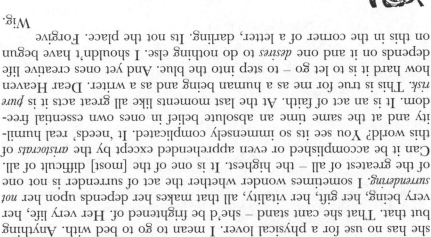

Darling Bogey
Kissing is a queer thing. I was standing under a tree just now – a tree that is shedding exquisite golden yellow leaves all over my garden path. And suddenly one leaf made the most ethereal advances to me and in another moment we were kissing each other. Through the silvery branches one can see the deep blue sky . . . lapis lazuli.
I think the time has come for it really has come for us to do a little courting. Have we ever had time to stand under trees and tell our love? Or to sit down by the sea and make fragrant zones for each other? The tea

roses are in flower. Do you know the peculiar exquisite scent of a tea rose? Do you know how the bud opens – so unlike other roses and how deep red the thorns are and almost purple the leaves?

I think it must be the orange flower which Marie has brought home from market. I have been arranging branches of it in jars and little slips of it in shallow glass bowls. And the house has a perfume as tho the Sultan were expecting the première visite of his youngest bride. Marie, standing over me chanted the while – almost sang a hymn to the cyclamen sauvage qu'on trouve dans les montagnes and the little violettes de mon pays which grow so thick that one trempe ses pieds dedans.

If I live here much longer I shall become a bush of daphne or you'll find no one to welcome you but a jasmine. Perhaps its the effect of receiving the Sun every morning – très intime – the lady clad only in a black paper fan. But you must come here, you must live here in the South and forget greyness. It is *divine* here – no less.

Wig.

MS ATL. *LKM* II. 78; *LJMM*, 588–9.

---

¹ Murry's letter describing the novelist Rose Macaulay (1881–1958), with others from this period, does not survive. KM had reviewed her *What Not* in the *Athenaeum*, 4 Apr. 1919, and her *Potterism*, 4 June 1920. The earlier review spoke of her 'nice sense of humour' and 'fine, sensitive style', but the second emphasized 'a strange confusion in our minds'.

² Naomi Royde Smith (d. 1964), novelist, playwright, and biographer, was literary editor of the *Westminster Gazette* 1912–22.

To J. M. Murry, [12 November 1920]

[Villa Isola Bella, Garavan, Menton]

My precious Bogey

I am awfully excited today. Its for this reason. I have made an offer to Jinnie for this villa for one year from May 1st next and tho' the offer has not been accepted it has also not been refused. Chances are even. *Oh dear what torture.* Perhaps you don't know that my feelings towards this villa are so fearfully intense that I think I shall have to be evicted if she doesn't give it to me. Its the first real home of my own I have ever loved. Pauline – yes, it wasn't home tho', neither was Runcton, not even Hampstead.¹ Not really – not with this thrill. This little place is and always will be for me the one and only place, I feel. My heart beats for it like it beats for Karori. Isn't it awful. And for US it is made in every single particular. True theres no salle de bain. But theres a huge saucer bath and a spung as big as me. So what matters! The divine incomparable situation is the trick, I suppose. Heaven from dawn to dawn. Walking on the terrace by starlight looking up through my vieux palmier I could weep for joy. Running into the garden to see how many more buds are out in the morning is to run straight at – into – a blessing. The fires all burn – but not frightfully. The doors shut. The kitchen is big & the larder is down 10 steps that send a chill to ones knees. The garde-linge is immense, all fitted with cupboards & shelves. The luggage is kept there & the umbrellas & the flags that flew at my gate on the 11th.[2] One gets ones parasol from the garde-linge. Your feltie would be there, too. There's enough garden for you to bien gratter in. At the back we could grow veg. In fack it is the dearest most ideal little corner. And private – just the next thing to an island.

If Jinnie accepts I thought we'd stay on here until le grand chaleur. Then take the funicular to Annunciata for those weeks & leave Marie here. She could come up & take away our laundry & bring it back & generally keep our things in order while we were there. I mean shed come by the day. It only takes 40 minutes to the hotel. We'd be back here in September & plant a *terrific* garden. Do you like the plan? You see we'd know just where we were for that first year. No worry. No moving. You'd REST. No responsibility. You'd just get rested & happy & loaf about & garden & play with me & whistle on the stairs. There are 3 bedrooms not counting Maries room so you could have a guest if you liked.

Bogey – hold thumbs for me. Truly this is a great turning point. Im trying to be calm but its not easy with such bliss in the balance. I had to offer an immense sum – 6000 francs. That means your share of the rent is 3000 for the year and the franc is at present at 57.

Am I a little bit mad? You will find ISOLA BELLA in poker work on my heart. The baths are only 10 minutes away for you in the summer – sea baths with splash boards – no springboard for you to plop off. I wait outside with a bun for you with big currant eyes (the bun I mean). Je t'aime. But *do* wish it will come true!!!

Wig.
Do you love me as I love you? Its getting frightfully urgent. I mean a kind of sweet blissful longing excitement & joy – always JOY.

MS Mention. *LKM* II. 74–5; *LJMM* 591–2.

1 The Villa Pauline, Bandol, for the first three months of 1916; Runcton Cottage, near Chichester, Sept.–Nov. 1912; 2 Portland Villas, Hampstead, since Aug. 1918.
2 The day before, which was the anniversary of the Armistice.

To J. M. Murry, [12 November 1920]

[Villa Isola Bella, Garavan, Menton]

My own Love

While I think of it: Would it worry you very much to bring your big suet case (registered) with clothes in it? Things to wear. The point is this. No, I DONT want you to dress up, or to worry, but it would be most awfully nice if you brought a clean suit for here and a pair of grey trousers to wear with your jaegar jersey – or a grey suit – I cant remember what you've got. But I fearfully want you to look a little bit pretty – for Marie, for the doctor – for Jinnie – for . . . At the same time I know you may be a little fed up with me for suggesting it. But the journey isn't very grubby nowadays so if you do bring your not oldest overcoat it won't get spoilt. And a Hat. I don't want to make you feel I ask you to spend DS.

Bring as much as you like: I can guard it for you here, & keep my book money in future (if you agree to the scheme) to pay for the registration. I know you thought of coming in a rucksack & spegchicks [spectacles]: thats why I write. Its 2 cold at Xmas for white Duck [drawing of a duck sitting on top of the D] trousers. Now just absolutely straight dinkum would a cheque for £5 help with clothes? *Please answer.* Praps it would be more convenient for you to send the big suit case on? In front of you. But I don't think so. It means a tagseye across Paris but thats worth it. The metro's *inferno* at present.

What are your idears?

Wig.

MS C. Murry. *LJMM*, 586–7.

To J. M. Murry, [13 November 1920]

[Villa Isola Bella, Garavan, Menton]
Isola Bella *until* May 1922

My darling Bogey

Did I tell you yesterday that Jinnie has accepted my offer for this villa? So its mine until *May 1922*. I hope when you have seen it you will be happy to think that its our pied-à-terre. I cant expect you to feel about it as I do. For me its for some reason the place to work in. Found at last. Its the writing table. But I only want to sit & write here until May 1922. Ive a horror of people or distractions — the time is more than ripe. And here at long last Life seems to have adjusted itself so that work is possible. Even if our finances went down & down we could live here more cheaply than anywhere else. I want you to plant veg. if you will at Christmas. Très important. Even if we had no maid we could live here (tho' God forbid). We should just eat bread & lettuce on the Terrace & dust once a fortnight. I really feel it may not be notwendig even to go up into the Mountains. We'll have the whole garden of the Louise for ourselves after May (when Jinnie & Connie go) and as Jinnie points out the fruit & veg. Thats bonzer cherries, oranges, tomates, pimentos, figs, grapes. The garden is simply divine with grass in it and trees. Its romantic, too, and very big with lemon groves. Their villa and ours always seem to me to be on an island. You see weve no neighbours. Only, out of sight up the hill a chateau which belongs to some Spaniards[1] & *that* garden we can wander in too, for they never come & la guardienne is a friend of Marie's. It takes the ultimate biscuit.

But Isola Bella's the thing. Now, if you ever want to send anything over, dearest, like a bit of cretonne or — no, Ill get Ida to bring what I want after Christmas. For of course the furniture isn't pretty. Still, it somehow, even as it *is*, looks . . . to my doting eye.

Youll have a whole year here. Last night I walked about and saw the new moon with the old moon in her arms[2] & the lights in the water & the hollow pools full of stars — and lamented there was no God. But I came in and wrote Miss Brill instead, which is my insect magnificat now & always. Goodbye, my precious for now. BE HAPPY. Your last letters have been so fearfully woeful. Such a fool I was to have told you about my head. I *was confiding*. And the worst of it is I felt so infinitely better till I got your sad, desolate, crushed reply: "*Not long now*" as tho' we were waiting for le dernier soupir. Oh Boge Boge Boge — Do lets try & not fall over! Or if we do — lets explain to each other (as I tried to) that we are falling. Do please come back to me. I feel you've gone away and are queerly *angry* — with life — *not* as you were.

Your true love
Wig.

MS ATL. *LJMM*, 592–3.

¹ KM did not know that this belonged to the Spanish writer Vicente Blasco Ibáñez (1867–1928), whose novel *The Four Horsemen* she reviewed as 'powerful and distinguished' in the *Athenaeum*, 11 July 1919.

2   Late, late yestreen I saw the new moone
                               Wi the auld moon in hir arme.

                                             (Anon. Scots ballad, 'Sir Patrick Spens')

To J. M. Murry, [14 November 1920]

[Menton]

INTREAT YOU LET NOONE HAVE HIDEOUS OLD PHOTOGRAPH¹ PUBLISHED IN SPHERE IMPORTANT BURN IT

TIG

Telegram ATL.

¹ A photograph taken in 1913 of a fuller-faced KM than is usual in her photographs, wearing a greenstone ear-ring. It appeared in the *Sphere* on 6 Nov.

To J. M. Murry, [14 November 1920]

[Villa Isola Bella, Garavan, Menton]

Dearest Bogey

I wired today about my photograph in the Sphere. I can't think who gave it to the papers. My vanity is awfully wounded. What a dogs life it is! Really I haven't got such beastly eyes & long poodle hair & a streaky fringe. Thats one for R.M. [Rose Macaulay] and Sheila K.¹ & all the rest of them. I feel quite ill with outraged vanity. Ive written to Sadler & sent him a postcard. Ill take the front page of the Daily Mirror for two pins & denige this other. I know you know how I *detest* it. Its not me. Its a HORROR. If its given to anyone please get it back. Fool I was not to have burnt it!

Tig.

MS ATL. *LJMM*, 595–6.

¹ KM had reviewed Sheila K. Smith's *Green Apple Harvest* in the *Athenaeum*, 3 Sept. 1920. She criticized it for its too obvious division into rustic and sophisticated levels: 'If the novel were ever alive it would be pulled to death between them.'

To Michael Sadleir,[1] [14 November 1920]

Villa Isola Bella | Garavan-Menton.

Dear Michael Sadleir,

My press agency posted me today a most AWFUL photograph of myself published in The Sphere. It was like a turnip or even a turnip manqué. Where it came from I dont know. But only beautiful people can afford to let such frights of themselves be laughed at; plain ones have to be more cautious. So, in case anyone should ask my publishers for a more-or-less likeness would you see they are given this postcard? Its very unlikely the occasion will arise but after my horrid shock this morning I'd like to be prepared. With all good wishes –

Yours sincerely
Katherine Mansfield.

MS Targ.

[1] Michael Sadleir (1888–1957), educated at Rugby and Balliol, was a friend of Murry's at Oxford, assisted in establishing Rhythm, and after a brief diplomatic career was now a publishing editor with Constable. He would become a director of the firm the next year. Also an eminent book collector and bibliographer, he wrote on Trollope and the history of publishing, and became a popular novelist, his Fanny by Gaslight (1940) achieving vast commercial success.

To Richard Murry, [15 November 1920]

[Villa Isola Bella, Garavan, Menton]
Sunday.

My dear Richard,

Its 7.15 a.m. and Ive just had breakfast in a room lit with great gorse yellow patches of sunlight. Across one patch there's a feathery pattern that dances, thats from the mimosa tree outside. The two long windows are wide open – they are the kind that open in half – with wings, you know – so much more generous than the English kind. A wasp is paddling his petticoes in the honey glass and the sky is a sort of pale lapis lazuli. Big glancing silver ducks of light dive in and out of the sea. This kind of weather has gone on for over a week without one single pause. I take a sunbath every morning. Costume de bain: a black paper fan and it has an awfully queer effect on one. I mean all this radiance has. You know those rare moments when its warm enough to lie on your back & bask – its a kind of prolongation of that. One tries to behave like a sober sensible creature & to say 'thank you' to the postman and no thank you to the umbrella mender but all the time one is hiding broad beams. So I slink away out of sight of everybody, down the steps from the terrace and stand underneath a tree called a datura and there, privately, I gloat. This tree, Sir, is a sight for you. It has small close, grey-green leaves; the buds in their first stage are soft green pods. They open and the flower, tightly folded, springs out and gradually it opens into a long bell-like trumpet about 8 inches long – gold coloured with touches of pale red. But the drawing in the buds and the petals! The gaiety of the edges – the freedom with which Papa Cosmos has let hisself go on them! I have looked at this tree so long that it is transplanted to some part of my brain – for a further transplanting into a story one day.

You must come here one day, Richard and live here for a bit. I dont see how you couldn't be happy. I appreciate your feeling that you would not care to work on a large canvas in England. I feel just the same about writing. Im always afraid my feeling won't last long enough for me to have expressed all that I wanted to. There's something in the atmosphere which *may* blow cold. And there's always a sense of rush – a strain. If the Muse does deign to visit me Im conscious all the time that shes got her eye on the clock – she's catching the funicular to Olympus at 5.30 or the special to Parnassus at 5.15. Whereas here, one begins to tell the time by the skies again.

I love hearing about your work: you must know I do always. What's this Christmas Jamboree? Tell's about it! As for little K.M. she's agoing it as usual. The more I do the more I *want* to do: it will always be the same. The further one climbs the more tops of mountains one sees. But its a matter for rejoicing – as long as one can keep the coffin from the door. I don't care a pin about the old *wolf.* I must get up & take the ear-wigs out of the roses. Why should they choose roses? But they do & I go against Nature in casting them forth. Dear Richard, don't forget your loving – really awfully loving X

Katherine.

MS R. Murry. *LKM* II. 78–80.

To J. M. Murry, [15 November 1920]

[Villa Isola Bella, Garavan, Menton]

My darling

Your letter saying I could knock off (no need thanks) came today & you sound better. You told me too about the Part Eyes. If I were you Id never go – never. Why should you? They must be simply *too* awful – I don't believe I could go. Id change into something frozen. Leave them alone. Sullivan & his Sullivanchen can go. Hes queerly insensitive & proud of being invited to such affairs mais ils ne sont pas pour nous.

113

Tchekhov hated them just as we do. At any rate its not worth while to sit up till 1.20 for Sullivan – ever. I hate Sullivan for that.[1] If I could see him now here Id say 'no'. I feel I don't ever want to speak to him again. Such disgusting indifference. He is a *clumsy* creature. I think Im terribly intolerant of *clumsiness*.

Fine shades – fine shades – Im all for them. Life is made up of nuances. One must be sensitive to the very last nerve – or I must.

If I didn't live with you Id live solitary. Id go further & further away. I love to watch my people to know them but I like to keep very very free – what I suppose you accused me – aloof. In fact, I confess that except with you I do feel aloof and remote and rather fastidious. Ill only be familiar with *you*. Du reste j'ai mon travail. But just shaking those parties at me makes me . . . feel like Mother. Oh people are careless, clumsy – the days when I could stand them are over. Dont ever ask Sullivan here – will you?
Your own
Wig.

MS ATL. LJMM, 596.

[1] KM's attitude to Murry's friend and assistant editor, Sullivan, fluctuated. He was invited, and stayed at Isola Bella, the following April.

To Sydney Schiff [c.15 November 1920]

[Villa Isola Bella, Garavan, Menton]

My dear Sydney
Will you and she forgive me if I do not write a letter just now? I am overworked. C'est un mauvais moment. Please accept my love instead. I long to see you both. I rejoice with all my heart that you are better, dearest Violet. May you both be happy!
The weather here is divine. It is almost unbearably beautiful. I have taken this villa for two years – for my lifetime, I feel.
But dear friends, my friends whom I think of with – how much – love – forgive me for just now.
Je suis tellement fatiguée.
Katherine.

MS BL. *Adam* 300, 105.

To J. M. Murry, [17 November 1920]

[Villa Isola Bella, Garavan, Menton]
Thank you for the flower. Yes, it *did* touch me.

No, darling, If I let this other letter go I shall repent it. For it is not all. Its true I am hurt as Ive never been. Perhaps it is your carelessness. But then carelessness in love is so dreadful. And yet what else can it be? Even after getting my present which I tried to make perfect for you in a case which I chose awfully carefully and you never even *gave one word to*. You didn't mention this other photograph. And to talk about too much fragility and so on – I hang my head. I feel timid and faint. I am not an ox. I *am* weak: I feel my hold on life is fainting-weak. But that is ME, the real real me. I cant help it. Didn't you know? And then when you toss off my letter about "passports, kisses, OBE" – oh, I am so *ashamed*. What anguish to have written as I did about kisses. Was that what I wrote about? Let me creep away and fold my wings. They quiver – you hurt me.

I must tell you; no one else will. I am not like other women. I am not this great girl. Whether you did tell Sadler it was precious or not I don't know. I scarcely hear you saying that to him.

But I must tell you something else. I have been ill for nearly four years – and Im changed changed – not the same. You gave twice to your work (which I couldn't see) what you gave my story. I dont want dismissing as a masterpiece. Who is going to mention "the first snow"?[1] I haven't anything like as long to live as you have. Ive *scarcely any time I feel*. Arthur will draw posters 100 years. Praise him when Im dead. Talk to ME. Im lonely. I havent ONE single soul . . .

MS ATL. *LJMM*, 596–7.

---

[1] Murry points out (*LJMM*, 597) that this is a reference to a sentence in her story 'The Stranger', which she had sent him on 3 Nov.: 'But her words, so light, so soft, so chill, seemed to hover in the air, to rain into his breast like snow.'

To J. M. Murry, [18 November 1920]

[Villa Isola Bella, Garavan, Menton]
Dear Bogey,

For this one occasion I have the use of the Corona. It's an opportunity to write you a legible business letter. Will you regard it as such, as just the letter of one writer to another? That's to say – don't, I beg, think it is just my little joke. I am in dead earnest.

I have your letter saying you gave that picture to the press. Now I must ask you to see that it is destroyed at once. And in future please do not act on my behalf without sending me a wire. Nothing is so urgent it cannot wait twenty-four hours. No earthly publicity is worth such a price. I am more or less helpless over here, as you know. But that has got to be changed. I beg you not to publish one single solitary thing that I may have left in England.

And I want to put my work and publicity into the hands of an agent with whom I shall communicate direct. Is Pinker[1] the best man? I shall be doing a great deal of work from now on, and I want to free myself from journalism, which I hate, at the first possible moment. At the same time I must have money. If you do not understand my feelings about that photograph – could you do this? Could you ACT as if you did?

And why on earth did you not go direct to Constable at once. Why write to Sadler's wife?[2] That's not business, surely. I am so bitterly ashamed of this affair that I'd pay for bookmarkers with my new photograph.

You do not understand. I cannot make you. But at least you did know – tho' you may have forgotten – that I hated this thing. And you did possess other photographs of mine that you knew I did not mind.

I can't write to you personally, tonight. The other face gets in the way! Is that the person you've been writing to for the last four years?

I am terribly sorry about it all. But please for my sake – I'll even stoop and mention my health – put me out of my anxiety and let me feel that you will always send me a wire – at my expense – before you act for me. Dont misunderstand your.

Wig.

Until I do get an agent – you will act for me? Im sending another story[3] tonight. And Id be immensely grateful if you'd suggest what I ought to do with it.

Wig.

TS/MS ATL. *LJMM*, 597–8.

1 James Pinker represented the literary interests of Henry James and Joseph Conrad, among others.

2 In an attempt to clear up his inadvertent mistake in sending the wrong photograph for Constable's publicity, Murry had written to Michael Sadler's wife, Edith.

3 This was 'Poison'. See letter on p. 119.

To Constable & Co Ltd, [19 *November 1920*]

[Menton]
COULD YOU ARRANGE FOR NEW PHOTOGRAPH ALREADY SENT BY ME TO APPEAR ON WRAPPER OF BLISS BLOCK WILL BE SUPPLIED BY MURRY.

KATHERINE MANSFIELD

Telegram Targ.

To Constable & Co. Ltd., [c.21 November 1920]

Villa Isola Bella | Garavan | Menton |
A/M

Dear Madam,

I am greatly obliged to you for your letter. I am sorry it has not been found possible, even by the substitution of other blocks, to stop that horrible photograph. But it is a relief to know you will see it is not used for publicity purposes on any further occasion. Instead of advertising Bliss it looked to *me* as though it ought to describe How I Gained 28 lbs. in One Month. However –

Would you kindly see that all further communications respecting my book are addressed to me personally at the above my permanent address.

Letters do not take more than 2½ days & if the matter is urgent I will avail myself of the electric telegraph.

Yours very faithfully

Katherine Mansfield

MS Targ.

To J. M. Murry, [21 November 1920]

[Villa Isola Bella, Garavan, Menton]

Dearest Bogey

Thank you very much for all my little drawings. The nicest you ever made was the hobgoblin with the fork dashing off to eat that sole. "Be sprightly – thou'rt among friends" he seemed to be saying.

I am very glad you liked Miss Brill.[1] I liked her, too. One writes (*one* reason why is) because one does care so passionately that one *must* show it – one must declare ones love. But oh – there are so many stories to write and they are all so different.

The paper came this morning & 2 Newses & the Literary Supplement. The *News* is sordid; theres no other word for it – and such sordid news. Dreadful people behaving in such an odious way. One feels – not frightened but that never never will one return to such a city.

The paper . . . wasn't a very good number was it? In fact I think you must have driven your cold into it & there it *rages*. Poor Athenaeum! Let me be frank. The tone isn't quite certain, either. "A trumpet to the soul of the nation".[2] That doesn't ring: its common property: it has been blown by so many writers that its gone dull. Perhaps Im out of sympathy. I suppose those leading pars must be topical – now Im referring to the later ones. Beresfords story was just so bad that I could hardly credit it![3]

I had been waiting for the review of the Grenfell brothers. This book must have been an *astonishing* document; but no one has discovered it. The quotations in the A. are enough to make one glimpse what a feast was there. But C. *F!*[4] Ye – Gods – in the name of Psychology what balderdash is this! I think its far the worst review thats been in the paper. E.B. had Masefield delivered into his hands.[5] Its queer how an author always gives away finally his *secret weakness*. Here is *anatomy of description instead of creative power* – it comes of course from a weakness of creative power. One thinks the effect can be producing [sic] by an *infinite piling on.* But theres a whole fascinating argument dropped there. E.B. evidently wishes to keep in with J.M. (or perhaps thats unkind of me).

The review of Ruskin, too.[6] Fancy talking of Ruskins "marvellous confidence in himself". Fancy being taken in to that extent! If the reverse was ever true of a man it was of R: his efforts are pitifully obvious to overcome this.

Sullivan tries to be a little knowing about Russia but its rather talks to our readers. D.L.M. is always good but Dent is disappointing – isn't he?[7] Poor old Aldous almost waves the flag off the stick![8] He's very exhausted on his book diet. He seems only to turn *from* books *to* books. I hope you wont be offended by my saying all this, Boge. Its just how it struck me. The truth is Im not in a mood for papers & perhaps not sympathetic. I appreciate tremendously your difficulties. Oh what a trial it must be! Do you enjoy it at all?

We shall talk about all this when you come over. Youre not going to tell a soul about your giving up the paper till then – are you?

Moults novel[9] is here. Je tremble dans mes souliers de fourrure. The worst of it is I shall tell the truth. I shant know Moult while I read it. I shan't be able to help myself. I posted you 4 novels today. I don't want any money for them. Keep the money – you can call it *telegraph money.* Its so cold here today – glacial. I wish I could draw you my fire – my golden stag. Or the blue glass bowl of orange blossom.

Your

Tig.

Are you doing any of your own work?

MS ATL. *LJMM,* 598–9.

[1] The story was published in the *Athenaeum,* 26 Nov. 1920.

[2] Murry's opening paragraph in 'Notes and Comments', the *Athenaeum,* 19 Nov., spoke of the publication in *The Times* on Armistice Day of Thomas Hardy's poem 'And There was a Great Calm'. Murry wrote: 'The voice of resignation and pity in his poem should sound like a trumpet to the soul of the nation.'

[3] The short story 'The Hidden Beast' by J. D. Beresford.

[4] John Buchan's *Francis and Riversdale Grenfell: A Memoir,* the life of rather privileged twin brothers, both of whom died in the First World War, was reviewed by Cyril Falls.

[5] Edmund Blunden reviewed John Masefield's long horse-racing poem, *Right Royal.*

[6] An unsigned review by E. Muir of Ruskin *the Prophet and Other Centenary Essays,* edited by J. Howard Whitehouse, and *The Harvest of Ruskin,* by John W. Graham.

7 J. W. N. Sullivan reviewed Bertrand Russell's *The Practice and Theory of Bolshevism*; D. L. Murray wrote on 'The Theatre in America'; and Edward J. Dent discussed 'The Tradition of German Music'.

8 As 'Autolycus', Aldous Huxley contributed his usual page 'Marginalia', covering bestiaries to Francis Bacon's *De Sapientia Veterum*.

9 See p. 120 n. 3.

To J. M. Murry, [23 November 1920]

[Villa Isola Bella, Garavan, Menton]

My darling Bogey

I have so much to say that I don't know what to start with. Yes, I do. First, foremost, most important, nearest is

Je t'aime

'coeur petit'

If only I could make that warm – or make a beam fly out of it into your heart. Your letters make me long to hold you tight and tell you that the golden thread never COULD be broken between us. Oh, don't you know that. The golden thread is always there. Bogey, you must believe that my little drawing of a heart IS a sign a symbol. You know whom it comes from, don't you, darling? You are my Boge my 'Veen' (who ever he is: he's *very* important). You are also Basil-love and Jag-Boge. If you were here you would believe me. When you come – you will! You *are* coming at Xmas? I am preparing for you every single day. 'I should like it done before Xmas' is my one date when I give orders.

Darling, your letter enclosing the cover of Bliss came today.[1] Thats alright. Thank you for sending it to me. You must [not] be my dog any more tho'. Pinker must. He sounds a perfectly *horrid* dog, doesn't he: one that runs sideways – do you know the kind?

I want to tell you I have had a chill. Its over now or rather its turned the corner. Never was serious. But it took it out of me & I have been a farthing candle for light & warmth. I wouldn't bother to mention it except that I feel my novel review suffered so dreadfully in consequence. It took me 11 hours!! and the result was only that!! Is it too bad to print. I simply could not squeeze a review out of my head. But Ill make up for it this week & try & send you two bonzers.

About the punctuation in The Stranger. Thank you, Bogey. No, my dash isn't quite a feminine dash (certainly when I was young it was). But it was intentional in that story. I was trying to do away with the three dots. They have been so abused by female & male writers that I fight shy of them – *much* tho' I need them. The truth is – punctuation is infernally difficult. If I had time Id like to write an open letter to the A. on the subject. Its boundaries need to be enlarged. But I wont go into it now. Ill try however to remember *commas*. Its a fascinating subject, ça, one that Id like to talk over with you. If only there was time to write all one wants to write. There seems less & less time. And more & more books arrive. Thats not a complaint. But it *is* rather cursed that we should have to worry about Louis Golding[2] when we might be writing our own books – isn't it?

Oh darling, Heres a Perfectly Dreadful Discovery of mine. Poor little Moult's book is the continuation of Opal Whiteley's Diary.[3] He is in fact (this is for your ear alone) Opal Whiteley. Even the cat is called William Shakespeare & there are bits about roses in her cheeks & babies coming & horses having some tired feelings. In fact if I didn't know poor Tom I should have said so in print.

And about Poison. I could write about that for pages. But Ill try & condense what Ive got to say. The story is told by (evidently) a worldly, rather cynical (not wholly cynical) man *against* himself (but not altogether) when he was so absurdly young. You know how young by his idea of what woman is. She has been up till now only the *vision*, only she who passes. You realise that? And here he has put *all* his passion into this Beatrice. Its *promiscuous love* not understood as such by him, perfectly understood as such by her. But you realise the vie de luxe they are living – the very table, sweets, liqueurs, lilies, pearls. And you realise? she expects a letter from someone calling her away? *Fully* expects it? which accounts for her farewell & her declaration. And when it doesn't come even her *commonness* peeps out – the newspaper touch of such a woman. She can't disguise her chagrin. She gives herself away . . . He of course laughs at it now, & laughs at her. Take what he says about her 'sense of order' & the crocodile. But he also regrets the self who dead privately would have been young enough to have actually wanted to *Mary* such a woman. But I meant it to be light – tossed off, & yet through it – oh – subly – the lament for youthful belief. These are the rapid confessions one receives sometimes from a glove or a cigarette or a hat. I suppose I haven't brought it off in 'Poison'.[4] It wanted a light, light hand – and then with that newspaper a sudden . . . let me see *lowering* of it all – just what happens in promiscuous love after passion. A glimpse of staleness. And the story is told by the man who gives himself away & hides his traces at the same moment.

I realise its quite a different kind to Miss Brill or the Young Girl (she's not 'little', Bogey; in fact I saw her big, slender, like a colt). Will you tell me if you see my point at all? Or do you still feel its no go?

Here is an inside and an outside photograph of me in and out of my Isola Bella. Would you like some more? I have more here if you'd like them. And shall I tell you the conversation which just went on between Marie & the carpet woman? Oh, no, its not interesting really without the voices. Even old Marie *attend Monsieur* now. J'ai l'idee Madame d'acheter une belle tranche de veau – *alors* de faire une poch-e dedans et de la farcir avec un peu de jambon, *un* oeuf, and so on & on and on – the song becoming more & more triumphant & ending *mais* peut-être il faudrait mieux que nous attendions l'arrivée de Monsieur pour *ça*. En effet un bon plat de nouilles est toujours un bon plat & then she puts her head on one side & says Monsieur aime le veau?

Pleased to tell you mice have made a nest in my old letters to Ida. Would that I could always be certain of such behaviour. The mice in this house are upstarts.

Goodbye for now darling

I am your

                                                                                    Tig.

MS ATL. *LKM* II. 81–2, 84–5; *LJMM*, 603–5.

[1] *Bliss and Other Stories* was published on 2 Dec.
[2] Louis Golding (1895–1958), prolific romantic novelist, whose most recent work was *Forward to Babylon* (1920). KM did not review anything by him.
[3] KM stopped reviewing for the *Athenaeum* from 10 Dec., and so was spared having to discuss her friend Thomas Moult's new novel *Snow Over Eden, A Story of Today*. She is noting the similarity in style between her friend's novel and the recently published *The Diary of Opal Whiteley*, which claimed to be assembled from the torn-up fragments of a young American girl's diary. Written in a naïve and 'cute' style, it was mainly a record of thoughts on nature and animals.
[4] The story KM sent to Murry on 18 Nov., which he chose not to run in the *Athenaeum*. The narrator is a 24-year-old Englishman living with his older mistress in the south of France, while she waits for a letter from a new admirer. The young man is devoted to her, admires her 'exquisite sense of order', and when she asks for an orange juice, 'I would gladly, willingly, have dived for an orange into the jaws of a crocodile – if a crocodile ate oranges.' When no letter arrives, but only a newspaper, the woman discourses on the theme of poison and the way all lovers eventually administer or receive it.

To J. M. Murry, [24 November 1920]

[Villa Isola Bella, Garavan, Menton]
Heres a photograph of the girl you are NOT in love with – sitting on the steps of her vegetable garden. It is one of her hiding places.

Answering your Sunday letter.
Dearest Bogey,

I do wish youd send me your article Art & Morality[1] as soon as you can. Id immensely like to see it. All my ideas on this subject are VERY lively just now but I simply haven't the time to write them. They will have to *filter through*. But all I know I have learnt by studying divine Shakespeare. I feel that only NOW do I begin to understand how mighty he is – but one feels that once every six months at least . . . "Chief nour-isher at Life's feast'.[2]

However let me commend to your notice perhaps the most perfect written phrase in all literature: "*Reverence – that angel of the world*"[3] I am going to ask it to go before my new book. It says all I would say. Merciful Powers! What a man is this!

Will you send me too, my copy of Cinnamon and Angelica?[4] I am very anxious to re-read it. Im a little bit sorry you are writing on Art and Morality just now, because "a clear logical statement" is nothing like enough! The breath of life is in the subject – and it must blow easy, easy, filling the sail. Perhaps thats only an uneasy fear on my part of which I ought to be ashamed.

But *do* send me the article. The subject is of FIRST importance. Its still cold – ice cold here. Snow on the mountains. The thermome-ter dropped 10 degrees in 24 hours. I fear for the anemones – they are just about 5 inches high – très frisé – lovely – and the ranoncules are smaller still. They want sun. I tried to comfort them yesterday but they only referred me to my own nose! Which *was* in very truth all but bit-ten off.

I am making my *Isola Bella* very nice. It is shabby beyond words inside with old faded papers & ceilings that are sickled o'er with pale casts[5] of dear knows what. But who cares? The windows of the salon have dear little cotton corduroy velveteen trousers to keep them warm at 10.50 the mètre.

Youll see at Christmas.

Your loving

Wig.

MS ATL. *LJMM*, 599–600.

[1] Murry must have mentioned that he was working on such an essay, but nothing with that title appeared.

[2] 'Sleep . . . | Balm of hurt minds, great nature's second cause, | Chief nourisher in life's feast': *Macbeth*, II. ii. 34–7.

[3] '. . . yet reverence | (That angel of the world) doth make distinction | of place 'tween high and low: *Cymbeline*, IV. iv. 248–50. Thomas Moult, in 'Katherine Mansfield as I Knew Her', *TP's Weekly*, 1 Dec. 1928, quoted from an otherwise undated vanished letter from KM to himself: 'Reading Shakespeare today I found this perfect phrase "Reverence, that angel of the world." When one thinks of it – it fills the sky.'

[4] Murry's verse drama, published earlier in 1920.

[5] 'Thus the native hue of resolution | Is sicklied o'er with the pale cast of thought': *Hamlet*, III. i. 85–6.

To J. M. Murry, [c.25 November 1920]

[Villa Isola Bella, Garavan, Menton]

Dear Bogey,

NO { You know that blue-green curtain that used to be on the sofa in the studio – an indian thing – a djellim I think. You know the one I mean? Its on the top shelf of the linen cupboard. Could you SEND it here to me if its worth it? I have a dark red velvet sofa which is too dreadfully gory. I cannot afford to buy a cover for it here and I don't want a loose cover made for thats just waste.

YES { If you think it would be better to send a new one (to "go with" old gold curtains) would you call at Libertys,[1] buy one give them this address & Ill send you X a cheque by return.

♡

S

D[2]

Yes, thats all the best. I don't want that dirty old one again, & they can post it and pack it & send it for tea.[3] But the colours must be not extreme you know, not the old djinnies, not violent – just what you would put with OLD GOLD. And if this is too much trouble – well – just dont do it for

Wig.

Heres a card for them – and Ill enclose the cheque for you to make out. DO be careful of the cheque, Boge, wont you. No, Im frightened to enclose a blank cheque. Ill send it filled as soon as I hear.

MS ATL. *LJMM*, 607.

---

[1] The large store in Regent Street.
[2] KM is indicating one of her favourite phrases, 'Cross my heart straight dinkum'.
[3] KM's adaptation of the infant's ditty, first recorded in 1698:
        Pat-a-cake, pat-a-cake, baker's man,
        Bake me a cake as fast as you can;
        Pat it and prick it and mark it with B . . .

To J. M. Murry, [27 November 1920]

[Menton]

BELIEVE THIS TELEGRAM ALL MY LOVE.

TIG.

Telegram ATL.

To J. M. Murry, [27 November 1920]

[Menton]

YOUR WIRE CAME JUST AFTER SENT MINE ALL WELL DEAREST LOVE WRITTEN
TIG.

Telegram ATL.

To J. M. Murry, [27 November 1920]

[Villa Isola Bella, Garavan, Menton]

Dearest Bogey

Dont lets speak of it again.[1] These things are simply part of life. Why? Ones question whispers out & out into the darkness: there *is* no answer. And you have got a terrific case against me which is: I am OVER sensitive – *impossible* – Life being what it is. Also it is not within the bounds of possibility that we should be in quite the same worlds. I have hiding places – so have you. They are very different ones. We do though emerge from them strange to each other & its only when the strangeness wears off that we are together. This must ever be so. We share *something* – not *all*, I think, by recognising that fully we shall cease hurting each other ever. What we share we prize enough to wish to share it: the rest is our own. And forgive me if I hurt you – *ever*. Oh, I can't *bear* to hurt people! Least of all my dear Bogey.

Ill write to Pinker. I have a long story here[2] – very long which I want to get published serially. Its supremely suitable for such a purpose. And it would bring me in money. Its form is the form of The Prelude BUT written today – not then. The Prelude is a child's story. But I shall not sell it unless I am offered a good deal of money. Yes, please send The Stranger to the Mercury as soon as possible – will you?

I didn't think for one infinitesimal moment that you deliberately gave that photograph to anybody. How *could* I think such a vile thing? I thought you didn't think at all . . .

Just a breath of something else. Anthony Asquith[3] has sent me a letter which makes me feel that there are young people for whom one writes! He must be a darling boy. I wrote to him explaining how youd sent his letter to me *privately* & he says of course he couldn't be angry! Oh but its such a real *boy's* letter – my kind of boy, at any rate. And those quick words which are scratched out – how they express the lovely impatience of youth which knows what it wants to say & chafes at the rein! If you see him please give him my love. All is well, darling?

Wig.

MS ATL. *LJMM*, 600–1.

[1] The problem over the photograph he sent to Constable.

[2] KM was working on 'The Daughters of the Late Colonel' under the tentative title of 'Non-Compounders', the term used at Queen's College, London, for students who attended only some of the college's courses or for girls who did not board but lived at home. Ida Baker, on whom Constantia is based, had been a 'non-compounder' when they were fellow pupils between 1903 and 1906. The story bears some resemblance to Ida's family circumstances at the time, when she and her sister May lived with their dominating father, a medical practitioner who had served in Burma.

[3] Anthony Asquith (1902–68), then a student at Balliol College, Oxford, was the son of Margot and Henry Asquith and the brother of Elizabeth, Princess Bibesco (see p. 127, n. 1). He later became an eminent film director.

To J. M. Murry, [28 November 1920]

[Villa Isola Bella, Garavan, Menton]

Dearest Bogey

Your new book[1] arrived today. Let me congratulate you on its appearance, darling. I wish it – Ah you know! I wish it Every Success. I greatly look forward to reading it carefully before you come & discussing it with you. Collins has certainly done you proud. It is a pleasant & entirely dignified volume. I am very fond of a longish shaped book with a narrow page: it is especially suited to criticism, somehow.

Yesterday I had your letter *re* the finances of the A. Really there is nothing to be said. Bonwick[2] has sat on the poor egg to some purpose. I hate the directors for their stupidity and I detest that queer equine-faced nimrod Bonwick. The picture of you was lifelike. Your very legs were under the table. I would have known them among a million pairs. But child! you have a terrible pen for these small drawings. Dear! Dear!

they are so pathetical. When Mother came back from Switzerland 1894 she brought me a tiepin made like a violet & one shut ones eye & looked through it at the Lion of Lucerne!! *Your* tiepins, darling, all are made of a diamond that's really a tear drop. I shut one eye & look through at my own little Lion – & my heart *faints* to see his sweet mane all in knots over his sums.

However, Liony dear, I am very happy to hear of your costume de Hannelle, & I think rich brown gravy shoes would look awfully nice with it. What about a *Daily Mail hat*?[3] They look, in pictures, really top-hole. Orpen[4] I saw in one & thought immediately of you. They are, I imagine the result of leaving a bowler & a felt hat between the hatters sheets. Will you try and get one? They haven't got Daily Mail written on em. Yes, Ill send a Christmas Story before the end of the 2nd week in December. And when you know when you are coming you'll let *me* know, won't you dearest?

Its still freezing cold. Oh, I do feel the cold most cruelly. I *cannot* keep warm. Blankets over my knees, two pairs of everything that one has two of, a fire, soup – nothing saves me. I frissonne and fade & curl up. And as soon as the sun so shakes his fiery head I feel better. Bogey, when I leave here it will be to go further South.

My good Marie is ill with rheumatisme dans les reins & a fierce cold. Jinnie is laid low; Connie too. As to L.M. we have just had a fearful fight on the subject of MEN and I think she must be frozen. She always talks of "a man is a man", "thats a man all over", "clearing up after men". This is so extremely offensive to me – so *repellent* that I could bear it no longer. Why are people so coarse. Its unthinkable. I mean – & I always expect mean by coarse – why do they *so offend against human dignity*? Also, I expect its nature speaks in her tho', too. Its not all her fault. Nature is starved & shes provided no kind of substitute for what would have been for her the real thing.

I confess since Ive been away this time my need or my wish for my people has absolutely fled. I don't know what it is to be *lonely* and I love to be *solitary*.

Bogey, if my book is to be reviewed in the paper who is to do it? May I have a say? Of course you cant and I dont want V.W.[5] to, because I don't like her work at all at all. It wasn't for nothing that she got so excited by a mark on the wall,[6] my Jo! that was a revelation. Id prefer to have it done by someone who'll – oh, I don't know – *Santayana* I prefer. Now Im not being serious. I mean of course darling thats only my wicked preference. But his idea of friendship[7] & mine is alike – that is beaucoup – isn't it.

Your very cold but loving
Wig.

Did you read in the Times that Shelley left on his table a bit of paper with a blot on it & a flung down quill. Mary S. *had a glass case* put over same & carried it all the way to London *on her knees.*[8] Did you ever *hear* such rubbish!! Thats her final give away for me. Did she keep it on her knees while she ate her sangwiches. Did everybody know. Oh − *didn't* they just. Ive done with her.

I was fearfully shocked by D.L.M.'s stupidity about Juliet.[9] That *was* a blow. He has never had the faintest idea about the whole play, evidently. What a *foolish* article. But it was worse than that. It was very ignorant and stupid.

MS ATL. *LKM* II. 83; *LJMM*, 605−7.

[1] *Aspects of Literature*, a selection of Murry's essays and reviews from the *Times Literary Supplement*, the *Athenaeum*, and the *Nation*, was published by Collins.

[2] Business manager for Arthur Rowntree, proprietor of the *Athenaeum*.

[3] The 'Salisbury', a type of felt hat whose design had won a competition run by the *Daily Mail*.

[4] William Orpen (1878−1931), an Irish painter of historical set pieces and fashionable portraits.

[5] A considerable change of heart, for Virginia Woolf recorded in her diary, 4 Aug. 1920, her visiting KM a week before, 'when she asked me to review her book. I cried off on the ground that to review spoils the reading' (*Diary of Virginia Woolf*, II. 55).

[6] Woolf's short story 'The Mark on the Wall' was in *Two Stories*, published by the Hogarth Press in 1917, when KM wrote telling Woolf she had reread the story 'and liked it tre-*men*dously' (*CLKM* II. 170).

[7] George Santayana (1863−1952) was born in Spain, and was professor of philosophy at Harvard 1889−1912. He and Murry met at Garsington, and he wrote six 'Soliloquys on England' for the *Athenaeum*. The fifth of these, 'Cross Lights', published 26 Nov. 1920, concluded: 'But when minds being naturally akin and each alone in its own heaven, *soliloquize in harmony*, saying compatible things only because their hearts are similar, then society is friendship in the spirit; and the vision of many thoughts twinkles happily in the night across the void of separation.' He did not review KM's new collection, as she hoped.

[8] A detail in a letter from J. E. Panton in the *Times Literary Supplement*, 19 Nov. 1922.

[9] In reviewing a production of *Romeo and Juliet* at the Everyman Theatre, Hampstead, in the *Athenaeum*, 26 Nov., D. L. Murray emphasized Juliet's childishness, claiming that she 'has not quite definitely outgrown her dolls'.

To J. M. Murry, [29 November 1920]

[Villa Isola Bella, Garavan, Menton]

Darling Bogey

Just a line in reply to your letter all about Elizabeth Asquith[1] & Mary H.[2] I *should* resent the getting there as Im sure you wont get Godber to take you. But I expect you'll enjoy the rest. Mary H. understood food very well & an atmosphere of admiration is never wholly unpleasant at 31 − is it, Monsieur? I dont *quite* believe in your cry against fine ladies. At least I take a big grain of salt out of my salt cellar while youre telling me & *say*: "I think your hair wants parting a little more to the left." Mary H. too, is no end artful with those she wants to please.

I was walking about in the garden last night. It was wonderfully starry. Not a breath stirring. How pleasant it is to walk in and out of ones windows as one does in France – I'd much much rather look at the stars alone than at the bubbles in my glass in *any* company.

But Im very sorry you're so pressé, darling. For *heavens sake* don't bother to tell me all about it!

Yours,

Wig the eremite.

MS ATL. *LJMM*, 609.

---

1 KM was not yet aware of the deepening friendship between Murry and Margaret Elizabeth Bibesco, Margot Asquith's daughter.
2 Mary Hutchinson (1887–1977), a cousin of Lytton Strachey, who had been close to KM for a time in 1915 (see *CLKM* I. 198). An energetic hostess to intellectual gatherings, she had phoned Murry on Friday 26 Nov., inviting him to dine with her and Elizabeth Bibesco on Monday, 29 Nov., at her home in Hammersmith.

Richard Murry, [late November 1920]

[Villa Isola Bella, Garavan, Menton]

Dear Richard

Just two lines to thank you for your letters. I wish it wasn't such a JOB to write to me. Bother it. Why don't you just send me anything. But I want you to know that Im holding thumbs about your new idear. All success to it, my dear old boy. I await the portraits. I bet you'll do them. What an awful pull you have over us aged flowers at being such a little short of spring yourself. You're no older than a jonquil for all your big overcoats & Im a kind of late – late – lets see – Ill say marigold because I love them. Thats unblushing; I didn't mean it to be.

Bretts advice to her grandson amused me. If she does give you eggs to suck they might be fresh eggs. But she means well. Shes pathetic, really. Ill never see her as a painter – only as a reflector.

Well – Ive got a chill which Ill sell for a handkerchief. My temperature is sitting on a top branch & it wont come down. Its work: Ive done a bit too much. Oh, Richard – *dear* Richard cant you cut poor little K. a new pair of lungs out of strong untearable impermeable paper and send them over. If you knew what it was to be getting always knocked over. And Im so full of stories that if I was strong they'd come flying out like doves from a tower.

Did you 'note' my praise of your FIRM just because my little brother-in-law was in it?[1] I expected you to commend me for that.

I must climb up the stairs & under the eiderdown.

Goodnight. This isn't a letter. Its just a note under the door – or a pebble flung at your window. Yes, come to the S. of France one day and we'll tame lizards & paint & write and be happy.

Love for ever from

Katherine

MS R. Murry. *Adam* 370–5, 26.

¹ Richard Murry worked as a book designer for the publisher Richard Cobden-Sanderson. In her review of E. B. C. Jones's *Quiet Interior* in the *Athenaeum*, 19 Nov. 1920, KM asked: 'Why is it that some publishers are compelled to print their books on grey, black-haired paper, to squeeze them between the covers that used to contain "ninepennies" in the old days and to price them at nine shillings, when Mr. Cobden-Sanderson can produce a volume as attractive in appearance as "Quiet Interior" at eight? . . . Miss Jones' novel in a blue linen-faced cover with the title in plain lettering attracts one immediately.'

*To J. C. Squire,*¹ *1 December 1920*

Villa Isola Bella | Garavan | Menton
A/M
December 1st 1920.

Dear Mr Squire,

Murry sent me on your kind letter this morning. I am very happy to know that you think of publishing my story 'The Stranger'.

May I try and explain why I ended with that sentence 'They would never be alone together again'.² Yes, of course, I agree with you that man will forget – almost immediately, really – it certainly won't be true of his future relations with Janey. But in the 'keyed up' state he was in, and remembering how it was natural to him to exaggerate everything – to take the most extreme view of everything, and remembering too, his *childishness* – his childish desire for everything to be alright and really his childish grief that it wasn't – I feel that nothing less than such an unqualified statement would fit. There in its glimpse of falsity, too, you had him . . . It was all up with him, for ever. (Of course, it wasn't!)

I cannot hope to change your opinion. But I'll be awfully sorry if this point prevents you from publishing my story.

If you knew what The London Mercury means to an exile! It is devoured even to the covers – and the last number always seems the best.

Yours sincerely,

Katherine Mansfield.

TC Stanford. Cited Meyers, 215.

[1] John Collings Squire (1884–1958), journalist and poet, was editor of the *New Statesman* from 1913 to 1919, when he established the *London Mercury*.

[2] The last sentence of a story in which a loving but possessive husband, after waiting on a wharf for his wife to return from Europe, is appalled to hear that a stranger, a male passenger, has died in her arms. Although the setting is Auckland, the event on which it was based had occurred to KM's mother in 1909, while her father waited her arrival in Hobart.

To J. M. Murry, 1 December 1920

[Villa Isola Bella, Garavan, Menton]
December 1st

My darling,

Two letters today from you. You are generous not to have resented what I said about *Art & Morality*. Its a queer thing. You always manage to surprise me whatever I think (and you know how highly I do esteem) of your powers as a critic. I don't agree with all of your book, rather I feel you yourself would *enlarge* and *expand* much now. But your book is ASTONISHING as a whole. Theres a note in it, not always loud, but clear and challenging and absolutely new, my boy. It rings through the forest of literature, my child – it is so finely purposeful. What do I mean by that? I mean you are not thinking for thinking's sake, or reading for reading's sake. One has the feeling that you are out to discover, to explore literature in the name of Life. I am only saying general things now – for Ive only read through your book – but trust me, Bogey. Trust my 'flair' (if you like). I still think your Sorleys[1] a mistake, for example. You've made him up. But your Hardy – your remarks on Coleridge & above all – much above all – your first essay[2] BRAVO. It is very very thrilling when the one you believe in – calmly goes one better. So, just to go on with, accept my admiration, please. (Here a salute of guns is heard.)

I have written to Squire. His letter tho' was a boule-versement. He'd never even begun to see what I was getting at. Of course I cant change the sentence. I *want* the L.M. to publish my serial in the spring. I am so glad you feel like that about Anne. Them's my sentiments exactly. And nothing really suits my feelings except to hug her.

I had a letter from Schiff today, telling me Miss Brill[3] was *quite* good, quite *nice* & full of *feeling* and happy phrase. But didn't I think that it was a mistake to rate the Russians above de Maupassant? And that Proust is not only the greatest living writer but perhaps (I like the perhaps) the greatest novelist that ever has been!!!!! And what a dastardly shame to have dismissed Ludovici's novel[4] (one of the "*freshest*" voices of our day) in a short notice. And – but that's enough. And to spare. If he comes to Roquebrune Ill never be able to see them. I will reply I would give every single word de Maupassant and Tumpany ever wrote for one short story by Anton Tchekhov. As to Proust with his Morceaux de Salon (who cares if the salon is 'literary') let him tinkle away. He must be beaten simply. In very truth Bogey, Koteliansky's saying: 'this man must be beaten plainly' is *profound*.

Oh, by the way, Sullivan's a silly about Santayana – and his 'scornful stare'.[5] Rubbish! Thats romancing. Its far too obvious & its not even true. Sullivan isn't finely subtle enough for Santayana – scientific carefulness won't do. You can't dissect him with an instrument; hes not the kind. And I do wish S. would eat his dinner for once without a bottle of G.K.C. on the table.[6] Even if he doesn't dash his viands with it he always points to the bottle . . . Let me be as bad as I can. Es gibt etwas inferior in Sullivan. His shoes will always carry a trace of *Fleet Street* & he's too proud of the trace to have 'em cleaned.

Oh dear what a bother!

I am fainting with hunger. Its choux farcie for dinner with puree of pommes de terre, salade de rave & roquefort cheese & fresh oranges. Un jour demi-maigre, as Marie says.

My last preparation for you is a yellow tin of Berlingots de Carpentras. Well, my dear darling. Try & be a good boy – and don't forget to now and then think of

Tig.

MS ATL. *LJMM*, 608–9.

[1] Murry's essay 'The Lost Legions', on Charles Sorley's letters, reprinted in *Aspects of Literature*.

[2] 'The Poetry of Thomas Hardy', 'Coleridge's Criticism', 'The Function of Criticism.' All the essays in the volume were reprinted from articles in periodicals.

[3] Which had appeared in the *Athenaeum*, 26 Nov.

[4] In the same issue, under 'Novels in Brief', an unsigned notice by Camilla Jebb of Anthony M. Ludovici's *Too Old for Dolls* reproved the novel's 'repellent subject – the jealousy of an elder sister for her more attractive junior'.

[5] Under 'The Wisdom of Mr Santayana', J. W. N. Sullivan had reviewed George Santayana's *Character and Opinion in the United States*, judging him 'not the cleverest or most learned, but the wisest philosopher of our time'. He found also: 'His irony is not accompanied with a smile and a shrug, but rather with a scornful stare.'

To Sydney Schiff 1 December 1920

Isola Bella | Caravan-Menton
A/M
1.XII.1920

My dear Sydney,

I must answer your letter at once – though Id a thousand times rather talk and talk it over with you and with Violet.

First – about Violet. I think you are very wise not to attempt a journey while she has a temperature. This climate, as you know better than do I, is the very devil for a temperature. It is divine, but its changeable. L'autre jour the thermometer in my room dropped 10 degrees in 24 hours. Il faut avoir de la force to combat that. But it *is* an adorable climate when its radiant. Yesterday and today have been supremely beautiful. I think, like one of those mythological ladies Im really married to the sun . . .

Im sorry aout Ludovici's book: it didn't come my way. Im *tired* of extinguishing Benson,[1] especially as he shines as bright as ever the moment after. Plague take these books. If it wasnt a question of money – what wouldn't I give to leave them alone & only do my own work. Its an awful wrench to turn from ones work & take up Stacpoole or Pett Ridge[2] (what names the fellows have, too!) However – Squire has taken my last long story for the Mercury. I don't know when it will appear. Its a study of a man and a woman. People won't like it.

About the Russians. I agree that translations are perfectly terrible. The peculiar *flatness* of them is so strange and its just that flatness which the story or whatever it is mustnt have. One feels its superimposed. And yet – and yet – though I hate to agree with so many silly voices I confess that Tchekhov does seem to me a marvellous writer. I do think a story like '*In Exile*' or '*Misery*'[3] is frankly incomparable. (Its years since I read De Maupassant! I must read him again.) And then Tolstoi – well, you know, Anna's journey in the train when she finds Vronsky is travelling to St. Petersburg too[4] – and the whole figure of Anna – – when I think how real, how vital, how vivid she is to me, I feel I cant be grateful enough to Tolstoi. By grateful I mean full of praise to him for his works.

Will you lend me Marcel Proust when you come out this time? I don't feel qualified to speak of him.

I wonder what you'll think of this little Isola Bella. Its very small. The windows have got little cotton velveteen trousers put up by me in place

---

6 KM is saying that Sullivan is too influenced by G. K. Chesterton (1874–1936), poet, novelist, and critic, but is also playing with the trade name of O.K. sauce.

of the dreadful little chemises that hung there on my arrival. And I have an old servant, a butter and sugar thief, who is an *artist* in her way – a *joy*. Her feeling for hot plates & for what dear Henry James[5] might call the *real right* gravy is supreme. These things are so important. I don't think I could love a person who liked gravylene or browno or whatever they call it.

Heaven bless you both!

Katherine.

MS BL. *LKM* II. 82.

---

[1] KM had written two dismissive reviews of E. F. Benson's novels in the *Athenaeum*, one of *Queen Lucia* on 20 Aug. 1920, another on *The Countess of Lowndes Square and Other Stories*, on 26 Nov. 1920.

[2] In 26 Nov. she had bitingly dismissed *Just Open*, by W. Pett Ridge, and *A Man of the Islands*, by H. de Vere Stacpoole.

[3] Both stories were in Constance Garnett's translation of *The Schoolmistress and Other Stories*, published the previous Nov.

[4] *Anna Karenina*, pt. 1, ch. 20.

[5] Her true opinion of Henry James was quite different, repelled as she was by his 'arrogant, monstrous pomposity – even from early youth' (*CLKM* III. 284).

To J. M. Murry, [3 December 1920]

[Villa Isola Bella, Garavan, Menton]

My darling Bogey

I am so very sorry you've had all that extry hard labour. And I hope your boats out of the storm now, at any rate & that it will sail in smoother waters until youve had a holiday. I 'note' youll get here about the 22nd; youre very sensible to travel 1st class. Its madness to risk 2nd class anything, anywhere for the next 50 years at least. Ill go all through the paper today with a pencil & give you *my* views. Also your Art & Morality is come. Ill read that, today too. I sent off my reviews last night. Tomorrow Im going to *wade* into my story. Oh dear – curse this question of time! Its terrible here. I want to work all day. I shall never have the whole afternoon to spend looking at things or talking darling if you do come in Avrilo. Im simply *rushing* to catch up & shall be for evermore – what ever evermore may mean . . .

You see I was right about the dinner, after all. It was very wise of the Princess B. to give you a lift home.[1] I hope you do meet Anthony; I heard from him again today. Hes a very nice little friend to have out of the blue. Dont be suspicious about women. Are you really? Or is that *your way*. You're very attractive to women, as you know, but as long as they don't interfere – surely you like knowing them. And you always can escape, darling, for though you are so tender hearted you're ruthless too. I mean if it was a question of a woman or your work – there wouldn't *be* a question would there? Otherwise I think you ought to enjoy them. There is even a strong dash of the lady killer in you! And think of the way you look at yourself in a glass if a glass is in the room. You return & return to it; its like a woman to you. I have often noticed that. Don't forget you're only 31, Boge, and get all you can out of Life! You see Bogey, your position is difficult. Im a writer first & a woman after. .'. I can't give you *all* you want – above all a kind of easy relaxation which is essential to you – and which the glass (I don't mean that in the least scornfully) provides. A man with your kind of mind cant go on being strenuous and exerting himself the *whole* time – for your mental activity is, as it were, separate from your life. Mine is all one – so its no effort to me. The story isn't always at a crisis, don't you know, but it is all part of the story. This is an essential difference. I was blind not to have understood it in the Brett affair – but no – that *was* "wrong", as we say. However – *do feel free.* I mean that.

Its a lovely day – but by the time you come all the leaves will be gone. The last are falling. I don't know about mes roses; at present the whole garden is roses – where its not violets. The different smells of different roses – Ive only this year realised. There are 6 in my garden. I go from one to the other until I feel like a bee.

Well, darling I must go out & sit in my tent with the A. & a pencil.
Take care of yourself.

Tig.

MS ATL. LJMM, 610–11.

[1] After the dinner at Mary Hutchinson's on 29 Nov, Murry's letter of 10 Dec. expands on the episode (Murry, 317–20).

To J. M. Murry, [4 December 1920]

[Villa Isola Bella, Garavan, Menton]

Darling Bogey,

I hasten to return this story which I haven't read & wouldn't read for £5.[1] Oh no! no! no! Im sorry, Sir, but Im MUCH too busy – and Im not a bit – not a morsel interested. That is the harsh truth. And please, darling dont tell me about Madame la Princesse. Forgive me for saying this. But – – the love story in the motor and so on – – – oh, *dont* tell me! For I can't just listen & keep quiet & if I do reply I shall only offend you. So, I am sitting here with about 5 bearing reins . . . & one bulls eye to keep quiet.

Thank you most awfully for all you say about Poison.[2] I agree. If DeLaMare would do my book – I'd rather him than anyone.[3]

Otherwise if you'll do it unsigned, love. If not – E.M. Forster. I mean *yes*, E.M.F.

And Id love a striped silk piece for my sofa – any colour you like.

Oh Bogey I caught your glimpse of Clovelly so plainly.[4] I often turn & turn those days over – hold them up to the light – almost wear them again.

What I thought I drew was a dove with a laurel wreath, Sir Peckham.[5] You arent much of a finder out. The little picture of your in the D.M. hat is simply ravishing. Have you a revolver in one hand too? *Boge* – off to see his Fine Ladyes – is my name for it & it makes me laugh.

Its a pure silver day. I have a blue & white glass of tiny blue hyacinths on my table. The day & the flowers say – Greece, to me & if I were a poet they would have a poem. Its cold, though. I must knock off now. Tomorrow Ill write *re* Art & Morality & Paper.

Yours for ever

Tig.

MS ATL. *LJMM*, 611.

[1] Murry's letter, like most of his communications at this time, does not survive. But soon after the dinner at Mary Hutchinson's, Elizabeth Bibesco had given Murry a short story which he thought clever and tentatively accepted for publication. It was this which he now sent on to KM. She was not to know that the beginning of the story, 'An Ordinary Man', with passion first revealed in a taxi, bore a striking similarity to the details Murry later told her (see Murry, 318–19) of his lift home with Elizabeth the Monday before. But there were other details which must have struck her. In a fairly obvious reversal of roles, the man in the story became ill, and corresponded with a devoted woman – 'twice every day he wrote to her from his chaise-lounge, and twice every day she wrote to him in order that no post should be a disappointment. She never could resist illness.' Murry ran the story in the *Athenaeum*, 14 Jan. 1921.

[2] Murry did not care for the story, and it was not published until after her death.

[3] Walter de la Mare reviewed *Bliss* in the *Athenaeum*, 21 Jan. 1921.

[4] KM was living in 69 Clovelly Mansions, Gray's Inn Road, when she met Murry at the end of 1912. He moved in with her in Apr. 1913.

[5] Presumably a reference to her tiny drawing of a bird on the capital D of 'Duck trousers' in her letter to Murry, 12 Nov.

To J. M. Murry, [5 December 1920]

[Villa Isola Bella, Garavan, Menton]

Business
D. Bogey
re The Athenaeum.

I think the list suggested by you cannot be improved on. Its a pity the *exhibitions of the week* has to go because its awfully readable at present. I don't know how sound Drey is but he certainly seems to me to have improved greatly.[1] Pity he cant do something on the paper. I think poetry ought not to be cut down & its hard to get a story shorter than between 2½ & 3 cols.

Novels ought to be 2 only and I think you ought to aim at getting more 1 col reviews – I mean for books generally. Have you got your number for Nov. 19. Turn it up if you have. As regards its make-up its awfully good. The reviews are fairly short & yet the paper has not a scrappy appearance. I think its rather a no. to aim at.

Correspondence ought to be 2 cols only – don't you think? And D.L.M.[2] ought not to be more than 2.

The whole paper needs a stricter form – or could do with one, I feel – a more [stringent][3] form that is scrupulously adhered to. But I realise the difficulty of this with writers like K.M. & Co who never seem to learn the length of a page. Still they ought to be hauled over the coals. A big nasty cut now & again would larn em.

The front pars are . . . not very interesting, are they? They want more diversity. One *par* one subject. If they run on you might as well have a short article. I think the Science article is valuable. Its a pity it cant be more varied. Where's your medical man the man who wrote about the fatigued frog?[4] *Orion*[5] ought to be sent a book or two for 1 col reviews, too.

Marginalia is utterly feeble. It had a moment, a little spurt, a few weeks ago but ever since then it has been dead as a nib. 100 years ago[6] is the dustbin, tho, Boge.

If the paper is shorter it wants to be more *defined, braced up, tighter.* In my reckless way I would suggest all reviews were signed & all were put into the first person. I think that would give the whole paper an amazing lift up. A paper that length must be *definite, personal,* or die. It cant afford the "we", "in our opinion". To sign reviews, to put them in the 1st person stimulates curiosity, *makes for correspondence,* gives it (to be 19-eleventyish) GUTS.[7] You see its a case of leaning out of the window with a board & a nail, *or* a bouquet *or* a flag – administering whichever it is & retiring *sharp.* This seems to me essential. Signed reviews are tonic: the time has gone by for any others. I do wish you could work this. Im sure it would attract the public. And theres rather a "*trop de livres trop de livres*" faint cry in it. I read the first par – of about 4 reviews & I begin to whimper faintly.

YOU'RE alright but the others are not. A letter ought to be drafted to your regular contributors asking them, now that the reviews are to be signed (supposing that were to happen) asking them to pull themselves together & make their *attack* stronger. Do you know what I mean? I feel inclined to say to them, as if I were taking their photographs: "*Look Fearless*". They are huddled up.

I think the shorter paper might be all to the good. But it *must* be swifter too. If all those cobwebs are gone we must show the bare boards. I do wish you were here to talk it over. Writing is the very devil – specially as my pen wont go. Its not out of order its merely wicked – sitting

on its hind legs & scratching its ear. As I write this I burn with enthusiasm for the paper – yes, its as undiminished as ever. And this new form seems to me a great clearing of the ground, & easier for you [to] manage. Only wish I had more to say darling. Is this any good?
Ever your

K.M.

MS ATL. *LJMM*, 612–13.

---

[1] Signed O. R. D., the weekly report on current art exhibitions was written by O. Raymond Drey, husband of KM's close friend Anne Estelle Drey.

[2] D. L. Murry, the drama critic.

[3] Word supplied by Murry.

[4] An unsigned article on 'Fatigue', the *Athenaeum*, 31 Oct. 1919, by Geoffrey Keynes.

[5] William Orton, friend and admirer of KM before she met Murry, whose autobiographical novel *The Last Romantic* (1937) is an important source for KM biography in 1910. (See *CLKM* I. 99–102.) He was an occasional contributor to the *Athenaeum*.

[6] 'Marginalia' was regularly written by Aldous Huxley. 'A Hundred Years Ago' was an unsigned column concerning publications a century earlier.

[7] As part of the determined programme for Modernism that he declared in the first editorial of *Rhythm* in 1911, Murry took a stand for 'guts and bloodiness' (F. A. Lea, *The Life of John Middleton Murry* (1954), 24).

To J. M. Murry, [6 December 1920]

[Villa Isola Bella, Garavan, Menton]

Darling Bogey

Ive just finished a story called *The Ladies Maid*[1] which Im sending for the paper. I do hope you will care to print it. Its what I meant when I said a Xmas story. Dear knows Xmas doesn't come in it after all and you may think Im a fraud. But I think, all the same, people might like to read it at Xmas time. The number of letters Ive had about Miss Brill! I think I am very fortunate to have people like my stories – don't you? But I must say it does surprise me. *This* one I'd like you and de la Mare to like – other people don't matter.

Curtis Browns[2] letter & your reply came today. I am deeply grateful to you. Yes, I feel I may make enough money in America to free myself to make money. Its *hell* to know one could do so much & be bound to journalism for bread. If I was a proper journalist Id give the day to reviewing & so on – but no! Reviewing is on my chest – AND a sense of GUILT the whole week! However it cant be helped. Ill win out and then I dont want to read another novel for ——— But isn't it grim to be reviewing Benson when one might be writing ones own stories which one will never have time to write, on the best showing!

Ive not written to Pinker yet, for the reason that I have not any reserve stock to offer him. I hope after Xmas to have at least 3 stories ready. But it only confuses things to get into touch with him & not have the goods. Hes bound not to have any interest. So Brown had better go ahead with 'The Stranger', & Ill write promising him my 3 stories which will be ready at the end of this month. It was a nice letter. Personally I want to make money by my stories *now*. I cant live poor – cant worry about but- ter and cabs and woolen dresses & the chemists bill and work too. I don't want to *live rich* – God forbid – but I must be free – and ca coute cher aujourdhui. Its most awfully kind of you, darling, to have written to Brown.

Just while Im on the subject I suppose you will think I am an ego- centric to mind the way Constable has advertised my book & the para- graph that is on the paper cover. Id like to say I mind so much so terribly that there are no words for me. No – Im *dumb!!* I think it so insulting & disgusting and undignified that – well – there you are! Its no good suf- fering all over again. But the bit about ''women will learn by heart and not repeat''[1] – Gods! Why didn't they have a photograph of me looking through a garter! But I was helpless here – too late to stop it – so now I *must* prove – no – convince people ce n'est pas moi. At least if I'd known they were going to say that no power on earth would have made me cut a word. I wish I hadn't. I was wrong – very wrong.

The story will go to you Wednesday morning. A typist has been found at 7 francs a 1000. I think she is mad as well. But I can't afford not to send corrected copies.

What a horrible note this is. And there's the evening star – like an emerald hanging over the palm. Forgive me, evening star. Bogey, for- give me. These are only sparks on my coat – they are not my real fur. But the ancien couteau turns faintly in my left lung tonight, & that makes me wicked. Wicked – but loving – loving.

Tig.

MS ATL, *LJMM*, 613–14.

1 'The Lady's Maid' appeared in the *Athenaeum*, 24 Dec. 1920.

2 KM presumably had written to the American A. Curtis Brown (1866–1945), managing direc- tor of Curtis Brown Ltd., an international publishing agency.

3 The jacket blurb for *Bliss and Other Stories* which KM so objected to read: 'Katherine Mansfield is already well known to discriminating critics as the author of *In a German Pension*, published before the war and long since out of print.

'This book of her stories represents her principal work during the last six years. In theme, in mor- dant humour, and in keen realistic outlook, she is the nearest thing to the modern Russian story writers and to de Maupassant that England has produced.

BLISS will create delight, surprise, alarm and possibly anger. The stories have a wry chic, and tell, with a cruel and detached irony, of sorrows and of sudden brutal joys.

BLISS is the "something new," in short stories that men will read and talk about and women learn by heart but not repeat.'

To J. M. Murry, [c.6 December 1920]

I made these notes. Read them, will you?

The Lost Girl

Its important. It ought not to be allowed to pass.

The Times gave no inkling of what it was – never even hinted at its dark secret.[1]

Lawrence denies his humanity. He denies the powers of the Imagination. He denies Life – I mean *human* life. His hero and heroine are non-human. They are animals on the prowl. They do not feel: they scarcely speak. There is not one memorable *word*. They submit to the physical response and for the rest go veiled – blind – *faceless* – *mindless*. This is the doctrine of mindlessness.

He says his heroine is extraordinary, and rails against the ordinary. Isn't that significant? But look at her. Take her youth – her thriving on the horse-play with the doctors. They might be beasts butting each other – no more. Take the scene where the hero throws her in the kitchen, possesses her, and she returns singing to the washing-up. It's a *disgrace*. Take the rotten rubbishy scene of the woman in labour asking the Italian into her bedroom. All false. All a pack of lies![2]

Take the nature-study at the end. It's no more than the grazing -place for Alvina and her sire. What was the 'green hellebore' to her? Of course, there is a great deal of racy, bright, competent writing in the early part – the 'shop' part. But it doesn't take a writer to tell all that.

The whole is false – *ashes*. The preposterous Indian troupe of four young men is – a fake. But how on earth he can keep it up is the problem. No, it's not. He has 'given way'. Why stop then? Oh, don't forget where Alvina feels '*a trill in her bowels*' and discovers herself with child.[3] A TRILL – what does that mean÷ And why is it so peculiarly offensive from a man? Because it is *not on this plane* that the emotions of others are conveyed to our imagination. It's a kind of sinning against art.

Earth closets, too.[4] Do they exist *quâ* earth closets? No. I might describe the queer noises coming from one when old Grandpa X was there – very strange cries and moans – and how the women who were washing stopped and shook their heads and pitied him and even the children didn't laugh. Yes, I can imagine that. But that's not the same as to build an earth-closet because the former one was so exposed. No.

Am I prejudiced? Be careful. I feel privately as though Lawrence had possessed an animal and fallen under a curse. But I can't say that. All I know is, This is bad and ought not to be allowed. I feel a horror of it – a shrinking. But that's not criticism. But here is life where one has blasphemed against the spirit of reverence.

MS lacking. *Scrapbook*, 156–7.

To J. M. Murry, [7 December 1920]

[Villa Isola Bella, Garavan, Menton]

About your Book.

My dear Bogey

I have now read your book and though we can't really discuss it until you come I should feel ungracious were I not to write you quelques mots. Well, Bogey, Im your admirer. Accept my admiration. Its from my very heart & head! There is real achievement in that book. While I read you on Tchekhov, Butler, the first essay, Shakespeare criticism,[1] I liked to pretend you were a stranger. I imagined what Id feel like if this book had fallen out of the sky – and that really gave me your measure. (There's a female standard!) At your best no one can touch you. You simply are first chop. For the first time je me trouve underlining your sentences – putting marks in the margin – as one so *very* seldom does, Boge. You recreate – no less – Tchekhov, for instance. I want to make you feel what a great little fellow I think you are for this book! And how it makes me believe in you – stand by you in my thoughts and respect you. There! Shake hands with me. And of course I want to 'criticise' – to tell you all I feel. But not before you realise how firm and unyielding are the foundations of my praise. Here goes.

Your Hardy[2] doesn't quite come off to my thinking. You seem to be hinting at a special understanding between yourself and the author. That's not fair: it puts me off. You (in the name of your age, true, but not quite not wholly) intrude your age, your experience of suffering. This destroys the balance.

---

[1] D. H. Lawrence's novel *The Lost Girl* was published on 25 Nov. 1920, and reviewed in the *Times Literary Supplement* on 2 Dec., under 'Postscript or Prelude', as a study in social realism. KM did not know that the unsigned review was by Virginia Woolf; Murry, in the *Athenaeum*, 17 Dec., under 'The Decay of Mr D. H. Lawrence', regarded it as 'degraded by a corrupt mysticism'.

[2] The novel follows the passion and eventual marriage between Alvina Houghton, only child of a declining Midlands merchant, and Ciccio Marasca, an Italian member of a shabby troupe of continental entertainers who dress and perform as Red Indians under the name of the Natcha-Kee-Tawaras. In ch. 3 Alvina trains as a midwife, and 'liked the sort of intimacy' the young doctors pressed on her; in ch. 10 Alvina and Ciccio make love in her old home, between her starting the breakfast dishes and finishing them. In ch. 12 the temporarily rejected Ciccio serenades Alvina as she professionally attends a friend who is about to go into labour, but who insists that he is invited in to satisfy her curiosity. The woman declares 'Your friend is a hefty brute', and argues philosophy as the delivery begins (*The Lost Girl*, ed. John Worthen (1981), 37, 232, 283).

[3] Towards the end of the novel, Alvina goes to Ciccio's small village in the Abruzzi where she is both repelled by its bleakness and enchanted by its beauty and vegetation, including 'green belle-bore . . . a fascinating plant'. She realizes on a market-day that she is pregnant when 'she felt a strange thrilling in her bowels: a sort of trill strangely within her, yet extraneous to her. She caught her hand to her flank' (ibid. 332, 320).

[4] Ciccio builds his wife an earth closet, as 'the obvious and unscreened place outside was impossible' (ibid. 323).

Your Keats is performance right enough, but its more promise. Makes me feel you ought to write a book on Keats.[3] Its deeply interesting. The last paragraph is a pity – when you praise Sir Sidney. Here again I seem to catch a faint breath of *pride.*[4]I think Edward Thomas[5] is seen out of proportion. Its not in his poems; he's not *all that.* Your emotions are too apparent. I feel one ought to replace Thomas with another & say it all about *him.* There was the beginning of all that in Thomas but you've filled it out yourself, to suit what you wanted him to be. Its not wholly sincere, either, for that reason. Let me make my meaning clearer. Take your Tchekhov. Now you make Tchekhov 'greater' than one sees him but NOT greater than he was. This is an *important dangerous* distinction. A critic must see a man as great as his potentialities but NOT greater. Falsity creeps in immediately then. You ought to guard against this. Its another 'aspect' of your special pleading danger – as in your essay on Hardy. In your tremendously just desire to prove him a major poet you mustn't make yourself Counsel for the Prisoner! I mean that in all its implications . . .

You might have borne this trick of yours in mind when you are so down on S.T.C. for his idolatry.[6] Remember how Shakespeare *was* regarded at that time – the extraordinary ignorance, stupidity and meanness of the point of view. I don't think you take that into account enough. Its too easy to talk of laudanum & soft brainedness. The reason for his überfluss is more psychological. I don't defend S.T.C. but I think he and you are both wrong in 'considering' far too specially a 'special' audience. On the other hand you are splendidly just to his amazing Venus and Adonis criticism. (I must say that chapter on V. & A. is a gem of the first water.)

Ronsard[7] is interesting because you've conveyed the chap's quality so well tho' I deeply disagree with one of the 'charming' quotations – the complexion one is perfect. Now Ill be franker still. There are still traces of what I call your sham personality in this book & they mar it – the personality that expressed itself in the opening paragraphs of your Santayana review in the Nation.[8] Can't you see what a *farce* it makes of your preaching the good Life. The good Life indeed, rowing about in your little boat with the worm eaten ship & chaos! Look here! How *can* you! How can you lay up your sweat in a phial for future generations! I dont ask for false courage from anyone, but I do think that even if you are shivering it is your duty as an artist and a man *not* to shiver. The devil & the angel in you both fight in that review. I must speak out plainly because your friends flatter you. They are not really taken in by your "sham personality" but they are too uncertain of themselves not to pretend they are and you are deceived by their pretence because you want to be. It is this which mars you, and it is for this reason you will not be popular. Its the

BAD in you people can't stomach – not the good. But tho' they dont understand it they sense it as treachery – as something that *is not done.* Dont be proud of your unpopularity, Bogey. It is right you should be unpopular for this.

Now let me point to your remark in the preface that you can "do no less than afford your readers . . . a similar enjoyment in your case." My dear Bogey! How could a person say such a thing.[9] Its so naive as to be silly, or so arrogant as to be fantastique. Suppose I wrote "I have dated my stories as I venture to hope my readers may enjoy tracing my development, the ripening of my powers . . ." What *would* you think! You'd faint! It is indecent – no less – to say such things. And one doesn't think them!

It always seems to me you let yourself go in the Nation especially; you count on Massingham's[10] weakness. The worst of it is that when-ever one is less than true to oneself in work, even what *is* true becomes tainted. I feel whenever I *am* true my good angel wipes out one bad mark – doesn't give me a good one – but at any rate, next time, there is one bad mark the less to get over. Now you only get half marks, and they are no marks at all, because you cannot resist this awful insidious temptation to show your wounds. Until you do, you are a great writer marred. Lynd called it "highbrowism". Its much more subtle.

There you are. If you were to send me back my 1/9 wedding ring for this letter I should send the letter just the same & keep the ring in a matchbox & be very sorry.

I must risk being wrong. In my efforts to be clear I am crude. I must risk that. For as long as I live I never will be other than dead honest and dead sincere with you, as I would have you with me. Do not think I imagine I know all about you. Ah, my darling – I never shall. Forgive me if I hurt you – please forgive me!
But I love you and I believe in you.
Thats all.
Wig.

MS ATL, *LJMM*, 617-20.

---

1 The chapters in *Aspects of Literature* entitled 'Thoughts on Tchekhov', 'Samuel Butler', 'The Function of Criticism', 'Shakespeare Criticism'.
2 'The Poetry of Thomas Hardy.'
3 'The Problem of Keats'. Murry published *Keats and Shakespeare* in 1925, *Studies in Keats* in 1930.
4 In writing of Sir Sidney Colvin's *John Keats: His Life and Poetry, His Friends, Critics, and After-fame*, Murry concludes that 'in the few places where Sir Sidney falls short of the spirit of com-plete acceptance, we discern behind the words of rebuke and regret only the idealisation of a love which we are proud to share'.
5 'The Poetry of Edward Thomas'.
6 'Coleridge's Criticism'.

⁷ In his essay 'Ronsard' Murry quotes

> De vif cinabre estoit faicte sa joue,
> Pareille au teint d'un rougissant oeillet,
> Ou d'une fraize, alors que dans de laict
> Dessus le hault de la cresme se joue.
>
> (Pierre de Ronsard (1524–85), 'La Charite', stanza 16)

⁸ 'The Detachment of Mr Santayana', Murry's review of *Character and Opinion in the United States*, in the *Nation*, 4 Dec. 1920.

⁹ His statement in the 'Preface', pp. vii–viii, 'I make no apology for not having rewritten the essays. As a critic I enjoy nothing more than to trace the development of a writer's attitude through its various phases; I could do no less than afford my readers the opportunity of a similar enjoyment in my own case.'

¹⁰ H. M. Massingham, editor of the *Nation* and a close friend of Murry's.

To J. M. Murry, [8 December 1920]

[Villa Isola Bella, Garavan, Menton]

I have sent back the books today.

My dear Bogey

It is with the most extreme reluctance that I am writing to tell you K.M. cant go on. The fact is she ought to have given up months ago but money was so urgent that she dared not. I know you suggested a months holiday – but a months holiday doesn't fit the case. She wont be well in a month. The strain will begin all over again, and I think she has told you fairly often *what* a strain it is.

She would not, however, have taken this step if Doctor Bouchage had not made her realise it was *absolutely necessary*. He has. It is not that her health is worse than it was in London. But its no better. She has good days she didn't have then; but she has BAD ones she didn't, either. And she is not improving, as they say.

In two words – & plain ones: its a question of shortening her life, to keep on. And that she cant do.

But you must realise how deeply she 'appreciates' the awkwardness of this for you. She knows it all: feels it all.

One thing must be perfectly clear. She wants NO money from you and no sacrifice. She hates even discussing money affairs with you. She knows you have paid debts of hers; she hopes they are the last you'll ever pay. *This is final.* You may smile at this and say: 'I haven't any money to give her, at any rate' – Right-o. But she just had to tell you.

And now Ill be personal, darling. Look here you ought to have sent me that Corona! You really ought to have. Can't you possibly imagine what all this writing out has been to a person as weak as I *damnably* am?

You can't or a stone would have sent it. You knew what a help it was to me in London.

But oh dear I don't mean to accuse you – because I cant bear, as you know, to make you feel unhappy. But what you would have saved me – I cant *say*! Isn't it awful that I have not dared to *add to your burdens* by reminding you before? Thats Mother in me. And you rather count on it, my darling.

But don't feel sad – or knocked over – or don't take any of this too seriously. Easy to say – isn't it. Yes, all the same its not RIGHT to LIVE among mountains of gloom – or to sweat blood as one climbs them. One must just run on top and be careless. I don't now mean that in putting you in this hole Im laughing at the hole. But think of the hole that I might so easily trip into!! Its far bigger – far blacker – but I WONT moan. This is a very mixed letter. You ought just to love me – thats all the best – and you *must* understand.

Your own
Tig.

Darling
I open this letter to say Ive just got yours of the 5th. The Morning Post is very 'whiskery' – isn't it. But oh, I didn't have to send my letter! Your letter makes it so hard.

My chill is a bit better today but always there. 'C'est pas gran'chose mais enfin' is the feeling.

Ive had a letter from Squire saying my story is at the printers & asking for another as soon as & whenever I have one. Ill give you one to take back.

Now about things you ought to bring. Do you mean – for me? I have no commissions for you. Bring warm clothes for yourself. Its v. cold here & the last leaves are gone. We are very exposed – all our lovely trees are bare. I fear you will not think it is very pretty at all. The lemons shine on bare boughs, & the freckled tangerines have two little leaves left to fly with.

I feel so queer – so *abnormal* – shorn of my job that I can scarcely write to you until I have heard. And it pains me to think I shant be there in the paper. Im shut out. But it cant be helped. No complaining!
Farewell my darling
Wig.

MS ATL. *LJMM*, 615–6.

To Michael Sadleir, 8 December 1920

Villa Isola Bella | Garavan | Menton
A/M
8.XII.1920

Dear Michael Sadler,

Thank you so much for your letter. I am sorry I lifted up my voice so loud − and I fully appreciate the position . . . Perhaps I ought to be thankful that J.M.M. didn't send you a photograph of a complete stranger − by mistake − whom he'd "always thought" was K.M!

Its awfully kind of you to have bothered to write.

Yours,

Katherine Mansfield.

MS Targ.

To Dorothy Brett, 9 December 1920

Villa Isola Bella | Garavan | Menton
9 xii 1920

My dear Brett,

I have just received your letter. Do not fear your letters. Let me try and explain why I did not reply to you. I felt, somehow, that you felt it necessary to assume a personality with me that wasn't wholly you. Perhaps I was quite wrong. But I feel there was a strain − an uneasiness. And then − I must own − after talking so much about imagination it seemed to me impossible for you to have understood Gertler so little as to *mind* his being cross − and to almost boast that you wouldn't cook eggs for him any longer but just gave him the saucepan and let him look after himself! Now I feel sure that was not true. I feel certain you have looked after Gertler to the very limit of your powers − but why did you think I'd admire you for being such a poor artist as not to understand a sick person's psychology? There was (or I felt; please forgive me if I am wrong) a kind of frosty breath, light but chill, of falseness in this . . . and so I kept silent.

But, dear Brett, don't worry about telling me everything. We shall know each other by our work. The time to work is here. We cannot afford to delay. I have chosen deliberately to leave my friends for a time. If they do not understand then I must do without their understanding. I have left the company and gone away and I can neither return nor welcome my friends until some of this work is done. You see, Brett, the days are so short and who knows whether there is going to be a long evening? I, for one, don't dare count on one.

But forgive me for failing you as a friend. If you knew how I wish you Joy!

Yours

Tig

Would you give my love to Koteliansky if you ever see him?

MS Newberry.

To J. M. Murry, [9 December 1920]

[Villa Isola Bella, Garavan, Menton]

Darling little Fellow,

Il fait beau, aujourd'hui. I am sitting in my long chair on the terrace. The wind of the last days has scattered almost the last of the fig leaves & now through those candle shaped boughs I love so much there is a beautiful glimpse of the old town. Some fowls are making no end of a noise. Ive just been for a walk on my small boulevard & looking down below at the houses all bright in the sun and housewives washing their linen in great tubs of glittering water & flinging it over the orange trees to dry. Perhaps all human activity is beautiful in the sunlight. Certainly these women lifting their arms, turning to the sun to shake out the wet clothes were supremely beautiful. I couldn't help feeling – and after they have lived they will die and it wont matter. It will be alright, they wont regret it.

A small slender bird is pecking the blue bay berries. Birds are much wilder here, much quicker: properly on the qui vive, you know. Bogey dear, do you mind? Ive *done* with England. I dont even want to see England again. Is that awful? I feel it is rather. I know you will always want to go back. I am collecting possessions at an awful rate. All my pennies go on them. Dont expect your Wig to have 2 pairs of flannel trousers; she only buys 2 pairs of curtains or a pair of coffee pots. But they are all movables. They can all be carried up the mountains. Wander with me 10 years, will you darling? Ten years in the sun. Its not long – only 10 springs. If I manage to live for 10 years I don't think Id mind dying at 42 and then you'd be about the age of Johnny Fergusson – very beautiful and brown and free and easy moving in your ways.

But as to starting a theatre for Schiffs to come to! Lord – Lord – not I!

You are coming quite soon now – aren't you Boge? I shant come & meet you at the station. This station is an absolute *death trap*. Trains are always late; you have to wait in the open and horrid men wave you away from the barriers even. Perhaps our own station! will be open by then.

That would be perfect for its only one minute off. But otherwise I shall send my special cocher for you wearing some outstanding mark for you to find him by − a red rose − and Ill be here at the gate. You cant arrive at the gate for no horse can mount the tiny sentier. But that doesn't matter. I only hope youll like my little Isola Bella like I do. I dont suppose its perfect or anything like perfect − but − well − it *suits me*. Tchekhov would be happy here. Of that Im *certain*.

There is a train now which arrives in the early afternoon. Its a very fast train. Had you better ask about it? It leaves Paris (I believe) sometime after 8 and arrives here shortly after 2. Be sure you take some FORMAMINT to suck in the train in case people have colds. Frenchies are so careless. Its a pity you cant come in a box, darling. But you know about keeping warm & eating plenty − they are the essentials of right conduct on a journey. *Dont buy biscuits*. Eat dejeuners & diners whatever they cost.

MS ATL. *LKM* II. 84; *LJMM*, 601–3.

¹ The new station at Garavan, a few hundred yards from the Isola Bella.

To J. M. Murry, [c.10 December 1920]

[Villa Isola Bella, Garavan, Menton]

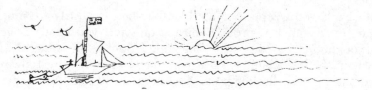

Darling little Fellow

Ive just had the wire about the £30. Now this is just what I wanted to avoid. I presume it is my A. cheque for this month augmenté to that sum by you. Will you believe me or I shall be cross − I am in NO need of money. Ill pay you back every cent il y a de plus. Im as rich as Croesus (who was *Croesus*¹). My kine are fat; my sheep are all jaeger. Stop now! Calmez vous! What do you mean by jumping up − you Jack-in-the-Box. What can I do with you?

Doctor B. has just gone. We talked over the affair again. He was quite definite. I shall now tell you exactly so that you know where you are.

I *have* injured my heart for the moment by overwork − but not permanently. If I had persisted I should have endangered my life. It is difficult to explain to anyone as wise as you the gigantic strain of one weekly article – to a person as 'weakly' (as Pa would say) as I am. It sounds fantastic. It hung over me like a cloud. But ① money and ② my feeling for the paper and you and so on made me cling. However it was ① which has kept me at it too long, I fear. At present, too, both my lungs are inflammés as a result of a chill. Its not serious or urgent but if I tried to exert myself it would be. My heart is however the ''trouble'' at the moment. It needs rest. So I have to lie low and rest the little *fiend*. It will then get better.

However I am not forlorn. Je suis si bien ici. J'ai ma petite villa, ma bonne, un fer d'enfer flamme dans la cheminée – & lying here I can do my own work when Im not too tired. I can take it up & put it down à mon aise.

There. I only tell you all this because youre such a bad wicked Boge to worry. Stop! Ill tell you when to worry. Oh darling – take a long breath – *now*. Are you afraid of anything. I solemnly assure you I am afraid of NOTHING. I mean that. I do not want to die because Ive done nothing to justify having lived yet. But if I *had* done my work Id even go so far as to die. I mean to jolly well keep alive with the flag fly-ing until there is a modest shelf of books with K.M. backs. Which reminds me I do think Constable might have sent me a copy of Bliss – don't you? But only vanity makes me want to see it. *Confession:* I want to leave it about for Marie to find and exclaim over.

Goodbye darling. Help me to keep all fair – all serene and fine. Why should it be otherwise? No, you are not a Teddy Bear you are a *Boge* and I am a *Wig*.

MS ATL, *LJMM*, 616–17.

¹ Croesus, king of Lydia (c.560–546 BC), famous for his fabulous wealth.

To Richard Murry, [c. 10 December 1920]

VILLA ISOLA BELLA | CARAVAN | MENTON
A/M
Richard

About that primitive outlook. It doesn't need reviving. We've got it. It comes with seeing & feeling as deeply and truly as we are capable of. I mean by that nothing self conscious – God forbid – but just a kind of simple acceptance of Life as an artist must see it. The freshness is all there. Everything is to our hand. The whole secret is to give ourselves up to it in the right way.

What you quote from Van Gogh is *very fine*.[1] I could give you its twin sentence if I had Tchekhov's letters here. Tchekhov felt just *like that*. I too, suspect and don't feel comfortable in this "art life". What I mean is when Brett used to write me endless pages about good & bad art I always wanted to hang my head because I felt she wasn't *working*. She wasn't really *getting down to it* (dont misunderstand me) humbly.

See dear Richard you show your reverence for your job in the way you approach it. I don't believe there are any short cuts to Art. Victory is the reward of battle just exactly as it is in Life. And the more one knows of ones 'soldiers' the better chance one has. Thats not an absolutely true analogy tho'. The thing is more subtle.

But what I do believe with my whole soul is that one's *outlook* is the climate in which ones art either thrives or doesn't grow. I am dead[2] certain that there is no separating Art & Life. And no artist can afford to leave out Life. If we mean to work we must go straight to Life for our nourishment. There's no substitute. But I am violent on this subjeck. I must leave it.

About your Easter holiday. Just feel as free as air. Come when you like – how you like. Make your Easter at Christmas or your Christmas at Easter. Dont feel bound.

I am stuck in bed, by my old doctor who says I must stay here another week at least. Pity poor little K. I hate bed. I shall never go to bed in Heaven or eat anything off a tray. If a cherubim & seraphim come winging their way towards me with some toast & jelly I shall pop like a chestnut into Hell & be roasted.

Look after your baby brother, and *be sure* he does not fall out of the gocart on to his boko.[3]

Goodbye my dear

Katherine.

MS R. Murry. *LKM* II. 80.

[1] As Murry explained in a footnote (*LKM* II. 80) the extract quoted read: 'Nevertheless I find in my work a certain reverberation of what fascinated me. I know that Nature told me something, that she spoke to me, and that I took down her message in shorthand. Perhaps my transcript contains words that are undecipherable; belike there are faults and omissions in it too, – still it may possess something that the wood, the beach or the figures said.' The quotation is from an undated letter from Vincent van Gogh to his brother Theo, in *The Letters of a Post-Impressionist*, a selection translated by Anthony M. Ludovici (1912), 9. The letter is no. 228, Autumn 1882, in *The Letters of Vincent van Gogh to his Brother*, i (1927), ed. J. van Gogh-Bonger.

[2] Above 'I am dead' in par. 4 (the top of p. 3 in her manuscript) KM had initially written to Murry "D. B. [Dear Bogey] I return this proof. Send it straight to the M, will you?" This was then crossed out, and beside it she wrote "Sorry but cant was' paper".

[3] Richard Murry's typescript note recalls that at Portland Villas 'Katherine asked me what I thought was the funniest word in the English language: she said hers was "boko" cockney and I daresay N.Z. slang for the human head. . . . I suggested "go-cart", the name for a small low perambulator. . . . Jack, called in later, said judiciously: "Then I suppose the funniest sentence . . . must be 'He fell out of the go-cart on his boko.' " '

To J. M. Murry, [12 December 1920]

[Menton]

STOP TORMENTING ME WITH THESE FALSE DEPRESSING LETTERS AT ONCE BE
A MAN OR DONT WRITE ME

TIG

Telegram ATL. Alpers 1980, 323.

To J. M. Murry, [12 December 1920]

[Villa Isola Bella, Garavan, Menton]

Bogey

A letter has come from you in which you say you are 'annihilated' & tell me of Madame la Princesse because you think your[1] – – what shall I call it – meeting her may have had something to do with my illness. Well, Bogey – please let me speak.

I told you to be free – because I meant it. What happens in your personal life does NOT affect me. I have of you what I want – a relationship which is unique but it is not what the world understands by *marriage*. That is to say I do not in any way *depend* on you, neither can you shake me.

Nobody can. I do not know how it is but I live *withdrawn* from my personal life. (This is hard to say.) I am a writer first. In the past, it is true, when I worked less, my writing self was merged in my personal self. I felt conscious of you – to the exclusion of almost everything, at times. (All this is just outline.)

But now I do not. You are dearer than anyone in the world to me – but more than anything else – more even than talking or laughing or being happy I want to write. This sounds so ugly; I wish I didn't have to say it. But your letter makes me feel you would be relieved if it were said.

Cant we stop this *horrible drama!* I hate explaining myself: its so unnatural to me. It makes me feel indecent.

Let us quit ourselves like men.

Tig.

This is much harsher than I feel, but you compel me to speak out. It isn't even *as* I feel; its so crude. But I simply CANT – – bear your lack of a sense of proportion. It *will* be the ruin of us both.

MS ATL. *LJMM*, 621-2.

¹ Murry's letter of 10 Dec., the only one that survives from this period, was among several whose 'fearful pain' distressed her (*Journal*, 229). It gave a meticulous account of his kissing several women,

his involvement with Elizabeth Bibesco, and conveyed a painful sense of attempting to be utterly frank with his wife. The full text of his letter is in Murry, 317–20.

To J. M. Murry, [15 December 1920]

[Menton]

PAY NO HEED MY LETTERS[1] ILLNESS EXASPERATED ME ARE YOU ARRIVING TUESDAY IF SO WONT WRITE AGAIN FONDEST LOVE REPLY

TIG

Telegram ATL. *LJMM*, 622.

[1] It is likely that some of KM's letters from this period, as well as Murry's, were not kept. But Murry quickly made arrangements to leave London, and arrived in Menton *c.*20 Dec. On 15 Dec. she recorded in a notebook that she was 'ill, unhappy, despondent', but reading Chekhov's story 'The Duel' made her laugh. On 19 Dec. she made a much fuller and considered entry.

'I should like this to be accepted as my confession.

'There is no limit to human suffering. When one thinks "Now I have touched the bottom of the sea – now I can go no deeper," one goes deeper. And so it is for ever. I thought last year in Italy: Any shadow more would be death. But this year has been so much more terrible that I think with affection of the Casetta! Suffering is boundless, it is eternity. One pang is eternal torment. Physical suffering is – child's play. To have one's breast crushed by a great stone – one could laugh!

'I do not want to die without leaving a record of my belief that suffering can be overcome. For I do believe it. What must one do? There is no question of what Jack calls "passing beyond it". This is false.

'One must *submit*. Do not resist. Take it. Be overwhelmed. Accept it fully. Make it *part of life*.

'Everything in life that we really accept undergoes a change. So suffering must become Love. This is the mystery. This is what I must do. I must pass from personal love which has failed me to greater love. I must give to the whole of life what I gave to him. The present agony will pass – if it doesn't kill.

'It won't last. Now I am like a man who has had his heart torn out – but – bear it – bear it! As in the physical world, so in the spiritual world, pain does not last for ever. It is only so terribly acute now. It is as though a ghastly accident had happened. If I can cease reliving all the shock and horror of it, cease going over it, I will get stronger.

'Here, for a strange reason, there rises the figure of Doctor Sorapure. He was a good man. He helped me not only to bear pain, but suggested that perhaps bodily ill-health is necessary, is a repairing process, and he was always telling me to consider how man plays but a part in the history of the world. My simple kindly doctor was pure of heart, as Tchehov is pure of heart. But for these ills one is one's own doctor. If "suffering" is not a repairing process I will make it so. I will learn the lesson it teaches. These are not idle words. These are not the consolations of the sick.

'Life is a mystery. The fearful pain of these letters of the knowledge that Jack wishes me dead, and of his killing me, will fade. I must turn to *work*. I must put my agony into something, change it. "Sorrow shall be changed into joy."

'It is to lose oneself more utterly, to love more deeply, to feel oneself part of life – not separate. Oh Life! accept me – make me worthy – teach me.

'I write that. I look up. The leaves move in the garden, the sky is pale, and I catch myself weeping. It is hard – it is hard to make a good death . . . and the horrible vulgar letters of this woman about "[?]" and so on. And this cruel insulting letter about "*no physical attraction*" (!!) "I think she is in love with me" and so on – were they necessary? He now claims his right not to suffer on my account anymore – oh god! How *base* in its selfishness.

'But *no, no*! I must not blame him anymore, and I must not go back. Thus was it. Let it be.

To Dorothy Brett, 22 December 1920

Villa Isola Bella | Garavan-Menton
A/M.
22 xii 1920

Dearest Brett,

I have to thank you for a most lovely sumptuous garment. One feels like a bird with its winter wooly wings on in it. And the colouring is so lovely and fair. I want to scold you for having sent it to me and at the same time to make you feel how admiringly Im saying: "Thank you very much indeed, please".

I wonder where you will be for Christmas. Having M. with me has turned it into a fête. My treasured Marie is determined that Christmas shall be kept here & bought the mistletoe all in readiness for the arrival of Monsieur. The kitchen is a progression of still lives from a poor dead bird leaning its tired head on a tuft of watercress (oh how *awful* it looks!) onwards. And because the weather is chill, blue & white weather, log fires roar in the chimleys. This little house is a perfect darling. Its not beautiful, its shabby and the bedroom wallpaper is baskets of pink flowers and in the dining room there is a big corpse of a clock that sometimes at dreadful intervals & for no reason begins to *chime* – never to tick. But there is a feeling over everything as though it were a real resting place. I have taken it until the end of 1922 and even so Im frightened at the idea of saying goodbye to it then. I love this country, too, more and more. It is winter now – many trees are bare but the oranges, tanger-ines & lemons are all ripe; they burn in this clear atmosphere – the lemons with gentle flames, the tangerines with bright flashes & the oranges sombre. My tiny peach tree still clings to a few exquisite leaves – curved like peaches & the violets are just beginning. More and more (for how long? No matter. A moment is forever) one *lives* – really lives. M. says you have painted a lovely picture of asters in sunlight. I wish I could see it.

Are you childish about the New Year? Do you feel it is a mystery & that if your friends wish you a happy one – happiness does come beat-ing its beautiful wings out of the darkness toward you?

Dearest Brett – I hope you will be happy. I salute your work for 1921. May it bring you joy. And I send my love and friendship – From

Tig

'To live – to live! And to leave life on this earth as Tchehov left life and Tolstoi.

'After a dreadful operation, I remember that when I thought of the pain of having stitches out, I used to cry. Every time, I felt it again, and winced, and it was unbearable.

'That is what one must control. Queer! The two people left are Tchehov – dead – and unheed-ing, indifferent Doctor Sorapure. They are the two good men I have known.' (*Journal* 1954, 228-9)

M. brought over my Japanese doll. I wish you had painted his portrait. He really is a lovely little creature!

MS Newberry. *LKM* II. 85–6.

To Anne Drey, 26 December 1920

Villa Isola Bella | Garavan | Menton
A/M.
26 xii 1920

My Precious Friend,

The parcel arrived on Xmas morning but it was a separate fête by itself – just your letter & the two enchanting sketches. I love them, Anne. They remind me of our spring together & the laburnum seems hung with little laughs. If you knew how often I think of that time at Looe[1] – our pic-nic, the white-eyed Kaffir, the midget infant hurling large pieces of Cornwall into the sea on the beach that afternoon! Its all as clear as today.

But you know – dont you? – that all the times we have ever spent together are clear like that. And here – I am always sending you greetings – always sharing things with you. I salute you in tangerines and the curved petals of roses thé and the crocus colour of the sea & in the moonlight on the poire sauvage. Many many other things. It will *always* be so with me however seldom I see you. I shall just go on rejoicing in the fact of you and loving you and feeling in that family where Monsieur le Beau Soleil est notre père nous sommes des soeurs. But all that's jolly fine. I shan't be content, darling, unless we do have a real summer together one day with the blessed enfant pouring sand down our necks. . . .

Murry tells me you are working. I hope it goes very well. I hope there are a whole flock of masterpieces with canvas wings flying towards you from shadowy 1921. Whenever I *examine* things here – the lovely springing line of flowers & peach leaves, par exemple, I realise what a marvellous painter you are – the beauty of your line – the *life* behind it.

I am still hard at the story writing and still feeling that only now do I begin to see what I want to do. Im sending you my book. Its not a good one. I promise the next will be better but I just wanted you to have a copy. Living solitary these last months with a servant who is a born artist & says "un ou deux bananes faisent plus *intrigantes* le compotier" & who returns from market with a basket which just to see on the kitchen table is *food* for the day – makes work a great deal easier to get at. The *strain* is removed. At last one doesn't worry any more. And fancy ones domestique having an idea of what work is! She won't even let a person talk at the front door if Im working. She whispers to them to go to la porte de la cuisine. . . . parce que c'est tres enervant pour Madame d'entendre causer quelqu'un pendant qu'elle travaille! Its like being in Heaven with an ange gardienne.

Murry is here for Christmas. The weather is superb & champagne is only 30 francs a bottle. There is always un feu d'enfer in my chambre à coucher. The result is, chère (oh I can only say these things to you!) we are continually suggesting to Marie she should go to Vespers, Bénédiction, la messe. The poor old creature can't understand this mania de la pousser vers l'église. Its a mystery! But what is one to do? The house is so small. I send her to market, to the poste, out to see her friends – anywhere . . . and when she comes back she cries Dieu me gardé! Que Madame et Monsieur ont bonne mine! Champagne in this air & this sun is unsafe for all people under – say ninety-nine. Queer it is. I believe if I lived in England I could be a eunuch quite cheerfully, but . . . there's something in the air of France – – – which is very restora- tive, lets say.

To turn to more serious subjects. How awfully well Drey writes in The Athenaeum. I do so immensely enjoy his articles. He's the only man who seems to write about painting as though it wasn't first put through the intellectual mincing machine. Will you tell him how awfully I like his work & serre lui la main pour moi? I hear that he has been to MY Sorapure. There's a doctor – and a very fine honest man.[2]

Darling – its lunch time – I tremble de faim. Bless you for Ever. Take care of your self. Come to France soon. Let us meet one day soon – and until then know you have my deep love & devotion.

Toujours
Your
Katherine

MS ATL. LKM II. 86–7.

[1] Anne Drey had been staying nearby, and saw a good deal of KM when she was at the Headland Hotel, Looe, in May 1918.
[2] KM had written on the manuscript of 'The Daughters of the Late Colonel', completed 13 Dec.: 'To Doctor Sorapure. Were my gratitude to equal my admiration, my admiration would still out-step my gratitude' (ATL).

To Virginia Woolf, 27 December 1920

Villa Isola Bella | Garavan | Menton
A/M
27. XII.1920

My dear Virginia

Please don't talk of a triumph,[1] even in jest. It makes me hang my head. I wish some day I might deserve your long generous letter − but the day is far off, I realise that. Thank you for it all the same. It came on Xmas day too, and so was a two-fold gift.

I think of you often − very often. I long to talk to you. Here, at last there is time to talk. If Virginia were to come through the gate & were to say "Well − Katherine" − oh, there are a thousand things Id like to discuss.

I wonder if you know what your visits were to me − or how much I miss them. You are the only woman with whom I long to talk *work*. There will never be another.

But leagues divide us. I have taken this little house until the end of 1922. Perhaps you will come here before then. It is in the country & there is a garden & a stone terrace. It is solitary but not lonely. One lives by the sky again − by the changes of cloud & light. Whenever I think of Asheham[2] it is of clouds − big golden clouds, hazy, spinning slowly over the downs − −

Oh, how beautiful Life is, Virginia, it is marvellously beautiful. Were one to live for ever it would not be long enough. Sometimes I sit on the wall watching the sun & the wind shake over the long grass & the wild orchid cups & I feel − − − simply helpless before this wonder.

Farewell dear friend. (May I call you that).

Yours ever

Katherine.

MS Sussex. *Adam* 370−5, 24.

[1] On 19 Dec. Virginia Woolf had written: 'I wish you were here to enjoy your triumph − still more that we might talk about your book − For what's the use of telling you how glad and indeed proud I am?' (*The Question of Things Happening, the Letters of Virginia Woolf 1912−1922*, ed. Nigel Nicholson and Joanne Trautmann (1976), 422).
[2] Where Virginia Woolf lived when she was first friendly with KM, before moving to Monks House, Rodmell, Sussex, in Sept. 1919.

To Herbert Palmer,[1] [? late December 1920]

[Villa Isola Bella, Garavan, Menton]

Dear Herbert Palmer,

I am sorry that your letter to me should have been opened at the Office. But anything that looks like MSS suffers the same fate before it's sent across to me.

Now for your letter. Don't think me unsympathetic. I am not. But look here! There is one thing you must discover, if you want to do your work in this world, and that is that it is no good crying out. Perhaps it helps us to bear our pain but that's all. It stops the ears of those whom we would have listen to us; they hear nothing but the crying. And that – hard as it sounds – antagonises them. It isn't wrong this should be so. It's hard but it's necessary – Life being what it is. There is a law against letting ourselves go. Warriors must be men as well as warriors, or we shall all be shouting together.

Do you know, the line in your poem which makes me feel your suffering more than any other – the *powerful* line? It's: 'I want to walk with the sheep and swell the fern . . .' All things have their flower and their fruit – Pride, Love, Fear, Sorrow, Hysteria.' The greater part of your poem seems to me the flower and the fruit of hysteria. It's a fine harvest but cultivate other ground. Don't waste yourself, don't spend your manhood.

And you must – at whatever cost – rid yourself of these feelings of rage and spite and the idea that every man's hand is against you. You can't afford to feed such vile guests. If you do they will steal every gift you have and poison you into the bargain. Write to me again. I want you to feel I am your friend; I am anxious for you and I wish I could help you. But understand that I think you must change – I think you must make the effort of your life and *throw away* all your marks of battle before you are a real poet. I know they are your treasure. But that's just why they must go. You are too proud of them.

It is useless to write less than the truth to anyone. Forgive me if I hurt you.

Yours ever,
J.M.M.

MS ATL.

1 Herbert Palmer (1880–1961), educated at Birmingham and Bonn universities, worked as a teacher in Germany, France, and England, before deciding on a literary career in 1921. A prolific and minor poet, two of his poems were published in the *Athenaeum*, 1 Oct. and 26 Nov. 1920, and his second book of verse, *Two Foemen*, was reviewed by Edmund Blunden on 26 Nov. Since this letter was written in KM's hand but signed JMM, Palmer's own letter was presumably received at the *Athenaeum* office after Murry had joined his wife in France, then sent on to Menton, where KM rejected a submitted manuscript on the editor's behalf, but also seems to be clearing up a heated complaint.

To Richard Murry, 1 January 1921

[Villa Isola Bella, Garavan, Menton]
January 1st 1921

Dear Richard

A Happy New Year. As I made up the fire just now, laid the fresh logs across & neatly disposed of the half consumed ones I found myself sending you a greeting. I hoped this year would be a very special, an extra special one for you & that all the milestones dotted through it were canvases by our young painter Richard M. Good luck – dear little brother – now and always. On Xmas day we drank your health in real live champagne. I hope you had a good Xmas. Jack has brought me up to date in your news even down to a description of your new overcoat (which is very powerful for Jack). I hope he will tell you of this place. He likes it and he looks very well and eats something tremenjous. We spend our time talking, reading Shakespeare, discussing the 'future' and what we want to do, and more talking. Its years since we have been quite alone together like this. Everything seems so simple – so easy. Its like being a child and grown up at the same time. The chief feeling is though – that marvellous sense of ease – which seems to me the rarest thing in Life for two people to share. I have written a huge long story of a rather new kind. Its the outcome of the *Prelude* method – it just unfolds and opens. But I hope its an advance on Prelude. In fact I know its that because the technique is stronger. Its a queer tale, though. I hope you'll like it.

Arnold G. sent a story[1] for the paper which I read the other day. It interested me *very* much. One felt he'd been reading Tchekhov but in the good sense – Tchekhov had fired him, given him the courage to be himself. I thought it a remarkable piece of work. But then again it set me thinking of you. For you are the real New Generation to me, and I wondered what you were doing & feeling about "this painting business", and Life, generally. If you ever feel inclined to – tell me a little, will you?

We had a marvellous drive up into the mountains here the other day to a very ancient small village called Castellar. These roads wind & wind higher and higher – one seems to drive through the centuries too – the boy with the oxen who stands on the hillside with a green branch in his hand, the old woman gathering twigs among the olives, the blind peasant with wild violet pinned to his cap – all these figures seem to belong to any time. And then the tiny walled village with a great tree in the cobbled square and the lovely young girl looking out of the window of flower pots in the Inn. Its all something one seems to have known for ever. I could live here for years and years – I mean away from what they call "the world".

Here's Jack, back from a walk & here's old Marie with the tea and honey cake.

Fare well. I send you my love. May we meet before this year is ended.

Katherine.

MS R. Murry. *LKM* II. 87.

1 Arnold Gibbons was a school friend of Richard's, who had visited KM in Hampstead and tried his hand at writing after winning an essay prize. As Murry resigned as editor in Hampstead later in the month, even a recommendation from KM would not have had time to get his work in the *Athenaeum*. He soon after settled on becoming an engineer, and finally an expert on theatre lighting.

To Richard Murry, [early January 1921]

VILLA ISOLA BELLA | CARAVAN | MENTON
A/M

Dear little Bruvver,

It occurs to me that a more reasonable 'kick off' would have been to send you a très late Christmas present. I therefore enclose a small cheque. *Spend it*, thats all I ask. Don't save it. Enjoy yourself, Richard dear. Buy yourself a book you want or take Mam'selle out to dinner or – do what you like. Thats all the bes'.¹

And never think any money I send you deprives Jack of anything. As you know we keep our money affairs entirely separate. He doesn't give me a penny & never has. So feel as free as air.

I decided this morn to make my will in case I should go off suddin like. I dont suppose Ill leave more than 4d but after mature considera-tion Ive pitched on ce jeune peintre Richard Murry to be my heir.

Addio, caro mio

Catherina

Cheque enclosed.

MS R. Murry. *Adam* 370-5, 25.

1 Richard Murry's note explains that as a young child, in exasperation with his older brother on holiday from Christ's Hospital, he declared: 'You go back to your school – that's all the best for you!' This amused John and was remembered by him – thence to Katherine. She frequently used this phrase, or some variant of it.

To Sydney Schiff, [early January 1921]

VILLA ISOLA BELLA | GARAVAN | MENTON
A/M

My dear Sydney,

If only you did write the story from Janey's point of view![1] What wouldn't I give to see it . . . That my attempt gave you some pleasure is a great reward for me. Its such *encouragement* to know I have a critic. You understand that? And I value every word & suggestion. Let us speak about it, if you please, one time when Violet you and I are together. Murry has changed his opinion. He likes it almost more than my other stories now.

But that brings me to the triangle talk of the other evening, about which a *book* would not be enough. Yes, of course you were right, we were 'happier' when you left – rather, the strangest thing happened to Murry. No, I can't write it. Its so involved. I could only tell it in one of our talks.

M: . . . "When we started talking, as I listened to Schiff & you I suddenly felt that I was outside it all, that I had been for months really, a false personality. And when I came out of the corner & sat in the other chair I felt this false personality gradually being shed. Everything began to get simpler . . ." But thats only the beginning.

You know those people who with a wand can divine the presence of a spring of clear water, can trace the source of a spring that flows deep underground.

Quite apart from all your conscious gifts as a psychologist, I feel you, too, are a *diviner* in just this way. I thought of the analogy the other day . . . when Violet & I were together in the car. You remember, Violet? And how are you, today? I know you have exquisite courage. Dont put it to the test too much. Id *love* to see you – to know you are really better. I keep looking at my books. Is there one you would care for – one worth sending? But they look dull dogs. Few are the books one really wants to see. Are you in bed still? I should very much like to give you a small quick hug & say how glad I am you're better . . .

Yours ever with love

Katherine.

MS BL. *Adam* 300, 106–7.

---

[1] Janey was the wife in KM's story 'The Stranger', published in the *London Mercury*, Jan. 1921. The perspective of the story is that of her husband.

To Dorothy Brett, 9 January 1921

Villa Isola Bella | Menton | Caravan A/M
9. I. 1921

Dear Brett

Its *very* nice of you to send us all those good wishes. We have had a wonderful Xmas and New Year. The weather is absolutely divine today – like mid-June! But the day won't come when I shall say I was wrong. Why should it? How have I been *wrong?* I don't think I even understand. And I don't want to protest about it. It makes me feel uncomfortable and inclined to hang my head. Its undignified. What is in the Past had a great deal better be buried – bury the good even to get the bad safely under – and begin again. I think the important thing is to make ones Life part of ones work – to live as honestly as one paints or writes. But there mustn't be "weak spots". One can no more afford to give way in Life than one can in Art. If you really want nothing so much as to be an artist you must accept the discipline to obtain the joy. You *can't pre-tend* for a moment.

Dear Brett, there is so much that is good and fine in you, so much to admire and love. But *don't be frightened.* Of all devils Fear is the most subtle; he takes all sorts of forms and disguises. Perhaps he is the most powerful, too. The curse of him is he eats away ones strength and he confounds ones vision.

I would wish you a triumphant victory over Fear in 1921. Dont give way!

There. I expect you are very angry with me by now. Forgive me, Brett, I speak as one workman to another.

Yours ever

Tig

MS Newberry.

To Anne Drey, 9 January 1921

Isola Bella | Caravan | Menton
A/M.
9. I. 1921.

Darling Anne

May I ask you to do a Vile Deed for me? If you feel that vraiment c'est un peu trop just ignore my letter.

But you know darling it was through you I first met milanese silk stockings & since then I have used no other. But la belle France or at any rate sur le bord de la Riviera doesn't wear them – & only sells fiendishly dear ladder traps. Would it be a bother for you to send me 3 pairs of grey ones? I will send a cheque by return. Id be more than grateful. If youd put them in an envelope with *bas usés* written on it. The last ones I bought were twenty something & six – but if you would buy me what you buy for yourself, ma chère, c'a serait parfait.

Forgive me for asking this. Ill never do it again. And please dont hesitate to refuse your

Darned for the last time

Katherine

P.S. I take 4's in shoes!

MS ATL. *Adam* 300, 93.

To Alfred A. Knopf,[1] 10 January 1921

Villa Isola Bella | Garavan |Menton
France
10
i
1921

Dear Mr Knopf,

Very many thanks for your letter and for the perfectly charming Borzoi book.[2] I have read it with great interest & pleasure. Its a delightful idea – to give a party for your authors & invite their readers to come, too, and just what the readers long to have happen – – –

I hope you are a little bit unduly pessimistic about my book.[3] If I may say so – it has had a very good press indeed over here – and there is every sign that it is a biggish success. Would it be worth while my sending you a few of the particularly favourable notices?

I must say frankly I don't think "Bliss" deserved so much notice. I hope my next one will be a different affair altogether. I wish "Bliss" were better – for all that.

With Best Wishes to you for the New Year

Yours faithfully
Katherine Mansfield

Alfred A Knopf, Esq
220 West Forty Second Street
New York.

MS Texas. Cited *Exhibition*, 46.

---

[1] Alfred A. Knopf (1892–1984) was born in New York, and graduated from Columbia University in 1912. In 1915 he began a publishing firm under his own name, and soon acquired a reputation

for the quality of his authors, both American and foreign, and for the emphasis he placed on handsome book production. He had met KM in the summer of 1913, at Dan Rider's bookshop off St. Martin's Lane, a gathering place for writers. (See *CLKM*, I, 334).

[2] Knopf's distinctive publisher's device was a Russian long-haired greyhound running. The book he sent KM would have been *The Borzoi 1920*, being a sort of record of five years publishing. This was a bibliographical survey of books published by Knopf since the establishment of the firm five years before.

[3] Knopf published *Bliss, and Other Stories* in February 1921, in sheets supplied by Constable.

To J. M. Murry, 11 January 1921

VILLA ISOLA BELLA | GARAVAN | MENTON A/M
11.I.1921

My precious darling,

I shall never forget your beautiful gesture in handing me that letter.[1] I read it and I drove home with you and you are still here. You have been in every moment of the day; it is as though you had gone up to the mountains for a long afternoon. I have never loved you so. No, my precious, until now I did not know what it was to love *like this*. This peace and this wonderful certainty are quite new.

Take care of yourself. Depend on me. Tell me anything, and feel that I am with you. My one drop of 'sorrow' is that I am not helping you. But you *know* how I am with you. Oh, my Veen, how happy you have made me! I sit here on the striped couch & Rib does sentry go up & down the back of it with the feather for a gun and I am still possessed by memories of my darling. On the red box there is the snail shell. It said to me this evening: "am I not one of your treasures, too". Darling little snail shell – found by Boge – perfect little blue flowers brought by him. Oh, my Heart, how can I ever thank you for everything! Wig.

This exquisite paper has just arrived. I must send a note to the Villa Louise – to impress them . . . Bogey, our photographs are *very* important

. . .

MS ATL. LJMM 622–3.

[1] Murry left that day for a short trip to England, and his departing letter told her: 'I am going away with absolute peace in my heart, and the knowledge certain & sure, like a warm thing curled up inside me, that I love you more, far more than ever. With all its horrors these three weeks have been a taste of our true serenity' (Murry, 321).

To J. M. Murry, 12 January 1921

VILLA ISOLA BELLA | GARAVAN | MENTON A/M
12.I.1921

My precious Boge,

It has been a perfect day. I was out on the terrasse from ten o'clock on: Marie even brought me my dejeuner there sur une petite table. I wished you had been there to share it.

I sent you a wire this afternoon, for it will be so long before my letters arrive & I don't want you to be without a sign.

Yes, I *miss* you, my darling. But tout va bien & I am working & that marvellous serenity is unchanged.

Marie has got her bitter oranges. A small pot of the confiture is to be sent to Monsieur. Now that she knows "us" I think she will turn into our nurse.

When I emerge from my work it is to follow my darling's journey. I see him take out his pocketbook, put it up, read, (but I never can think of him asleep – ça me serre le coeur). And now you go up the gangway & now you are on deck. Oh, my beloved Veen!

Goodbye.

Your
Wig.

MS ATL. *LJMM*, 623.

To Sydney Schiff, 12 January 1921

VILLA ISOLA BELLA | GARAVAN | MENTON A/M
XII.I.1921

Dear Sydney

I promised J.M.M. yesterday before he left that I would without fail write to you & say how sorry he was to have seen so little of you and Violet. "I wish to God the others had gone & they had stayed", said he. "I felt we could have talked no end if only we'd been alone." And: "Be sure to give my love to them both."

I am wondering if you are in your Villa yet; I hope you are. And I have a feeling that drive was too long for Violet. It tired her. You were tired, my dear, weren't you? And not a bit in the mood for Mary C's quick chatter . . . I wish I could have prevented it.

Its delightful to know you are both near. I hope we shall meet soon.

Yours ever

Katherine M.

MS BL.

To J. M. Murry, [13 January 1921]

VILLA ISOLA BELLA | CARAVAN | MENTON A/M

Dear Bogey

Thank you for your little letter 'en route'. Dear Bandol![1] I should like to see it again. Do you really imagine those days . . . incorrigible optimist!

All is as usual here. My cough is a great deal worse pour le moment. It has never ceased, so it seems, since yesterday morning. But perhaps it will be quieter today. Its devastating.

The more I think of it the more I hope the Athenaeum shuts down. But I *feel* it wont. Bonwick is now going to prove what he is capable of . . . I mustn't let my fancy run on.

Lebe wohl

Wig.

MS ATL. LJMM 623–4.

[1] Murry had referred to their happy months together in Bandol in 1916. KM, more concerned with their recent difficulties, copied in a notebook the following day a sentence from Keats to Fanny Brawne, Aug. 1820: 'To be happy with you seems such an impossibility. It requires a luckier Star than mine . . . The world is too brutal for me' (*Journal* 1954, 237).

To Orlo Williams,[1] 17 January 1921

VILLA ISOLA BELLA | CARAVAN | MENTON A/M

17
I
1921

Dear Mr Orlo Williams,

Will you forgive me for having delayed so long to thank you for the delightful small book. The truth is I *did* write to you, but just before I sat down to do so I re-read your sympathetic note and away flew my pen in answer in a terrible way that exiles pens have of flying. I quite forgot that I'd only met you twice or thrice at luncheon – I only remembered that you had said you knew the unhappiness of separation & the happiness of being together & sympathised with Murry and me.

Before I knew where I was I found myself telling you what it *did* mean to us . . . which wasn't at all the way to repay a kindness.

But sympathy is so rare – so awfully rare – it went to my head –

I want to tell you how much I admired your story *The Wild Thing*.[2] Perhaps Murry told you. It made me want very much to see other stories of yours.

I re-read '*Gusev*'[3] the other day – Oh, Heavens! What a marvellous thing this writing is!

With my sincerest thanks

Yours ever
Katherine Mansfield.

MS Cains.

[1] Orlo Williams (1883–1967), educated at Eton and Balliol College, Oxford, became a successful Civil Servant, served in the Middle East during the First World War, and later published extensively fiction, criticism, translation, and parliamentary history. His *The Good Englishman* was published in 1920.

[2] Williams contributed reviews to the *Athenaeum*, and his story 'The Wild Thing' was published there on 3 Dec. 1920.

[3] Chekov's story 'Gusev' was translated in both *The House with the Mezzanine Floor* (1917) by S. S. Koteliansky and Gilbert Cannan, and Constance Garnett's *The Witch and Other Stories* (1918).

To Richard Murry, 17 January 1921

VILLA ISOLA BELLA | GARAVAN | MENTON A/M
17.I.1921.

My dear Richard,

If you knew how I love hearing from you and how honoured I am by your confidence! I want you to feel I am a *real* sister to you. Will you? Remember that here is your sister Katherine who is not only interested in everything that you do but who wants to be made use of. Treat me as a person you have the right to ask things of. Look here – if you want anything & you haven't the dibs – come to me *bang* off and if I have the money you're welcome to it – without a single hesitation. Ill always be truthful with you, that's a promise. Ill be dead straight with you in everything.

Why I am saying all this is (I see your eyes rolling and your hair rising in festoons of amazement and I dont care!) Well, why I am saying it is that we "artists" are not like ordinary people and there are times when to know we have a fellow workman who's ready to do all in his power, because he loves you and believes in you, is a nice comfortable feeling. I adore *Life* but my experience of the world is that its pretty terrible. I hope yours will be a very different one dear old boy, but just in case . . . you'd like to shout Katherine at any moment – here she is – See?

Having got that off my ches' (which is at this moment more like a chest of super-sharp-edged cutlery) let me say how I appreciate all you feel about *craft*. Yes, I think youre absolutely right. I see your *approach* to painting as very individual. Emotion for you seems to grow out of deliberation – looking long at a thing. Am I getting at anything right? In the way a thing is made – it may be a tree or a woman or a gazelle or a dish of fruit – you get your inspiration. This sounds a bit too simple when it is written down & rather like "Professor Leonard The Indian Palmist". I mean something though. Its a very queer thing how *craft* comes into writing. I mean down to details. Par exemple. In Miss Brill I chose not only the length of every sentence, but even the sound of every sentence – I chose the rise and fall of every paragraph to fit her – and to fit her on that day at that very moment. After Id written it I read it aloud – numbers of times – just as one would *play over* a musical composition, trying to get nearer and nearer to the expression of Miss Brill – until it fitted her.

Don't think Im in vain about the little sketch. Its only the method I wanted to explain. I often wonder whether other writers do the same. If a thing has really come off it seems to me there mustn't be one single word out of place or one word that could be taken out. Thats how I AIM at writing. It will take some time to get anywhere near there.

But you know Richard, I was only thinking last night people have hardly begun to write yet. Put poetry out of it for a moment & leave out Shakespeare – now I mean prose. Take the very best of it. Aren't they still cutting up sections rather than tackling the whole of a mind? I had a moment of absolute terror in the night. I suddenly thought of a *living mind* – a whole mind – with absolutely nothing left out. With *all* that one knows how much does one *not* know? I used to fancy one knew all but some kind of mysterious core (or one could). But now I believe just the opposite. The unknown is far far greater than the known. The known is only a mere shadow. This is a fearful thing and terribly hard to face. But it must be faced.

Well, thats enough at a time for you. I hope you're not bored. I long to see the landscape. Am I to be allowed to hang it on my walls to bear me company?

With my love to you
Ever

Katherine.

≈

MS R. Murry, *LKM* II. 88–9.

To J. M. Murry [19 January 1921]

VILLA ISOLA BELLA | CARAVAN | MENTON A/M

Dear Bogey

No post today
Ida brought me a copy of the horrid Daily Mail which says the weather is appaling in London. Do try & see that you dont catch cold. The London climate is *infinitely* {Wednesday | Tuesday}

dangerous. By the way I chanced to read a doctors letter which said that tuberculosis transferred from a wife to a husband or vice versa was so rare as to be absolutely left out of account. It is perhaps the rarest form of contagion. This may reassure you in a mauvais moment.[1]

No news. No change. I hear the walking world go up & down le petit sentier outside. But they don't realise their good their *heavenly* fortune.

Lebe wohl

Wig.

MS ATL. *LJMM*, 624.

---

[1] KM may have had in mind her notebook entry on 12 Aug. 1920, where she recorded Murry's reaction to her coughing. 'And J. is silent, hangs his head, hides his face with his fingers *as though* it were unendurable' (*Journal* 1954, 207).

To Violet Schiff, 19 January 1921

VILLA ISOLA BELLA | GARAVAN | MENTON A/M
19.1.1921

My dear Violet

This morning at about ten o'clock Murry arrived. My telegram saying I would send no more work had frightened him & he caught the next train. He felt there was "something up" and that I must be ill.

I had to let you know . . . I feel *fearfully* sorry for him – overwhelmingly so. I suppose my love is the desire to protect a person who is in such need of protection. I didn't realise, myself, until this morning, the extent of his need. Its strange – so strange that I feel only now I "know" of what human beings are capable.

He is staying for a week, then returning for a week *with Jones* to look after things. Then he comes out here for good. Are you laughing at the idea of "accompanied by Jones"?

Yesterday was one of those days that only come with Sydney and you. It goes on and on in ones mind.

Take care of yourself, my dear. May we meet again soon! The very curtains in this house behave as though they were in the presence of a drama & even the fire looks artificial.

But perhaps that sounds cynical and coldhearted. I don't feel either. Far from it.

But Violet I DO feel blessed in having you two for my friends.

Ever

Katherine.

MS BL. *Adam* 300, 105–6.

To Sydney Waterlow, [27] *January 1921*

VILLA ISOLA BELLA | GARAVAN | MENTON A/M

January 1921.

My dear Sydney

Quite by chance, I learned while talking to J.M.M. that you had received no reply to the letter you sent me in Italy.[1] I answered it. To the best of my memory it was even on the same day. But it was the time of that cursed Postal Strike, and my letter must have miscarried. Friendly letters, letters such as you wrote me, dear Sydney, are so rare — so awfully rare in my life, it grieves me to think I should have appeared unappreciative . . . Oh dear! why does Life make us so timid. I want to tell you Ive always felt such real affection for you; it has always been so very pleasant to hear your "well, Katherine", & I have regretted we have seen so little of each other.

But perhaps, by now, I am talking to no end of an enemy — I hope not . . .

The fact, too that we were cousins. I confess that apart from all else my esprit de famille delighted in that —

Well, here's so very late in the day my thanks & my love to you for the Italian letter.

Katherine.

MS ATL.

---

1 Clearly KM had not seen Waterlow during her summer in England. She had left Ospedaletti in Italy just over a year before, on 21 Jan. 1920.

To Sydney Schiff [c.29 *January* 1921]

VILLA ISOLA BELLA | GARAVAN | MENTON A/M

My dear Sydney

Our letters crossed. And now Jones tells me she did not post mine but delivered it by hand. First — will you tell me how Violet is? I am so anxious for you both. Thank goodness that cold wind has stopped today. Dear woman! Tell her how I sympathise.

There are times when a letter seems to fit the moment almost miraculously. I was . . . tired and not too happy last evening. And the voice of a friend speaking to me so as I understood and reciprocated was more precious than I can say. Thank you.

If I can really do what I want to do — it will be because of the way you and Violet have 'helped' me. I mean that, I mean by 'help', now, something very deep, that would take a lifetime of explanation. But there it is. Its one of the joys of life to be with you and to talk.

Murry is terribly tired. He goes back on Tuesday.[1] Its difficult. Its the morning after an earthquake. One has to go warily, one does not know what is *not* going to shake.

Your understanding of Murry is of course, simply too amazing. It is your great *gift* – this 'finding' the secret of another's being.

My love to you both

Katherine.

MS BL. *Adam* 300, 106.

[1] Murry left for England again early in Feb.

To Anne Drey, [January 1921]

VILLA ISOLA BELLA | GARAVAN | MENTON A/M

Dearest

I have just received your blue & cherry letter. What a perfect colour for a lining – Id rather have one cherry lining than 50 silver ones!

The stockings are so cheap that I can hardly believe my eyes. I thought theyd be at least 25/6 a pair – which was the price I paid for them at good old Swan & Ed.[1] Don't bother about any more – I know how hateful it is to shop for another. I send my cheque with a thousand thanks.

I tremendously enjoyed hearing of the Gwen Otter[2] dinner. I could see it & hear it. Gwen in gold trousers & that long long après midi d'un Faune.[3] Poor dear! It will never be over for me. I have a warm corner in my heart for that woman always. There's something very fine in her & yet she has *missed* Life.

Its terrific news to hear you are working. I am in the middle of a new long story called Family Life which may surprise people a bit.[4] I try & make Family Life so gorgeous – not hatred and cold linoleum – but warmth & hydrangeas –

Addio, mia bella

Katherine.

MS ATL. *Adam* 300, 93.

[1] Swan and Edgar, the large department store on the corner of Regent Street and Piccadilly.
[2] Gwen Otter, who claimed the American Indian princess Pocohontas among her forebears, was for decades a Chelsea hostess to artists of all kinds, 'almost an institution', who 'entertained both the obscure and the famous with equal lavishness' (Douglas Goldring, *South Lodge* (1943), 44).
[3] 'Après midi d'un faune', a poem by Stéphane Mallarmé (1848–92), on which Claude Debussy (1862–1918) based his tone-poem 'Prelude à L'après midi d'un faune' in 1894.
[4] No story with this title survives.

To Anne Drey, [January 1921]

VILLA ISOLA BELLA | GARAVAN | MENTON A/M

My darling Anne

I feel just the same about the drawings as le petit does. Im sure we should have the same point of view. They are simply ravishing. What must it feel like to have a Maman who can make you pictures like these. That grey horse, par exemple, is such a nice horse that you want to give a loud squeak of joy at sight of him and the rabbits, rather coy, as the best rabbits always are make me want to touch em too. Your other two Christmas drawings framed in blue frames hang on the walls. They are a constant delight. Your work gives me always such a deep joy — its all part of my love of you. I mean I have the feeling that I understand your work — without a word spoken, almost fundamentally, or organically — sounds rather funny when I write it. . . . . .

It is indeed good news that stockings are coming down — as they say. In France they are still going up. To make a bad small joke ils montent par les échelles. I should have to paint my jambes & have done with it if I had to pay these prices.

Don't bother to get me any more tho'. Its such a *bore* for you. Heres my cheque.

The garden is full of double pink stocks. Gorgeous flowers, so strong and so sturdy. I wish I could send you an armful.

Say no more about my old book. I must get a new one out — thats what I feel. The others not good enough to stand alone — though its lovely to feel that it gave you a little pleasure.

Give the Blessed Infant a butterfly kiss from me & tell him that hes my *favourite.*I suppose he won't care a straw; he's everybody's favourite. How you must love him to play with. Is he going to be a great laugher? Shall we have a laugh à trois one of these days? How I hope so!

I feel I shall be away for years from England. I can't bear the idea of seeing it again. Yet, somewhere there's always a pinch of feeling for it *when* one is abroad — never otherwise! I prefer to keep the pinch, how-ever. Once I put my toe on Folkestone Pier it goes.

All Blessings be yours darling.

Ever your
Katherine.

MS ATL. *Adam* 300, 94.

To Ottoline Morrell, [late January 1921]

[Villa Isola Bella, Garavan, Menton]

Dearest Ottoline,

Do come! We shall be delighted. But won't you come before 4; it gets dark so soon. I was only wishing to hear from you this morning when lo! the post came.[1]

Yours ever

Katherine.

Postcard Texas.

[1] After arriving in Marseilles in Nov., Lady Ottoline had been staying in Paris, and now passed through the Riviera on her way to Italy.

To ? [early 1921]

[Villa Isola Bella, Garavan, Menton]

Your letters sounded insincere to me; I did not believe them. People *don't write* such things; they only think they do, or they read them in books. But real life is on quite another plane. If I were not ill, I still would have withdrawn from 'the world' because of my hatred of insincerity. It makes me dreadfully uncomfortable and unhappy. I could have answered your letter just in your vein and 'accepted' it, you knowing how I accepted it and I knowing that you knew – but it wouldn't have lasted. It would have been another *cul de sac* relationship. What good would that have been to either of us?

You see – to me – life and work are two things indivisible. It's only by being true to life that I can be true to art. And to be true to life is to be *good, sincere, simple, honest.* I think other people have given you a wrong idea of me, perhaps. I only like to love my friends. I have no time for anything less 'precious'. Friendship *is* an adventure; but do we agree about the meaning of the word 'adventure'? That's so important! That's where I feel we would quarrel. If you came on to *our* boat should we have understood one another?

You must not think I am 'prejudiced' or unfair. I am not. I still wish it were possible; but I cannot, and I won't pretend. Let us really and truly know where we are first. Let us be open with each other and not concealing anything.

MS lacking. *Journal* 1954, 236–7.

To Ottoline Morrell [2 February 1921]

VILLA ISOLA BELLA | GARAVAN | MENTON A/M

My dear Ottoline,

I am very happy to have your cards & to know that you have found Italy so lovely. I have been wondering where you were & hoping, for selfish reasons, that you would come back here. I did long for *one talk* . . . But perhaps that was like my impudence. All the same, I must say that on the last afternoon when you & Julian & Murry & I sat together in that little yellow room with the beetle carpet there were moments when I felt it was like being goldfish in a forgotten – cruelly neglected! – goldfish bowl. Was that nonsense? Was it quite all right, really? Oh, surely not. When I think of all we have lived through – the really precious moments and of all that we have felt & seen it was *melancholy* to be no nearer. It can't be helped, I suppose. And here's to the wonderful times we *have* had – they are unforgettable!

This card Il Trono di Venere[1] is simply divine. What exquisite grace. What beautiful obedience to the movement of the whole. I wish I could see such things.

J.M.M. is still here. He came back, very suddenly, & now he is going to England tomorrow only to arrange to leave for good. – I *dont* know. I hope he will be happy. When he is away – yes – I do miss his COMPANIONSHIP. I miss talking with a man, and its very lonely here when he's in London – for the Mountain & I only agree when we are silent or out of each other's sight! But I mean to leave the Riviera as soon as possible. Ive *turned frightfully* against it & the French. Life seems to me ignoble here. It all turns on money. Everything is money. When I read Balzac I always feel a peculiar odious exasperation because according to him the whole of Life is founded on the question of money. But he is right. It is – for the French. I wish the horrid old Riviera would fall into the sea. Its just like an exhibition where every single sideshow costs another sixpence. But I paid goodness knows what to come in.

Where can one go, I wonder. Italy? Dear Ottoline, do tell me if you find a lovely place in Italy . . . As to England – I never want to see it again. I read J.M.M's letters from Clive and Co.[2] & they horrify me. Did one know all the wrong people? Is that why nobody remains? Not a soul remains to me – not one – except Delamare whom I never knew when I was there . . .

However, one goes on believing. Life *might be* marvellous. One keeps faith with that belief in ones work. Ive been writing of a dance this after-noon & remembering how one polished the floor was so thrilling that everything was forgotten . . .

Please give my love to Julian[3] Goodbye, dear Ottoline.

I rejoice to know you are happy.
Yours ever with love

Katherine.

MS Texas. *LKM* II. 89–90.

[1] Probably a card of the so-called 'Ludovisi Throne', a Greek work of the 5th century BC depicting Venus rising from the sea, in the Museo Nazionale Romano.

[2] KM's brief friendship with the art critic Clive Bell (1881–1964) had soured by mid-1917 because of his propensity for gossip – "What wretched little bones has Clive been stealing from grubby little plates & tossing to his friends now. . . . He is an appalling creature' (*CLKM* I. 308–9). She continued to associate him with much that she disliked in the Bloomsbury 'group'.

[3] Miranda Seymour, *Ottoline Morrell: Life on the Grand Scale* (1992), 431, records that 'the 14 year old Julian refused to visit KM with her mother', and 'an angry scene' ensued.

To Richard Murry, 3 February 1921

VILLA ISOLA BELLA | GARAVAN | MENTON A/M.
February 3rd 1921

My dear Richard,

I dont suppose you really realise what your two last letters to me have been like. Well, I must say Ive *never* had any letters to beat them, and when you are in Paradise I hope the Lord will present you with two brushes of comets hair in token of appreciation for same. Paint brushes, of course I mean. In the meantime je vous serre le main bien fort as they say, for them . . . I'll take em in order.

The first, I must say, was what the French newspapers call un espèce de bowl-over! Your interview with Fate (not forgetting his Secretary) written on that beautiful leming coloured paper was simply a proof of what you could do at this imaginative short story writing if you really got going. Richard Murry enters the ring & shows Kid Mansfield How to Do it. I leave the drawing of the scene to you – me, in black welvet shorts with a crochet lace collar and you in a kind of zebra tights costume . . . Well, dear old boy you wiped the ring with me. Not only that I do really think that things have taken a Turn and that Jack and I have seen our worst days. Hope so, at any rate.

I think your Easter plan is a first rate one. Its down in my diary as a certainty. Do lets bring it off! Dont worry about the fare. When the time comes just put your toospeg brush, pyjames and a collar (for Sundays & fête days) into a handkerchief & Ill send along the ticket & a dotted line for you to follow. Seriously a rucksack is all you'll need. My grandpa[1] said a man could travel all over the world with a clean pair of socks and a rook rifle. At the age of 70 odd he started for England thus equipped but Mother took fright & added a handkerchief or two. When he returned he was shorn of everything but a large watering can which he'd bought in London for his young marrows. I don't suggest him as a Man to be Followed, however. Already, just with the idea of you coming Ive seen you on the terrace – the three of us, talking. Ive packed the picnic basket & weve gone off for the day. Lunch under the olive trees . . . and so on . . . Richard dear, it will be awful if it doesn't come true! We must make it. Jack has a scheme to meet you in Paris & convey you to and from The Louvre on your way.

Well, I now come to your Letter II containing your photograph. I love having it. You have, as Koteliansky used to say, an "extremely nice face", Richard. Being fond of you as I am I read into it all sorts of signs of the future painter . . . I believe they are all there.

My honest opinion is that if there is a person going on the right lines – you are he. I can't tell you how right I feel you are. It seems to me like this. Here is painting, and here is life. We can't separate them. Both of them have suffered an upheaval extraordinary in the last few years. There is a kind of tremendous agitation going on still, but so far anything that has come to the surface seems to have been experimental or a fluke – a lucky accident. I believe the only way to *live* as artists under these new conditions in art and life is to put everything to the test for ourselves. We've got, in the long run, to be our own teachers. There's no getting away from that. We've got to win through by ourselves. Well, as I see it, the only way to do that honestly, dead truthfully, shirking nothing and leaving nothing out, is to put everything to the test. (Your desire for technical knowledge is a kind of profound *symbol*.) Not only to face things, but really to find out of what they are composed. How can we know where we are, otherwise? How can we prevent ourselves being weak in certain places? To be *thorough*, to be *honest*, I think if artists were really thorough & honest they would save the world. Its the lack of those things & the reverse of them that [are] putting a deadly blight on life. Good work takes upon itself a Life – bad work has death in it.

Well, (forgive me if Im dull, old boy) your longing for technical knowledge seems to me profoundly what an artist OUGHT to feel today. Its a kind of deep sign of the times – rather the Zeitgeist – thats the better word. Your generation & mine too has been 'put off' with imitations of the real thing and we're bound to react violently if we're sincere. This takes so long to write & it sounds so heavy. Have I conveyed what I mean to even? You see I too have a passion for technique. I have a passion for making the thing into a *whole* if you know what I mean. Out of technique is born real style, I believe. There are no short cuts.

Look out! I mustn't get off the lines. Ive just read your last pages again. An aesthetic emotion is what we feel in front of *a work of art* – one doesn't feel an aesthetic emotion about a thing, but about its artistic representation. Example: Richard Murry in front of Portrait of Madame Manet.2

Oh Richard! Believe me! I think you're terribly right to feel as you do and not to pretend. Only, dear old boy, the price you pay for your honesty is you don't have any false thrills about the pose & the form & the vision. I don't mean the chaps in your class are insincere, but evidently you are coming to it in a different way. Don't forget that intellectually you are stages beyond the men you draw with. That makes you critical in a way its very rare to be when one is starting out.

But I wish you were not so far away. I wish the garden gate flew open for you often & that you came in & out & we talked – not as in London – more easily and more happily. I shall pin the sun into the sky for every day of your holiday and at night I shall arrange for a constant supply of the best moonlight.

Well, my fellow worker – lets get on with the job. If its any help to you to know theres someone who believes in you . . . here she is. The House Flag is always flying.

Goodbye for now.

With a whole mountain of love

Katherine

Jack will be in London on Bunday. (sic)

MS R. Murry. *LKM* II. 90–2.

---

¹ Her grandfather Arthur Beauchamp, who frequently moved his large family.

² Edouard Manet (1832–83) painted several pictures of his wife. KM would have seen *Mme. Edouard Manet on a Blue Sofa* at the Jeu de Paumes, the Louvre.

To Alexander Kay, 6 February 1921

VILLA ISOLA BELLA | GARAVAN | MENTON A/M.
6 ii 1921

Dear Mr. Kay,

May I please have my passbook sent to me as soon as is possible?¹ I am not quite certain what monies I have in the Bank & I must pay out a large amount this month.

I am sitting up proper for the first time today – in bed, still, however. Jack has been over with me. He returned to London this morning, but only to fix up things preparatory to his coming out here permanently. My health is so precarious just now that it seems the only way to make sure he won't be late for the funeral! But one never knows. I feel I shall

tire my audience out & last for goodness knows how many rounds more.
I hope so.

With very best wishes & love

Yours ever
Cathy.

MS Parker.

[1] KM had found out that her passbook had been sent on to Harold Beauchamp for inspection. This may have anticipated the payment of royalties which she did not want her father to know of, as she later opened another account at Barclays Bank, Hampstead.

To Sylvia Lynd, 6 February 1921

VILLA ISOLA BELLA | GARAVAN | MENTON A/M.
February 6th 1921

My dear 'Sylvia Lynd',

I was simply horrified today to open a copy of last week's Athenaeum & to read that disgusting review of your novel.[1] What can I say? I had to give up all my reviewing work weeks ago – in November, but nevertheless I feel I must apologise that a paper which Ive *anything* to do [with] should treat a delicate sensitive artist in such a way. Murry had to come over here suddenly a short time ago on account of my health; he only returned today. He was with me when the post arrived and shared my dismay and anger. He begged me to include him in my telegram. I scarcely know Mr Lynd, but I felt that a telegram to him might reach you sooner & I wanted to reach you *at once*.

My dear fellow–writer, I would give anything for this not to have happened. I long to read your novel . . . Don't bother to answer this, but please accept my admiration and love.

Katherine Mansfield.

PC ATL.

[1] A dismissive, unsigned review of *A Swallow Dive* appeared in the *Athenaeum*, 4 Feb. 1921.

To J. M. Murry, 7 February 1921

VILLA ISOLA BELLA | GARAVAN | MENTON A/M.
7.II.1921

Dear Bogey
I haven't a postcard but this will serve. All goes well here. I mean there is no change at all.

Try not to rush things. Dont hurry back. If you want to stay longer Ill arrange to go away as soon as I am "up & about again", as they say. I hope your journey was not too horrid.

Yours ever

Wig.

MS ATL. *LJMM*, 625.

To Michael Sadleir, 7 February 1921

VILLA ISOLA BELLA | GARAVAN | MENTON A/M.
7.II.1921

Dear Michael Sadleir

I am v. sorry not to have answered your letter sooner. I have been – I *am* ill, & am only just at the sitting up stage. I am glad to hear that Bliss has done fairly well. It has brought me an extraordinary number of letters. One, by the way, I enclose.

My new book won't be ready until the end of this month. When it is I shall give it to my agent with instructions to send it first to you for consideration. It will be long short stories: Ill *never* write a real live novel.

I must congratulate you upon the great success yours is having.

Yours sincerely

Katherine Mansfield.

MS Targ.

To Constance Garnett,[1] 8 February 1921

VILLA ISOLA BELLA | GARAVAN | MENTON A/M.
8.II.1921

Dear Madam,

As I laid down my copy of War & Peace tonight I felt I could no longer refrain from thanking you for the whole other world that you have revealed to us through these marvellous translations from the Russian. Your beautiful industry ends Madam in making us almost ungrateful. We are almost inclined to take for granted the fact that the new book is translated by Mrs Constance Garnett. Yet my generation (I am 32) and the younger generation owe you more than we ourselves are able to realise. These books have changed our lives, no less. What would it be like to be without them!

I am only one voice among so many – I do appreciate the greatness of your task, the marvel of your achievement. I beg you to accept my admiration and my deepest gratitude.

Yours faithfully

Katherine Mansfield.

MS Texas. Cited *Exhibition*, 46.

[1] Constance Garnett (1862-1946) was the most important translator of Russian fiction for Mansfield's generation. She translated numerous volumes of Chekhov, Dostoevsky, Gogol, Turgenev, and Tolstoy.

To A. R. Orage,[1] *[9 February 1921]*

[Villa Isola Bella, Garavan, Menton]

Dear Orage,

This letter has been on the tip of my pen for many months.

I want to tell you how sensible I am of your wonderful unfailing kindness to me in the "old days." And to thank you for all you let me learn from you. I am still – more shame to me – very low down in the school. But you taught me to write, you taught me to think; you showed me what there was to be done and what not to do.

My dear Orage, I cannot tell you how often I call to mind your conversation or how often, in *writing*, I remember my master. Does that sound impertinent? Forgive me if it does.

But let me thank you, Orage – *Thank you for everything*. If only one day I might write a book of stories good enough to "offer" you . . . If I *don't* succeed in keeping the coffin from the door you will know this was my ambition.

Yours in admiration and gratitude

Katherine Mansfield

I haven't said a bit of what I wanted to say. This letter sounds as if it was written by a screw driver, and I wanted it to sound like an admiring, respectful, but warm piping beneath your windows. I'd like to send my love, too, if I wasn't so frightened. K.M.

MS lacking. Cited Mairet, 121; Alpers 1980, 325.

[1] Alfred Richard Orage (1875-1934), whom KM first knew as the gifted editor of the *New Age*, the lively Fabian weekly, when she took her story 'The Child who was Tired' to his office. He published it at once, on 24 Feb. 1910. A further nine of her stories were published in the same year. She was strongly influenced by Orage as editor and by her friendship with his difficult mistress, Beatrice Hastings, and she lived with them for a time in the summer of 1910. Her closeness with both lessened after she took up with Murry and began to write for *Rhythm* and the *Blue Review*. Under his pseudonym 'R. H. Congreve', Orage ran a savage series of satirical pieces on KM as 'A Fourth Tale for Men Only', the *New Age*, 2 May–6 June 1912. As 'Mrs Marcia Foisacre', she was put down

for her taste, her intelligence, and her morality. KM was again writing for the *New Age* in 1917, however, and although she came to dislike Hastings bitterly, her affection and respect for Orage remained. He later became an important influence on her life as an evangelist of Gurdjieff.

To Sydney Waterlow, 9 February 1921

VILLA ISOLA BELLA | GARAVAN | MENTON A/M.
9 II 1921

My dear Sydney,

Don't feel bound to answer this, but I can't *enjoy* a letter as I did yours without saying thank you . . . And I want to tell you a queer thing. You know where you speak of your "superiority of apprehension" . . . God knows we have seen little enough of each other, & I hadn't (to be frank) the faintest idea that you thought of me other than as a "cold aloof little creature" − that you shared the general opinion, in fact. And yet, just before Christmas I wrote a very long story & YOU were my reader. I hope that doesn't sound impertinent. I confess the impression was that you enjoyed the story, *saw* it, *felt* it, as I did − in a quite special way that outsiders wouldn't appreciate. I even had a mental picture of you sitting in an armchair, reading it. It is called, in case you should ever see it "The Daughters of the Late Colonel" . . . and Squire is going to publish it in The Mercury.

Let me salute you, Sydney, through my story; let us be friends because of it. Good Heavens if you knew how pleasant it is to know there is someone who cares to tell you he makes his fire first arranging the twigs in a pyramid, & that the logs are "self cut". I share that delicious first moment & while I warm my fingers I forget these nasty foreign palms . . . Your room sounds lovely.

I shall never live in England again. I recognise Englands admirable qualities, but we simply don't get on. We have nothing to say to each other; we are always meeting as strangers. Murry, on the other hand is *made* for England and I am certain he will not remain abroad for long. I understand that very well in him. No, Ill go finally to some place like Yalta & build a little house at Oreanda[1] − if I *do* succeed in keeping the coffin from the door for so long.

What are you going to do in the immediate future, I wonder. Where are you going to live. And I wonder if you are happy and what you really think about Life & if you have friends − real friends.

I am sitting up in bed in an ugly little room with a huge dead clock in it & a pink screen worked with a needlework picture. *Scène*: Game of billiards *sur l'herbe fraiche*. Lady with die-away look being kissed by military party & very impertinent dog looking on. At moments it seems to me that ALL French literature is in that picture. The wind is blowing. Strange shadows fly over the walls & ceiling from the palm outside, and these quick shadows are awfully beautiful . . .

Lebe wohl
With love from

Katherine.

MS ATL. *Selected*, 198–9.

¹ KM is apparently thinking of the years Chekhov spent at Yalta, as well as either the house he build in the Crimea or the small house he bought in Kuchokoi in 1898. Oreanda was where he took Olga Knipper, and is mentioned in his story 'The Lady with the Dog'.

To J. M. Murry, [10 February 1921]

VILLA ISOLA BELLA | GARAVAN | MENTON A/M.
Thursday.

Dear Bogey,

This letter has come for you. That's all the post there was. As soon as you know your plans you might send me a wire – will you? Then I shall know when to stop writing. I have an idea you will be away a good deal longer than you arranged for. Please tell me straight out if this is so, and don't bother de faire des explications . . . Find I can't get a room in Bordighera for weeks . . .

I hope things are going well with you & that Bonwick et Cie are not putting too much pressure on you.

All serene here. I am still in bed, of course.

Yours
Wig.

MS ATL. *LJMM*, 624.

To J. M. Murry, [11 February 1921]

[Menton]

NO NEED WHATEVER FOR YOU TO HURRY BACK TAKE YOUR TIME BUT PLEASE KEEP ME INFORMED OF YOUR PLANS ALL SERENE BORDIGHERA OFF
WIG

Telegram ATL.

To Sylvia Lynd [c.12 February 1921]

VILLA ISOLA BELLA | GARAVAN | MENTON A/M.

My dear Sylvia Lynd

Your letter and your book made a sort of *Fête de Saint Sylvie* of yesterday. Your lovely little letter brought you back to me so clearly – very radiant, in air blue and primrose, sitting for a moment in time on my small sofa – the one which in private life is known as 'the stickleback' . . .

Thank you very much-indeed-please for The Swallow Dive. It is full of the most beautiful things. You turn to Beauty like a flower to the light (I must put it in the third person. Its easier to say.) She fills and glows with it and is like a shining transparent cup of praise . . . Early morning light, I feel, with the grass still pearled, and long, slender shadows . . . If you were here I should like to say . . . "Caroline crying after she had heard of Ethel's engagement", "her moment of leaving her Aunt Mildred's house for ever", "her top of the bus ride",[1] her pink cotton frock drifting through July in London. As to The Fall of Antioch, I *hear* it, *smell* it, *know* it as if I had played in it. But above all *Ashleem!*[2] Your early morning description of Ashleem, Miss, took away my breff.

Forgive an impudent woman. Shes very very serious really. And because we are *fellow-workmen* may I say I think you sometimes know more than you say & sometimes you say less than you know . . . Does that convey anything?

I find my great difficulty in writing is to learn to submit. Not that one ought to be without resistance – of course I dont mean that. But – when I am writing of 'another' I want so to lose myself in the soul of the other that I am not . . .

I wish we could have a talk about writing one of these days.

Was there really a new baby in your letter? Oh dear some people have all the babies in this world . . . And as sometimes happens to us women just before your letter came I found myself tossing a little creature up in the air and saying: "Whose boy are you?" But he was far too shadowy, too far away to reply.

So tell me about *your* baby – will you? And when I do get out of this old bed I shall drive to the lace shop & buy a cobweb to make a cap for himher. Farewell. May the Fairies attend you. No, dear woman, it is grim work – having babies. Accept my love and my sympathy.

Yours ever
Katherine Mansfield

MS ATL. *LKM* II. 92–3.

---

[1] Events in the life of the novel's heroine, Caroline, the daughter of poor parents, who is brought up by relatives. She is variously distressed by the engagement of her cousin Ethel to a much older

man, leaves her aunt's home to chance her luck as an actress, and takes a bus ride during which she is flattered by a young writer.

2 Caroline finds a small part in a sumptuously described production of a historical play set in Antioch, and later spends time at Ashleem, an artists' colony in Ireland.

To J. M. Murry, [13 February 1921]

[Menton]

BEG YOU NOT TO HASTEN YOUR RETURN TAKE YOUR TIME I AM MUCH BET-
TER WRITTEN TODAY WIG

Telegram ATL.

To Sydney Schiff [? mid-February 1921]

VILLA ISOLA BELLA | GARAVAN | MENTON A/M.

Dear Sydney – dear friend,

Let me add one word to our all too brief conversation this afternoon. Alas! what a plague is Time. No sooner has one begun to *appreciate* what the other is seeing than – its as though, at a turn of the planet, he is whirled away. And just supposing that by some heavenly chance there *was* Immortality the question of the Artist and his Time *won't* be so pressing, so vital, so infinitely important as it is now . . .

It is, I am sure, the Question of Questions. The artist who denies his Time, who turns away from it even as much as the fraction of a hair is false. First, he must be free; that is, he must be controlled by none other than his deepest self, his truest self. And then he must accept Life, he must submit, give himself so utterly to Life that no personal qua personal self remains. Does that convey anything? Its so hard to state. 'Bitterness' is a difficult word for me to disentangle from a sense of personal wrong, a "this is what Life has done to me". But I know you don't mean that. You mean a bigger thing – the gesture with which one turns aside today from what might have been, what ought to have been. There is humour in it, of a kind, and inevitable sadness . . .

But let me confess, Sydney, I feel something else as well – and that is *Love*. But thats so difficult to explain. Its not pity or rainbows or anything up in the air. Perhaps its *feeling* FEELING.

Goodbye. Heres my hand in devoted friendship to you and to Violet. May we meet again soon!

Katherine.

MS BL, *LKM* II. 94.

To Richard Murry (? mid-Feb. 1921)

[Villa Isola Bella, Garavan, Menton]

Dearest Richard,

Just a word to accompany our telegram. It's superb news[1] and I am flying the Heron flag from my window . . . And you deserved it beyond words. Jack sent me a note with your postcard. You can imagine how bucked he is. Now I long to know 'what nex'?' But that will have to wait, I suppose until Big Brother comes back from his journey to England. It does not much matter. In the meantime I shall go on seeing you emerging from the river with the Scholarship (like a very friendly crocodile) clasped in your arms and a card round its neck – *this size £160.*

With love, Riccardo mio, and 'May good fortune fall ever more deeply in love with thee'.

Yours ever,

Katherine.

I enclose a little photo taken in the garden. Do you like it? Brother and sister of the painter, R.M., you observe.

R. Murry. *Adam* 370–5, 28.

[1] Richard had received word of a London County Council Scholarship to the Slade School of Art.

To Richard Murry, [17 February 1921]

VILLA ISOLA BELLA | GARAVAN | MENTON A/M.
Thursday.

What's this Ive been hearing about you Riccardo Murryo.

The Big Bear has written to say that he has seen the Little Bear's drawings & he's persuaded hes the *real thing* & hes made very Great and Important Progress.

If you were here Tiny Bear would have to give you a small hug for that or a piece of wild honey out of a hollow tree. (Little Bear: "Yes, thats all the best.")

But it really is thrilling news & I wish I could see them too.

A big fat Catholic priest has just been to see me, sitting by my bedside in a red plush armchair. I thought, as I listened, and looked *meek*: Richard would have de faire son portrait with cocobutter, lamp black, and a little rich gravy-out-of-the-dish for the cheek bones. But being a perlite little thing, I didn't say it out loud.

(1) Theres a Chinese Magnolia out in the garden. Oh, Sir, you never *see* such a Beauty.

(2) The peach tree is in flower. I noticed it at the same moment as a young bee. The young bee *literally* fell down about 3 feet of air in its astonishment. As for roman hyacinths & violets & gilly flowers they are just bread and butter here.

Im going to get up tomorrow. Please fly the flag. Goodbye little Painter-Brother

Katherine.

MS R. Murry. *Adam* 370–5, 27.

To S. S. Koteliansky,[1] *[19 February 1921]*

VILLA ISOLA BELLA | GARAVAN | MENTON A/M.

What has happened to the inkstand with the elephants on it — mother-of-pearl, inlay — or was it ivory. Some of the inlay had begun to come off; I fancy one of the elephants had lost one eye. And that dim little picture of a snowy landscape hanging on the wall in your room. Where is it now? And where are the kittens and the children and Christ, who looked awfully like a kitten, too, who used to hang in the dining room. And that leather furniture with the tufts of horsehair stuffing coming out. Where are all the hats from the hatstand. And do you remember for how long the bell was broken. Then there was the statue on the stairs, smiling, the fair caretaker, always washing up, the little children always falling through her door.

And your little room with the tiny mirror and the broken window & the piano sounding from outside. Those were very nice teacups — thin — a nice shape, and the tea was awfully good — so hot. "At the Vienna Café[2] there is good bread." And the cigarettes. The packet done up in writing paper you take from your pocket. It is folded so neatly at the ends like a parcel from the chemists.

And then Slatkovsky[3] — his *beard*, his 'glad eye', his sister, who sat in front of the fire and took off her boot. The two girls who came to see him the Classic Day his Father died.

And the view from your window — you remember? The typist sits there & her hat & coat hang in the hall. Now an Indian in a turban walks up that street opposite to the British Museum *quarter.*

It begins to rain. The streets are very crowded. It is dusky. Now people are running downstairs. That heavy outer door slams. And now the umbrellas go up in the street and it is much darker, suddenly. Dear friend — do not think evil of me — forgive me.

Kissienka.

MS BL. *LKM* II. 94–5.

¹ Although it was over a year since KM had written to Koteliansky (see *CLKM* III. 160–2), their friendship survived distance, spells of silence, and his recent irritation that she had lost some of his Chekhov translations. He was now to become a major influence on decisions she took on the treatment of her tuberculosis.

² At 22–4 New Oxford Street, a favourite of KM's since her early years in London.

³ R. S. Slatkowsky, proprietor of the Russian Law Bureau where Koteliansky had worked translating and certifying Russian documents.

To Alice Jones,¹ 23 February 1921

[Villa Isola Bella, Garavan, Menton]
23.II.1921

Dear Mrs Jones,

Here have all these weeks gone by & I have never thanked you for so kindly sending me those papers. Thank you now. It was v. good of you to have gone to the trouble for me.

Although it was inevitable it is sad to think there is no more Athenaeum.² I wish things had fallen out differently. And I never saw your little boy after all. Miss Baker is bringing him a tiny present with best wishes from us both.

Yours sincerely

Katherine Mansfield Murry.

MS Texas.

¹ Murry's secretary at the *Athenaeum*.

² Murry's final number as editor was 11 Feb. 1921. From 19 Feb. the paper continued as an amalgamation, the *Nation and the Athenaeum*, and although it announced that KM would continue reviewing, she did not do so.

To Edward Marsh,¹ 26 February 1921

[VILLA ISOLA BELLA | GARAVAN | MENTON A/M.]
26.ii.1921

Dear Eddie Marsh,

I feel I must write and thank you for the delight of meeting Mrs Belloc Lowndes² this afternoon. I can hardly believe that I met her for the first time today for she is one of those rare *loveable* women whom one's heart goes out to.

Visits from the 'outside world' are small events here. The memory of them, long after they are past goes on reverberating . . . It's late evening

To Violet Schiff [? *late February 1921*]

VILLA ISOLA BELLA | CARAVAN | MENTON A/M.

Dearest Violet,

I was on the point of writing to you this morning when I received your dear letter. How can I say how sorry I am that you should be ill again. Of course I have known you were not at all yourself ever since you came here; your courage couldn't disguise it. But my heart goes out to you; it is dreadful to be losing precious moments. I love you and Sydney deeply, warmly, and I always wish you happiness and freedom from all those things that interfere with your beautiful *understanding* of Life.

It is very good news that you have discovered Doctor Bouchage. He is extremely intelligent and sympathetic – I mean in the 'professional' sense. Hes quite the most satisfactory doctor I have ever met, except my London one. How I should love a long talk with you. Plague take the ugly road that divides us![1] Now I am coming through your gate & I see, in the garden, my two dear friends whose *appearance* apart from all else is always a delight. There is a very long book about you and Sydney – never to be written by me, but its one of those books a writer always has on hand for himself alone.

Dont worry about my old cook, Violet dear. I shall keep this serpent until Murry goes to England in May.[2] I suppose Ive as much peace with her as I should have with anybody. Thanks most awfully for suggesting the other, but to tell the truth, Im frightened of any change for the moment.

Here's Murry come for the Post. "Cant wait. You ought to be ready." What does that mean?

now & there is nobody here but the fire, but the little salon is still sounding faintly with those warm, sincere, generous tones. I loved seeing her.
It was so nice hearing of you from Jack.
With kindest remembrances,
Yours ever,
Katherine Mansfield.

MS Berg.

1 Edward Marsh (1872-1953), Cambridge-educated, Civil Servant, patron of the arts, and editor of *Georgian Poetry*, had assisted Murry financially at the time of *Rhythm's* collapse in late 1912.
2 The novelist with whom KM soon after corresponded. See p. 204.

Goodbye for now. Its very queer to have a grown up son. But there's no doubt Ive got one.

Love and Blessings

Katherine.

MS BL.

---

¹ Roquebrune was only a few miles to the west of Menton, but over a steep and difficult road.
² Clearly there has been a major falling out with Marie, whose praises KM had sung so highly earlier on.

To Dorothy Brett, [1 March 1921]

VILLA ISOLA BELLA | GARAVAN | MENTON A/M.

Dear Brett

You sound so rich in plans, determinations, adventures and '*Revelations*' that I feel my ambling nag can scarce keep pace with such a swift charger. And then – what do you mean exactly by revelations? And how do they beget other revelations? I don't know – I feel mystified . . .

Im sure its an awfully good plan to go into the country for the summer, and what luck to have Sylvia Sullivan¹ to paint. She would be a lovely little creature under a tree, I should think. I feel I have been awfully wanting in kindness to Sylvia Sullivan: Im sure she's simple and very lovable really. But you'll find out in the summer.

Don't blame your parents too much! We *all* had parents. There is only one way of escaping from their influence and that is by going into the matter with yourself – examining yourself & making perfectly sure of their share.

It can be done. One is *NEVER* free until one has done blaming somebody or praising somebody for what is bad & good in one. Don't you feel that? By that I dont mean we ought to live each of us on an island. On the contrary – Life is relationship – its giving & taking – but thats not quite the same as making others *responsible*, is it? There lies the danger. Dont think I underestimate the enormous power that parents can have. I dont. Its staggering – its titanic. After all they are real giants when we are only table high & they act according. But like everything else in Life – I mean all suffering, however great – we have to get over it, to cease from harking back to it, to grin & bear it & to hide our wounds. More than that and far more true is we have to find the *gift* in it. We cant afford to waste such an expenditure of feeling; we have to learn from it – and we DO, I most deeply believe come to be thankful for

it. By saying we cant afford to waste – – feeling I sound odious & cyni-
cal. I don't feel it. What I mean is – *everything must be accepted.*
But I run on – and Im dull. How lovely your Down country sounded.
Larks, too!

I am only on nodding acquaintance with Spring. We talk from the
window. But she looks from this distance fairer than ever, more radiant,
more exquisite. It is marvellous to know the earth is turned to the light.
Murry is very well. He looks and sounds happy. I don't see a great deal
of him as Im finishing a book & he's terribly busy. I wonder what you
think of the fat Nation or the thin Athenaeum[2] – like Jack Spratt & his
wife.[3] Fare well. Be happy!

K.M.

MS Newberry. *LKM* II. 95–6.

1 The wife of Murry's friend, J. W. N. Sullivan.
2 After the *Nation* had merged with the *Athenaeum* at the end of Jan., the first section was still
concerned more with politics and public affairs, the second and thinner section with literature and
the arts.
3   Jack Sprat could eat no fat
     His wife could eat no lean.
                    (rhyme first recorded in the mid-seventeenth century)

To Ida Baker [8 March 1921]

[Villa Isola Bella, Garavan, Menton]
Tuesday.

This is just a note to let you know that tout va bien à la maison.[1] It is
the late afternoon of an exquisite day. That heavy evening rain that
made water spouts of Jack's trousers fell like a blessing upon the garden.
When I went out today the air smelt like moss, and there was a bee to
every wallflower. The peach leaves are like linnet wings; the branches of
the fig are touched with green, the bush of may is just not in flower. I
had to lift up the daffodils & set them on their legs again and to give a
finger to the reclining freezias. But nothing had come to harm. As to that
white rose bush over the gate & the gas meter it is sprinkled with thousands of tiny satin fine clusters. This is a darling little garden when one
can get out of ones shell & look at it. But what does it profit a man to
look at anything if he is not *free?*[2] Unless one is free to offer oneself up
wholly and solely to the pansy – one receives nothing. Its promiscuous
love instead of a living relationship – a dead thing. But there it is – And
my gland is a great deal more swollen for some reason. The blood goes
on tapping squeezing through like a continual small hammering and all
that side of my head is numb. Its a vile thing.

I hope you had a good journey. Will you please wire me immediately if you want any money & Ill wire it to you., I am now v. serious. Don't go to other people first. I can so easily overdraw for now: I dont care a button. But you must feed properly in London, eat nourishing food – not scones & coffee, and you must take taxis. Dont buy things in bags & eat them. Make Violet cook you porridge, bacon & eggs & toast for breakfast. That climate is the devil. And wear a thick scarf when you go out & change your shoes & stockings when you come in. And burn the anthracite. And get people to come & see you if you want to see them & make Violet cook for them. I feel you will never be sensible enough to keep warm, dry shod and fed. I have no confidence in you.

I wish I were back in that Hampstead house, wafted to the top landing, allowed to linger on the stairs to look out of the windows to see if the lemon verbena is still alive. It should have been a perfect little house: it never came to flower. And the view of the willows – bare now, and the room that was mine – so lovely. The light was always like the light in a pale shell.

Tell me what happens. Take things easy. I beg you to wire me for money without hesitating. Dont work too hard.

Try and be happy; be sure to keep well

Katherine.

MS BL. *MLM*, 157–8.

[1] Ida had left Menton a few days earlier, to return to London and arrange the removal from Portland Villas.
[2] Cf. Mark 8: 32: 'For what shall it profit a man, if he shall gain the whole world, and lose his own soul?'

To Ida Baker, [11 March 1921]

[Villa Isola Bella, Garavan, Menton]
Friday night.

Your telegram re the house arrived today. I like your habit of sending telegrams with windows in them. I *saw* Athenaeum. Speaking of windows, look out, in the evening for the little stray, will you? I feel if he's alive he may come back on a moonbeam. A box from The Printemps came, too. The veil is exquisite. Thank you. Saw Bouchage today & am going to see Le Blanc,[1] chirurgien, with him tomorrow, to get the latters advice about not cutting, but puncturing this gland. This is an operation as simple as an intramuscular injection. It is done with a large needle & nobody is any the worse for it. I think its a good idea. Ill let you know what they decide on. Any move is a good move if one is in prison. But one learns at grim cost that its only the prisoner who NEVER gets tired of trying to escape. There's been a terrific East wind today. Positive scythes hurtling through the air. Good old Marie II broke a windy in her excitement. Can't you imagine the unholy joy of Marie I? But M. Allasena has of course leapt into the breach. I shant want you to hurry for any sort of reason because of this gland. I am now serious: I mean that.

At 9 a.m. today I met Bouchage at the clinic of Le Blanc the surgeon & after some consultation the gland was punctured and a large quantity of pus removed. It was very skilfully done. Bouchage was most kind and helpful. He saw me off the premises & even drove back with me . . . I feel rather tired but Im glad its done. It will have to be repeated, this small operation, two or three times. But now one knows the worst, theres nothing to mind about it. Heres something for your amusement. Marie was at market, Jack ranging the streets for a voiture, I trying to dress in haste, when *Jinnie* came in from mass, to *be with me* (!) while I was alone. And of course she simply delayed me tidying up & so on. Finally she kissed me & said "I shall pray for you, Katie dear." I feel almost revolted by this.

Excuse this egoism. I feel its awfully stupid to make a fuss about une affaire si mineure. There wont even be an honourable scar!
Yours
Katherine.

MS BL.

1 Georges Leblanc, a Menton surgeon.

To Ida Baker, [13 March 1921]

[Villa Isola Bella, Garavan, Menton]
(Confidential)
Sunday.
I really must tell you this or jump out of bed or out of the window. You'll appreciate it so. I paid the surgeon on the nail yesterday. That was all right. I expected to. Only 100. But Jack came down & paid the cocher. When I said Id paid the surgeon he replied "The cocher is mine.I agreed on the price 20 francs beforehand". Just now – making out the weeks bills he asked me for 11 francs for the carriage – half, plus a 2 franc tip! I think its awful to have to say it. But fancy not paying for your wifes carriage to & from the surgery! Is that simply extraordinary or am I? I really am staggered. I think it is the meanest thing I ever heard of. Its not the fact which is so queer but the lack of fine feeling. I suppose if

one fainted he would make one pay 3d for a 6d glass of sal volatile and 1d on the glass. That really does beat Father.

Things are serene otherwise. My head hurts but not more than is to be expected. Cousin Lou[1] has been in today. Shes infinitely kind and affectionate. In fact she lavishes kindness on me in an old fashioned family way.

The old villain is being as sweet as sugar. Hangs up my dresses, puts away my hats, brings up supper for 2 into this room without a murmur. I feel like Koteliansky when he says: "Let her be beaten – simply – but to death!" I hope to hear from you tomorrow.

Dont rush things. Keep well & be happy!
ALL IS WELL

Katherine.

MS BL. *MLM*, 158–9.

---

[1] Connie Beauchamp's sister.

To Ida Baker, [14 March 1921]

[Villa Isola Bella, Garavan, Menton]

The apprentice just came to be paid 80 francs for the hat. Had we paid? She swore no. So I paid. But you'll remember.
Monday.

This is in answer to your letter. About the house – I regret it. I often think of it but its too painful to dwell upon. If I were rich Id buy it. But I suppose that would be foolish . . . However.

Jacks clothes. (a) He tells me they were arranged in a certain order to be called for by Arthur. What A. does not take had better be kept. Perhaps if there is time youd send him a list.

(b) Please store furniture in my name.

(c)   Dont store kitchen lino or those trays.

(d)   Give V. the bango of course with my love. I wld like – and I think it would be right to give her all we are selling. ⟨In fact what about seeing what price it will fetch, wiring me the price & then giving it to V & Ill pay Jack.⟩ NO. Dont do that. We cant. Ill make it up to V. one day as soon as I can. But of course let her have what she wants for a song.

(e)   Shepherdess had better be thrown in the dustbin.

(f)   Yes, I want Mother's photograph *very much*. The last one of her. Send it – will you? I am always wanting it.

(g)   What the large file of papers & the typed sheets is and are I don't know. They'd better be stored. The brown photographs are Jacks – to go with his papers.

Important

If you find a Fry's Chocolate box the one I had in Italy. For Gods sake keep it & bring it over. It is full of papers in my & Kots writing. *Please do tell me about this.* It must not be stored. As to the Athenaeums, Nations & Je ne Parle Pas Jack says they are to be kept. Is that possible? I *detest* this habit of keeping old papers.

I note Brett has been up. She sent Jack a most typical letter t'other day. He was immensely charmed. It was all reverence & a kind of tender fear. "*Master*" and a looking after *their* child – Arthur. You know he, Jack, will marry her one day. It would be an ideal marriage. She worships him and her flattery, reverence, adoration are just what he needs from a wife. Also he can lay down the law to her on art and life to his heart's desire. I *know* they will marry. Cant you hear the proposal? And cant you see Jack with Lord Esher,[1] his father-in-law? Also Brett's £550 – which is bound to be more! I long to have this happen. Id send such a nice present & Id go and have tea with them – joyfully.

Roger[2] sounds nice. What does he look like? Not like his Da, I hope. No, I mustn't be horrid from afar & Ive no doubt your brother in law is being the "decentest sort". However I cant bear him and thats the truth.

Its fine today. I am hiding (in vain) from the house the servants & Jack. It would be marvellously beautiful if one were alone. As soon as this gland is on the way to mending, as soon as it is in control I swear I shall go away. To Sospel.[3] Jack can stay here & write his lectures. He'd love it and Ill go up there for a complete change. I wonder if it can be done. This letter sounds disagreeable. Its not meant to be. I am angry with 'people' with Brett & Co. with Vera for writing me a false, coldhearted snobbish letter "so glad you are nearing normal again". Typical! It cant be helped. I hope you go and stay with Mrs Scriven before you come back. I feel you ought to. Take things easy. Keep me informed when you can.

Yours

Katherine.

MS BL.

1 Brett's father was Reginald Baliol Brett, 2nd Viscount Esher (1852–1930), a distinguished Civil Servant.
2 The child of Ida's sister, May.
3 A small town, inland from Menton.

To Ottoline Morrell, [14 March 1921]

VILLA ISOLA BELLA | GARAVAN | MENTON A/M.
Monday.

Dearest Ottoline,

I want to write you a long letter but I know this will only be a mingy scrap. But I must tell you how much I loved hearing from you, and how sorry I am that we are in the same boat! I had been in bed for six weeks with my lungs & heart; then "they" have decided that my heart trouble is caused by a very swollen gland which presses, with intense pain on an artery. This the surgeon tapped on Saturday & intends to tap 2 or 3 times again. And so on and so on and so on. The Mountain is in England pendant cette crise. But I'll not go on.

The weather is really exquisite. Today was perfection. Radiant, crystal clear, one of those days when the earth seems to pause, enchanted with its beauty, when every new leaf whispers: "am I not heavenly fair!" The sun is quite warm. It is tame again. It comes & curls up in your arms. Beautiful Life! In spite of everything one cannot but praise Life. I have been watching the peach tree outside my window from the very first moment, and now it is all in flowers and the leaves are come, small stiff clusters like linnets wings.

Yes. *I do understand.* But even now I cant explain. Something happened – a kind of earthquake that shook everything and I lost faith and touch with everybody. I cannot write what it was. And perhaps I shall never meet you again so that I can tell you. This is sad. Blame me if you must. How can you do otherwise? I expect this all sounds fantastic. I hate people who hint at secrets in letters. You will hate this. Let me say I was almost out of my mind with misery last year.

J.M.M. is here for the moment. He goes back to England at the end of April. His typewriter ticks away here.

Yes, I know what you must have felt about Keats. I have just been looking at the Keats Memorial Volume. It is simply *indescribable* in its vulgarity. But theres a letter by Keats in it,[1] so full of power, gaiety, 'fun' that it mocks the book as he would have mocked it!

I wish we could meet in Florence, but I have forfeited those happy chances.

Would that you were better! At any rate, in that other world, that world which we share, *there* I meet you, *there* I know – and sympathise as others cannot.

Ill write again if I may.

Goodnight dearest Ottoline. With my love,

Ever yours
Katherine.

MS Texas. *LKM* II. 96–7.

1 *The John Keats Memorial Volume* was issued by the Keats House Committee in 1921, and was comprised for the most part of essays by Keats scholars. But there was also a long, hitherto lost letter of 22 Sept. 1819 from Keats to Richard Woodhouse, including the "Ode to Autumn" and sections of "Hyperion".

To Sydney Waterlow, 16 March 1921

VILLA ISOLA BELLA | GARAVAN | MENTON A/M.
16.III.1921

Dear Sydney

Since receiving your letter Life has driven me through dark little door-ways, down underground passages which ended this week in one of those white tiled rooms, with glass shelves, a fine display of delicate steel, too many wash basins, a frosted windy glass & a narrow little black sofa with steel grips for the patient to cling to. Here the surgeon & my doctor decided to risk it and plunged about 2½ inches of hollow knitting nee-dle into my neck & withdrew it. Success triumphant. This process, repeated twice or thrice will, they hope, in time, relieve the accumula-tion . . . And so on so and on so and on . . .

Brett sends me a silly letter: I return a tart reply. But really to emerge, to be above ground long enough, peacefully enough to take my friend by the hand & beg him not to talk of "boring me" and not to imagine Ill accept "obvious explanations" – thats been awfully difficult. In fact its not been possible. So Ive had to risk your cursing me and turning away from me and thinking your very worst.

All the same, *I* shall risk coming back to my small place by the fire. I shall even pretend (until I know) that you understand and are not at all fierce . . . I loved your letter. Life is so very short. Let me say again, quickly, nothing you can tell me *bores* me. The only thing in the world that bores me is falsity, insincerity. I cannot tell you how I value, how I appreciate, anything you may ever care to tell me. But I wish you may soon know me well enough to feel I do not misunderstand you — — —

Yes, I feel you are going to write. Its in your letters. They have that curious deliberate quality of one who is revolving something in his mind. What is it? I feel that you can afford to, and you do, see Life as you see it at present because you are absorbed in something else.

And heres a queer idea for which I've no justification. I feel certain that one day you'll write a play. But a very fine play. Or is that wide of the mark.

You see, as I 'see' you (forgive me if I ever sound impertinent. Its so hard to speak from a distance) you have been moving hidden through Life. You have been a hidden, secret spectator when *les autres* did not even know that YOU were by. You have lived by apprehensions far far more than most people, I imagine. But I am timid of talking to you about yourself – even though I want to so much. You may dislike it extremely.

Is your new room your real *writing room*? Will you be working late there at the weekends? And what do your windows look out on. It will be lovely as the spring advances. I love a room that is a fortress and I love to work at night. To be free to get up and lean out of [the] window into that dark, airy stillness – is happiness. Dear Heaven! How little has been written about the extraordinary charm of NOT going to bed at night! Only to think of it and one passes into a whole strange world where to be awake is enough. As long as one isn't at a London party, or taking dinner with the Hutchinsons.[1]

But I remember, I expect you do, too, walks, drives, walking over wet lawns and down dark garden paths, finding oneself on the wharf or the station at a quarter to two in the morning, exploring empty kitchens long after midnight, watching the light change while you lie on the divan smoking and listening – one could go on for ever. And thats all too trivial – I mean something more – which makes every breath one takes, as it were – an emotion.

It is very mysterious how, in spite of everything, we find ourselves at the last *praising Life*.

But this disjointed letter must end. Big green stars glitter in the deep sky; the frogs are shrilling and the sea beats 'A-Ah'. It is like summer.

Goodnight. I ought to give you news of Murry, tho'. Let me see . . . As far as I know he is quite unchanged. He is working, but not too hard. And in the intervals he smokes his pipe, sews, and irons his trousers.

Salute your New Baby[2] for me and her fortunate mother. I hope they are both well.

Je vous serre le main

Ever

                                                        Katherine.

MS ATL. *Selected*, 204–6.

---

[1] See p. 202, n. 2.
[2] Sydney and Helen Waterlow's first child, John.

To Ida Baker, [*16 March 1921*]

[Villa Isola Bella, Garavan, Menton]
Thursday.[1]

I shall try and reply to your two letters. I wish to Heaven you didn't refer some of these silly little points to me. Its really idiotic to ask me if I wish to take the advice re cleaning of Shoolbreds man. Of course I do. Why not? Am I an idiot? They sound all right and satisfactory. Go ahead.
(a) Yes, sell mattress of camp bed. Keep mattress of grey bed.
(b) Ill send a note to Broomies.
(c) Arthur had better have the letter paper for scribbling paper.
(d) Of course give the rabbit or any other small thing to the baby.
(e) Let both the wooden clocks go – especially the beehive one. I mean I do not want them kept.

Do you mean *destroy* by *put away*? Is that a delicate refined way of referring to the morts des objets chers. I don't know. May I put them away? What does it mean? You'd scarcely be silly enough to destroy my old blotter if it were possible to keep it, and the velvet curtain you say has only one small hole. ∴ its not bad enough to destroy. And does *keep* mean *store.* For I asked you to bring my Chinese skirt & yet I certainly don't want these other things. As to the remains of that rubbishy plaid velvet – I groan with horror at the thought of its perpetuity. It is extremely confusing. I have wired you about Jack's things. Its no good saying if you dont hear by Thursday youll do so & so. Today is Thursday & your letter is only just come.

The weather is v. fine here. All is as usual. The house 'goes' & the servants are just the same. Please do not hurry back. That is my one really urgent cry. My health is also – the same.

Katherine.

Dont, as a result of this letter stop writing to me – *please.*

MS BL, *MLM,* 160–1.

[1] The letter is postmarked 16 Mar., which was Wednesday.

To Ida Baker, [*18 March 1921*]

[Villa Isola Bella, Garavan, Menton]
Friday.

About the key of Broomies. I don't think A. ought to have it. He would forget to lock the door or he'd leave the windows or lose the key. I don't think he is reliable really. I have had rather a horrid shock about him.

Hes got the family complex. When he wrote me all that about taking less money & so on Brett was giving him £50 a year and paying for all his colours etc. So be cautious with him, will you? Brett has, in fact, completely adopted him and I don't come in at all. That I don't mind, but I do mind his plea of poverty. Its a trifle too familiar. Ive an idea you feel rather sentimental about him & may take him out & pay for him and all that kind of thing. Thats why I warn you.

I must say I loathe money but its the lack of it I hate most. If Father would settle £500 a year on me – but what nonsense! All the same Sorapure haunts me. I cant write to him or ask him a thing. It does seem preposterous that J. could not pay that.

The serpent in the kitchen has taken to gardening. I hear her raking & watering now (8 A.M.) The kitchen is *as usual*. She rakes the heads off anything in her way, too. The other Marie has been very good, lately, or so it appears. This one is going to Nice on Monday for the day "pour chercher le clef de mon appartement." I wish shed be drowned there. Friday (later).

I haven't heard from you today. Again I have forgotten your letter for Broomies. Here it is.

Bouchage came today & my neck was again tapped. But it was no go. He was not very satisfactory or helpful, I must say. I think he is tired of the patient for the moment. He has exhausted his not v. rich resources. But he did say most definitely that I cant stay here later than May. Positively not. This means, therefore, finding another place for four months at least. I should like to try Switzerland. Its not really fashionable & there are doctors there. Peira Cava, par exemple is no good. I couldn't bear hotels for so long & I don't imagine there is any medical man there. I *feel* Switzerland might be much the best place. Would you go & look at it for me? I mean – when you come back. Would you, as soon as possible, go off there & look for a v. small chalet?

I shall write Marie Dahlerup[1] to send me a list of places near Geneva. And perhaps there is a bureau – I am *sure* there is in London where you can get information. Do try & find one. The Swiss Consulate would put you on its tracks, wouldn't it? You see there is no time to be lost. Here's March over. Therell be nothing left if we leave it any longer. I had hoped, *in a way*, *only* not *really*, to stay off and on here until the end of July but its definitely out of the question. And I shant come back here until the end of September. I have a vague idea Ive seen advertised a *Swiss Information Bureau* but I can't be certain.

What about going to Switzerland from – No, you have a return ticket & besides one cant talk out such important plans from afar.

I think thats all. Im sorry your little neffy is ill with malaria. How unfair for a child to have fever.

The weather has quite changed this last week. Spring has really 'set in'

as they say. The air is different & now at night one hears, not one moustique, but a regular tuning up. I wish I could change too. Perhaps
Switzerland will do the trick. In spite of what Bouchage says to the contrary I have a perpetual suspicion that this place is a bad place. Lovely,
and dear, in a way, but *bad*. And it has caused these glands. For they are
now plural – another having been discovered at the apex of the right
lung, pressing on the bronchial tube. GOOD. I believe it may be all the
fault of this relaxing climate. At any rate the climate is never helpful. You
have to do all your own bracing, as it were. It clings round your neck.
So help me to get to Switzerland soon, will you? And always we must
behave as though J. were a 'visitor'. *Not* a person to consult, or to expect
from or to count on. If he *comes* along – he *comes* and thats all.
Fare well.

Katherine.

MS BL, *MLM*, 159–60.

---

1 An old but shadowy friend from KM's early years in London, turned to in moments of
need, but also quickly put aside. There had been a proposal in 1920 that she replace Ida Baker
as a companion on the Riviera. (See *CLKM* III. 176–7.)

To Ida Baker, [20 March 1921]

[Villa Isola Bella, Garavan, Menton]
Sunday.
D.I.

Your telegram about Wingley came late last night. It was very thrilling.
I long to know how he was found, and even more, if possible, what was
the meeting like between Athy and him. I envy you seeing that. I hope
you really saw it and can tell me what happened. It is a great triumph
to have found him. But now the question is – what to do with them? If
we were not leaving for Switzerland I wouldn't hesitate. But all these
train journeys – arriving at hotels, and so on? Would it be torture for
cats? I feel the cats' first need is a settled home; a home that never
changeth. And I know that is just what I am not going to have. At the
same time the idea that they should be destroyed is *horrible!* You see, just
suppose you and I hear, when we are in Switzerland, of another place
& decide to try it. Or decide to make a sea voyage. Or . . . so much is
possible. We couldn't ever leave the cats with Jack, & to take cats where
they are not wanted is cruelty. I confess I don't see a way out. If Richard
were older Id suggest asking him to mind them. Id better leave it like
this. If when you have thought it over you decide it would be an
unhappy life for them or impractical for you – have them destroyed.

Elizabeth Bibesco has shown signs of life again. A letter yesterday begging him to resist Katherine. "You have withstood her so gallantly so far how can you give way now". And "you swore nothing on earth should ever come between us". From the letter I feel they are wonderfully suited and I hope he will go on with the affair. He *wants to*. "How can I exist without your literary advice", she asks. That is a very fascinating question. I shall write to the silly little creature & tell her I have no desire to come between them only she must not make love to him while he is living with me, because that is undignified. He'll never break off these affairs, tho', and I dont see why he should. I wish hed take one *on* really seriously – and leave me. Every day I long more to be alone.

My life is the same. I get up at about 11, go downstairs until 2, come up & lie on my bed until five when I get back into it again. So I am infinitely worse than when I left England. There's no comparison. I wish I could consult Sorapure. Its all a great bother. I 'note' what you say about your Thursday letter. I'll destroy it.

I find it possible to speak to you today. I am not in despair about my health. But I must make every effort to get it better *soon*, very *soon*. You see Jack 'accepts' it; it even suits him that I should be so subdued & helpless. And it is deadly to know he NEVER tries to help. But I was not born an invalid and I want to get well – I long for – Do you understand? I feel every day must be the last day of such a life – but I have now felt that for years. Ida – let us both try. Will you? Bouchage has failed. Help me to escape!

Later.

Your Wednesday letter has come re the furniture. I'd take what they will offer. Perhaps £8 is rather too little, tho.

I have decided to give up this villa for good & to really try Switzerland. I shall try & find that man *Spahlinger*[1] & see if his treatment suits me. Jack goes to England in the first week in May. I have arranged with him not to return abroad, at any rate until the winter. But to spend the summer in the English country, with a bicycle. It would be *impossible* to have him in Switzerland while one was "looking round" & deciding. I can imagine it too well. He is v. willing not to come. So we'll burn our French boats & go off together. I wish you could get Spahlingers address or an address where the treatment is followed. But how can you? I don't know . . . I must now make a real effort to make money for this. Somehow, it *must* be done.

Take things easy – & look after yourself. I hope the little boy is better.

Yours

Katherine.

MS BL. *MLM*, 161–3.

---

[1] Henry Spahlinger, a Swiss doctor whose course of treatment KM was now thinking of taking.

To Ida Baker, [21 March 1921]

[Villa Isola Bella, Garavan, Menton]

Important Letter explaining my telegram. Please read it carefully.

Some time ago I read in the paper of the results of the SPALINGER treatment – a vaccine treatment – for advanced cases of tuberculosis. An English doctor – Doctor Leonard Williams[1] had applied it to himself with excellent results. I think Doctor Leonard Williams is a Harley Street man. I am under the impression, also, that he is connected with The French Hospital. It further stated that this treatment was being given in Switzerland and France, and it *implied* that Spalinger was in Geneva. Doctor Bouchage knows Williams personally. I am sending Jack to him tomorrow to ask if he will give you a letter of introduction, mentioning my case. I hope he will. If he does I want you to go and ask him where there is an institution or sanatorium in Switzerland where this treatment is followed & if I am likely to be accepted. Just go quietly and do this for me will you? I am willing to go into any sanatorium, of course.

Katherine.

MS BL.

¹ Leonard Williams, a graduate of Glasgow University and now a Harley Street specialist, had published on a wide range of medical subjects.

To Princess Bibesco,[1] 24 March 1921

[Villa Isola Bella, Garavan, Menton]
24 III 1921

Dear Princess Bibesco,

I am afraid you must stop writing these little love letters to my husband while he and I live together. It is one of the things which is not done in our world.

You are very young. Wont you ask your husband to explain to you the impossibility of such a situation.

Please do not make me have to write to you again. I do not like scolding people and I simply hate having to teach them manners.

Yours sincerely
Katherine Mansfield.

TC Texas. Meyers, 211.

¹ Elizabeth Asquith (1897–1945), only surviving daughter of Herbert Henry Asquith, Liberal Prime Minister 1908–16, defeated in the general election of 1918, but again in Parliament in 1920, and Margot Asquith. She had married Prince Antoine Bibesco, formerly First Secretary at the

Rumanian Legation in London. Her collection of short stories *I Have Only Myself to Blame* was published in 1921.

Murry's relationship with her disturbed KM rather more than she conceded publicly. Murry had
become infatuated with her when they met the previous summer at The Wharf, the Asquiths' country house in Berkshire, and by 27 Dec. 1920 KM wrote: 'I thought also of the Princess B. It's a bit
bewildering − her unlikeness to the faces "we" recognise or would recognise. She has a quick rapa-
cious look − in fact she made me think of a *gull*, with an absolutely insatiable appetite for bread.
And all her vitality, her cries, her movements, her wheelings, depend upon the person on the bridge
who carries the loaf. This would of course *be hidden*. But this is what she is when she is really *she*,
and not "enchanted" ' (*Journal* 1954, 233).

Early in the new year KM also noted: 'Does one ever know? One never knows. She realised how
foolish it would be to ask the question: "What are you thinking of?" And yet if she did not ask this
question she would never be sure he was not thinking of . . . Even if she asked it how could she be
certain he did not make up the answer' (*Journal* 1954, 236).

To Ida Baker, [26 March 1921]

[Villa Isola Bella, Garavan, Menton]
Saturday.

Dear Ida

After some days without news I received a kind of note from you this
morning, which, from its tone, convinces me that something serious has
happened. You tell me nothing. Please tell me the truth. As to all you
say about Switzerland − it is out of all proportion. Thank you v. much.
You misunderstood me. I am going to Switzerland myself in April or the
middle of May. But I shall not need the kind of 'taking' that your letter
conveys. However − all that does not matter. What does is − I wish you
would tell me the truth. I know that it is impossible for you to be like
this unless something has happened. For have we not both experienced
what it is like to be without letters, news, to be 'put off' and told nothing − to be left in the dark.

I am *very* anxious.

MS BL.

To Sydney Waterlow, [late March 1921]

VILLA ISOLA BELLA | GARAVAN | MENTON A/M.

Dear Sydney,

This little room with its pale walls, yellow velvet curtains, faded gilt
mirror and large jars of wide open roses and marigolds is the salon. Its
wonderfully still; even the clock seems to have stopped exprès, but outside the windows the young peach leaves are shaking and big silvery
clouds spin over the blue.

Murry and Sullivan[1] are somewhere, ranging the mountains. We have been talking of you so much these last few days that your letter seemed almost to bring you here. I shall (if I may) read the Tom Eliot part to these two young men over déjeuner.

It was an immensely interesting letter – a delight. Thank you for it. Just a word about a cursed subject. Its beautifully kind of you to worry about Switzerland. I wonder what J.M.M. said to you. I wish I knew. For my part I am decided to go to Genève in May & to see there a man called Spahlinger. Ill get him to treat me & then I shall stay in die Schweiz until such time as it shall please the Lord to leave plaguing me but NOT in a sanatorium. I want to find a little chalet if possible near *Thun* – in German Switzerland. J.M.M. can of course be there when he likes, and there seems a chance that Sullivan may find a pied à terre in the neighbourhood. Also a Dane, a friend of mine, [Marie Dahlerup] wants to come from time to time. This project seems to me engaging. Shall we be able to persuade you to come & make holiday – too?

The curse is still heavy on me – but I ignore it all I can, and, merciful Powers! What strange compensations there are! Yesterday for instance, as I waited for the surgeon in a huge, grim ante-chamber, I thought as I watched my companions – especially the poor ones – as I realised the immense gulf between those who have a perfect right to be ill if they choose & can pay whatever is necessary to be well again, and the others for whom illness is the mysterious *ill fortune* for which they are somehow to blame . . . "kindly excuse us, but even an insect will live" . . . I felt, more sincerely than I can say: "I would not be anywhere else for worlds. I would not have missed this." But Im writing quickly, and I haven't expressed what really was there – *Beauty* . . . Do you know what I mean that word to convey? No, I must turn it into a story before its really intelligible.

Thank you for telling me about O'Malley.
Ive been feeling these last weeks that its only *now* that I know what I *want* the short story to be . . .

Yes, Brett is a brick. I get impatient with her sometimes because she will think it necessary to write to me about what Kotelansky used to call "extremely serious questions". And somehow these questions ring a little false from Brett. They are not what one wants from her. But I do appreciate my wickedness.

Later.

At this point they came in and we began with olives and sausage and very good herrings. M. saw the point of the affaire Elliot perhaps better than I did. I didn't know he had been spending his very spare time with the Hutchinsons[2] and not with the likes of you. Hes a rare, delightful being – isn't he? Thats what I always feel, even when the bluff oppresses me. But Prufrock[3] remains. I think thats what I want modern poetry to be. I even have a feeling (this is private!) that Johnny Keats would have admired it immensely and written Elliot no end of a letter.

I confess Im a *moralist* enough to think no man can afford to run with the Hutchinsons, more especially if he feels about them as Elliot does.

But I don't know. One must lay down the law for nobody except one-self . . . but Life is so precious, so marvellous – can one afford to pour it out for the Hutchinsons – afford to waste it except – gloriously – with ones friends?

Later still. This letter is fated to be interrupted. Now Sullivan, having drunk 2 bottles of wine and a wineglass of brandy has gone off to Marseilles. J.M.M. is in his bedroom which adjoins mine, preparing to go to bed. We have been having a tremendous discussion on personal freedom. *He* has come to the conclusion that to be honest is the whole of the law. You cannot be a 'good' artist if you are a hypocrite – but – thats as much as one can say. The rest is personal freedom . . . He looks youthful, excited and gay as he stalks about declaiming this. I imagine he sees white arms beckoning; I imagine he is sloping over Europe with a ruck sack, meeting – whom? A young man on the threshold of Life, in fact.

Whereas my personal freedom is a big table, and to lose myself in work.

Goodnight. Forgive this letter. *Be happy*.

Katherine.

MS ATL.

---

¹ J. W. N. Sullivan was staying at the Isola Bella.
² St John (Jack) Hutchinson (1884–1942), an Oxford graduate and barrister, and his wife Mary Hutchinson (1889–1977), a cousin of Lytton Strachey's, were the centre of a fashionable and intellectually élite social circle. KM had been close to Mary for a time in 1915–16. (See *CLKM* I, 198, 293.)
³ KM admired T. S. Eliot's *Prufrock and Other Poems* when it was published in June 1917.

To Ida Baker, *[early April 1921]*

Isola Bella

Dear Ida

I have not written to you quite lately because I did not know how soon you intended leaving London. All your letters have come.

Will you come here tomorrow at about 10.30? Then I shall be free & able to talk to you in the salon. The early morning, here, is as you know rather a distracting time. I am v. anxious to hear your news.

In this month that you have been away I have discovered I am not nearly so in need of assistance as I thought I was. So will you, as far as possible, forget our relationship of the past four years and look on me not as a friend who needs looking after, but only as a friend? I mean that in all its implications.

I hope you are not too tired after your journey.

Yours

Katherine.

MS BL, *MLM*, 163–4.

To Dorothy Brett, [early April 1921]

VILLA ISOLA BELLA | CARAVAN | MENTON A/M

My dear Brett,

I am afraid I shan't be here when JMM goes to England.[1] I intend, if Im above ground to disappear and view the solid earth from another angle. Just for a change. But why don't you arrange to go to Paris when he returns from England & go over together & spend some days there looking at pictures. That seems to me no end of a good plan. Don't put it forward as mine. Tackle him on your own account. You'd both enjoy it so – wouldn't you? – and have such fun into the bargain. Murry knows Paris awfully well; he'd be a good person to go with – Paris is divine in June. I can see you both, in my minds eye, sitting under the stars & talking about art with a VERY big A. If I were there Id take out a small mouth organ and spoil everything . . . Im writing in the garden under a big striped umbrella. Its the most perfect day but the butterflies go to ones head rather, and you feel the bees are coming to tickle you when they hover so near and buzz so awfully nicely. The little darling, precious bees! I love bees! Through the rather shabby lattice wood fence (which is covered with tiny rose clusters) one can see winking-fire diamonds of sea. And heres a visitor – I smell his pipe. He's coming in.

He came and stayed, and he and JMM talked clothes until the sky changed for the evening. I shall have to write one day a masculine dissertation on clothes. I've listened to so many. JMM is just as interested in his clothes as a woman, tho' in a different way. As to sewing – he loves it, and performs miracles of *patching*. You would laugh to hear him say in the middle of a conversation on, say, Burtons Anatomy of Melancholy:[2] "Ive got a hellishly difficult piece of hem stitching here. I have to keep it tucked under with one hand and bind it with the other . . ." He's very well and I think, quite happy. Good food does wonders for him.

Goodbye for now. I hope your Thursdays are a success. Yours ever

K.M.

MS Newberry.

¹ Murry would leave in early May to lecture in Oxford.
² Robert Burton, *The Anatomy of Melancholy* (1621).

To J. C. Squire, [10 April 1921]

Villa Isola Bella | Garavan | Menton A/M
10.V.1921¹

Dear Mr Squire,

I am returning my proofs of the Story The Daughters of the Late Col. today. May I say, without impertinence that I wrote this story for the Mercury? Your kind letter giving me leave to send another started me off that very afternoon. But of course there was the risk of your not liking it or not thinking it good enough.

But it really was a kind of thank offering for that letter. And much the more grateful am I to you now for your review of Bliss in the Observer.² Of course its delightful and unexpected if people like ones work. But you told me so exactly where I failed, what I'd left undone and what I ought to do.

One knows these things but it is the most precious encouragement to feel there is someone who realises what one is getting at!

I hope my next work will please you better.

Yours sincerely,

Katherine Mansfield.

P.S. On page 5 of the MS old grandfather Pinner, whose teeth have gone and whose tongue is stiff can't say *extraordinary*. I hope the word is all right as it stands 'esstrodinary'.

TC Stanford.

¹ As KM had left Menton on 4 May, and the story appeared in the May issue of the *London Magazine*, this date is clearly an error.
² Squire had written an admiring review in the *Observer*, 23 Jan. 1921.

To Marie Belloc-Lowndes,¹ [? mid-April 1921]

Villa Isola Bella | Garavan | Menton A/M

Dear Mrs Belloc-Lowndes,

Ariane arrived at 6 o'clock this evening and I have just (10 P.M.) taken leave of her. I think its an enchanting little book and amazingly well done.² Thank you very much for sending it to me. Yes I have enjoyed it immensely.

But *not* improper – is it? There's something so delicate, supple, warm, in the style – the emotion is so sensitive . . .

I wish there were more books of this kind. But they wont be written in England.

I confess to an awful feeling of wickedness after reading Ariane – some feeling almost like a dégout for those solid boiled puddings that those good young men & serious young women cook with such Awful Care. But that lovely little creature en chemise is responsible –

Yours very sincerely
Katherine Mansfield.

MS Texas.

1 Marie Belloc-Lowndes (1868–1947), sister of Hilaire Belloc (1870–1953), was of French-English descent and a prolific writer of novels that were often fictional treatments of actual crimes. Her autobiography, *I, Too, Have Lived in Arcadia*, was published in 1942.
2 *Ariane, Jeune Fille Russe* (1920), by Claude Anet, was the story of a young woman who combined childishness and sensuality, devotion and perversity.

To Sydney Schiff [c. 18 April 1921]

Isola Bella | Garavan-Menton

Dear Sydney

I was more sorry than I can say not to have been able to come on Thursday. Fate is against me in these matters. I wish I knew why. But we shall meet again? Yes, I am sure we shall. My plans, however seem more & more vague. The Swiss doctor maintains his silence, & I continue to receive letters for & against his treatment. Jones is going to Switzerland this week.1 To a little place called Baugy – above Montreux & on to Chateau d'œux to 'spy out the land'.

I am simply staggered there's no other word for it, by your analysis – heaven knows its infinitely more – of Sullivan. Perfect! From the first word (oh, how suble that is!) to the last. And that "he has less imagination than he thinks", that "his future lies in the development of his powers of application." My dear Sydney. That is divination indeed.

I am fond of Sullivan – and I am his friend – but with *reservations* . . . His lack of what we mean by sensitiveness is hard to bear, so too is his lack of self discipline. I mean that in every sense. I think it is still a toss-up whether he finds his true approach or whether he fritters his Life away. He wants to live somewhere near me for the next few years &, privately, I shrink from the idea. But he's a vague creature. Perhaps I'll never see him again. At the moment this thought is pleasing. How hateful I am! My excuse is he has been staying here – here all day long until 10 o'clock at night – and Sydney – one is so *infernally watchful*. His habit of going into the dining room, taking an orange, bringing it to the salon, tossing the peel into the fireplace. Oh! Oh! But thats only one 'obvious' small horror . . . I want to live among mountains and hide from nearly all mankind – not *all*, thank God.

I shall long to hear how you and Violet fare. This country has been really horrible these last few days. A woman came to tea yesterday & spoke of Switzerland in the spring as though it were a paradise. And outside the window the heavy sky and grey old palm mocked us. I fancy Germany might be the place to live in. No, perhaps not. But its wretched to be a wanderer with all this work which waits for a peaceful room.

We have not seen the Mercury for April. I shall write for a copy. My long story "The Daughters of the Late Colonel" comes out next month. I hope you will care for it. It means more to me than any other. I wish I could think your next novel would soon be written. One *needs* it.

The two young men were very happy on Thursday. Murry said *he* was dull but Sullivan was a success. I wonder. M. and I are happy just now. He is quite different after we have been alone together for a time.

I hope big, fair Marie Dahlerup will not bore you. I have not seen her since . . . I was 16. From her letters she is a dear creature.

May you both be happy, dear Sydney. I shall think of you constantly. I press you hand.

With love from

Katherine.

MS BL. *Adam* 300, 107–8.

---

[1] Ida Baker returned to Menton in mid-April. This visit to Switzerland must have been a brief reconnaissance, as she was with KM later in the month, helping her prepare for the move.

To Violet Schiff, [c.18 April 1921]

Isola Bella | Garavan-Menton.

Dearest Violet,

Goodbye for just now. Ive not seen half as much of you as I had hoped. But I shall still look forward. It is good to think you are better than when you came. I hope with all my heart that you will keep well.

Murry begs me to send his greetings to you both. He will be in London in the second week of May. Its curious, although I have seen you and Sydney so seldom – now that you are gone I feel that everybody is going. The Riviera is finished. Little Doctor Bouchage came this morning. He told me Doctor Marmel had been to see them yesterday. He came at 3 and stayed until 8.30 & "talked incessantly all the time". When he did not talk he whistled. I feel I could write a whole life of

Doctor Marmel Id even like to. The Swiss doctor, Spahlinger has never answered, so I don't know whether his treatment is available or not. Its a disappointment. It sounded very marvellous. One didn't only get better – one became perfectly well & able to fly again as high as ever.

Dearest Violet – I hope youll read my story in the Mercury. Its not pride that makes me say that. Its only that you & Sydney are my two readers in such a *special* sense. I don't care a farthing for what the others think. They don't know what I am trying to do – but you know.

I hope you will have a happy journey. Let me hear from you when you can – will you? Jones goes to Switzerland on Wednesday. I think I shall go the last week in May.

Goodbye again. With my warm love
Ever yours
Katherine.

MS BL. *Adam* 300, 108-9.

To Dorothy Brett [20 April 1921]

I.B. | G.-M. | A/M.
Sunday

Dear Brett

Don't have those dreams about me. I don't feel the least in the world inclined to snub you, my dear. And I thank you most awfully for your letter & for the little box which hasn't come yet. They take a long time coming – little boxes – weeks & weeks sometimes, but they always *do* arrive, finally, & are carried up the hill to this little villa by a black man who gets a franc for his pains.

About Love. Well, each of us thinks differently. For M. & for me love IS possessive. We make terrific demands on each other & if we are not all in all then we are *wrong*. We feel we *have* the right to each other & are exclusive & jealous and fierce. If we fail from this the heavens fall & have to be builded up again before we can go on. But that is personal to us. No two people are alike. Its the only way we can be free as artists. But it has taken years to discover this & it will take all the years there are to hold to and to *enjoy* this. You see, one cant *say* what is freedom for another. One can only find out. I think its the hardest thing on earth to divine.

About Toronto. You weren't really quite serious in asking me that – were you? You couldn't do it. You don't live on *that plane*. I feel a little bit disgusted with Toronto¹ and with the people who say such things. Love isn't a *new dish*, after all, & physical love is such rare rare delight that its only to be taken in hand lightly and wantonly by *both* parties.

Equally! Unless its a purely trade affair I imagine you want a lover to give yourself to. No woman wants less. And no man either, if he is worth loving. Im *all for love* & for people enjoying themselves, but its a pity when they enjoy themselves *less* than they might, that's my feeling. And I think any relation which is not *fastidious* is not worth having.

We are wondering if that Strike has really struck. There is no way of knowing here. It must be horrible in London. Bernard Shaw had a letter in the D.N.[2] which explained it all away. Its a pity he's not King. But the very sound of a soldier fills me with horror, and as to all these pictures of young giants joining up & saying goodbye to Daddy — the falsity of it, the waste of Life — even if not a man is killed — is appaling. And all the while the trees come out & the year begins to ripen . . . If there were a God he'd be a Queer Fellow.

Here it is so cold that it might be November. We are both frozen. We shiver all day. I get up from 11–5.30 & turn the clock round so as to get back in bed more quickly. Ive been spitting blood since last Tuesday too — which is horrid. It makes one feel that while one sits at the window the house is on fire. And the servants have gone mad or bad or both. One has completely disappeared. Only her feather duster remains. She wasn't a little one either. But I expect we shall come across her one day. I have a fancy she's in one of the chimneys. All our flags are pinned on Switzerland. Meadows, trees, mountings, and kind air. I hope we shall get there in time.

I *saw* your party at Iris Moffatts. I envied you seeing Koteliansky. Isn't St. Johns Wood lovely in the spring? It seems to me always especially lovely. The houses are so white & the trees so plumy & one hears a piano. It is a romantic spot. I wish 5 Acacia Road[3] were mine. You paid too much for the sticks from Portland Villa. One day I shall come & weep over them. Goodbye for now, dear Brett. I hope London is calm. I hope you are *happy*.

With love from
Tig

MS Newberry. *LKM* II. 97–8.

[1] Brett's friend, the part Sioux Indian Frank 'Toronto' Prewitt (1893–1962) whose poems were published by Hogarth Press in 1921.

[2] 'Coal Consumer's Point of View', *Daily News*, 14 Apr. 1921.

[3] Which KM and Murry rented from June–Nov. 1915, and where Koteliansky now lived.

To Michael Sadler, 30 April 1921

c/o The Nation & Athenaeum | 10 Adelphi Terrace | London W.C.2
30.IV.1921

Dear Michael Sadler

Im leaving for Switzerland next week and my address is a little in the vague. If you have cause to write to me will you send the letters to the office below?

Yours very sincerely
Katherine Mansfield.

Postcard Targ.

To Violet Hunt,[1] 30 April 1921

c/o The Nation & Athenaeum | 10 Adelphi Terrace | London W.C.2
30.iv.1921

Dear Mrs Hueffer

We should have loved to come to your Party on May the fifth but we are too far away. Thank you so much for asking us. Your note sent us whirling back to that afternoon visit in the little house near Chichester I feel shortly after Queen Victoria came to the throne. But it must have been a little later than that really.

With warm remembrances from us both.
Yours very sincerely,
Katherine Mansfield.

MS Berg.

[1] Violet Hunt (1866–1942) lived with the novelist Ford Maddox Ford (1873–1939) under his family name of Hueffer. A flamboyant personality and a strongly feminist novelist, her autobiography *The Flurried Years* was published in 1926. She had lived close by when Murry and KM rented Runcton Cottage, Chichester, from Sept. 1912 to early 1913.

To Marie Belloc-Lowndes, 3 May 1921

Villa Isola Bella | Garavan. Menton.
After today:
C/o The Nation and Athenaeum | 10 Adelphi Terrace W.C.2
3 V 1921

Dear Mrs Belloc-Lowndes,

I ought to have sent back the books you lent me – I ought to have written to you about them. But I only posted them yesterday and I never sent a word of thanks. Please do not think me the black and graceless creature I appear. But the Lord, for some reason, has seen fit to visit me with a New Curse and I have been "in the surgeon's hands" as they say. They were very expert, professional French surgeons hands which made a difference & they didn't have to do anything very fearful. But this little affair was horrid enough to be my excuse for "creeping into my shelly cave." Forgive me.

Tomorrow I am going to Switzerland – first to an hotel in a little place near Montreux & then later to some convenient mountain. If I may Id like to write to you about the Mrs A. book from there. It was *awfully* interesting.

It has been cold and grey and frileux here & all the english papers show people trying to get a cool breath from the river or eating ices in Trafalgar Square. But its always thus . . .

My husband sends his warm remembrances. I *do* hope we shall meet again one day not too far-away.

Yours very sincerely
Katherine Mansfield Murry.

MS Texas.

III

SWITZERLAND – MONTREUX
AND SIERRE
MAY–DECEMBER 1921

By the time KM left Menton for Switzerland in May 1921, it was not simply a new phase of health she hoped for in the specialist treatment she had heard of; it was a fresh spiritual orientation as well. She spoke of this obliquely, hinting at possibilities rather than claiming certainty of any kind. Her writing, as much as her response to experience, was to be a focused celebration, an answer, in its deliberately unspectacular way, to what she believed was the debilitating intellectualism that followed the First World War.

After almost two months of living in hotels in Montreux and Sierre, she settled at the Chalet des Sapins, Montana-sur-Sierre, in late June. It was here that she wrote several of her finest stories: 'At the Bay', 'The Doll's House', 'The Garden Party'. It was also to be her last period of concentrated work.

§

To J. M. Murry, [7 May 1921]

[Hotel Beau Site, Clarens-Montreux]
Saturday.

My darling Bogey,

I have been walking round and round this letter, treading on my toes & waving my tail and wondering where to settle. There's *too* much to say! Also, the least postcard or letter penned in view of these mountains is like presenting ones true account to ones Maker. Perhaps their effect will wear off. But at present, Boge . . . one keeps on murmuring that about cats looking at Kings but one feels a very small cat, sneezing, licking one's paw, making a dab or two at ones tail in the eye of Solemn Immensities. However the peasants don't mind, so why should I? They are cutting the long brilliant grass; they are wading waist high through the fields with silver stars – their scythes winking-bright in the sun – over their shoulders. A cart drawn by a *cow* (Im sure it is a cow) drags over a little bridge & the boy driver, lying like a drunken bee in his fresh green bed doesn't even *try* to drive. Its a perfect, windless day. Im, as you have gathered, sitting on the balcony outside my room. The sun is wonderfully warm, but the air is just a little too clean not to be chill. The cleanliness of Switzerland! Darling it is frightening. The chastity of my lily-white bed! The waxy-fine floors! The huge bouquet of white lilac, fresh, crisp from the laundry in my little salon! Every daisy in the grass below has a starched frill – the very bird droppings are dazzling.

Bogey: But Wig – this is all jolly fine but why dont you tell me things. Get down to it!

I'm sorry, my precious. Ill have another try. You got my telegram. The journey was excellent. The lits salons were horrid – when they unfolded they were covered thickly with buttons so that one felt like a very sensitive bun having its currants put in. But it was soon morning & my mountains appeared as of yore with snow, like silver light on their tops, and beautiful clouds above, rolling solid white masses. We passed little watery villages clinging to the banks of rivers, it was raining, the trees dripped, and everybody carried a gleaming umbrella. Even the fishers fished under umbrellas, their line looked like the huge feeler of a large water beetle. And then the rain stopped, the cows began to fatten, the houses had broad eaves, the women at the bookstalls got broader & broader & it was Switzerland. I sat on a neat green velvet chair in Geneva for 3 hours. L.M. brought tea on a tray – do you see her, coming from afar, holding the tray high, her head bent, a kind of reverent beam on her face, & the smoke of the teapot mounting like the smoke of sacrifiges? Then we mounted an omnibus train & *bummelt*ed round the lake. The carriage was full of germans; I was imbedded in huge ones. When they saw a lilac bush, Vater und die Mamma and even little Hansi all cried *Schön*. It was very old world. Also they each & all read aloud the notice in the carriage that a cabinet was provided for the convenience of the passengers! (What other earthly reason would it have been there for?) We reached Clarens at 7. The station clock was chiming. It was a cuckoo clock. Touching – don't you think, darling? I was *v.* touched. But I didn't cry. And then a motorcar, like a coffee mill, flew round & round the fields to Baugy. The manager, who is very like a goldfish, flashed through the glass doors and our journey was over . . . This hotel is admirable. The food is prodigious. At breakfast one eats little white rolls with butter & fresh plum jam & cream. At lunch one eats – but no, I can't describe it. It could not be better though. I suppose, in the fullness of time I shall take soup at midday, too. But at present I can only watch and listen. My rooms are like a small appartement. They are quite cut off & the balcony is as big as another room. The sun rises in the morning vers les sept heures & it sets or it begins to set, for it takes its setting immensely seriously here, at seven in the evening. It has no connection whatever with the S. of France sun. This is le soleil père – and she's a wanton daughter whose name is never mentioned here. The air, darling, is all they say. I am posing here as a lady with a weak heart & lungs of Spanish leather-o. And so far, I confess, I hardly cough except in the morning. One mustn't be too enthusiastic though. Perhaps its the hypnotic effect of *knowing* one is so high up. But the air is amazing!

Its all very German. Early German. Fat little birds, tame as can be – they look as though their heads unscrewed & revealed marzipan tummies – fat little children, peasants, and – I regret to say – ugly women. In fact everybody seems to me awfully ugly. Young men with red noses & stuffy check suits & feathers in their hats ogling young females in mackintoshes with hats tied with ribbons under the chin! Oh weh, Oh weh! And if they try to be 'chic' – to be French – its worse still. Legs – but legs of mutton, Boge, in silk stockings & powder which one feels sure is die Mamma's icing sugar.

Of course I quite see the difficulty of being chic in this landscape. I can't quite see . . . yet. Perhaps a white woolen dress, a Saint Bernard, a woolen viking helmet with snowy wings. And for you . . . more wool, with your knees bare, dearest, and boots with fringèd tongues . . . But I don't know – I don't know . . .

I am sure you will like Switzerland. I want to tell you nicer things. What shall I tell you? I should like to dangle some very fascinating & compelling young carrots before your eminent nose. The furniture of my salon is green velvet inlaid with flesh pink satin, & the picture on the wall is Jugendidylle. There is also an immense copper jug with lovely hearts of imitation verdigris.

Goodbye, my darling. I love you v. much & Im fond of you and I long to hear from you.

Wig.[1]

MS ATL. *LKM* II. 98–100.

[1] A draft of this letter survives in one of KM's notebooks:

7.30. A.M. Hotel Beau Site.

My precious Bogey,

I keep walking & walking round this letter, treading on my toes & with my tail in the air; I dont know where to settle. There's so much to say & the day is so fine – Well here goes, darling.

The journey to Geneva took no time. My watchet seemed to be racing the train. We arrived some time after one & I went & sat in a green velvet chair while L.M. saw to things. I suppose we had a long wait there; it did not seem long. Ever since early morning those mountains that I remembered from last time had been there – huge, glittering, with snow like silver light on their tops. It was absolutely windless, and though the air was cold, it was cold like Spring. In fact (perhaps you realise Im putting a terrific curb on myself) it was delicious. Only to breathe was enough. Then we got into an omnibus train & it waddled slowly round the lake, stopping at every tiny station. Germans were in the carriage; in fact I was embedded in Germans, huge ones, Vater und die Mama und Hänsl. Every time we saw a lilac bush they all cried *schön*. This was very *old world*. There was also a notice in the carriage to say that the company had thoughtfully provided a cabinet. This they read aloud (1) Vater – then die Mama & then little Hänsl. We arrived at Clarens just as the station clock (which was a cuckoo clock: that seems to me awfully touching doesn't it to you?) struck seven & a motor car, like a coffee mill, flew round & round the fields to Baugy. Oh dear, you realise Im just telling you facts. The *embroidery* Ill have to leave for now. The hotel is simply admirable so far. Too clean. Spick is not the word nor is span. Even the sprays of white lilac in my salon were fresh from the laundry. I have two rooms and a huge balcony, and so many mountains that I havent even begun to climb them yet. They are superb. The views from the windows, Betsy love, over fields, little mushroom-like chalets, lake, trees, & then mountains are overwhelming. So is the green velvet & flesh pink satin suite in the salon, with copper jugs for ornaments & a picture on the wall called Jugendidyle. More of all this later.

I am posing here as a lady with a weak heart & lungs of spanish leather! It seems to 'go down' for the present. Well, I had dinner in my room – consommé, fish, cream sauce, roast turkey new potatoes braised laitue & 2 little tiny babas smothered in cream. I had to send the turkey & trimmings away. Even then . . .

Saint Galmier is superseded by Montreux[1] which the label says is saturated with carbonic acid gas. But my physiology book said this was deadly poison & we only breathed it out – never unless we were desperate took it in. However according to Doctors Ritter, Spingel and Knechtli its marvellous for gravel and makes the urine sparkil like champagne. These are the *minor* mysteries.

MS Draft ATL. *Journal*, 1954, 248–50.

[1] Saint Galmier and Montreux are both mineral waters.

To Ottoline Morrell, [c.8 May 1921]

Hotel Beau-Site | Clarens-Montreux

Dearest Ottoline,

Are you still in Lausanne?[1] Is there a possible chance of our seeing each other? I am sending this letter just *in case*. If I don't hear from you I will write to Garsington.

I can't tell you how glad I was to hear from you, and how sorry to

know you have been in such pain. It's devilish! I hope the doctor did
find out what was causing it and succeed in really helping you.

All news when I hear from you. If you would come here for a night
as my guest . . . Would you? Then we could *really* talk. That is my – I
hope it doesn't sound *wild* – idear.

Yours ever with love,

Katherine.

MS Texas.

[1] In April Lady Ottoline had gone to Lausanne for medical reasons, but KM's letter was too late
to bring about a meeting.

To J. M. Murry, [9 May] 1921

[Hotel Beau Site, Clarens-Montreux]
Monday.

Dearest Bogey

It was a great pleasure to hear from you today & to get your postcards
of Bandol & Arles. *This* time I am numbering & keeping your letters . .
. You took me back to Graviers – especially those big pebbles. They are
so plain in my memory, big, round, smooth. I see them. I am glad you
saw the Allègres, even tho' it was sad.[1] The postcards are v. impressive.
So was your desire to see a bullfight. I rolled my eyes.

After my hymn in praise of the weather it changed on Saturday night,
to heavy rolling mists & thick, soft rain. The mountains disappeared,
very beautifully, one by one. The lake became grave and one felt the
silence. This, instead of being depressing as it is in the South, had a sober
charm. I don't know how it is with you; but I feel the South is not made
pour le grand travail. There is *too much light*. Does that sound heresy?
But to work one needs a place (or so I find) where one can spiritually
dig oneself in . . . And I defy anybody to do that on the Riviera. Now
this morning the mist is rolling up, wave on wave, and the pines & the
firs, exquisitely clear, green and violet-blue show on the mountain sides.
This grass, too, in the foreground, waving high, with one o'clocks like
bubbles & flowering fruit trees like branches of pink & white coral . . .
One looks & one becomes absorbed. Do you know what I mean? This
outer man retires and the other takes the pen . . . In the South it is one
long fête for the outer man. But perhaps, after your Tour in Provence
you won't be inclined to agree. (I mean about it being not ideal for working.)

I feel, at present, I should like to have a small chalet, high high up
somewhere & live there for a round year – working as one wants to

work. The London Mercury came on Saturday with my story. Tell me if anybody says they like it, will you? Thats not vanity. Reading it again I felt it might fall quite dead flat. Its so plain and unadorned. Tommy & DeLamare are the people Id *like* to please. But don't bother to reply to this request, dearest. Its just a queer feeling – after one has dropped a pebble in. Will there be a ripple or not? . . .

You know how much I shall want to hear about your lectures. Tell me what you want to. No more. I expect youll be busy & not inclined for letters. All the same I shall expect letters.

What do you feel about Broomies now? This weather, so soft, so quiet, makes me realise what early autumn there might be. Its weather to go & find apples, to stand in the grass & hear them drop. Its Spring & Autumn with their arms round each other – like your two little girls in Garavan.

The packet arrived safely, thank you, darling. Your remark about Tis reminded me that in a paper here I read a little letter by Gaby Delys saying that Feudels Bath Saltrates made her feet 'feel so nice'.[2] A little, laughing picture & a bright string of bébé French. I felt if I went on read-ing – there'd come a phrase "quand on est mort, tu sais . . ."

Goodbye for now, dear darling Bogey.

MS ATL. *LKM* II. 101–2.

---

[1] On his way back to London, Murry had stayed for a night at the Hotel Beau Rivage, Bandol, where KM had spent most of Dec. 1915, before moving to the Villa Pauline. He had walked to the beach at Graviers, and called on their old friends the Allègres, who were in poor health and con-siderably aged.

[2] Murry's postcard on 7 May (ATL) had complained of tired feet and described drinking tea [tisane]. Gaby Deslys (1884–1920), a French music-hall *danseuse* who had been a favourite of KM's. (See *CLKM* III. 220.)

To J. C. Squire, 12 May 1921

Hotel Beau Site | Clarens-Montreux | La Suisse
12.V.1921

Dear Mr Squire,

Just in case anyone should write to me c/o The Mercury would you kindly readdress the letter to 10 Adelphi Terrace c/o The Nation and Athenaeum. I have left the South of France for good but I haven't found my mountain yet and letters are so rare in my world that I cant bear the thought of them being lost.

Yours very sincerely

Katherine Mansfield.

TC Stanford.

To J. M. Murry 12 May 1921

[Hotel Beau Site, Clarens-Montreux]
12.V.1921.

Dearest Bogey

The inventory came from Pope's[1] last night. I am keeping it in the file. We don't pay this bill, do we? (Re money: L.M. destroyed that cheque you gave her. I don't know why.) The list of our furniture would make any homme de coeur weep.

1 Tin Box Dolls Tea Service
 China Figure of Sailor
2 Liqueur Decanters
1   "   Glass
3 Light Dresden Girandole
1 Glass Bowl
9 Paper Knives

Doesn't it sound a heavenly dustbin? Did you know there was a Fluted Comport? And a Parian Flower Jar?

Since my first letter the mountains have been mobled kings.[2] They have unveiled themselves today, tho'. I have not had one word sent on from the office, nor a paper. This is *queer* isn't it? I am glad it was "rather beastly" to feel absolutely cut off. Thank you for this Houré smale.[3] Goodbye dear Love. Is it to be postcards postcards *all* the way?[4]
Tig.

MS ATL. *LKM* II. 104–5.

1 The agency that handled the shift from Portland Villas.
2 'But who, O, who has seen the mobled queen': *Hamlet*, II. ii. 525.
3 During these weeks while she was reading Chaucer, KM frequently affected Chaucerian spelling and phrases.
4 Cf. 'It was roses, roses all the way', Robert Browning, 'The Patriot' (1855).

To Anne Drey, [12 May 1921]

Hotel Beau Site, | Clarens-Montreux | La Suisse suisse SUISSE.

My Precious Darling Anne,

If I were in Paris wouldn't I fly to where you were! Its so perfect of you even to think Im there. I feel as though I was. Or at least that for two quite inferior pins I could pack up and go. But, chère, at the moment I can only walk from the kerridge to the door and from the door to the ker- ridge. Cant mount a stair, cant do *anything* but lie in a chaise longue look- ing at mountains that make one feel one is living in the Eye of the Lord. Its all temporary – I am full of beans and full of fight, but unfortunately darling Im full of Bacilli too. Which is a bother. If you came here Id simply have such a laugh about it that this rotten old chaise longue would break its Swiss legs. Instead Im waiting for docteur Figli (good name that!) and Ive got a very nice little booklet of information to give him about 2 little guineas which have just died for my sake. The number of guinea pigs Anne that Ive murdered! So that, my precious dear, is *that*. Paris might be – might very *well* be la pleine lune for me.

I left my dear little Isola Bella last week. The South of France is fever to the feverish. Thats my experience. Adorable pays – Ill go back there one day but sans un thermomètre. Switzerland, which I have always managed to avoid is the very devil. I knew it would be. I mean the people are so UGLY; they are simply hideous. They have no shape. All the women have pear shaped derrières, ugly heads, awful feet. All the men wear ready made check flannelette suits, six sizes too small and felt hats another six sizes too small with a little pre-war feather sticking up behind. Curse them. And the FOOD. Its got no nerves. You know what I mean? It seems to lie down and wait for you; the very steaks are meek. Theres no contact between you and it. You're not attracted. You don't feel that keeness to meet it and know more of it and get on very intimate terms. The asparagus is always stone dead. As to the puree de pommes de terre you feel inclined to call it 'uncle'. Now I had food in the South that made me feel – should there be a Paradis you and I shall have one lunch cooked by my old Marie which will atone for years of not meeting. And then Anne, Switzerland is revoltingly clean. My bed! Its enough to unmake any man – the sight of it. Dead white – tucked in so tight that you have to insert yourself like a knife into an oyster. I got up the first night and almost whimpering like Stepan in The Possessed[1] I put my old wild jackal skin over the counterpane. But this cleanliness persists in everything. Even the bird droppings on the terrasse are immaculate and every inch of lilac is crisp home from the laundry. Its a cursed country. And added to this there are these terrific mountains. I keep saying that about cats looking at Kings but one feels a very small cat, licking ones paw, making a dab or two at ones tail in the face of Immensities.

However, darling, I believe it is the only place where they do give one back ones wings and I cant go on crawling any longer. Its beyond a joke.

I hope you have a perfect time in Paris. Murry has been there. He was very happy. He's at present lecturing in Oxford on Style.[2] I had a very long story in The Mercury this month which I rather hoped you'd see because you'd see the point of it. I hope you do. Tell me about your work when you have time. The precious babe's little picture follows me everywhere. The one in the pram – looking out.

I shant stay here at this hotel long so my London address is best. The sight of distant Montreux is altogether too powerful. As to the people in this hotel – it is like a living cemetery. I never saw such deadness. I mean belonging to a by gone period. Collar supports (do you remember them?) are the height of fashion here & hair nets and silver belt buckles and button boots. Face powder hasn't been *invented* yet.

Its a queer world, but in spite of everything, darling, its a rare rare joy to be alive – and I salute you and it & kiss you both together – but you I kiss more warmly. Love please to Drey.

Goodbye for now.

Toujours, ma bien-chère

Ta

Katherine.

MS ATL. *LKM* II. 102–4.

[1] Stepan Trofimovitch Verkhovensky, a garrulous dandy and inept liberal in Dostoevsky's *The Possessed* (1871).

[2] The six lectures that Murry delivered at the School of English during the summer term were published in the following year as *The Problem of Style*.

To J. M. Murry, [12 May 1921]

[Hotel Beau Site, Clarens-Montreux]

Its a chill, strange day. I can just get about. I decided this morning to write to Sorapure about the Swiss Spahlinger treatment: whether it would be suitable for me, etc. And I shall wire you to-morrow, asking you to go and see Sorapure. Say what you like. But let him know that I am practically a hopeless invalid. I have tried to explain about money to him; why I haven't paid him, and I have promised to pay the first moment I can. . . .

'Mistress, I dug upon your grave
To bury a bone, in case
I should be hungry near this spot
When passing on my daily trot.
I am sorry, but I quite forgot
It was your resting place.'

(Thomas Hardy)[1]

Wing would do this.

MS lacking. *Journal* 1954, 258–9.

[1] The final stanza of Thomas Hardy's 'Ah, Are You Digging Up My Grave', from *Satires of Circumstance* (1914).

To J. M. Murry, 13 May 1921.

[Clarens-Montreux]

Tout va bien.

Telegram ATL. Text: letter of Murry, 13 May 1921. Murry, 326.

To J. M. Murry, [14 May 1921]

[Château Bellevue] Sierre,
Saturday,

I am in the middle of one of my *Giant Coups*. Yesterday evening I decided to look no longer for doctors in Montreux. In fact I felt the hour had come for something quite extraordinary. So I phone Montana – asked Dr. Stephani to descend by funiculaire to Sierre and meet me here at the Château Bellevue at 3 o'clock today – then engaged a car and started off this morning shortly after 9 o'clock. It is years since I have done such things. It is like a dream.

MS lacking, Scrapbook, 178–9.

To J. M. Murry, [15 May 1921]

[Hotel Beau Site, Clarens-Montreux]
Sunday.

Sweethert myn

I got back from Sierre at about 7.30 last night. I rather wish I hadn't sent you that little note from there. It was so confuged. Tear it up, love. While I write a man is playing the Zither so sweetly and gaily that ones heart dances to hear. Its a very warm, still day.

Will you please look at this picture of the lake at Sierre? Do you like it? Its lovely, really it is. Bogey if we spend a year here in Switzerland I don't think you will regret it. I think you would be happy. Yesterday gave me such a wonderful idea of it all. I feel I have been through & through Switzerland. And up there, at Sierre & in the tiny mountain towns on the way to Sierre it is absolutely unspoilt. I mean its so unlike, so remote from the Riviera in that sense. There are *no* tourists to be seen. It is a whole complete life. The only person I could think of meeting would have been Lawrence before the war. The only thing which is modern (and this makes me feel the Lord is on our side) is the postal service: it is excellent everywhere in Switzerland even in the villages. There are two posts a day everywhere. As to telegrams they simply fly. And your letter posted 8.30 p.m. May 12th arrived here at 9.30 a.m. May 14th. All these remarks are, again of the carrot family. I heard there are any number of small chalets to be had in Sierre and in Montana. We should take one, don't you think, darling? And have a Swiss bonne. As to cream-cows, they abound. And the whole countryside is full of fruit and of vines. Its famous for its small grapes, and for a wine which the peasants make. The father brews for his sons, and the sons for their sons. Its drunk when its about 20 years old & I believe it is superb.

Queer thing is that all the country near Sierre is like the Middle Ages. There are ancient tiny castles on small round wooded knolls, and the towns are solid, built round a square. Yesterday as we came to one part of the valley – it was a road with a *solid* avenue of poplars – a green wall on either side – little wooden carts came spanking towards us. The man sat on the shafts. The woman, in black with a flat black hat, ear rings & a white kerchief sat in front with the children. Nearly all the women carried huge bunches of crimson peonies – flashing bright. A stream of these little carts passed & then we came to a town & there was a huge fair going on in the market square. In the middle people were dancing, round the sides they were buying pigs and lemonade, in the cafés under the white & pink flowering chestnut trees there were more people & at the windows of the house there were set pots of white narcissi and girls looked out – they had orange & cherry handkerchiefs on their heads. It was beyond words gay and delightful. Then further on we came to a village where some fête was being arranged. The square was hung with garlands & there were cherry coloured masts with flags flying from them and each mast had a motto – framed in leaves – AMITIE – TRAVAIL – HONNEUR – DEVOIR. All the men of the village in white shirts & breeches were stringing more flags across & a very old man sat on a heap of logs plaiting green branches. He had a huge pipe with *brass fittings.*

Oh dear. In some parts of the Rhone valley there are deep, deep meadows. Little herd boys lie on their backs or their bellies & their tiny white goats spring about on the mountain slopes. These mountains have little lawns set with trees, little glades & miniature woods & torrents on the lower slopes & all kinds of different trees are there in their beauty. Then come the pines & the firs, then the undergrowth, then the rock & the snow. You meet tiny girls all alone with flocks of *black* sheep or herds of huge yellow cows. Perhaps they are sitting on the bank of a stream with their feet in the water or stripping a wand. And houses are so few, so remote. I dont know what it is, but I think you would feel as I did *deeply pleased* at all this. I like to imagine (am I right, my own?) that you would muse as you read: yes, I could do with a year there . . . And you must know that *from Sierre* one can go far and wide – in no time. I believe the flowers are in their perfection in June & July and again the *alpine flora* in September and October.

I see a small chalet with a garden, near the pine forests. I see it all very simple, with big white china stoves and a very pleasant woman with a tanned face & sun bleached hair bringing in the coffee. I see winter – snow & a load of wood coming at our door. I see us going off in a little sleigh – with huge fur gloves on & having a picnic in the forest & eating ham & fur sanwiches. Then there is a lamp – très important. There are our books. Its very still. The frost is on the pane. You are in your room writing. I in mine. Outside the stars are shining & the pine trees are dark like velvet.

Farewell, Bogey. I love you dearly dearly.

Tig.

Thank you for Mrs H[ardy]'s nice letter.[1] I long to hear of your time there. I was not surprised at Sullivan. Hes so *uncertain* at present I mean in his own being that it will come natural to him to pose. I don't know how far you realise you *make* him what he is with you – or how different he is with others. Also at present S. has no real self respect and that makes him *boast*. Like all of us he wants to feel important & thats a *right* feeling – we *ought* to feel important – but while he remains undisciplined & dans le vague he *can't be* important.[2] So he has to boast. I mustn't go on. You are calling me a school mistress . . .

Please give Mother & Richard[3] my love.

MS ATL. *LKM* II. 107–10.

---

[1] Murry had sent on a letter from Thomas Hardy's wife Florence, saying how much her husband admired 'The Daughters of the Late Colonel'.

[2] Since Sullivan's visit to Menton, and his ongoing domestic difficulties, Murry found his playing the role of abandoned lover tiresome.

[3] Murry was staying with his parents at 2 Acris Street, Wandsworth.

To J. M. Murry, [16 May 1921]

[Hotel Beau Site, Clarens-Montreux]
Monday.

My darling,

I feel certain this letter from Father contains that Blow I am always expecting. Will you open it & read it & *wire* me what result?[1] That sounds extravagant but you know the feeling? Ive got it v. strong this morning. Perhaps I ought to cable Pa. I don't know. I suppose *you* couldn't write a line just to report? To say what old Stephani said (1) There is still hope *provided* I have no more fever *and provided* I can get strong enough to stand treatment.

Those are the unblushing facts.

I havent heard from you today yet. I expect Ill hear by the afternoon post. Don't know what it is Bogey but

I have never loved you as I love you now.

This must be our Indian summer, I think.

I send you my love. It is safe with you & you will send it back to me. I know it won't be lost. Keep it, dearest dearest Hert.

Tig.

Dont spare me any of Pa's letter. I can hear anything from you.

MS ATL. Cited Alpers 1980, 335.

[1] KM feared that her father had cut her £300 annual allowance. He did not in fact do so, although he felt strongly that it was Murry's duty to provide for his wife.

To J. M. Murry, [17 May 1921]

[Hotel Beau Site, Clarens-Montreux]   Tuesday, 4.30 p.m.

My darling Bogey

About the Journal. I wish it were ever so many times as long again.[1] You can imagine how I read it, a kind of special façon de lire. Really there is nothing more fascinating than this vision of the others mind – independent, personal, detached as it can't be in letters – and yet intimate as it cant be in another form of writing. Bandol is *beautiful* – there is no other word – theres such 'leisure' – a dreaming quality . . . Its like a boat swinging idle on a still sea. I feel you were at the place, at Arles[2] for instance for months. That your room there *was* your room. You did without a carafe *the whole time*. I have now an idea of all that country, and of the kind of life which I did not even glimpse before. The farmer class, the asparagus, the grossness, the lovely tiles, the talk. Good heavens! Are there really only a few pages of it? The procession seen from the window might be the middle of the book.

As to Paris. I never have read anything about a child more exquisite than your little girls remark il pleut when someone put a sunshade up. Its the most profound thing about a very young baby's vision of the world Ive ever struck. *Its what babies in prams think.* Its what you say long before you can talk. Shes altogether a ravishing person – no, so much more than that. Shes a tiny vision there in those gardens for ever. Your tenderness is perfect – its so *true*.

I liked Valéry and his household.[3] It seemed somehow 'extremely right' as Kot would say that his mother should be there & that she should be so small. I expect she thought you were a boy. I should like to have been there.

(I am writing in the thick of a thunderstorm. They are regular items now in the late afternoon. It gets misty, the birds sound loud, it smells of irises & then it thunders. I love such summer storms. I love hearing the maids run in the passages to shut the windows & draw up the sun blinds, & then you see on the road between the vineyards people hurrying to take shelter. Besides Ive such a great part of the sky to see that I can watch the beginning the middle and the end . . .)

Darling I cant thank you properly for the blue book. Ill take care of it for you.

Lets see. What is the news of the outside world. A letter from Sorapure – *awfully nice*.[4] A letter from Bouchage & his bill – 2000 francs. Awfully nasty. A letter from Tom Moult appealing to the past when he first knew us & quoting your old letters to him. Yes, it *did* touch me. A bundle of press cuttings – stray shoots that ought to have been cut off long ago. And Jeanne, in Montreal and Jinnie just off to Rome – and so on, love. Its so hot that one pulls up ones sleeves to write – above the elbow, you know – & thinks in terms of fans. I decided last night that we should have our first dinner up here in the little salon. It was the first – in fact it was the airy fairy *foundation stone* of the dream which is called *Arrival of Bogey*.

Tig.

MS ATL. *LKM* II. 114; *LJMM*, 632–3.

[1] Murry had started keeping a daily journal, which he sent on to KM.
[2] Murry visited Arles after he left Bandol on 7 May.
[3] Murry had become friendly some years before with the French poet Paul Valéry (1871–1945).
[4] Probably the letter which he wrote to her on 4 May 1921, which would have been sent to Menton, then to Switzerland. He reprimanded her for an earlier, lost letter, in which she seems to have attacked him: 'I am indeed sorry that you have read me so unkindly. I have put your horrid little note into the fire, and with it the unpleasant memory of your mistake.' His letter went on to compliment her on her courage and her gifts, and offer the following advice: 'You must know that there are phases in life that we all have the right to share with others' (ATL). It is perhaps as a result of this 'awfully nice' second letter that she wrote him a long account of her experience of tuberculosis (see next letter).

To Victor Sorapure,[1] *[? mid-May 1921]*

[Hotel Beau Site, Clarens-Montreux]

Dear Dr Sorapure

About a year ago you taught me how to breathe and how to sit and how to make my feet warm. Those 'lessons' started me thinking over – or rather observing one or two other little things. And I wonder whether you might be interested in what a tubercular patient has noticed. They are very slight; I only send you one or two out of a sheaf-full. Other people might think I was morbidly selfconscious in thus giving expression to my symptoms but I know you will understand I do so because I have learned to think (and try to act by it) that "what is the matter?" is a ques-tion of no value whatever unless it is tripped up by "How can I put it right" –

I submit them in all humility.

K.M.

('I' is of course just 'x' or 'the patient'. I hope this doesn't sound like Mrs Eustache Miles[2] or that you will not think me impertinent in imagining that you might be interested in "what the patient feels".)

Breathing: When I wake in the morning I keep very still, lie on the back, breathe as I have been taught to breathe and, in addition, slowly open the arms to their fullest extent. Quite slowly, without effort, imitating the action of an opera singer who makes just this gesture before taking a high note which he wants to 'hold' as long as possible. I do this very *thoughtfully*, half a dozen times at most and it seems to air the lungs – to, in fact, fill the lungs quite full. This particular movement of slowly, gen-tly, opening the arms is at all times extremely refreshing, but particularly in those peculiar moments of *sudden fatigue* which one feels.

Depression. When I am attacked by acute feelings of depression I find it a great help to change my position. If I am in bed I move, get an extra pillow, sit up if Im lying down, or lie down if Im sitting up. If I am not in bed I move gently about the room. The change of position seems to relieve a feeling of congestion, and that peculiar feeling that one is being smothered.

(I wonder if healthy people realise the effect of a *change of position* on the patients mind. I mean now, the difference it makes to change the 'site' of a bed, to make the patient face another way, or escape the pat-tern of the wallpaper. It is extraordinarily refreshing.)

Humming: When I am resting and breathing is easy I *hum*. I make no attempt to sing or indeed to raise the voice at all, but just hum softly "under the breath" as they say. This gentle sound distracts ones atten-tion from the act of breathing and I find that in a few minutes the breathing is taking care of itself and is easier and gentler. At the risk of an Americanism I do think its very well worth while for tubercular patients to "get the humming habit". Whistling is a nervous effort and singing out of the question but its not natural for a normal healthy per-son to make no sound other than speech – and this humming seems to break the feeling of 'isolation', as well as to relieve the breathing.

Appetite: I discovered that when I had no appetite my food gave me indigestion. At the sight of food I immediately felt nervous, and attacked it in a state of physical tension. Then I tried relaxing consciously for a minute or two before eating and this relaxation not only made me eat slowly when I did eat, it made it possible to eat a great deal more – and (though this is extravagant, I suppose) I find it cured my indigestion. Perhaps *grace before meat* wasn't only instituted so that infants should praise de Lord but also with a view of inducing this feeling of relaxation. *Breathing*: When the breathing is very troublesome and the weather is dark I find it a help to look at pictures. I should think little children would benefit greatly from this. Reading is no help, and either talking or listening less, but the sight of pictures seems to ease one. Healthy creatures *at sight* of anything that pleases them give a "*sigh* of pleasure"; it seems to provoke them to breathe deeply and lightly. They are not so much excited as steadied and made tranquil and if one is ill this feeling is accentuated – I have proved this often. It seems so important when there is difficulty in breathing to distract the patient from the act of breathing and yet keep him tranquil.

MS ATL. Cited *Exhibition*, 45.

[1] Victor Sorapure (1874–1933) was educated at St George's Jesuit College, Kingston, Jamaica, and, following his medical degree and postgraduate work at St Andrews University, he served as chief surgeon at Government Hospital, Kingston. After holding the chair of histology and pathology at Fordham University Medical School 1906–10, he returned to England, and was consultant physician at Hampstead General Hospital when she first visited him in 1918. He was the one of many doctors she consulted whom she continued to admire, and he seems to have acted almost as a kind of spiritual adviser as well as a physician. In July 1919 she wrote a series of light-hearted limericks relating to her health, the first of which read:

> A doctor who came from Jamaica
> Said: This time I'll mend her or break her.
> I'll plug her with serum
> And if she can't bear'em
> I'll call in the next undertaker.

(*Journal* 1954, 178)

[2] The wife of Eustace Miles (b. 1868) who wrote, as well as books on history, literary technique, and cricket, a number of volumes on health and fitness, including *Healthy Breathing* (1921).

To J. M. Murry, [19 May 1921]

[Hotel Beau Site, Clarens-Montreux]
Thursday.

Darling

I cant tell you how Tigs love to be told they are missed and that their Bogies think of them – especially when they are in 'some strange hotel'.[1] I shall be very glad when you can come back. I hope you will not have to go away too soon again . . . Sullivan has 'gone' for the time being – hasn't he? I confess I do not want to see him here – not now – nor Brett. In fact I *cannot* see Brett or other people just now. I wish they would

understand that. If they suggest coming across will you please tell the
plain truth which is I am too busy this year? Leave it to them to understand or not, darling. *There it is.*

I wish you weren't such a modest little fellow. I'd love an outside opinion of your lectures. *Are you happy about them?* No, you can't answer that.
You're feeling your way yourself. That is just the point. What about
heaving out that quotation from K.M. & replacing it by someone else.[2]
I don't think its in quite good taste. At any rate, I have a feeling about
it . . . What do you think? Of course I remember old Grundy.[3] It was
Goodyear's laugh I heard when I read his name – a kind of snorting
laugh, ending in a chuckle & then a sudden terrific *frown* and he got very
red. Do you remember? And you remember the stick he brought from
Bombay? He was very pleased with that stick. Your mention of Grundy
gave me Goodyear[4] again – living, young, a bit careless and *worried* – but
enjoying the worry – in the years before the war when a pale moon
shone above Piccadilly Circus and we three stood at the corner & didn't
want to separate or go home . . .

I went out yesterday in a Swiss kerridge to see Mercanton – who is
Stephanis man here. The Swiss kerridge was a rare old bumper and the
driver who weighed about 18 stone leaped into the air & then crashed
back on to the seat. It was raining. A massive hood was down. I could
just put forth a quivering horn from beneath it. Montreux is *very ugly* and
quite empty. But in the shops the people are awfully nice. They are simple, frank, honest beyond words & kind in the German way. The thing
about Switzerland is there is absolutely no *de luxe.* That makes an enormous difference. Its simply not understood. And one is not expected to
be rich. Far from it. One isn't expected to spend. This is very pleasant
indeed. I suppose there is a sort of surface scum of what the Daily Mail
calls the "Jazzing World" but it doesn't touch the place. To put it in a
gnutshell, love, there simply is no *fever* – no fret. The children are really
beautiful. I saw a baby boy yesterday who took my heart away. He was
a little grub in a blue tunic with a fistful of flowers – but his *eyes,* his *colour,*
his *health!* You want to lie in the grass here & have picnics – Monte Carlo
is not in the same world. Its on another planet almost. But you'll feel
what I mean.

Tig.

MS ATL. *LKM* II. 106–7; *LJMM* 634–5.

1 Murry notes (*LJMM,* 634) that this phrase was from a music-hall song.

2 Murry did not follow KM's advice. In his fifth lecture, 'The Process of Creative Style', he
advantageously set the opening paragraph of part II of *Prelude* against Arnold Bennett's 'At the Quai
d'Orsay Terminus, Paris', from *Things that Have Interested Me.*

3 Murry had written on 16 May that 'I met a ridiculous old tutor of mine – called Grundy –
you may have heard Goodyear and me speaking of him'. George Beardoe Grundy (1861–1948) was
a lecturer at Brasenose when Murry and Goodyear were undergraduates. A specialist in classical

geography, he published works on the Persian War and on Thucydides. He was an ardent sports-
man, but a rigid, limited teacher.

⁴ KM's admirer Frederick Goodyear (see *CLKM*, I, 248–50) was at Oxford with Murry, and for
a time worked for Oxford University Press in India.

To J. M. Murry, [19 May 1921]

[Hotel Beau Site, Clarens-Montreux]

Veen dear,

Read this criticism. It takes the bisquito. This gent is evidently playing Paris to Miss W's Helen.¹ But why a half-brick at me? They do hate
me, those young men. The Sat. Review said of my story "a dismal transcript of inefficiency".² What a bother! I suppose, that living alone as I
do, I get all out of touch & what seems to me even *lively* is ghostly glee.

Sorry your forgot your braces & your toothbrush. I cant imagine
either you or me without toospeg brushes. I feel theyd come flying after.
I am v. glad you lunched with the Luft Schiffs. Dont they get a funny
crew together!³ But they are a kind pair.

Oh my dear sweet hert, I like these 2 torn pages written at such a terrific lick – funny long y's and g's tearing along, like fishes in a river when
you are wading.

One word more.

I was not honest about not "facing all facts". Yes, I *do* believe one ought
to face facts. If you don't they get behind you & they become terrors,
nightmares, giants, horrors. As long as one faces them one is top dog.
The trouble is not to *steel oneself* – to face them calmly – easily – to have
the habit of facing them. I say this because I think nearly all my falsity
has come from *not* facing facts as I should have done & its only now that
Im beginning to learn to face them.

MS ATL. *LKM* II. 104.

¹ Not identified.
² From the one sentence referring to 'The Daughters of the Late Colonel' in an unsigned survey column 'Magazines', *Saturday Review*, 7 May 1921.
³ On 15 May Murry had lunched with the Schiffs in London. 'Your Mr. Tinayre was there –
also Ada Leverson' (Murry, 329). KM had met Tinayre at the Schiffs' villa in Roquebrune; the novelist Ada Leverson (1862–1933), a close and compassionate friend of Oscar Wilde, was Violet
Schiff's sister.

To Anne Drey, [19 May 1921]

Hotel Beau Site | Clarens-Montreux

I must write to you once again, darling woman, while you are in Paris.
Anne, if I were not to hear from you again ever I could live on your last

letter. To have taken the trouble – I know what writing means – to have sent me that whole great piece of Paris – complete with yourself and the traffic (Id love to be somewhere where taxis ran one over) and the tops, and Louise avec son plumeau, and the shops with the flowery saucissons, & that getting le petit déjeuner, and Wyndham Lewis[1] & – well – I walked through your letter once & then I just idled through it again & took my time and stopped to look & admire and *love* and smell and hear it all. It was a great gift, my dearest Anne – it was un cadeau superbe pour moi. How I *love* you for doing just that. Do you feel I do? You must. Now Ive been to Paris – and even to St. Cloud. For your idea of a house there started me dreaming of the house next door. Charming houses – two stories with lilac bushes at the gate. I made a hole in my fence big enough for an eye to flash through – and in the morning I spied through and called to the petit who was *gardening* "David" and he said – rather off hand – "Quoi?" And I said "Will you come to tea with me today?" and he turned his back on me & shouted up at his own house "She wants me to go to tea". At that your head appeared at a window & you said "Well do you want to go?" David replied – "Well what have we got for tea here?" . . . . . It was an *awfully sweet* dream. I wish it would come true. What fun we should have. In the evening there would be a lamp on the garden table. I see a whole lovely life – and more my life than cafés nowadays.

All the same Paris and London have their appeal. Its very good to talk at times & I love *watching* and *listening.* These mountains are crushing table companions. But all the same I lie all day looking at them and they are pretty terrific. . . . if one could get them into the story, you know – get them "place".

I saw the biggest specialist in Switzerland on Saturday, Anne. Thats what made your letter so wonderfully good just at the moment. It seemed to bring Life so near again. After Id seen this man it was just as if the landscape – everything changed a little – moved a little *further off.* I always expect these doctor men to say – "Get better?" Of course you will! We'll put you right in no time. Six months at the very most & youll be fit as a fiddle again.' But though this man was extremely nice he would not say more than – I still had a chance. That was all. I tried to get the word "guéri" but it was no good. All I could wangle out of him was: "If your digestion continues good you still have a chance".

Its an infernal nuisance to love Life as I do. I seem to love it more as time goes on rather than less. It never becomes a habit to me – its always a marvel. I do hope Ill be able to keep in it for long enough to do some really good work. Im sick of people dying who promise well. One doesn't want to join that crowd at all. So I shall go on lapping up jaunes d'oeufs and de la crème . . .

Anne will you greet Wyndham Lewis for me and say how I regret not knowing him. Hes one of the few people Id very much like to have had for a friend.

You gave the Joyce ménage perfectly. I *see* them. I suppose he is a very great man. I confess there is a quelque chose in his writing which I can't get on with – it to speak frankly – disgusts me. It strikes me as unhealthy in a peculiar way.[2] But I believe that Im not as modern as I ought to be. Jack Murry says Im a fearful moralist!!!

Its evening now. I expect the lights are just on in the streets. I see the round shadows of the trees, the warm white of the pavé. I see the people – flitting by. And here in the lake the mountains are bluish – cold. Only on the high tops the snow is a faint apricot colour. Beautiful Life! "To be alive and that is enough". I could *almost* say that – but not quite.

Farewell for now dear precious woman.

Toujours à toi
Katherine

The little photographs are just *exquisite*. It is his lovely little *fearless* look which is so remarkable. I think he's booked for an artist, Anne.

MS ATL. *LKM* II. 110–11.

---

[1] Wyndham Lewis (1882–1957), the Canadian-born novelist and painter, was a friend of both the Dreys and the Schiffs, but a later meeting with KM turned out acrimoniously.

[2] KM's view of Joyce fluctuated, as she found *Ulysses* both admirable and disturbing. She told Lady Ottoline Morrell in 1919 that 'In Joyce there is a peculiar *male* arrogance that revolts me more than I can say – it sickens me. I dislike his method equally with his mind & *cannot* see his power of writing' (*CLKM* II. 343). The Woolfs had been offered *Ulysses* for the Hogarth Press in Apr, 1918, but did not accept it. But Virginia Woolf remembered an event she recorded only in Jan. 1941: 'One day Katherine Mansfield came, & I had it out. She began to read, ridiculing: then suddenly said, But theres something in this: a scene that should figure I suppose in the history of literature' (*Diary of Virginia Woolf*, v. 353). See KM's letters to Sydney Schiff, 25 and 31 Dec. 1921, for the fullest expression of her opinion of Joyce.

To J. M. Murry, [21 May 1921]

[Hotel Beau Site, Clarens-Montreux]
Saturday evening.

My precious Bogey

I am rather conscious that my letters have fallen off just these last days. Especially so, since this evening I have read yours written at Oxford on Thursday. You know how it is when just the letter you get is the letter you would love to get? That was my experience with this one of yours, my darling. I dipped into that remote Oxford & discovered you there: I heard that click of the cricket ball, & I saw the trees & grass. I was with you, standing by you – not saying anything – but happy.

I love you with my whole heart, Bogey.

The reason why I haven't written is I am fighting a kind of Swiss chill. It will go off. Dont please give it another thought. I've got a tremendous equipment of weapons.

All day, in the sun, the men have been working in the vineyards. They have been hoeing between the vines & then an old man has been dust-ing certain rows with powder out of a Giant pepper pot. The heat has been terrific. The men have worn nothing but cotton trousers. Their bodies are tanned almost red brown – a very beautiful colour. And every now & then they stop work, lean on their pick, breathe deeply – look round. I feel I have been watching them for hundreds of years. Now the day is over, the shadows are long on the grass. The new trees hold the light – and wisps of white cloud move dreamily over the dreaming mountains. It is all very lovely . . . How hot is it in England? Here it is really, as Chaddie would say, almost tropical. The nights are hot, too. One lies with both windows wide open and my toes as usual get thirsty. Yes, what you say about your exercises. You know the vision of you with naked foot stalking within my chamber' is somehow most awfully *impor-tant* in the story of my love for you. And seeing you in the mirror & see-ing you on the floor . . . all so marvellously jewel clear! And you – a radiant, very free being – revealed in some way, in no need of the least 'protection' or 'covering.' I wonder if you see what I am getting at. It seems to me that my *false* idea of your helplessness was put absolutely beautifully *right* by the sight of your nakedness. But here I spec' you're smiling at Wig for making such a big bone about it. Nevertheless I mean something "very profound", love.

Thank you for the Tchek. Came tonight. I am simply captivated by Chaucer just now. I have had to throw a bow window into my coeur petit to include him with Shakespeare. Oh dear! His Troilus & Cressida!? And my joy at finding your remarks & your pencil notes.

I read today The Tale of Chaunticleer & Madame Pertelote – its the *Pardoner's Tale*.[3] Perfect in its way. But the *personality*, the *really* of the man. How his impatience, his pleasure, the very tone rings through. Its deep delight to read. Chaucer & Marlowe are my two at present. I don't mean theres any comparison between them. But I read Hero & Leander last night. Thats incredibly lovely. But how extremely amusing Chapman's *finish* is![4] Taking up that magical poem & pulling it into a body & skirt. Its V. funny! As I write theres a subdued roar from the *salle à manger* where Lunns Lions are being fed.[5] Fourteen arrived today for A Week by the Pearl of Lac Leman. Its nice to think I have this salon & dont need to go among them except when so disposed.

I do hope you'll be happy with Hardy.[6] I feel it ought to be most awfully nice. I feel they are simple. There'll be no need to explain things. The kind of people who understand making jam, even – & would love to hear of others making it. I liked so what she said about their way of living – it was almost egg-weggs for tea. I *look forward* to June. Be happy, dearest mine.

Tig.

MS ATL. *LKM* II. 105–6; *LJMM*, 635–7.

[1]
> They flee from me that sometime did me seek,
> With naked foot stalking in my chamber.

(Opening of Sir Thomas Wyatt's lyric, 1557)

[2] Chaucer''s long poem *Troilus and Criseyde, c.*1385.

[3] KM is confusing the 'Pardoner's Tale' with 'The Nun's Priest's Tale', which tells of Chauntecleer and Pertelote.

[4] The two sestiads of Christopher Marlowe's projected longer work *Hero and Leander* were published four years after the poet's death in 1598, with an additional four sestiads by George Chapman. KM copied in a notebook on 19 May a line from *Hero and Leander*, 1. 1. 242, which presumably she found apposite, 'Lone women like to empty houses perish' (*Journal* 1954, 251).

[5] Sir Henry Lunn was the founder of a prosperous group travel business.

[6] Murry would stay with the Hardys at Max Gate, Dorchester, on Saturday, 4 June.

To Ottoline Morrell, [c.22 May 1921]

Hotel Beau Site | Clarens-Montreux | Switzerland.

Dearest Ottoline,

I never felt more disappointed than that we should have been so near & yet so far, as they say. I wanted to telephone you, but that was no use. After the journey here my cough was so troublesome that I couldn't raise my voice at all. Oh dear! It was a melancholy business.

I do hope that you are feeling better and that the journey back was not too trying. Did the man really do you good in Lausanne? Is your neuralgia *really* better? Do let me know! I feel it must be a happiness for you to be at home again – especially after Lausanne! But one cant be really happy if ones body refuses to 'join in', if it persists in going its own way and *never* letting one forget it. But how is one to get cured? As to doctors – there aren't any. I have just paid little Bouchage 2000 francs for looking after me & Im 50 times worse than I was at Christmas. They know nothing. I had two really deadly experiences here with perfect fools and after all this long time they depressed me so much that I felt desperate & I motored off to Montana to see the specialist there. He's supposed to be the best man in Switzerland for lungs. He was better than the others and I am going to be under him in future – I dont know for how long. Its very vague. He would not say I can get better. All he would say was I still have a chance & he has known patients with lungs as far gone as mine who have recovered. I really don't mind a straw. It was a divine day – the day I met him – and the strange ancient room in an old hotel where we talked was so beautiful that the moment was enough. One must live for the moment, that is all I feel now. When he explained how the left lung was deeply engaged but the right was really the dangerous one I wanted to say: "Yes, but do listen to the bees outside. Ive never heard such bees. And theres some delicious plant growing outside the window. It reminds me of Africa."

But my health is such a frightfully boring subject that I won't talk about it.

Life in this hotel is a queer experience. I have two rooms and a balcony so I am, thank Heaven, quite cut off. They are corner rooms, too. But I descend for the meals – step into the whirlpool – and really one sees enough, hears enough at them to last one for ever. I have never *imagined* such people. I think they are chiefly composed of Tours – they are one composite person, being taken round for so much a week. Its hard to refrain from writing about them. But my balcony looks over Montreux and Clarens. Anything more hideous!! I think Switzerland has the very ugliest houses, people, food, furniture in the whole world. Theres something incredible in the solid ugliness of the people. The very newspapers full of advertisements for a "magnificent *porc*," or a batterie de cuisine comprising 75 pieces are typical. And the grossness of every-thing! I cant stand the narcissi even. I feel there are too many and the scent is too *cheap.* Yesterday L.M., who is staying at a place called Blonay brought me a bunch of lilies of the valley – an immense cauliflower it looked like and smelt like.

But I must say the country round Sierre is simply wonderful. Thats where I'd like to be. Its so unspoilt, too. I mean there are no Casinos, no *tea shops* and as far as I could see from my glimpse not a tourist to be seen. I shall go there at the end of June when Murry has joined me. I feel so remote, so cut off from everything here . . . I cant walk at all. I lie all day in the shade and write or read and thats all. Work is the only thing that never fails. Even if people don't like my stories I don't mind. Perhaps they will one day, or the stories will be better. Ive been reading *Chaucer.* Have you read his Troilus & Cressid lately? It is simply *perfect.* I have a passion for Chaucer just now. But England seems to think Miss Romer Wilson is so much the greatest writer that ever was born.[1] She *does* sound wonderful. I must say. Is it all true?

Goodbye dearest. Forgive a dull dog. I feel this is infernally dull. Its sent with so much love & *real* longing to hear you're better.

Ever

Katherine.

MS Stanford. *LKM* II. 115–17.

[1] The novelist Romer Wilson (1891–1930) was enjoying considerable vogue. Her new novel *The Death of Society* won the Hawthornden Prize, but in reviewing her first novel *All These Young Men* in the *Athenaeum*, 14 Nov. 1919, KM had observed how the main character merely 'gathers the scattered emotions of the moment into her bosom and pours them forth in song'.

To J. M. Murry, [23 May 1921]

[Hotel Beau Site, Clarens-Montreux]
Monday night.

Dearest Bogey darling

I have been trying to write out a long explanation of the reasons why I have felt out of touch with you. But I don't think such explanations are of the smallest good. If you were here I could tell you what I feel in a minute – but at a distance – its different – I dont think its good.

Do you know, darling, what I think Love is? It is drawing out all that is finest and noblest in the soul of the other. Perhaps the other isn't conscious this is what is happening & yet he feels at peace – and that is why. That is I think the *relationship* between lovers, and it is in this way that, because they give each other their freedom (for evil is slavery) they "ought" (not in the moral sense) to *serve* each other. By service I mean what Chaucer means when he makes his true Knights wonder what they can do that will give joy to their love[2]. (But the lady must, of course, serve equally.) And of course I dont mean anything in the least 'superficial'. Indeed I mean just what there was between us in the last months at the Isola Bella – that – more and more perfect.

You ask me how I am, darling. I am much the same. This chill has been the worst I have ever had since I was ill, and so I feel weak and rather shadowy, physically. My heart is the trouble. But otherwise I feel . . . well, Bogey, its difficult to say. No, one can't believe in *God*. But I must believe in something more *nearly* than I do. As I was lying here today I suddenly remembered that: "Oh ye of little faith!"[1] Not faith in a God. No, thats impossible. But do I live as though I believed in *anything*? Dont I live *in glimpses* only? There is something wrong; there is something small in such a life. One must live more fully and one must have more POWER of living and feeling. One must be true to ones vision of life – in every single particular. And I am not. The only thing to do is to try again from tonight to be stronger and better – to be *whole*.

Thats *how I am*, dear Love. Goodnight.

Tig.

MS ATL. *LKM* II. 112; *LJMM*, 637–8.

[1] Luke 12: 28.
[2] KM has in mind the contest between Arcite and Palamon in *The Knight's Tale*.

To J. M. Murry, [24 May 1921]

[Hotel Beau Site, Clarens-Montreux]

(I heard today that Spahlinger costs 14 horses to begin with!iiii)

Tuesday.

My dear Love,

Last evening came your perfect letter written on Friday.[1] I mean the one in which you wonder whether you 'ought' to have said more about Stephani's report.[2] Love, as I *read* it, I understood your saying you loved me was the answer & especially your speaking of our future. I wanted nothing else. It was just as though after Id said something important to you, you crossed the room & for some heavenly reason – kissed me. You see, my precious? It was a perfect reply.

The fact is Veen that we have decided (those mysterious two have) not to speak about my illness any more than is 'necessary'.[3] They just dont. There is no need to any more. Its for the same reason that when they are together it may happen that they don't talk to each other at all & even look out of different windows. It seems to me it all began one day going to Castellar. No, I could trace it back deeper still. But n'importe. It isn't possible to love anyone more than I love you. I wish I were a better girl in all ways. I mean to write a *work* which will be my kind of a love poem. Oh, Heavens! To think you're coming over here & we shall gather fruit together this autumn. Did I tell you Sierre is renommé for its golden grape? I told you about the wine. But in September, so they say, the whole little town goes into the vineyards. Shall you be there – shall I? Bogey & Wig with brown hands & leaves in their hair? Sitting at the foot of a tiny green mountain that has small leaping white goats on it. It makes an awfully nice piggcture.

Know that goldfinch I have *tamed* – he comes right into my bedroom now & eats breakfast crumbs beside the bed. He is a ravishing little bird. If only he were carpet trained. But Im afraid you can't train birds. He seems just as surprised as I am. The sparrows now that he has come in grow bold & come as far as the parquet, too. But I won't have them. I aspire to having taught this goldfinch to present arms with my founting pen by the time you come – to do you honour. I also dream of it singing an address of welcome – holding the address you know in one claw.

During the past two nights I have read *The Dynasts.*[4] Isn't it queer how a book eludes one. And then suddenly – it opens for you? I have looked into this book before now. But the night before last, when I opened it I suddenly understood what the poet meant & how he meant it should be read! *The point of view* which is like a light streaming from the imagination and over the imagination – over ones head, as it were, the chorus & the aerial music. I am talking carelessly, because I am talking to you & I am relying on you to more than understand me. But it did seem to me that if the *poetic drama* is still a possible 'form' it will be, in the future, like The Dynasts – AS IF for the stage and yet not to be played. That will give it its freedom. Now when one reads The Dynasts its *always* as though it were on the stage . . . But the stage is a different one – it is within us. This is all très vague. Yet on my life I saw a play by you . . . which was the outcome of this form. In fact – I LONG to talk about this.

Squire has written asking for another story & also begging me to write a novel. Mrs Belloc Lowndes says – won't you telephone her if you've time? Every single afternoon there is a thunderstorm. Here I stopped. The doctor came. Its really funny. I must tell you. My chill is slightly better but I have symptoms of whooping cough! Il n'a manqué que ça! Oh Boge!

I am yours

Wig.

MS ATL. *LKM* II. 114–15; *LJMM*, 638–9.

¹ See Murry, 334–5.
² She had sent on the report of the eminent Swiss specialist.
³ Murry had written on 20 May: 'I find it so hard to say anything about your illness. It's some shyness or delicacy that prevents me' (Murry, 334).
⁴ Thomas Hardy's long verse drama *The Dynasts*, subtitled 'an epic-drama of the War with Napolean in three Parts, nineteen Acts and one hundred and thirty scenes', was published sequentially in 1904, 1906, 1908.

To Violet Schiff, [24 May 1921]

Hotel Beau Site | Clarens-Montreux

Many thanks for your letter. I want to write to you; I shall as soon as Ive got over this chill. At present I am in the very midst of it. The *place* is marvellous; the doctors incredibly, fantastically, too hopelessly maddening. They *will* speak English, too. If I could only give you an imitation of the one who has just left me. "Dere is nudding for it but lie in de bed – *eat* – and tink of naice tings" . . . He wore a little tiny straw hat too, & brown cotton gloves . . . What is one to do, dearest? To shoot or not to shoot . . .   Katherine.

Postcard BL. *LKM* II. 112.

To J. M. Murry, [25 May 1921]

[Hotel Beau Site, Clarens-Montreux]

Darling Bogey

In a small letter from you last night you seem to suggest that my letters aren't arriving. When I read that all my peaceful thoughts flew out of the tower – wheeled – circled – wouldn't come back. Not getting my letters? Not hearing from me? Is there a letter-eater at the office? Someone steals them? I cant bear to think they disappear. Dear love, I write so often . . .

I understand exactly what you feel about Oxford.[1] I expect you will be glad to be in London for some days. Tell me what you do. Just the facts & Ill embroider them. I like to ponder over them . . . to see you & Raleigh[2] at dinner.

It seems to me – the more I read the papers & now from what you say, too – that you & I are in some way *really different* from other writers of our time. I mean it seems to us so natural & so easy to link up with Flaubert[3] or another. Its part of our *job*. And the people whom we read as we read Shakespeare are part of our *daily lives*. I mean it doesn't seem to me QUEER to be thinking about Othello at breqchick or to be wondering about The Phoenix & The Turtle[4] in my bath. Its all part of a whole. Just as that vineyard below me is the vineyard in the song of Solomon[5] – and that beautiful sound as the men hoe between the vines is almost part of my body – goes on in me. I shall never be the same as I was *before* I heard it – just as Ill never be the same as I was before I read the death of Cleopatra. One has willingly *given* oneself to all these things – one is the result of them all. Are you now saying ''intellectual detachment''? But Ive *allowed* for that.

Other people – I mean people today seem to look on in a way I don't understand. I don't want to boast. I don't feel at all arrogant, but I do feel they have not perhaps lived as fully as we have . . . However . . . Did you know that Turgenev's[6] brain pesait deux mille grammes? Horrible idea. I couldn't help seeing it au beurre noir when I read that. I shall never forget that brain at Isola Bella. It was still *warm from thinking.* Ugh! Oh Bogey, I shall be very very glad to see you darling & to start Life with you. I have a mass of things to talk about. The great artist is he who exalts difficulty. Do you believe that? And that its only the slave (using slave in our mystical sense) who pines for freedom. The free man the artist seeks to bind himself. No, these notes ain't any good. But I have been *finding out* more & more how true it is that its only the difficult thing which is worth doing – its the difficult thing that one deliberately chooses to do. I don't think Tchekhov was as aware of that as he should have been. Some of the stories in The Horse Stealers[7] are – rather a shock.

Tell me, love (Ive changed my pen & my sujet) how is this? There is no Saint Galmier here – only Eau de Montreux – which, according to the bottil is saturated with carbonic acid gas. But my physiology book said that carbolic acid gas was a dedly poison – we only breathed it out but never except at the last desperate moment took it in. And here are doctors Schnepsli, Rittchen and Kneebloo saying it is a sovereign cure for gravel & makes the urine sparkle like champagne.

It is all so very difficult, as Constantia[8] would say.

Be a Good Boy. And don't walk on both sides of the street at once. It distracts people & makes it difficult for them to continue the conversation.

As for me I simply love you. ⸬

Tig.

MS ATL. *LKM* II. 112–14; *LJMM*, 639–41.

[1] Murry found himself out of sympathy with Oxford and the donnish life while staying there for his lectures.

[2] Walter Raleigh (1861–1922), professor of English literature at Oxford University, had invited Murry to deliver his six lectures on 'Style'.

[3] Both KM and Murry were admirers of the French novelist Gustave Flaubert (1821–80), on whom Murry was to write at least ten articles.

[4] *The Phoenix and the Turtle*, Shakespeare's long allegorical poem published in 1601.

[5] 'My vineyard, which is mine, is before me': S. of S. 8: 12. There are frequent references to the vineyard in the S. of S.

[6] The Russian playwright and novelist Ivan Turgenev (1818–83).

[7] Chekhov's *The Horse Stealers and Other Stories*, translated by Constance Garnett, was published in 1921.

[8] One of the timid, evasive sisters in 'The Daughters of the Late Colonel'.

To Beatrice Campbell,[1] [c.25 May 1921]

For the moment only: Hotel Beau-Site | Baugy-sur-Clarens | La Suisse.

Belle Beatrice

I can't tell you how glad I am to hear you are dancing again – albeit 'delicately' as you say.

> Lo! how sweetly the Graces do it foot
> To the instrument!
> They dauncen deftly and singen sooth
> In their merriement.[2]

That means you are really better. Don't get ill again. Isn't it awful — being ill. I lie all day on my old balcony lapping up eggs and cream & butter with no-one but a pet goldfinch to bear me tompanée. I must say the goldfinch is a great lamb. He's jet tame & this morning, after it had rained he came for his Huntley & Palmer[3] crumb with a little twinkling raindrop on his head. I never saw anyone look more silly and nice. Switzerland is full of birds but they are mostly stodgy little german trots flown out of Appendrodt's catalogue. (Which reminds me of Bertha K, ma chère.) But all Switzerland is on the side of the stodges.

MS draft Newberry. *Journal* 1954, 248.

[1] Beatrice Elvery (1885–1970), later Lady Glenavy, was born in Dublin and trained at the Dublin Metropolitan School of Art, then the Slade School of Art in London, before marrying Murry's close friend, the barrister Gordon Campbell, 2nd Baron Glenavy (1885–1963). KM's closeness to her had lessened in recent years, although a genuine warmth continued. Beatrice Campbell recorded their friendship in her autobiography *Today We Will Only Gossip* (1964).

[2] Edmund Spenser, *The Shepherd's Calendar, April*, 109–12.

[3] Huntley and Palmer, a well-known brand of English biscuits.

To Marie Belloc-Lowndes, 26 May 1921

Hotel Beau-Site | Clarens-Montreux | Switzerland.
26 V 1921

Dear Mrs Belloc-Lowndes,

I was so delighted to hear from you & so sorry to know you have been ill. I hope your play has not meant too much work & that you are better now. Murry, who has been lecturing in Oxford writes that the weather in London has been exquisite. Are you enjoying it? I have such a romantic vision in my mind of your house in Barton Street.[1] Thank Heaven for dreams! I have *been* there on a warm spring afternoon, & there has been a room with open windows where you sat talking, wearing the same embroidered jacket . . . Outside one was *conscious* of trees — of their green gold light . . . But its all far away from my cursed Swiss balcony where Im lying lapping up the yellows of eggs & taking my temperature in the eye of Solemn Immensities — mobled Kings.[2]

Ive seen the best man in Switzerland and he says I still have a chance. But I don't feel in the least die-away. Illness is a great deal more mysterious than doctors imagine. I simply can't afford to die with one very half-and-half little book and one bad one & a few — — —? stories to my name. In spite of everything, in spite of all one knows and has felt — one has this longing to *praise* Life — to sing ones minute song of praise, and it doesn't seem to matter whether its listened to or no.[3] Will one ever be able to say how marvellously beautiful it all is? I long, above everything, to write about *family love*[4] – the love between growing children, and the love of a mother for her son, and the father's feeling – But warm, vivid, intimate – not 'made up' – not *self conscious*.

Dear Mrs Belloc-Lowndes – is it bad manners in me to write to you so frankly? Forgive me if it is. Whenever I think of you I cant help loving you – just as I did when you sat in the little salon of the Isola Bella & I wondered (though I didn't even know at the time I *was* wondering it) if you'd kiss me – & you did.

Goodbye – I hope you are *happy*. I hope your are well.

Yours ever

Katherine Mansfield.

MS Texas. Cited *Exhibition*, 47–8.

[1] Marie Belloc-Lowndes lived at 9 Barton Street, near Westminster Abbey.
[2] See p. 219, n. 2.
[3] An anticipation of her final story, 'The Canary', written in July 1922.
[4] Which is what KM would soon attempt in 'At the Bay'.

To J. M. Murry, (? late May 1921)

[Hotel Beau Site, Clarens-Montreux]

⟨Darling,

Do treat me just for once as a weekly paper that pays you let's say £950 a year for one article a week – a 'personal' article – intimate – only about yourself. For 3 days no-one has been near my bed with a letter. Your postcard in the train came this evening – but that's all.⟩
The *Tig Courier*, Sir is a weekly paper that pays you £950 a year for an article, personal as possible, the more intimate the better. For three days the editor has been waiting for your copy. Tonight she got a p.c. written in a train; but that was all. Will you tell her (a) your reasons for withholding it (as subtle as you like) or (b) when she may expect it.

Address:
    Tig
        Stillin
            Bedfordshire.

MS draft Newberry. *Journal* 1954, 248.

[1] Clearly there are missing letters to Murry between 25 May and his leaving London on 9 June. This draft was in a notebook KM was using during those weeks.

To J. M. Murry, [late May 1921]

[Hotel Beau Site, Clarens-Montreux]

Darling Veen,

It's like this. It's no good her being here any more – it's too hot & the food has gone off. Also I must tackle my affair seriously, you know. So I am going to Montana. Stephani says that he would far rather I went to him for a month at least so that he could keep my heart under his *eye* or *ear*. Good. I agree. But there's my Bogey. Will he go to a pension 5 minutes away for a month & visit me? As soon as I find out how the place suits me we can get a little chalet. I send you a p.c. of your pension. Stephani's place is not a real live – or dead – Sanatorium. He of course thinks you would like to be with me there. Why not? It is quite usual. But I sang *No* to that & I'm sure you agree. You'd hate it. So would I.

MS draft ATL. *Scrapbook*, 179.

To Ottoline Morrell, [late May 1921]

Hotel Chateau Belle Vue | Sierre | (Valais)[1]

Dearest Ottoline,

I have been hoping to hear from you; I am so glad to know how you are, though the news isn't at all satisfactory. How horrible to have to undergo another operation! It is simply devastating. The only consolation is you have your lovely home to go to after & will not be in a Swiss hotel. I only hope THEY will do you some read good.

I am leaving here tomorrow. If I look down upon Montreux another day I shall fly into pieces with rage at the ugliness of it all. Its like a painting on a mineral water bottle – *bâtiment des Eaux.* And then along the road that winds through (I must say lovely) vines go these awful, ugly people, & one can't help looking at them. Never have I seen such ugliness. Father, with a straw hat on the back of his head, coat off, waistness. coat unbuttoned & stiff shirt showing, marches ahead & Mother follows – with her enormous highly respectable derrière & after them tag the little Swisses – Oh! Oh! Oh!!! Matters have reached a crisis too, as these last 2 days there has been the Fête des Narcisses. Hoards of uglies rushing by on bicycles with prodigious bunches of these murdered flowers on the handlebars, all ready for the fray. Happily, it rained & became a Fête des Ombrelles instead. I think from the expressions of the company homeward bound the umbrellas had been thrown as well!

To me, though, the symbol of Switzerland is that large middle class female *behind.* It is the most respectable thing in the world. It is deathless. Everyone has one in this hotel; some of the elderly ladies have two.

I think Sierre may be better & there one is at least in reach of forests and tumbling rivers. The man from Montana who is going to keep an Eye on me is near too, but thinking him over (as one does) I believe he's no better than the rest of them and he overcharged me *horribly*. I shall pin my faith on forests. Bother all doctors!

I was so interested in what you told me about Gertler – and Brett. I know I *ought* to love Brett and she is such a "brick", they say. But when that brick comes flying in my direction – oh, I DO so want to dodge it! Why will she [be] so jocose? And why does she have a kind of *pet name* for everyone? And why does she talk of "streaming into pubs" or "tickle and run"? This last phrase is really *too* awful. And I think she makes such a dreadful mistake in being on *her* terms with all these men. Its too undignified. I ought not to say a word of this, but . . . you know the feeling? And I feel she has such an awful idea of me. Im not that person at all. I don't want to smile when she tells me she has been "sick"; I want to hang my head.

How lovely Garsington must be! The grass, the shadows of the trees, the lemon verbena in the flower garden. I can see it all. And always coming into the house from the garden – the still, delicate beauty of the house . . . It is a memory to keep for ever. I really cannot imagine a house more beautiful. I wish Chaucer had stayed there . . .

I hope you do see Murry but when he gets to England he simply disappears. I *never* know where he is. I only hear from him that his pursuit of pleasure is very wearying & painful. But once M. is out of sight he is swallowed up. However, other people tell me he is full of gaiety whereas he tells me how he is *suffering* from the Coal Strike!! Isn't that like Murry!

I have just read his review of the Tchekhov notebooks.[2] Did you see the book? It was a dreadful *ice bath*, & now the last book of stories "The Horse Stealers" is a cold douche to follow. I thought the notebooks were in a way almost funny – but its cruel to laugh. Its not fair to glean a man's buttons & pins & hawk them after his death. But the lack of humour on the part of the *translators*! Poor Leonard Woolf typing out all those Russian names! How absurd it is!

Have you read Virginia's stories?[3] I havent – yet. And I haven't read Queen Victoria either.[4] Its so dear to buy, & one cant borrow at this distance. But I mean to read it. I saw a quotation from the death of the Queen & that sounded very good. But from all the reviews it seemed to me that Lytton hadn't really spread his wings. It sounded, all, just a little *cramped*.

I read less and less, or fewer and fewer books. Not because I don't want to read them. I do – but they seem so high up on the tree. Its so hard to get at them & there is nobody near to help . . . On my bed at night there is a copy of Shakespeare, a copy of Chaucer, an automatic pistol & a black muslin fan. This is my whole little world.

Forgive this 'scrappy' letter. And the torn page with the great pin in it. I have just finished a new story⁵ which Im going to send on spec. to The Mercury. I hope someone will like it. Oh, I *have* enjoyed writing it.

With my sincerest good wishes for your *health*, dearest Ottoline and
my warm love
Ever yours
Katherine.

MS Texas. *LKM* II. 117–18; *Selected*, 214–17.

1 The address KM writes anticipates the hotel she would go to in a few days time.
2 Murry had reviewed *Tchehov's Notebooks*, translated by S. S. Koteliansky and Leonard Woolf, and published by the Hogarth Press, in the *Nation and the Athenaeum*, 4 June 1921.
3 *Monday or Tuesday*, also from the Hogarth Press, 1921.
4 Lytton Strachey's *Queen Victoria* (1921).
5 Alpers, in *Stories*, 569, suggests that this may refer to 'Sixpence', published in the *Sphere*, 6 Aug. 1921.

To J. M. Murry, [early June 1921]

[Pension du Lac, Sierre]

Look here my love & my dear,
I'm not really up to chalets yet. This is what would be BEST of all. Do you agree? We go to Montana. I go to Stephani's for a month at least — you have a room at this *pension du lac*. Stephani then can keep his eye & his ear on my heart & I can lie absolutely low for that month. *Then* in the meantime, we have looked around & we take a chalet.
[Does] that seem possible to you?

MS draft ATL. *Scrapbook*, 179–80.

To Dorothy Brett, [4 June 1921]

[Pension du Lac, Sierre]

Dearest Brett
I am awfully sorry to seem so horrid. But I am so fearfully busy that I simply cannot see people this year. Come 1922. It will all be much nicer then. You wouldn't enjoy it now. And indeed I couldn't have that laugh or that talk. Its no go for this year. I must finish my book & finish another before I can think of making holiday. Im *working*. And you know what that means. One simply is not as far as other people are

concerned. I sound horribly ungracious. I cannot help it. I am determined to finish something before my time is up. Perhaps Murry explained to you that the specialist only gives me a *chance* – no more. This makes a great difference, you know. It makes one want to hurry *in case* one is caught. Work to me is more important than anything, I fear, and Im working against time.

Please believe me. I cant expect you to forgive anyone who sounds so horrid. I hope you'll like France & have fun.

Tig.

MS Newberry.

To Richard Murry, [12 June 1921]

Hotel Chateau Belle Vue. Sierre (Valais)
Sunday.

Caro Riccardo

I keep on thinking about you. I am tired of having no news from you & now Jack has come down here for the weekend[1] & he has not heard.

Send me even a p.c. – will you? I don't want to ask you for news about things unless you are in the mood to talk about them, but a sight of my dear little brother's handwriting would be most awfully welcome.

Jack, as you know, will be in England for August – September . . .?

With so much love, Richard dear

Yours ever

Katherine.

MS R. Murry. *Adam* 370–5, 27.

---

[1] Murry had returned from London on 9 June, and joined KM at the new hotel where she had just taken rooms.

To Richard Murry, 20 June 1921

Chateau Belle Vue | Sierre | Valais
(*Im*permanent address. Ill send the other as soon as we have got there.)
20.VI.1921

Riccardo mio,

I answer your letter bang off. But so many thoughts go chasing through my head (do you see them? The last thought, rather slow, on a tricycle!) and there are so many things Id like to talk over that its not as easy as it sounds . . . You know – its queer – I feel so confident about you always. I feel that, the way you are building your boat, no harm can come to it. It will sail. You're building for the high seas, and once you *do* take her out nothing will stop her.

About the old masters. What I feel about them (all of them writers too of course) is the more one *lives* with them the better it is for ones work. Its almost a case of living *into* ones ideal world – the world that one desires to express. Do you know what I mean? For this reason I find that if I stick to men like Chaucer & Shakespeare & Marlowe & even Tolstoi I keep much nearer what I want to do than if I confuse things with read-ing a lot of lesser men. I'd like to make the old masters my *daily bread* – in the sense in which its used in the Lord's Prayer, really to make them a kind of essential nourishment. All the rest is – well – it *comes after*.

I think I understand exactly what you mean by "visionary conscious-ness". It fits the writer equally well. Its mysterious and its difficult to get into words. There is *this* world and there is the world that the artist cre-ates in this world which is nevertheless *his* world, and subject to *his* laws – his "vision". Does that sound highflown? I don't mean it to be. Its dif-ficult to get over in a letter a smile or a look or a something which makes it possible to say these things when ones with a person without that per-son feeling you are a bit of a piglet . . .

Jack told me you were working at technique. So am I. Its extraordi-narily difficult – don't you find? My particular difficulty is a kind of facil-ity – which I suspect very much. Its not solid enough. But I go at it every day. Its simply endlessly fascinating.

Jack arrived here with the Broomies sun still shining fully in his eyes *and* on his nose. I heard about your day. For some reason I feel awfully glad you'd drunk some of the well water. It made me feel we had begun to live there. In 2 years time I hope we shall have enough money to really make it a terrific little place. I say – what fun we shall have! Can you imagine it? I can. Jack, you and me down there looking at *our* cow and the smoke coming out of *our* chimney. In your second drawing I note that the larder has shelves. I began to fill them with strawberry jam and currant jelly. I think more fruit trees ought to be planted now. Very small cherry trees do amazingly here – I wonder if they would there? Also I do wish one could get in a large bush of lavender at the side of the front door. I've learnt a lot from these drawings – more than from anything else. How sensible of you to put in [a] *sloping* field – that gives it one at once and I didn't know there was a tree by the gate, before. One tree more makes a difference.

We are leaving here at the end of this week & creeping by funicular up to Montana. There I hope we shall stay for the next two years. We have our eye on a chalet called Les Sapins which is [in] the midst of the forests – pine forests – theres not even a fence or a bar between it and the trees. So you picture the wolves breathing under the front door, the bears looking through our keyhole and bright tigers dashing at the lighted window panes. Montana is on a small plateau ringed round by mountains. Ill tell you more about it when we get there. Jack has been up twice. *He* says its the best place he's ever seen.

This place, Sierre, is in a valley. Its only 1500 feet high – very sheltered. Fig trees grow big, vines are everywhere; large flowery trees shake in the light. Marvellous light, Richard – and small lakes, bright, clear blue, where you can swim. Switzerland makes us laugh. Its a comic country; the people are extraordinary like comic pictures and they are dead serious about it all. But there is something fine in it, too. They are 'simple', unspoilt, honest and real democrats. The 3rd class passenger is just as good as the 1st class passenger in Switzerland and the shabbier you are the *less* you are looked at. No one expects you to be rich or to spend money. This makes Life pleasant – very. They are not at all beautiful people; the men are very thick, stiff, ugly in the German way, & the women are nearly all *dead plain*. But seen from afar, in the fields, against mountains, they are all well in the picture. The Spring is a good time here. I arrived just as the field flowers were out; now the hay is gathered and the grapes are formed on the vines. I cant say, Richard, how I *love* the country. To watch the season through, to lose myself in love of the earth – that is Life to me. I don't feel I could ever live in a city again. First the bare tree, then the buds & the flowers, then the leaves, then the small fruit forming and swelling. If I only watch one tree a year one is richer for life.

Let me take the plunge. I feel, in a way, that you are the same. Does it sound cruel for me to talk like that about country life when you, dear little brother, are in the town? But its only a question of time. Jack & I had a big helping of town. You will have, I hope, a very much smaller one. I am so glad Jack stayed at home this time. Mother must have loved having him, and he was happy. We often and often talk of you. You don't feel far off – do you? Switzerland feels to me nearer than the S. of France. All the same it isn't near enough.

Goodbye for now

With *real* love from

Katherine.

MS R. Murry, *LKM* II. 118–20.

To William Gerhardi,[1] 23 June 1921

c/o The Nation & The Athenaeum | 10 Adelphi Terrace W.C.2
23.vi.1921

Dear Mr Gerhardi,

I cannot tell you how happy I am to know that The Daughters of the Late Colonel has given you pleasure.[2] While I was writing that story I lived for it but when it was finished, I confess I hoped very much that my readers would understand what I was trying to express. But very few did. They thought it was 'cruel'; they thought I was 'sneering' at Jug and Constantia; they thought it was 'drab'. And in the last paragraph I was 'poking fun at the poor old things'.

Its almost terrifying to be so misunderstood. There was a moment when I first had 'the idea' when I saw the two sisters as *amusing*; but the moment I looked deeper (let me be quite frank) I bowed down to the beauty that was hidden in their lives and to discover that was all my desire . . . All was meant, of course, to lead up to that last paragraph, when my two flowerless ones turned with that timid gesture, to the sun. "Perhaps *now*." And after that, it seemed to me, they died as truly as Father was dead.

You will understand, therefore, how I prize your wonderfully generous letter telling me my attempt was not in vain. I can only repay you by trying not to fail you in the future. And that, believe me, I shall do.

Yours sincerely,
Katherine Mansfield

Montana
Switzerland

MS ATL. *LKM* II. 120.

1 William Gerhardi (1895–1977) had not yet added the final 'e' to his surname when he wrote to KM from Worcester College, Oxford, on 17 June 1921. Born of English parents but brought up in St Petersburg, where his father was in business, Gerhardi served as military attaché in Petrograd during the First World War, and during the Russian Revolution was with the British Military Mission to Siberia, 1918–20. He returned to Oxford after the War, where he wrote his first novel *Futility* (1922). He wrote several other novels, a biography of Chekhov, and an autobiography, *The Memoirs of a Polyglot* (1931).

2 Gerhardi wrote enthusiastically about her story, telling her 'I think it is, and in particular the last long paragraph towards the end, of quite amazing beauty', and saying of the entire story, 'I don't remember ever reading anything so intolerably real – *stifling* – since [Chekhov's] "The Three Sisters".' (ATL).

To Elizabeth, Countess Russell,[1] [*25 June 1921*]

[Palace Hotel, Montana]
Saturday.

Dear Elizabeth,

Murry does not know the extent of my guilt towards you. He *thinks* he is bearing greetings. But the truth is this little letter hangs its head. Can you – dare I ask you to forgive what must appear to be just dreadful blackheartedness?

When your perfect letter came I was ill. I put off answering it until I was better. I *did* answer it and never sent the reply. And then my wicked-ness frightened me and I *hid*. But even if you never want to see such a horrid creature again, please let me say how I *did* appreciate – I did love the beautiful gesture that made you write to me.

It is one of the penalties of illness that one loses what one would give so much to hold. And you know, dear wonderful Elizabeth, I have always longed to be allowed to know you a little. But – there. I can only say I am sorry with all my heart.

Please never feel you have to even greet me: I understand too well.

Katherine.

MS BL. Cited Usborne, 227.

[1] Elizabeth, Countess Russell (1866–1941), christened Mary Annette Beauchamp, but known in her family as May, was the daughter of Henry Herron Beauchamp, a wealthy Sydney merchant who was the brother of KM's grandfather. As the wife of Count Henning von Arnim she wrote the enormously popular *Elizabeth and her German Garden* in 1898, and later several successful novels. She was an encouraging model but a condescending older cousin to the young KM. The two women met after several years in June 1919, after Elizabeth's separation from her second husband Francis, Earl Russell, brother of Bertrand Russell. Her home, the Chalet Soleil, at Randogne sur Sierre, was close to the Chalet des Sapins, to which KM and Murry would move that week.

Elizabeth's diary notes on 25 June: 'Middleton Murry suddenly walked in about 11 . . . He and Katherine are at Montana. Went up after lunch and saw her' (Huntington).

To J. C. Squire, 10 July 1921

Chalet des Sapins | Montana-sur-Sierre | Valais | Switzerland
10.7.1921[1]

Dear Mr Squire,

Many thanks for your letter . I am delighted that you care to publish my story. I feel very lucky. I hope you like it. For a week after it had gone I was lost. Perhaps that sounds absurd about *one* short story, but to have been back to the Bay after 21 years – no less – was a joy.

This is a good place for work. Remote from motors and the Rich-an-great. Its marvellously beautiful. We live in a forest clearing, overlooking a valley and very real live mountains the other side. One begins to tell the time again by the sky. Its a pity though, we are too high for the trees to turn. They stay green. Only the little wild strawberry turns, but it does seem to realise its responsibility; it does the turning for everything else. I was noticing it today. With your leave one has the whole autumn for reposing one's hand.

With best wishes
Yours very sincerely

Katherine Mansfield.

TC Stanford.

[1] This letter, wrongly dated by KM, should rightly appear on p. 294, after the letter of 10 Oct. to Michael Sadleir.

To Alice Jones, 24 July 1921

Chalet des Sapins | Montana-sur-Sierre | (Valais) | Switzerland
24.VII.1921

Dear Mrs Jones,

Please forgive me for not having written to you sooner but I have to keep all my letter writing for Sunday just now; I am so hard pressed with a book that *won't* be finished, during the week.

It is more than kind of you to have sent me the photograph of your perfectly lovely little boy! You must indeed be proud of him. Please give him my love & thanks for it, too . . . I think the way you have had it taken is so charming, too – showing his arms and hands. Children are a joy to look upon . . . I do hope I shall see the small original one day. I shall try not to tell him how lovely he is – but thats always rather hard. England seems to have had a real summer at last. The Daily News arrives here gasping & even The Nation looks warm. Here on our mountain tops we are hot, too, but never too hot. And we step out of our front door and our back door into a forest which is always cool.

With kindest regards
Yours very sincerely
Katherine Mansfield Murry.

MS ATL.

To Ottoline Morrell, 24 July 1921

Chalet des Sapins | Montana-sur-Sierre | (Valais) | Switzerland
24.VII.1921

Dearest Ottoline,

Will you write to me one day & tell me how you are? I should love to know. I think of you so often and wonder how you are passing this lovely summer. It *is lovely* in England too – isn't it? The papers groan and gasp but thats only in London. Surely its not too hot under the ilex tree – or *in* the pond.

Here it is simply exquisite weather. We are so high up (5000 feet above the sea) that a cool breeze filters through from Heaven, and the forests are always airy . . . I cant imagine anything lovelier than this end of Switzerland. Once one loses sight of that hideous Lac Leman & Co. everything is different. Sierre, a little warm, sunripe town in the valley was so perfect that I felt I would like to live there. It has all the flowers of the South and its gay and "queynt" and full of nightingales. But since we have come up the mountains it seems lovelier still. We have taken a small not very small chalet here for two years. It is quite remote – in a forest clearing. The windows look over treetops across a valley to snowy peaks the other side. The air feels wonderful but smells more wonderful still. I have never lived *in* a forest before. One steps out of the house & in a moment one is hidden among the trees. And there are little glades and groves full of flowers, with small ice-cold streams twinkling through. It is my joy to sit there on a tree trunk; if only one could make some small grasshoppery sound of praise to *someone* – thanks to *someone*. But who?

M. and I live like two small timetables. We work all the morning & from tea to supper. After supper we read aloud and smoke; in the afternoon he goes walking & I crawling. The days seem to go by faster and faster. One beaming servant who wears peasant 'bodies' & full skirts striped with velvet looks after everything. & though the chalet is so arcadian it *has* got a bathroom with hot water & central heating for the winter & a piano & thick carpets & sun blinds. I am too old not to rejoice in these creature comforts as well.

The only person whom we see is my Cousin Elizabeth who lives ½ an hours scramble away. We exchange Chateaubriand[1] and baskets of apricots and have occasional long talks which are rather like what talks in the afterlife will be like, I imagine . . . ruminative, and reminiscent – although dear knows what it is really all about. How strange talking is – what mists rise and fall – how one loses the other & then thinks to have found the other – then down comes another soft final curtain . . . But it is incredible, don't you feel, how mysterious and isolated we each of us are – at the last. I suppose one ought to make this discovery once & for all but I seem to be always making it again.

It seems to me that writers dont acknowledge it half enough. They pretend to know all there is in the parcel. But how *is* one to do it without seeming vague?

Some novels have been flung up our mountainside lately. Among them Lawrence's Women in Love. Really! Really!! Really!!! But it is so *absurd* that one cant say anything; it after all is almost purely pathological, as they say.[2] But its sad to think what might have been. Wasn't it Santyana who said: Every artist holds a lunatic in leash. That explains L. to me. You know I am Gudrun? Oh, what rubbish it all is, tho'. Secker is a little fool to publish such STUFF. I wish a writer would rise up – a new one – a really good one –

M. is engaged in a fat novel.[3] He is quite wrapt away in it. I keep on with my short stories. I have been doing a series for *The Sphere*,[4] because it pays better than any other paper I know. But now they are done I don't believe they are much good. Too simple. It is always the next story which is going to contain everything, and that next story is always just out of reach. One seems to be saving up for it. I have been reading Shakespeare *as usual*. The Winters Tale again. All the beginning is very dull – isn't it. That Leontes is an intolerable man and I *hate* gentle Hermione. Her strength of mind, too, in hiding just round the corner from him for 15 years is terrifying! But oh – the Shepherd scene is too perfect. Now I am embedded in Measure for Measure. I had no idea it was so good. M. reads aloud in the evening & we *make notes*. There are moments when our life is rather like a school for two! I see us walking out [in] crocodile for two and correcting each others exercises. But no – not really.

Dearest Ottoline. Is this a Fearfully dull letter? Im afraid it is. Im afraid "Katherine has become so boring nowadays".

But I send it with much love, very *very* much.

Katherine.

MS Texas. *LKM* II. 121–2.

[1] François-René Chateaubriand (1768–1848), a prolific writer of fiction and travel works, royal apologist, and precursor of Romanticism. Brownlee Kirkpatrick (*Bibliography*, 22) has identified the quotation from Chateaubriand's *Mémoires d'outre-tombe* that KM used as an epigraph for *The Garden Party*: 'Montaigne dit que les hommes vont béant aux choses futures; j'ai la manie de béer aux choses passées' ('Édition nouvelle . . . par Maurice Levaillant et Georges Moulinier, II (Paris, 1938), 157.

[2] Lady Ottoline had greatly resented Lawrence's depiction of her as Hermione Roddice when she read *Women in Love* in typescript at the end of 1916, and Philip Morrell had threatened libel action should it be published. After a small private edition in the United States, the novel was published in England by Martin Secker in 1921.

[3] *The Things We Are* (1922).

[4] At a time when her medical bills were considerable, KM accepted the offer of Clement Shorter, editor of the weekly, the *Sphere*, to write six stories at ten guineas each. These all appeared before the end of the year: 'Sixpence', 6 Aug.; 'Mr and Mrs Dove', 13 Aug.; 'An Ideal Family', 20 Aug.; 'Her First Ball', 28 Nov.; 'The Voyage', 24 Dec.; 'Marriage à la Mode', 31 Dec.

To Dorothy Brett [*25 July 1921*]

1921–1923

Chalet des Sapins | Montana-sur-Sierre (Valais)

My dear Brett,

I have been wanting to write to you for ever so long. The difficulty has been to know where to catch you. If you were not at your Paris hotel I knew from experience the letter would never be sent on & I couldn't decide whether to chance sending direct to the Pyrenees. I shall send this to Paris & hope for the best. We have been very interested to hear of your experiences. I somehow feel you haven't *really* enjoyed it much. Thats in my heart of hearts. Perhaps one hasn't any right to intrude into these intimate places. But you know the feeling? As though it has all been very delightful but the fly has been there in the amber. Was Mrs D. the fly, perhaps? But you say so much of what youve seen and little of what you – you yourself are feeling. Will you be glad to be back in your own studio? After all?

We couldn't help feeling just a little superior about your mountains. We are living on tops that are over 5,000 feet high and the only way to get here is to be drawn out of the valley up the sheer side in a little glass carriage that pauses and winds and sways like a spider in mid air. It is divinely beautiful up here. We have a small – not very small house in a forest clearing. The trees are only a few yards away. Theres no fence – nothing that separates us from them but a little rocky lawn covered with grass and wild pinks and yellow tufty plants. It is absolutely remote and unspoilt – we might be miles and ages away from all civilization. There is nothing to be seen but a ring of mountain tops & beyond that more mountains – dazzling white against the sky. I send you a picture of our house in winter – it gives an idea of what it is like. Its delightful inside too – very snug, with a sumptuous bathroom, central heating, electric light, and even a piano. We have a real peasant girl who looks after everything. I wish you could see her. She is made to be painted and she wears, always, the peasant dress – a short jacket & full skirt – and her BEAMING smile is a joy. When she comes back after her afternoon out with a great bouquet of flowers and stands at the door holding them I wish Van Gogh was still alive! But to tell you the truth, its all so lovely – so wonderful that I hardly dare write it down. I feel it will fly away – it *must* be faery. I am writing now on the balcony. The sweet scents – the sounds (there is a little flock of goats with bells nibbling on the lawn) and all round it the quiet – the butterflies – the goldfinches – the black squirrel scolding on a high branch – they are all the citizens of our new world. Murry is almost a rich-brown-gravy brown. He lives out of doors as much as I do.

Our nearest neighbour – about ½ an hours scramble away is my ravishing cousin "Elizabeth". We see her fairly often and Murry goes there. She is certainly the most fascinating small human being I have ever known – a real enchantress – and she is so lovely to look upon as well as to hear. We exchange books and flowers and fruits. This is a marvellous moment for peaches & apricots & wild strawberries. They grow lower down the mountains. Very little grows here except pines, wild flowers and occasional small bobbing cherries. I feel at present as though I could spend the rest of my life here, with occasional descents. But this is more what I would like for home than anything I have known. I don't know why. There is a kind of charm. For one thing its so unspoilt – no railways, no motorcars, no casinos or jazz bands. Every tiny flower seems to shine with a new radiance. That queer chain of modern life seems to be unknown. I feel one will get younger and younger here & its fatal to begin laughing – one never leaves off. Murry & I get up early & work every morning until lunch. Then we play until tea time & then work again until supper. After supper we smoke, read aloud, talk until bed time.

By the way can you tell me the address of a man who makes really well cut breeks? I foresee that with the fall of the first leaf the only thing to do will be to shed ones petticoats & go in mans attire until next spring. It will be much too cold for anything else. But I don't know a single tailor who really can cut WELL & who goes in for such things. Who cut your lovely ones? And was he a very frabjous price? I shall have to have 2 pairs & wear them with thick wooly cardigans – or what would you suggest? How charming you looked at Garsington – it seems such years ago since that time. There is a great gulf between.

Do tell me more about your painting next time you write. Has France changed your ideas? Have you been disappointed in French painters? What are you working at now? In London, I mean. Oh, Heavens – how difficult Art is. Its the perpetual work at technique which is so hard. Its not enough to know what you want to say – but to be able to say it – to be equipped to say it! That is a life's work.

– – – I loved your bits of news. Fancy Carrington Mrs. Partridge.[1] It sounds very right, somehow. Is she happy? Is she just the same? I should imagine marriage would change her. How is Gertler? Is he quite cured? Sullivan I am sure will wax very prosperous and shine with fatness. He has become a humorous character to me. Sydney W. is *very* nice – don't you think? But Id rather see Koteliansky than any of them & I suppose I never shall. We shall not be back in England for 2 years at least, perhaps longer. I have been away nearly a year now. How I have hated England! Never, never will I live there. Its a kind of *negation* to me and there is always a kind of silky web or net of complications spread to catch one. Nothing goes forward. But perhaps I am not fair.

Dear Brett have your next summer holiday here. Do you feel its too high? Even strong men feel it for a day or two but it goes off. Goodbye. Take care of your little self.

With love from
Tig.

MS Newberry.

[1] The painter Dora Carrington (1893-1932), a friend of Brett's since their time at the Slade School of Art and an acquaintance of KM's through Garsington, recently had married Reginald (Ralph) Partridge (1894-1960), after some years of a complex triangular relationship with Lytton Strachey.

To Dorothy Brett, 29 July 1921.

Chalet des Sapins | Montana-sur-Sierre (Valais)
29 vii 1921

Dearest Brett,

I tremendously enjoyed that long letter. I had been out with M. down the road a little way & then across a stream & into the forest. There are small glades & lawns among the trees filled with flowers. I sat under a big fir & he went gathering. It was a dazzling-bright day, big silvery clouds pressing hard on the mountain tops – not even the cotton grass moving. Lying on the moss I found minute strawberry plants and violets and baby fir cones – all looked faery – & M. moved near and far – calling out when he found anything special . . . Then he disappeared down into a valley & I got up & explored the little fir parlours and sat on tree stumps & watched ants & wondered where that apricot stone had come from. These forests are marvellous: one feels as though one were on a desert island somehow. There is a blissful feeling of remoteness. As to the butterflies & golden and green dragonflies and big tawny bumblebees they are a whole population. M. came back with a huge bunch of treasures & I walked home & found your letter in the hall. So I sat down on the bottom step of the stairs with the flowers in a wet hanky beside me & read it. Don't you think the stairs are a good place for reading letters? I do. One is somehow suspended. One is on neutral ground – not in ones own world nor in a strange one. They are an almost perfect meeting place. Oh Heavens! How stairs do fascinate me when I think of it. Waiting for people – sitting on strange stairs – hearing steps far above, watching the light *playing* by itself – hearing – far below a door, looking down into a kind of dim brightness, watching someone come up. But I could go on forever. *Must* put them in a story though! People come out of themselves on stairs – they issue forth, unprotected. And then the window on a *landing*. Why is it so different to all other windows? I must stop this . . .

I don't like your Dobs at all,[1] in spite of all her good qualities. I don't feel she is living. She isn't really positive; its only her attitude of defence I imagine to disguise and protect her lack of power to sympathise. And isn't she really boring? Self engrossed people are the only boring people, but they are a fearful trial. There they are slap in front of you with all the keys in all the drawers and all locked. How deadly. I feel there is no suppleness in Mrs D. She paints thinks & feels with those bed post legs. As to her eating the last chicken leg – thats a *very* bad sign. That chicken leg is very deep really. It would have infuriated me at last. She ought to have had it strung round her neck like the poor ancient mariner's bird.[2] What a fool the woman is, too, to imagine she knows you. I bet she does. Funny! I see her as somebody in broad stripes in my mind's eye. Do you know the stripes I mean – rather bright but *stupid*.

I am deeply interested in what you feel about Manet. For years he has meant more to me than any other of those French painters. He satisfies something deep in me. There is a kind of beautiful real *maturity* in his painting, as though he has come into his own and it is a rich heritage. I saw a reproduction of a very lovely Renoir the other day – a young woman, profile or three-quarter with the arm lazily outstretched, lovely throat, bosom, shoulder – such grace.[3] But I think that in his later paintings he is so often muzzy, I cant appreciate the queer woolly outline, & I feel it was so often as like as not *rheumatism* rather than *revelation*. But I don't know. Id like to have a feed of paintings one day – go from here to Madrid, say, and have a good look. I shall. Once one is out of England I always feel every thing & *place* is near. We are only four hours from Milan here. Well, even tho' one doesn't go – there it *is*. One *could* start on Saturday morning & be there for the opera that evening. Its the channel which is such a dividing line. It frightens me. It is so terrifically wide, really. And once one is across one is *on the island*.

Thanks so very much for the tailor's address. I shall write to him for a measurement form. I appreciate what you say about the size. As to any other garments I must wait until Constable makes up his accounts. It is *very particularly* nice of you to say youll look round for me then – – –

Brett, while I remember. Have you read *The Three Mulla-Mulgars* by DelaMare.[4] If you haven't *do* get it and read it to any infants you know. Its about three monkeys. One seems to read a lot here. Its the kind of house in which you go into a room to comb your hair, find Gulliver's Travels on the shelf behind the door and are immediately lost to the world. The bedroom walls are of wood; there are thick white carpets on some of the floors – outside the windows wide balconies, & thick striped cotton blinds shut out the midday glare. A great many flowers every-where – generally apricots ripening on a balcony ledge & looking rather gruesome like little decapitated chickens. If only I can make enough money so as never to leave here for good! One never gets old here. At 65 one is as spry as a two year old & (I suppose it is the climate) all is so *easy*. The strain is gone. One hasn't that feeling of dragging a great endless rope out of a dark sea. Do you hate London? No, I *do* see it has its beauty and its charm, too. But all the same one feels so like the swollen sheep that looks up & is not fed[5]. Its so hard, to put it "stuffily" to live from ones centre of being in London.

Now it will be will you who won't be able to read all this . . . Tell me what you are doing, my dear, if you are so inclined. Dont lose any more ½ stones! For Heavens sake put the half stone back again. Look at the Sargol advertisements & be wise in time. God only loves the Fat; the thin people he sticks pins into for ever & ever.

With love to you from

Tig

MS Newberry. *LKM* II. 123–5.

¹ Valentine Dobrée (1894–1974), a painter married to the literary scholar Bonamy Dobrée, who occasionally wrote for the *Athenaeum*. A close friend of Carrington's, she was also a lover of Ralph Partridge.
² The sailor's punishment for killing the albatross in S. T. Coleridge's 'The Rime of the Ancient Mariner'.
³ There are several works by August Renoir (1841–1919) which fit this description.
⁴ Walter de la Mare's *The Three Mulla-Mulgars* was published in 1910, and later retitled *The Three Royal Monkeys*.
⁵ 'The hungry sheep look up and are not fed, | But swoln with wind', Milton, *Lycidas*, II, 125–6. (See also *CLKM*, III, 97.)

To J. Ruddick[1], 30 July 1921

Chalet des Sapins | Montana-sur-Sierre | (Valais) | Switzerland.
30
vii
1921
Dear Mr Ruddick,

By this afternoon's post I received from my sister, Chaddie, two *old* and *quaint* photographs that you had very kindly asked her to send me. Is that so? Were they really sent to me? Thank you most sincerely. I cannot tell you how I love a glimpse into the past, even if its such a dreadfully unflattering one! But Leslie looks such a darling little fellow, and I think they are both sweet of Marion. (I wonder if she does . . .)

I hear often of you all from Chaddie & Jeanne, & I always think lovingly of Mrs Ruddick because she was such a friend of Mother's. I remember her very well too, & Marion was one of my first 'great friends'. I wonder if she has forgotten our games at Miss Partridges, or old Miss Partridges way of saying: "Oh, Im so tired!" or the cream buns we were given for tea. I must say I think the cream buns should have been with held from me, though. I always see Marion in a sailor suit with her straight fringe and pretty shoes. Please give her my love. It would be very nice to think we should meet one day and talk over old times . . . Does she remember Island Bay, I wonder, and bathing her doll in the rock pools with me. But perhaps so much has happened since then that these things have faded.

My sisters were very happy to see you all again; they wrote most warmly of their visit. I am hoping they may visit me this winter. I have a house in a forest clearing on the mountain tops – 5000 feet high. Its perfectly lovely in this summer weather but they tell us winter is even better. It will be our first experience of *real* snow as you get it in Canada – – –

Thank you again for the photographs. With my love to Mrs Ruddick and my best wishes to you all

Yours very sincerely
Katherine Middleton Murry
'Kass Beauchamp'

MS Spiro.
[Envelope addressed to:
J. Ruddick, Esq,
Dairy Commissioner,
Ottawa
Canada.]

¹ John Ruddick had represented the Canadian Dairy Board in Wellington when KM was a child, and his daughter Marion had been one of her closest friends.

To *Dorothy Brett, 4 August 1921*

Chalet des Sapins
4 viii 1921

Dearest Brett

Forgive this paper. I am at the top of the house & there is no other here. I am on the side balcony which leads out of my dressing room. Its early evening. All the tree tops are burnished gold, a light wind rocks in the branches. The mountains across the wide valley are still in sunlight. On the remote snowy peaks there are small cloud drifts – silvery. What I love to watch, what seems to become part of this vision, though, are the deep sharp shadows in the ravines & stretching across the slopes. But one could not imagine a more marvellous view or one more perfect to live by. I watch it from early morning until late night when bats are out & booming moths fly for ones hair. With intervals . . .

While you feel I am in any way a kindred spirit – write to me. A kindred spirit reads your letters; that you may be *sure* of. That scene in the summerhouse went to my heart. What a big blundering callous world it is! Its no good saying they know not what they do;¹ it doesn't stop them doing it. And it is bad bad – or so I feel – that one should have to shrink from human beings as one has to in such circumstances. Its a kind of suffering which (if you know what I mean) ones real positive nature rebels at and rejects, and so, as well as everything else one has ones own poor self to hush and comfort and sing lullaby to . . . I hope you won't be there long. Ice cream and strawberries & hot baths don't really compensate. No, you are right we have no ice cream here. But we have strawberries – the only kind – wild ones, little brilliant magic berries – *too* exquisite to eat really. But I wont fly off on to strawberries until I have said I *realise* what it is like up there. And I'd like to sit with you in

a field and draw your eyebrows with a grass & make you feel you were
– loved – gently – tenderly –

Its not v. nice to see Mr and Mrs Sullivan a-lapping up the cream &
licking of their paws somehow. I think Sullivans obsession is all a fake –
a make up. It fits in with his present 'idea' of himself. Isn't that more like
it? Its *not* pretty! Now I shall be indiscreet & trust to your discretion. S.
has a very vivid imagination. Beware of it! But perhaps you have discovered it already. Before listening take a very large grain of salt & let
it dissolve slowly in the mouth (without swallowing) as they say. That is
dead private!

Oh, about the Spahlinger. No, its not true. For one thing one can't
have the treatment for there is no serum, and for another I wouldn't
have it for any money. Its purely experimental & very terrifying in its
results at present. Please *please* never think I need money like that. I can
always get money. I can always go into some crowded place & hold out
my hat or sell 1d worth of boracic ointment for 2/6 net profit 2/5. No
– money has no terrors for me nowadays. And besides I am making
some, and its only a question of my own activity how much I make. At
present I am £30 *down*, and two nuns have just come with needlework
made by infants in their convent. The dear creatures (I have a romantic *love* of nuns), my two gentle columbines, blue hooded, mild, folded
over – took little garments out of a heavy box & breathed on them & I
spent £2.7.0 on minute flannel jackets & pinnies for Ernestine's[2] sisters
first not-yet-born baby. The butchers bill on *red* slaughtered butchers
paper is quite unpaid & now I cant pay it. But you see thats what I am
like about money – never to be pitied or helped!

What is your picture – the one you thought of in your bath? Yes, I
find hot baths very inspiring, so does my cousin Elizabeth. She reads
Shakespeare in hers. No, she wasn't the Von Hutton. She was Von
Arnheim – and now she's Countess Russell, Bertie's sister-in-law. Her
love of flowers is really her greatest charm. Not that she says very much,
but every word *tells*. A man wouldn't discover it in her – he wouldn't
realise how deep it is. For no man loves flowers as women *can*. Elizabeth
looks cooly at the exquisite petunias and says in a small faraway voice:
"They have a very perfect scent." And I feel I can hear oceans of love
breaking in her heart for petunias and nasturiums and snapdragons. I
believe you have been painting petunias – your purple velvety ones.
Were they? Oh, we have the most wonderful ones here – SUCH colours.
If I were an artist I could never resist them. But they must be difficult,
because in spite of the weight of colour there's a transparent light shining through look in them. The look one imagines the fruits had in
Aladdin's orchard . . .

Brett, don't let men worry you with sex. Be cold, be brutal. You can't
hurt their feelings. If they had delicate feelings they would realise they

outraged or disgusted or bored yours. But in the name of our sex make them feel how impudent they are! Intelligent men have no right to be so stupid. I must stop this letter & get on with my new story. Its called *At The Bay* & its (I hope) full of sand and seaweed and bathing dresses hanging over verandahs & sandshoes on window sills, and little pink 'sea' convolvulus, and rather gritty sandwiches and the tide coming in. And it smells (oh I do hope it smells) a little bit fishy. Addio

Ever
Tig.

M. had your letter. He is imbedded in a WORK just at present. I don't *think* he is writing letters for the moment. Let me know when you are leaving Scotland.

MS Newberry. *LKM* II. 125–6.

1 'Father, forgive them; for they know not what they do': Luke 23: 34.
2 Ernestine Rey, a local woman of 'good family', but an unimaginative cook, who worked for the Murrys.

To Richard Murry, 9 August 1921

Chalet des Sapins | Montana s. Sierre (Valais) | La Suisse
9.VIII.1921

Richard,

You sent me a beautiful postcard.[1] Yes I agree about the hands & the angle of the head is so lovely. I mean how the chin is tucked in – that gives a kind of little delicate spring to the eyebrows & even the corners of the lips . . . or doesn't it? A poor ignorant writer asks.

We have just been doing the flowers before we start work. Scene: the salle a manger, with windows wide open & pink curtains flapping. The table bare & heaped with petunias, snapdragons & nasturtiums. Glass vases & bowls full of water – a general sense of buds and wetness & that peculiar stickiness of fresh stalks. Jack – white shirt with sleeves up to his shoulders, white duck trousers & rope shoes snipping with a large pair of wet scissors. Me – blue cotton kimono & pink slippers afilling of the vases . . . Jack is *terribly* keen on petunias. I wish I could send you a whole great bastick full. They are wonderful flowers – almost pure light – and yet an exquisite starry shape. We have every colour from pale pink to almost blackish purple. And do you know the smell of snapdragons? My dear boy. I must here pause or you will walk away. But tell me – why do people paint for ever bottles and onions? A white snapdragon, for instance, just for a change would be worth it, surely. Richard – I wish I could unobtrusively give you these things – leave flowers instead of foundlings on your studio doorstep, in fact. Perhaps one day I shall be able to . . .

About people. Yes, I meant what you mean. One gets mortally tired of speedometers. But I have been looking at a good deal of modern 'work' lately & it almost seems to me that the blight upon it is a kind of *fear*. Writers, at any rate, are self-conscious to such a pitch now-adays that their feeling for life seems to be absolutely stopped – arrested. It is sad. They know they oughtn't to say 'driving fast eh'[2] & yet they don't know what they ought to say. If I am dead sincere Id say I think it is because people have so little love in their hearts for each other. "Love casteth out Fear"[3] is one of those truths that one goes on proving and proving. And if you are without fear you are free; its fear makes us slaves. But this sounds so prosy. You know it as well as I do. I hate to bore you.

Jack had a birthday on Saturday. His presents were (1) a panama hat (2) some coloured blotting paper (3) a cake (4) a ruler. We had a tea with candles complete & liqueur chocolates that were positively terrifying. The moment of agonising suspense when you had the chocolate in your mouth & had to bite through to the *mysterious* liqueur. However we survived.

The weather is superb, here. There has been a battle of the Wasps. Three hosts with their citadels have been routed from my balcony blind. In the swamps, still white with cotton grass, there are hundreds of grasshoppers. Jack saw an *accident* to one the other day. He jumped by mistake into a stream & was borne away. Body not recovered. When we thought about it – it was the first real accident to an insect that we remembered.

Richard I must start work. Jack's novel is going along at a fine pace. Ill tell you when the old Sphere prints any story of mine that might interest you.

I still have so much to tell you. Ive only unpacked the little small things on top. All the big heavy ones are underneath. What are you drawing? How are you? Is it still summery? Lovely summer is! Have you had any bathing this year? You always look awfully at home in a 'watery element'. Dont bother to answer these questions.

Goodbye for now.

Ida Baker, who lives about 2 miles from here, is going to England this month & is going to bring back Wingley. Athy is married to an elderly lady in Hampstead, I believe, a *widow*. She lost her first husband – a lovely tabby – some taime ago.

I have given your message to Jack.

MS R. Murry. *LKM* II. 126–8.

---

[1] Richard had sent her a reproduction of a Reubens portrait.
[2] Alpers 1980, 341, proposes that the imagery here is 'obviously alluding to the hurtling motor-

To J. B. Pinker,[1] 16 August 1921

Chalet des Sapins, | Montana-sur-Sierre, | Switzerland.
August 16 1921

Dear Sir,

I have been advised to ask you to act for me as my literary agent. It is possible that you may already be acquainted with my work, for a collection of my short stories entitled "Bliss" which appeared last winter attracted a good deal of attention.

I shall have another volume of stories ready by the end of the present month, and I should be obliged if you would dispose of the volume for me both in England and America.

But I am chiefly anxious to have serial publication arranged for my stories in America. I have not had any difficulty in disposing of the English rights, but America is so far an untouched market for my work. I should be most grateful if you would consent to act for me.

Yours very faithfully,
Katherine Mansfield

TS Newberry.

1 James Brand Pinker (1864–1922), a successful literary agent to whom KM had sent a story in 1911 (see CLKM I, 109).

To Ida Baker, [20 August 1921]

Chalet des Sapins | Montana-s-Sierre
Saturday.

Dear

Thank you for your letter. I would have written a card before but the Furies have been busy. I have been – am – ill ever since you left[1] with what Doctor H.[2] calls acute enteritis. High fever, sickness, dysentery and so on. I decided yesterday to go to the Palace[3] but today makes me feel Ill try & see it through here. Jack is awfully kind in the menial offices of nurse & as I cant 'take' anything except a little warm milk E. cant do her worst Its v. unfortunate because it holds up my work so. Just when I am busy. But cant be helped. If I were to tell you how Ive missed you even you might be satisfied! At the same time – this is serious – don't

car in the "Excurse" chapter' of Lawrence's Women in Love, which Murry reviewed under 'The Nostalgia of Mr. D. H. Lawrence', the Nation and the Athenaeum, 13 Aug. 1921. The editorially marked copy of the journal held at the City University, London, assigns this review to KM, however-ever.

3 'Perfect love casteth out fear': John 4: 18.

hurry back, will you? The worst is over. Dont rush. I shall manage. Dont come before you have arranged – i.e. the 6th. At the *same* time dont, just to oblige a Glasspool,[4] come *later!*

I am glad you are safely there. Not a word about your new neffy – or haven't you seen him yet. Oh, I would *hate* to be in England. If only, in the next two years I can make enough money to build something here. But my soul revolts at your pension-talk again. I suppose it gives you a trumpery sense of power to take on one job & pretend all the time you're perfectly free for any other that comes along. A pity you can't resist the female in you. You're the greatest *flirt* I ever have met – a real *flirt*. I do wish you weren't. With all my heart I do. It seems so utterly indecent at our age to be still all a-flutter at every possible glance. But – there – I still hope one day you will be yourself. I am not going to flirt back, Miss & say how I want you as part of my life and cant really imagine being without you. The ties that bind us! Heavens, they are so strong that youd bleed to death if you really cut away. But *don't*. Oh please don't make me have to protest. Accept! Take your place! Be my friend! Don't pay me out for what has been. But no more about this. Ive no doubt Ill get a card today saying your idea is to go out to Africa and so on and so on. I *really mean* it *is* detestable.

E. is as mad as a sober Swiss can be. I think she puts all the thick soups into my hot water bottils.

When you send papers – get a label the size of the paper! Otherwise the copy arrives *torn, black* & *disgusting*. Didn't you know that? And I cant help the illustrator[5]. It was so *like Clive* to ask who he was – so tactful!

You can, in spite of my rages, read as much love as you like into this letter. You won't read more than is there.

Katherine.

What about money? Be frank![6]

MS BL. *MLM*, 171–2.

[1] Ida Baker had left for London on 11 Aug., and stayed for four weeks.
[2] Bernard Hudson, a graduate of Cambridge and London universities, and an expert on tuberculosis of the lung.
[3] The Palace Hotel, in Montana, where KM stayed when she required medical treatment or went to visit Dr Hudson. It was as much an institution for invalids as a hotel.
[4] An English girl whom Ida accompanied back to Switzerland.
[5] See p. 271, n. 3.
[6] A draft of this letter also survives:
Dear Ida
    Thank you for your letter. I would have written a card before but I have been – am – ill, & todays the first day I 've taken a pen even so far. I've had an attack of what Doctor H. calls acute enteritis. I think it was poisoning. Very high fever & sickness & dysentery and so on. *Horrible.* I decided yesterday to go to the Palace but today makes me feel I'll try & see it out here. Jack is awfully kind in the menial offices of nurse and I have not been able to take any food except warm milk so E. can't work her worst on me. She seems poor creature to be much more stupid than ever! Burns everything! Leaves us without eggs & went off for her afternoon yesterday without a word. We didn't even know she was gone.

In fact you are awfully in request. My very soul revolted though at your letter about your pension again. How can you have such a *passion* for people to hold up their hands & tell you over & over & over that they need you!! Or are you simply insincere when you take on a job? You don't ever mean to make anything your job — you're just a kind of vaccuum. *I* don't know. It's difficult. It's maddening. I suppose it gives you a trumpery sense of power. But no-one wants a slave, you know. There's your mistake. One only wants to feel sure of another. That's all. A pity you can't resist the female in you. I like people to be 'gay' & to be happy but I can't bear *flirts* . . .

MS draft Newberry, *Journal* 1954, 259.

To Charlotte Beauchamp Perkins & Jeanne Beauchamp
Renshaw, 21 August 1921

Chalet des Sapins | Montana-sur-Sierre | (Valais) | Switzerland.

21?
viii
1921

My dear Sisters,

I meant to write to you last Sunday but when the day came I couldn't take a holiday after all as I was overdue with work for the old 'Sphere'. I have been awfully busy lately with various commissions; please excuse me.

You sounded so very cheerful & gay and happy that I expect you won't notice. How jolly for you to have a small car. Who makes the wheels go round? And how far do you go. I shall soon forget just what they look like as our tops & peaks could never support one. The carts here are funny even, rather like open appolinaris cases on wheels & the CAB is one of the first cabs I imagine, the true original vehicle. If ever I go out in it the driver to be really chic, flings the floormat over the seat! But Montana is a perfect place to live in. It could not be more beautiful. All my tap roots are fixed here. We have sold Broomies even & when my furniture comes out of store it will be to come up here. This our present chalet is ideal for the two years we have it. It is extremely comfortable in every way — snug & cushioned & warm & if one doesn't want to play the piano one can have a real shower bath — just to hover between two luxuries. I find I cant do without Ida. But she doesn't live or feed here. She *runs* the little house & maid and is in fact an exact "Universal Aunt" — and she lives close by. Its a very satisfactory arrangement. We have settled down here as we never did in the South of France. I don't know why it seems so easy to live here — to fit into this life. Squirrels, rainbows, troups of white goats, *flowers*, these are our real neighbours. And even real live people come & go. May [Elizabeth] is here of course for all the summer. We see a great deal of each other. We have had Hugh Walpole here too, & a party of *Wells* arrives next month. That is our Socierty gossip . . .

It has been tremendously cold lately. Even now I am writing with the radiator on & a fur rug. Snow fell and one tasted winter. I expect winter will be *very* fierce . . . Do you really think you will come, my dears? I quite know what you mean about staying with us; I expect you'd be happier on your own, too. Ida will of course find you a pension or an hotel. But I can't help wondering if it wouldn't be *too* cold to spring up to – – suddenly. It is 5000 feet, you know & it hasn't a really gay winter season like some of the other places. But you will decide.

I have been having a beastly time with my *gland*. (Like your dear Aunt Agnes[1].) But it won't go. And it is attacked with needles at least once a week as I can't have an operation. However, I hope to live this final thorn in the flesh down, sooner or later. I wish the Lord loved me less. I've also had the most horrible nightmares about Mrs B. She haunts my slumbers. I feel she must be on my path. What a bother! How are you both? Are you seeing many people? Are you looking after your garden? England feels far away – and I have an idea that you write to me as one writes to a sick person – you know – not quite *all*. You are a little specially cheerful as one is at bedsides and sofas. Is that not true? Am I being "too sensitive" – Marie?[2]

Thank you very much for the photographs (which I *buried* immediately!) & the letters you sent me. I loved seeing the photographs but one doesn't show such awful things outside the family. Our clothes, my dear and our hats. I don't see why we were made such little guys. And why was I stuffed – why wasn't I given lean meat & dry toast – so that I looked less like the Fat Girl from Fielding.[3] Even my curls were like luscious fried sausages. We had a really hard and unflattering childhood, I must say. And it can't have been 'the fashion' only. For Marion Ruddick[4] looks a charmingly dressed child. Old V's *lapels* brought Miss Reading back to me. The only precious little unspoilt dear was Chummie.

Well, dear sisters, I hear the tea party has arrived downstairs & I must go & greet it. Old Mrs Maxswell[5] (a great friend of a General Aeneas *Perkins*[6] out in India) and Doctor Hudson who wears sandshoes. Both dears, though.

We have made excellent greengage & apricot jam on our electric toaster and are preparing to make plum & quince. Is life easier in England now? Goodbye for today. With much love to you both,

Ever your devoted K.

MS Spiro.

[1] KM's maternal aunt, Agnes Waters.
[2] Her sister Chaddie's nickname, from her likeness to the music-hall actress Marie Tempest.

3 Marion, the daughter of John Ruddick to whom she wrote on 30 July, and her close friend as a child.
4 Feilding, a small town 80 miles north of Wellington.
5 Mrs Maxwell was the owner of the chalet; Dr Hudson was her son.
6 Chaddie has married Lieut.-Col. John Charles Campbell Perkins, DSO, Controller of Military Accounts for the Western Circle, India, in 1913, and was widowed three years later.

To Elizabeth, Countess Russell [22 August 1921]

[Chalet des Sapins, Montana-sur-Sierre]
Dear Elizabeth,

It seems so slight a return to make only une reverence nouvelle for these flowers! I have a whole petunia and nasturtium summer to thank you for – no less. Never shall I forget it. I know you will understand me when I say that every time I go into the salon they give me a fresh small shock of delight; every time one bends over them to greet them it is to discover fresh beauties. I have 'planted out' some of my petunias into a story so that they may live a little longer, and now I am looking for a favourable corner for a whole blaze of nasturtiums. Breathes there the man, do you think? – who understands a woman's love of flowers? Perhaps a very ancient Chinaman or two. But they, to judge by their poetry, found lettuces so moving, which I find a little hard to understand. Not that I don't fully *appreciate* a lettuce – but its green food to sing on – –

A thrill went through the Chalet des Sapins to hear you were gone to Italy! To Italy – no less. Italian airs sang at the windows, and we ate our small mountain grapes at supper with a difference. But I hope this rain – so lovely here – is not falling so far.

Shall we see you soon. Oh weh! Why cant I once run down the hill and pipe Elizabeth very small – just once – beneath your windows.

Farewell
With our loves
Katherine.

MS BL.

To Ida Baker, (25 August 1921)

[Chalet des Sapins, Montana-sur-Sierre]
Thursday.

Dear Ida.
Everything is in order here – and I am v. grateful. Really grateful! I wish I could make you feel it. Ernestine cant work for nuts but it doesn't

matter. She'll learn in time. I send you 100 francs. Do you want more? Let me know. And please order for yourself from the chemist some *Eastons Syrup*. There is nothing like it for a tonic, and its effect is immediate. Hudson says its the best *quick* restorer you can have. You need it. Do get it. Surely you realise what health means! Its criminal folly to be careless. Don't just shake your old bi-palatanoids at me.

K.M.

MS BL.

To J. B. Pinker, 26 August 1921

Chalet des Sapins, | Montana-sur-Sierre, | Switzerland.
August 26 1921

Dear Sir,

I thank you for your letter. It is a very great pleasure to know that you will act for me.

I note what you say about sending my new volume of stories in duplicate, and I will let you have two copies as soon as possible.

In the meantime I am sending you copies of the last three stories of a series of six which were commissioned by the Sphere. I am afraid they may be appearing at the time you receive this letter. But would it be worth while sending them to America?

In the matter of a publisher for my new book I have promised the first refusal of it to Constable's. But I am not bound to any publisher. As to America, Alfred Knopf, who bought Bliss in sheets, asked to see my new book. But of course I am not anxious to have it sold in sheets again.

Yours sincerely,
Katherine Mansfield

P.S. Your second letter suggesting that I should write something for the Daily Chronicle has just arrived. The subjects I can think of off-hand on which I should like to write a thousand words are: "Up the airy Mountains", "Jam", "Stairs", "On discovering Books".[1] I hope these or some of these will be suitable; but I cannot turn my light pen into a sword or a ploughshare.

TS Newberry.

---

[1] None of these proposed articles was ever written.

To Dorothy Brett. [29 *August 1921*]

[Chalet des Sapins, Montana-sur-Sierre]

Dearest Brett,

I would have written before but the Furies have had me until today. Something quite new for a change – high fever, deadly sickness and weakness. I haven't been able to lift my head from the pillow. I think it has been a breakdown from too much work.¹ I have felt exhausted with all those stories lately & yet – couldn't stop. Well, there has been a stop now & I am just putting forth my horns again & thinking of climbing up the hill . . . How I do abominate any kind of illness! Oh God, what it is to live in such a body! Well, it doesn't bear thinking about . . . As soon as I can get well enough to go downstairs I shall engage our one origi- nal cab & go for a long drive behind the old carthorse with his jingle- bells. The driver – as a great honour – throws the foot mat over the seat when one goes for a party of pleasure. He seems to think that is *very* chic! But this is such a beautiful country. Oh! It is so marvellous. Never the same – the air like old, still wine – sounds of bells & birds and grasshop- pers playing their fiddles & the wind shaking the trees. It rains & the drops in the fir trees afterwards are so flashing-bright & burning that one feels all is enchanted. It is cloudy – we live in fine white clouds for days & then suddenly at night all is crystal clear & the moon has gold wings. They have just taken the new honey from the hives. I wish I could send you a jar. All the summer is shut up in a little pot. But summer is on the wane – the wane. Now Murry brings back autumn crocuses and his handkerchief is full of mushrooms. I love the satiny colour of mush- rooms, & their *smell* & the soft stalk. The autumn crocuses push above short, mossy grass. Big red pears – monsters jostle in Ernestine's apron. Yes, ça commence, ma chère. And I feel as I always do that autumn is loveliest of all. There is such a sharpness with the sweetness – there is the sound of cold water running fast in the stream in the forest. Murry says the squirrels are tamer already. But Heavens Brett – Life is so mar- vellous, it is so rich – such a store of marvels that one cant say which one prefers.

I feel with you, most deeply and truly, that its not good to be 'per- manent'. Its the old cry: "Better be impermanent moveables". Now here for instance – we are only 4 hours from Italy. One can run into Italy for tea. Murry went down to see Elizabeth last week & she had so done. She had waked with a feeling for Italy that morning & behold she was flown. And that night she sat in the Opera House in Milan . . . *That is right* – I am sure. Thats why I hate England. I can't help it, Miss, downs or no downs. There is that Channel which lies like a great cold sword between you and your dear love Adventure. And by Adventure I mean – yes – the wonderful feeling that one can lean out of heaven knows what window tonight – one can wander under heaven knows what flowery trees. Strange songs sound at the windows, the wine bottle is a new shape, a perfectly new moon shines outside . . . No, don't settle. Dont ever have a convenient little gentleman's residence. Hot baths in ones own bathroom are fearfully nice – but they are too *dear*. I prefer to bath in a flower pot as I go on my way . . .

I absolutely agree with you, too, about Manet & Renoir. Renoir – at the last – bores me. His feeling for flesh is a kind of super butchers feeling about a lovely little cut of lamb. I am always fascinated by lovely bosoms but not without the heads & hands as well – and I want in fact the feeling that all this beauty is in the deepest sense attached to Life. Real Life! In fact I must confess it is the spirit which fascinates me in flesh. That does for me as far as modern painters are concerned, I suppose. But I feel bored to my last groan by all these pattern mongers. Ah, how wearying it is! I would die of it if I thought. And the writers are just the same. But they are worse than the painters because they are so many of them dirty minded as well. I don't deny – I even can admire a dung hill. But Virginia Woolf tittering over some little mechanical contrivance to "relieve virgins" – that I abhor & abominate & am ashamed of!

What makes Lawrence a *real* writer is his passion. Without passion one writes in the air or on the sands of the seashore. But L. has got it all wrong, I believe. He is right, I imagine or how shall I put it . . .? Its my belief too, that nothing will save the world but Love. But his tortured, satanic demon lover I think is all wrong. The whole subject is so mysterious, tho'; one could write about it for ever. But let me try & say something.

It seems to me that there is a great change come over the world since people like US believed in God. God is now gone for all of us. Yet we must believe and not only that we must carry our weakness and our sin and our devilish-ness to somebody. I don't mean in a bad, abasing way. But we must feel that we are *known* that our hearts are known as God knew us. Therefore Love today between "lovers" has to be not only human, but divine today. They love each other for everything and through everything, and their love is their religion. It cant become any-thing less – even affection – I mean it can't become less supreme because it is an act of faith to believe! But oh, it is no good. I can't write it all out. I should go into pages & pages. But I think L. is a sign of the times – just as M's reply was, too.

How lovely your children sound. I *saw* them. Leonora's hair, Angela's 'ways' the expression of the little boy & Marie Loo's sort of *plunge* into Life. You made them simply lovely and so real!! I do wish I could appear behind a bush & see you painting them.[2] How I love little children & being with them! I envy you them *fearfully*. What is your picture like? I *see* the little heads & the green leaves behind them, but what is it really like? Tell me, do, & the colours.

My stories for the *Sphere* are all done, thank the Lord. I have had copies with ILLUSTRATIONS! Oh Brett! Such fearful horrors[3] All my dear people looking like – well – Harrods[4] 29/6 crepe de chine blouses and young tailors gents. And my old men – stuffy old wooly sheep. Its a sad trial. I am at present imbedded in a terrific story[5] but it still frightens me. And now I have to emerge & write some special things for the old Daily Chronicle who [is] going to make a feature of 'em. The Mountain is in London buying sweaters & stockings for our winter outfit. She has become a very fierce Swiss patriot. Switzerland is her *home*; she's perfectly happy here & is getting awfully good looking. M. says he won't stir for 5 years from this spot. Then we *say* we will sail to New Zealing. But I don't know.

Goodbye for now, dear Brett.

I send you my love & my duties.

Yours

Tig.

MS Newberry. *LKM* II. 129–32.

1 KM was in the middle of her long story 'At the Bay', but had also in August written 'Marriage à la Mode' and the incomplete 'A Married Man's Story.'
2 Brett's group portrait of her brother Maurice's children.
3 Several of her recent stories in the *Sphere* were crudely illustrated by W. Smithson Broadhead.
4 The fashionable department store in Knightsbridge.
5 Almost certainly 'A Married Man's Story'.

To Ida Baker, 29 August 1921

[Chalet des Sapins, Montana-sur-Sierre]
Monday 29.VIII.1921

Dear Ida,

I shall destroy the other letter I have written. Perhaps Jack is right; I *am* a tyrant. But . . . look here.

(a) Will you please either date your letters or put the day on the top.

(b) Do you mind cutting out the descriptions as much as you *can?* That kind of yearning sentimental writing about a virginia creeper & the small haigh voices of rainy children is more than I can stick. It makes me hang my head; it makes Jack play the mouth organ whenever we meet it in females. But I shall say no more. This is where the tyrant comes in. Its so much worse when the spelling is wrong, too. Brett is just exactly the same in this respect . . . Its very queer. . .

I don't like any of the stuffs. Will you go to *Lewis Evans & Selfridge* or *Debenham*.[1] Number the patterns & Ill wire a reply. Miss Read won't get them done, of course, but arrange with her to send them over. Try for

ROYAL blue instead of cornflower. These are either 2 dark or 2 light. As for tartans – try for soft smoky checks on any coloured ground instead – like the red & black check we saw in Menton. You remember? Thats the kind of stuff I meant, too. They had both better be lined with v. fine silver grey *viyella* or cashmere, I think. And tell Miss Read to cut them on the big side so that I can wear my woolen jumpers underneath if necessary. Id rather have nothing than these ugly dull stuffs. I am a very MODERN woman. I like Life in my clothes. Its no good going to Liberty² for plain colours – ever. Try & think of a picture in a French pattern book or a figure on the stage, cant you?

Sorry to give you so much trouble. Id no idea it would be all so *very* difficult. My advice is to "concentrate more" & not worry about the golden leaves so much. Fall they will! I am up. I am better and at work again. Cheer up!

Katherine.

MS BL.

¹ All stores in Oxford Street.
² Liberty, in Regent Street.

To Elizabeth, Countess Russell (30 August 1921)

Chalet des Sapins. | [Montana-sur-Sierre]

Dear Elizabeth,

It is on my conscience that I was horribly ungracious the other afternoon.¹ I felt half scrubbed and half painted away and yet another workman had sung The merry Widow² in my window from dawn till noon. The Swiss are *very* vocal. But that doesn't excuse my being as horrid as I know I was. I would have telephoned you and asked you to forgive me but my breath fails me at [the] telephone & I pant like the hart³ . . . Please forgive me.

Would you and Miss Richie⁴ drink a dish of tea with us on Thursday? It would make us very happy –

And please – because I love your petunias so much – *don't* rob your garden. Eight shut-tight, sealed perfect little buds have come into flower from the last ones.

Here is John, standing over me with a revolver at least.

With love, dear Elizabeth

Katherine.

MS BL.

¹ When Elizabeth took flowers to KM on 27 Aug., her cousin was in bed, not well enough to see her.

2 *The Merry Widow*, the opera by Franz Lehar (1870–1948), written in 1905.

3 'As the hart panteth after the water brooks, so panteth my soul after thee, O God': Ps. 42: 1.

4 Elizabeth's close friend Maud Ritchie, daughter of Lord Ritchie of Dundee, was staying with her at the Chalet Soleil.

To J. B. Pinker, [early September 1921]

Chalet des Sapins | Montana-sur-Sierre | Valais

Dear Mr Pinker,

Thank you for your letter. I am afraid I cannot cut that story. If I took such a dreadfully big snip off its tail there would be no mouse left. I will write another for The Sketch[1] as soon as I can the length they want and at the price they mention. Would you try to dispose of *A Cup of Tea* else-where.[2] I would far rather it did not go to the Mercury, however, as I am writing a long story[3] now in the style of *The Daughters of the Late Colonel* which they published. I feel pretty certain they would take this new one. It is so difficult to place long stories in England. On the other hand I can't expect them to want more than a certain amount from me. Is there not a weekly that might take it? I suggest The Nation again. It is not too long for them.

As soon as my next book of stories is finished I mean to write a novel. I long to. Its only horrid circumstances that keep me back at present —

Yours sincerely
Katherine Mansfield

MS Newberry.

1 KM's only story in the *Sketch* was 'Taking the Veil', 22 Feb. 1922.

2 'A Cup of Tea' came out in the *Story-Teller*, May 1922.

3 'At the Bay', published in the *London Mercury*, Jan. 1922.

To Sylvia Lynd, [early September 1921]

CHALET DES SAPINS | MONTANA-SUR-SIERRE | (VALAIS)
Switzerland.

My dear Sylvia Lynd,

Forgive me. I hardly dare to say why I haven't written. Its so dread-fully the *same old reason*. And I waited until I was 'free' again because I wanted to send you more than a little note.

I was so happy to see your handwriting again. But your news was sor-rowful, dear woman. That must have been terribly hard to bear. But one can say nothing to help. Id like you to feel though how I appreciate your lovely courage, how I wish with all my heart that you are well again.

I often think of you here. Its such a perfect place − ever so much nicer than the South of France. There are no casinos, not motorcars, no rich-an'-great. Instead there are mountain tops & forests & little hoarse streams & small flowery lawns, & troops of white goats, and innocent rainbows. Would it be impossible for you and your husband to come & stay with us next summer? It isn't a hard place to find either. One takes the train direct from Paris to Sierre − the valley town − & then one winds up the mountain like a spider eating its web. As to the flowers − they are so many and so fair that J.M.M. and I have both 'taken' to botany. He does all the hunting though which is unfair. If only the Lord would leave off loving me − 'chastening' love is a horrid kind!

I feel far away from London just now. Things sound so queer by the time they reach us. What did you think about the Lawrence book? I agreed with what John wrote in The Nation.[1] It seems to me there is something hopelessly wrong with Lawrence now, & don't you feel, too theres a kind of devilish exasperation & even as he would say PURE stupidity? It makes me groan. I wish I could find a really good book for a change. Is Romer Wilson a great person? It is tiring not to be able to admire things; I always *long* to though my enemies don't believe me.

Are you at work on a new novel? I have just finished six stories and am imbedded in the seventh, at that stage when one is frightened of the story flying away before you really have caught it. Dear knows how long these have taken me, though . . . I wish I knew what you were feeling about your work. J.M.M. and I seem to be starting a small boarding school for 2 boarders only with a little mixed dormitory with our two beds setting to corners. One feels awfully *not* grown up in Switzerland. Do you know that feeling? Its the kind of place − or perhaps it is this house − where one sits on stairs & where the window on the landing becomes really important again not only a bowing acquaintance − Our servant too, wears a yellow velvet bodice with black stripes on Sunday & every day she is wreathed in positive beams.

And for Socierty Gossip . . . Mr Hugh Walpole[2] has been staying in the neighbourhood − on (most strangely!) his way to *Venice*. I mean, it seems such an out-of-the-way leap. If only I could think you would come next year!

Goodbye for now.

I am your loving

K.M.

PC ATL.

---

[1] Under 'The Nostalgia of Mr D. H. Lawrence', Murry had reviewed *Women in Love* in the *Nation and Athenaeum*, 13 Aug. 1921.

² Hugh Walpole was staying with Elizabeth at the Chalet Soleil during July and early August, when Murry's ferocious attack on Walpole's new novel *The Thirteen Travellers* appeared in the *Nation and Athenaeum*, 16 July 1921.

To Richard Murry, 5 September 1921

[Chalet des Sapins, Montana sur Sierre]
5.IX.1921

Richard

I have been too long in answering your last letter. Forgive me. They varnished the outside of this chalet and the 'niff' gave me white lead poisoning & I felt an awful worm with it. The whole world seemed varnish. Everything I ate had varnish sauce. Even Jack was overcome for a day. But its over now, and we appear to be living in a house beautifully basted with the best brown gravy – and the factory is in full blast² again. I must say we do manage to get through a great deal of work here, and there are always side issues – such as jam making, sewing on our buttings, cutting each others hair which fill up the margin of the days. We *try* to make it a rule not to talk in bed. Its queer how full life is once one gets free of wasted time . . .

I want to say a word about your new job. I hope it fits in with your scheme of life. Its not much good me saying much, for I don't really know what you feel about it. It gives you more freedom, though doesn't it – and independence. I hope you're happy and all goes well.

My ambition is to make enough money to build a small house here – near where we are – on a grassy slope with a wood behind & mountains before. It will take about five years to do it – get the money together. But it would be a very great satisfaction to design a really good place to work in – down to the last cupboard. But who am I to talk so lofty. When – if – the time comes & you're not too famous I'll beg you to lay aside your laurels & do it for us. Ill only look over your shoulder and breathe very hard when you make those lovely little lines that mean stairs.

Since I last wrote summer has gone. Its autumn. Now Jack brings home from his walks mushrooms and autumn crocuses. Little small girls knock at the door with pears to sell & blue black plums. The hives have been emptied; there's new honey and the stars look almost frosty. Speaking of stars reminds me – we were sitting on the balcony last night. It was dark. These huge fir trees 'take' the darkness marvellously. We had just counted four stars & remarked a light, high up – what was it? on the mountains opposite, when suddenly far away a little bell began ringing. Someone played a tune on it – something gay, merry, ancient, over and over. I suppose it was some priest or lay brother in a mountain village. But what we felt was – its good to think such things still happen – to think some peasant goes off in the late evening & delights to play that carillon. I sometimes have a fear that simple hearted people are no more. I was ashamed of that fear last night. The little bell seemed to say, but joyfully: 'Be not afraid. All is not lost.'

Do you know – its a year since we have seen each other. *How* I should like to see you again! But not for an hour or two – thats no good. Id like enough time to get over the novelty so that we really could talk. Id like to hear enough about your work – to begin with . . . But its hardly fair, although its a temptation, to ask you why painters so seldom paint flowers – when you go to the trouble of explaining with a whole lovely little drawing. Oh, why can't I sweep all these fruits into a bastick & send it flying to you. Its not fair you shouldn't see these red, gold flecked pears and these greengages. I never set eye on them but I think of you . . .

All being well as they say, Wingley should arrive this week. He'll be terrified after the journey. We shall have to get him snow boots for the winter and an airman's helmet made of mouse's skin.

This letter is all in pieces. Don't think evil of me for it, brother.

Je vous embrasse

Katherine.

Jack: "Ask the old boy if he has seen Charlie Chaplin in The Kid.[1] And tell him to let us know what he thinks of it."

K: "I will."

K. to R: ?

R:

MS R. Murry. *LKM* II. 132–3.

[1] Charlie Chaplin's new film with Jackie Coogan as the 'Kid', 1921.

To Ida Baker, 7 September 1921

[Chalet des Sapins, Montana-sur-Sierre]
7.IX.1921

My dear I,

Its not possible to say all I wish to. Ill write it. Do you feel inclined to take this *job*[1] – really? I mean to manage things for me as if I were a man. Its like this. I have gone to a new agent, he's got me work which will keep me busy until Christmas at earliest. Then the Daily N. has asked me to do some special articles for them and so has the Daily Chronicle. All this is *extra*. I cant devote myself to it if I have to look after the house & my clothes and so on. Its impossible. At the same time I *must* do it without delay. I can pay you between £10–12 a month. But tho' payment is important – its not the important thing. Can I rely on you? Can I ask you just simply to do what is necessary – i.e. what I should do if I hadn't a profession? In a word – can I feel, payment apart and *slavery* apart and false pride apart – that you are mine? That you will accept this situation as the outcome of our friendship? Does it satisfy you? May I consider you as permanently part of the scheme & will you consider me in the same light?

The truth is friendship is to me every bit as sacred and eternal as marriage. I want to know from you if you think the same.

Yours ever

K.M.

As for my *violence* and so on I could explain all that, too, but it takes too long. Try and accept it, while it lasts.

MS BL, *MiM*. 170.

1 Ida Baker had just returned from London, when KM put to her the new proposals for her acting as companion and aide, and followed up their conversation with this letter.

To Dorothy Brett. [12 September 1921]

[Chalet des Sapins, Montana-sur-Sierre]

In harbour. Monday.

Brett,

Take a long breath. Im going to write masses. First about your picture. I think the little girl in the front is amazingly good. She is beautifully felt. You have got the essential "childishness" of her and you've got it by *painting*. I mean all is so firm, so compact, modelled and simple. And it remains warm. I think you ought to pride yourself no end on that little girl et je vous serre la main pour elle. I have put the photograph on the top of this page so Im looking at it as I write. Please remember how Fearfully good I think that small child!

I don't think it comes off as a composition chiefly because of the big child. She seems to me too big, too pale (even tho' I realise you want to get her fairness over) too broad, too much an *expanse*. She [is] in a different world to the other child and therefore they cant be really related. Theres a kind of weakness, too, in the painting of the head. Its as though you haven't held it in your hands & felt it all over. While you were painting you were not touching her. Thats how it looks. And her size distracts one. The picture falls away in her corner. The boy seems to me just very nearly successful. But in his case your sympathies – your feeling for his disposition seem to me to have interfered with your tranquility. You know how, whatever one feels in ones excitement, when one sits down to work that goes. All must be smooth. No *novelty*, no appearance of effort. Thats the secret. It must appear so natural, so without effort. I feel you have strained a bit to get across the fact of the boy's sensitiveness, and so you show him off a little instead of paint him. See what I mean?

Look here, Brett. Don't be angry with me for saying all this. If I am your friend you have the right to expect the truth from me. I cant, in these days, give less. Life is too important as well as too short. So forgive me, my girl, if I hurt you. Three heads – a group like that – are – is – hard to manage. One wants to roll them round softly, until they combine. ℐ℈ ℈ They want to flow into each other a bit, especially if they are children. You want a kind of soft nudging if one of the children is your little girl. This doesn't upset their "differences" but it *does* make one feel the artist has seen them as a THREE not as a 1, 2, and 3.

I expect after this youll never send me another photograph. Well, I shall be awfully sorry if you dont. Good luck! All success to you!

The Cezanne book, Miss, you won't get back until you send a policeman or an urgent request for it. It is fascinating, & you can't think how one enjoys such a book on our mountain tops. He is awfully sympathetic to me. I am absolutely uneducated about painting. I can only look at it as a writer, but it seems to me the real thing. Its what one is aiming at. One of his men gave me quite a shock. He is the *spit* of a man Ive just written about – one Jonathan Trout.[1] To the life. I wish I could cut him out & put him in my book. Ive finished my new book. Finished last night at 10.30. Laid down the pen after writing 'Thanks be to God'. I wish there was a God. I am longing to (1) praise him (2) thank him. The title is *At The Bay*. Thats the name of the very long story in it, a continuation of 'Prelude'. Its about 60 pages. Ive been at it all last night. My precious children have sat in here playing cards.[2] Ive wandered about all sorts of places – in and out. I hope it is good. It is as good as I can do and all my heart and soul is in it – every single bit. Oh God, I hope it gives pleasure to someone . . . It is so strange to bring the dead to life again. Theres my grandmother, back in her chair with her pink knitting, there stalks my uncle over the grass. I feel as I write "you are not dead, my darlings. All is remembered. I bow down to you. I efface myself so that you may live again through me in your richness and beauty." And one feels *possessed*. And then the peace where it all happens. I have tried to make it as familiar to 'you' as it is to me. You know the marigolds? You know those pools in the rocks? You know the mousetrap on the wash house window sill? And, too, one tries to go deep – to speak to the secret self we all have – to acknowledge that. I mustn't say any more about it.

Im glad you have left Scotland. Its so bad to be with people who depress you. I felt that your wings, quivering and pressed together like a butterfly's opened wide & fanned with joy to breathe the air of your own room. When

do you give up your house? I think its not good to be alone. You want people for many reasons, even for the sense of security a lodger gives you at
night. Thats a very real thing! The point is to try to have a house with as
little 'trouble' as possible. How do you manage? And certainly to be a move-
able as often as you can. But don't you find housekeeping very difficult? I
have had to give it up entirely. If one has a profession one has no more time
for it than a man has. One cannot arrange food, do one's mending, see that
there are flowers and that all is in order and work too. Murry and I have
tried it and neither he nor I can bring it off. So we have engaged the 'mountain' quite finally to be a professional housekeeper – to be the 'mistress' of
the house in fact as a servant understands that word. It works well. When
the mountain feels that she is needed she is quite different. And what a joy
it is to be free and not to know what there is for dinner! The only perquisite
we retain is jam-making. Murry and I brew our jam on the electric toaster
in a big saucepan. We have just made red plum & aspire towards quince.
Its a thrilling job, especially taking 'specimens' in a saucer – one ends with
a ring of saucers.

No, we certainly shan't be back in England for years. Sometimes, in bed
at night, we plan one holiday a year but everywhere else feels nearer than
England. If we can get the money we shall build here in two or three years
time & we have already chosen the way to look – the way the house shall
face. And it is christened *Chalet Content*. We are both most fearful dreamers,
especially when its late & we lie staring at the ceiling. It begins with me. M.
declares he won't talk. Its too late. Then I hear "Certainly not more than
two floors & a large open fireplace." A long pause. K: "What about bees?"
J.M.: "Most certainly bees and I aspire to a goat." And it ends with us
getting fearfully hungry & J.M.M. going off for two small whacks of cake
while I heat two small milks on the spirit stove.

You know Wingley? The mountain brought him over. He arrayed with
immense eyes after having flashed through all that landscape & it was several hours before the famous purr came into action. Now he's completely
settled down & reads Shakespeare with us in the evening. I wonder what cat
Shakespeare is like. We expect him to write his reminiscences shortly. They
are to be bound in mouse's skin.

Goodbye dear Brett. Im taking a holiday today after my labours last week.
I wrote for 9 solid hours yesterday. But it has been such a pleasure to talk
to you. Id like to send my love to Kot, if he wasn't my enemy. Take care of
yourself. Keep well. Eat nourishing food. But one can't say to another Be
happy. One can only wish it. Yours, dear little painter

Tig.
Who do you think turned up at the end of this letter? Mrs H.G. Wells &
two young H.G. Wells.[3] *Very* nice boys. We feel full of gaiety.

MS Newberry. *LKM* II. 134–5. *Selected,* 224–7.

[1] The romantic and disappointed uncle in 'At the Bay', based on Val Waters, husband of her mother's sister, Agnes. What KM has in mind is probably the figure on the right in Cézanne's painting *The Card Players* (1892).

[2] The scene in sec. 9 of 'At the Bay'.

[3] Mrs Jane Wells and her two teenage sons, Frank and George, were staying with Elizabeth Russell.

To Richard Murry, [12 September 1921]

[Chalet des Sapins, Montana-sur-Sierre]

Caro Riccardo,

Just a note to say that Wingley, our gooseberry-eyed one has arrived. Thin – terribly – with the bones sticking out of his rump like a cow's bones do. A mingy little ruff & fur that has turned brown like an actor's black overcoat. You can imagine his *look* after the journey, flashing across the world on the end of a string. But when Jack lay on the floor & rubbed noses with him he turned over & showed off his white weskit in just his old way. He is now quite settled down, reads Shakespeare with us every night & marks the place in his copy with a dead fly. Its awfully nice to have him. He's like a little anchor, here. We hope later on he may be persuaded to write his reminiscences . . .

How are you – my dear old boy? I finished my new book last night – laid down my pen at 10.30 p.m. and wrote *Thanks be to God* under the last line. Queer! I really felt it, too. Oh Richard I do hope it will give you a little pleasure – the first long story, I mean. Its a continuation of Prelude, but better than Prelude I hope. 60 pages. Ive been at it for seven hours a day all this last week.

Your brother is very well. Hes the colour of a superfine apricot through walking in the sun without his hat. He has bought a pair of jae-gar shoes that come halfway up ones leg and are so large that one could almost sit in one. He also bought a TERRIFIC leather jerkin from Pontings, Kensington for 10/-. Pontings have a sale of these government airman clothes. Its worth knowing. All goes well here. We begin to look towards Christmas: I begin to wonder if that small black dot moving over the snow with 2 Xmas candles in his hair is Richard –

With warm love, dear little brother

Katherine.

MS R. Murry. *LKM* II. 135–6.

To J. B. Pinker, 13 September 1921

Chalet des Sapins | Montana-sur-Sierre | Switzerland
September 13 1921

Dear Mr Pinker,

In case it may help you to dispose of the three stories[1] I lately sent you in America, I now learn that they are not to be published in the "Sphere" until November, so that they will not necessarily have appeared already in England.

Yours very sincerely
Katherine Mansfield[2]

P.S. I hope to let you have the MS of the book by the end of this week.

MS Newberry.

---

[1] These were 'Her First Ball', 'The Voyage', and 'Marriage à la Mode', published in the *Sphere* on 28 Nov., 24 Dec., 31 Dec. respectively. Pinker did not place them in American publications.
[2] The letter is written by Murry, but signed by KM.

To J. B. Pinker, 14 September 1921

Chalet des Sapins | Montana-sur-Sierre | Switzerland.
Sep 14 1921

Dear Mr Pinker,

Under separate cover I am sending the Ms of my new book "At The Bay and Other Stories".[1] Of the two copies one only is complete. The story that is missing from the other I am having sent round to you immediately. Even now I send only two copies of the first long story, "At The Bay", instead of four. This story has not yet been published serially. Would you try to sell it separately for me in England and America? I hope I am not troubling you too much by asking if you would have two copies typed for me for that purpose. I believe that Mr Squire might care to have it for the London Mercury. He has asked me for a new story.

Naturally I should like to get as large an advance as possible for this book; it has taken me over a year to compose. Of course I am very anxious to sell it separately in America, and not in sheets.

When you send me the account for the typing would you charge me with a telegram also, to say the MS has reached you safely.

Yours sincerely
Katherine Mansfield.[2]

I enclose two photographs of myself in case the press or the publishers would care for them.

TS Newberry.

To Richard Murry (17 September 1921)

[Chalet des Sapins, Montana sur Sierre]
Sunday

We thought your criticism of "The Kid" was extremely interesting. At last we got an idea what it really was like. It's a pity Charles lets these other things creep in – a great pity. I should very much like to see him with the infant. I feel that would be fine. But most of the rest – dear me, *no*! As to the tabloid of the lady with the cross – such things make one hang one's head.

We have been squirrel-gazing this afternoon through field-glasses. They are exquisite little creatures – so intent, preoccupied, as it were, and so careless. They flop softly from branch to branch, hang upside down, just for the sake of hanging. Some here are as small as rats, with reddish coats and silver bellies. The point about looking at birds and so on through glasses is one sees them in their own world, off their guard. One spies, in fact.

I'd like to send you some *moss*. Do you like moss? There are many kinds here, and just now it is in its beauty. It's nice to sit down and ruffle it with one's hand. Flowers are gone. A few remain, but they are flat on the grass without their stalks – dandelions and purple ones. The mountain ash is *terrific* against the blue. There aren't many leaves here to turn, but the wild strawberry makes up for them. Minute leaves of every colour are scattered on the ground.

In fact, if possible, this early autumn is all the bes' – even better than summer or spring. I mustn't send you a catalogue, though. I must refrain.

MS lacking. *LKM* II. 136.

To Michael Sadleir, 24 September 1921

Chalet des Sapins | Montana-sur-Sierre | Valais
Switzerland
24.IX.1921

Dear Michael Sadleir,

Some days ago I sent my new book off to Pinker – – at long last. Never have I had my pen so snatched away by The Furies. But I think these mountain tops are too high for them. Works much easier. I have asked Pinker to let you see the book. I hope it will be published by you . . .

Is it not time I heard some account of the sales of Bliss.[1] Its nearly a year now since it has been published.

I hope all goes well with you.
Yours sincerely
Katherine Mansfield.

MS Targ.

---

[1] Brownlee Kirkpatrick, *Bibliography*, 17, suggests that 'with four reprints between December 1920 and the end of 1921 sales would probably reach 3,000–4,000'.

To Sylvia Lynd, 24 September 1921

Chalet des Sapins | Montana-sur-Sierre | Valais
Switzerland
24.IX.1921

Most dear Sylvia Lynd,

I have been waiting to talk to you – to have you to myself, no less – until I could chase my new book out of the house. I thought it never would go. Its last moments lingered on and on. It got up, turned again, took *off* its gloves, again sat down, reached the door, came back, until finally J.M.M. marked it down lassooed it with a stout string & hurled it at Pinker. Since when there's been an ominous silence. True, I haven't had time to hear yet, but one has a shameful feeling that it ought to have been 'recognised' even at the bottom of the first mountain and a feeble cheer – a cheer left over from Charlie C. – might have been raised . . .

No, that sounds proud. Its not really pride but FEAR!

But its gone. May I give you a small hug for your marvellous letter. It really is a heavenly gift to be able to put yourself, jasmine, summer grass, a kingfisher, a poet, the pony, an excursion and the new sponge bag & bedroom slippers all into an envelope. How does one return thanks for a piece of somebody's life? When I am depressed by the superiority of men I comfort myself with the thought that they can't write letters like that. You make me feel, too, that whatever star they were born under, it wasn't the dancing one.' Keep well! Never be ill again!

About 'plans'. (Have you a passion for making plans? I have. Its a vice with me, like strong drink. When I am by myself, out comes the bottle and glass so to say, & I begin to sip at the idea of a winter in Spitzbergen, a summer in Spain, a cruise in a tramp steamer, a little house remote . . . remote until the servant comes in and catches at my flying head with the laundry bill or a parcel from the chemist.) But about Montana and pensions. The idea that you should come here with your daughters & your novel is fearfully tempting. It makes me want to hide the truth about the between season fogs and cost of living. Let me be 'resolute and calm'. Montana is a small village (one street of new & ugly shops) on a plateau surrounded by mountains. Its 5000 feet high. Except for that street its all fir and pine forests, little lawny pastures, ice cold streams and air like old wine. Its expensive. A pension costs about 16 francs a day, per persing. That seems to me terrible. There is, about ½ an hour's climb down from here an hotel in a forest clearing which I have heard is extremely comfortable in every way. Its not a horrid palace with waiters on the lawn but a 'simple' place managed by two comfortable parties who take an interest in your sanwiches if you want to go off for the day. I will send my (what is she? Friend? Not quite. Housekeeper? No. Invaluable Person?) Invaluable Person to examine it thoroughly and to photograph it if you would like me to. The position is – in the sun's eye & facing huge snow covered almighty ones. Its forests are real forests – almost fairy ones.

But *facts* are. That in either October or November the weather changes here. We are in the clouds, in a fine thick white drizzle for about 6 weeks before the winter begins. Then, so everybody says it is nothing but bright sun, calm, snow, ice, sleighs, little bells, tame squirrels and fir trees like polar bears rampant. But the interval? Could you bear it? And again theres the question of advantages. I don't know if a Mademoiselle could be found. I imagine it wouldn't be safe to count on finding one here. That, too, I'll ask my I.P. to inquire into.

Its 'lovely' here, as they say. There is a winter season though which of course we have never seen. I think for a place to work, its ideal. It will be very cold. One must be wool without & wool within. One must count the Swiss franc as a shilling. The post is superb, absolutely reliable. You can buy everything in that little village and I suggest a weekly toffee party here for your daughters to be allowed to make the toffee *themselves*. But I really must refrain from saying 'do come!' as I'd like to. There it is. I will tell you more at a hint, at a sign from you . . .

I lapped up the gossip . . . What is happening to 'married pairs'? They are almost extinct. I confess, for my part I believe in marriage. It seems to me the only possible relation that really is satisfying. And how else is one to have peace of mind to enjoy life and to do ones work? To know *one other* seems to me a far greater adventure than to be on kissing acquaintance with dear knows how many. It certainly takes a lifetime and its far more 'wonderful' as time goes on. Does this sound hopelessly oldfashioned? I suppose it does. But there it is – to make jam with J.M.M., to look for the flowers that NEVER are in the Alpine Flora book, to talk, to grow things, even to watch J.M.M. darning his socks over a *lemon* seems to me to take up all the time one isn't working. People

nowadays seem to live in such confusion. I have a horror of dark mud-
dles. Not that life is easy, really, or that one can be "a child all the time",
but time to *live* is needed. These complications take years to settle, years
to get over. I wish you'd write a novel about married happiness. It is
time for one . . . It is time for a *good* novel on any subject, though.
Perhaps we don't see them here. I've only just read Virginia Woolfs
Monday or Tuesday stories. I didn't care for them. She's detached from
life – it won't do – will it? Nothing grows. Its not even cut flowers, but
flower heads in flat dishes. I don't think one can 'scrap' form like that.
In fact I suspect novelty *as* novelty – don't you? Was Romer Wilson very
superb? Ah, my dear S.L. I shall never have a silver medal. I don't
expect such exotics. For long now my garden has only produced

Doctors' bills.
And chemists pills
And hot bottuls all in a row . . .

The *bills* persist & flourish. The rest I am determined to root out. They
are going . . . And speaking of ones poverty reminds me I would be most
awfully grateful for any work Mr Lynd cared to try me with.

I immensely enjoy *his* articles in the D.N., and I rejoiced in his letter
in The Nation this week about Wordsworth & Abrahams bosom.[2]

One thing one does miss here, and that is seeing people. One doesn't
ask for many but there come moments when I long to *see* & *hear* and listen . . . that most of all.

Otherwise this September has been perfect. Every day is finer. There's
a kind of greengage light on the trees. The flowers are gone, all except
flat starry yellow & silver ones that lie tight to the turf. J.M.M. is a fierce
mushroom hunter. He spares none. Little mushroom 'tots' swim in the
soup & make me feel a criminal. The mountain ash is brilliant – flashing bright against the blue. And the quince jam is boiling something
beautiful, M'm, as I write. I love autumn. I feel its better than summer
even. Oh, the moss here! Ive never seen such moss, & the colour of the
little wild strawberry leaves that are threaded through. They are almost
the only leaf that turns, here, so turn they do with a vengeance.

I hardly dare mention birds. Its rather hard Harold M. should have
had such a very large bird in his bonnet; it makes all the rest of us go
without. There are some salmon pink ones here just now, passing
through, which but for Harold M. I should enjoy . . .

But this letter is unmercifully long. Goodbye for now, dear S.L.
'May Good Fortune fall ever deeper in love with thee'.

Katherine.

PC ATL. *LKM* II. 137–9.

1 'There was a star danced, and under that I was born': *Much Ado about Nothing*, II. i. 349.

2 Robert Lynd had written to the *Nation and the Athenaeum* on 17 Sept. 1921, arguing that

Wordsworth's sonnet 'It is a beauteous evening, calm and free,' was addressed to a child, and that the line 'Thou liest in Abraham's bosom all the year' would be inappropriate if addressed to an adult.

To J. B. Pinker, 29 September 1921

Chalet des Sapins | Montana-sur-Sierre | Valais
Switzerland.
29.IX.1921

Dear Mr Pinker,

I received the enclosed letter today from Mr Michael Sadlier on behalf of Constable. If you are satisfied with their offer, I personally should like to accept it. They treated me very well over 'Bliss', and I imagine it is a good idea for a writer to keep with one publisher . . .

There is no chance – is there? – of the typist correcting my spelling in the long story *At The Bay*. There are several words which appear to be spelt wrong – i.e. emer*al* for emer*ald*, ninseck for insect and so on. These words are not in inverted commas, so the typist may just think its wanton ignorance on my part. But my hand on my heart I mean every spelling mistake! It interferes with the naturalness of childrens' or servants' speech if one isolates words with commas or puts them in italics. Thats my reason for leaving them plain.

Please excuse me for troubling you with this matter.

Yours sincerely
Katherine Mansfield

MS Newberry.

To Dorothy Brett, [1 October 1921]

Chalet des Sapins | Montana-sur-Sierre | (Valais)

Dearest Brett

Be gentle! Have pity on your Swiss friend. The staggering letter from Leila about Godfrey was almost too much. Its a perfect letter. Never never let it go. His desire for Panama is so touching & his Horror of putting on his dress clothes to go into Socierty. Such things cant be intended. The very mountains are laughing. But Brett – you must get to know him, you must stalk this wild shy creature – don't you think. And the OPeration? What can it be. I don't dare to *brood* over this aspeck of the affair. For Heavens sake and on my knees I beg (as Shakespeare put it) keep me posted in this affair![1]

I am sitting writing to you on the balcony among teacups, grapes, a brown loaf shaped like a bean, a plaited cake with almond paste inside & nuts out. M. has just forsaken it to join our cousin Elizabeth. She appeared today behind a bouquet – never smaller woman carried bigger bouquets. She looks like a garden walking – of asters, late sweet peas, stocks, & always petunias. She herself wore a frock like a spider's web, a hat like a berry and gloves that reminded me of thistles in seed. Oh, how I love the appearance of people – how I delight in it if I love them. I have gathered Elizabeth's frocks to my bosom as if they were part of her flowers. And then when she smiles a ravishing wrinkle appears on her nose – and never have I seen more exquisite hands. Oh dear I do hope we shall manage to keep her in our life. Its terrible how ones friends disappear & how quickly one runs after to lock the door & close the shutters. The point about her is that one loves her and is proud of her. Ah, thats so important! To be proud of the person one loves. Its essential. Its deep – deep. Theres no wound more bitter to love than not to be able to be proud of the other. Its the unpardonable offence, I think.

But no doubt Elizabeth is far more important to me than I am to her. Shes surrounded, lapped in lovely friends. Read her last book if you can get hold of it. Its called *Vera* & published by Macmillan. Its amazingly good?

Except for her we are lost in our forest. And next month the weather will change. Six weeks or two months in the clouds with nothing to see but more cloud before it clears & the snow falls. Other people who flee from the mountains in the between seasons seem to think it will be a very awful time. But there is so much to do. And I love to be in a place all the year round – to know it in all its changes. Ive been away from England for over a year now. Why does England sound so horrid? I suppose its not really, but the smell of the newspaper even frightens me. J.M.M. has just the same horror of it. Its a kind of nightmare.

I am very interested in your doll still life. Ive always wondered why nobody really saw the beauty of dolls – the *dollishness* of them. People make them look like cricket bats with eyes as a rule. But there is a kind of smugness & rakishness combined in dolls & heaven knows how much else that's exquisite & the only word I can think of is *precious*. What a life one leads with them. How complete. Their hats – how perfect – and their shoes, or even minute boots. And the pose of a dolls hand – very dimpled with spreading fingers. Female dolls in their nakedness are the most female things on earth. . . .

I keep on being interrupted by the sound in the trees. Its getting late – the tree tops look as though they have been dipped into the gold-pot & there's a kind of soft happy sighing or swinging or ruffling – all three going on. A bird, bright salmon pink with mouse grey wings hangs upside down pecking a fir cone – the shadows are growing long on the mountains. But its impossible to describe this place. It has so brought back my love of nature that I shall spend all the rest of my life – trekking. A winter in Spitzbergen is an ambition of ours after some photographs in The Sphere. It looks marvellous. The only question is – will our cat be able to stand it? The nearest other cat is China.

Do you enjoy your Thursdays? Are the talks interesting? Who holds forth? Sullivan, I expect, & is seconded by Waterlow. I like Milne – don't you? Sullivan sounds happy. There is no reason why he and Mrs S. plus the motor car shouldn't do very well. Is her baby coming? Babies are in the air just now. I heard via the Mountain, via Miss Reade that Miss-Carrington-that-was – was expecting.[3] She ought to have babies. Theyd be lovely – like sunflowers. How silly of Gertler.[4] Thats the worst of being a sentimentalist, one is landed in places where one looks silly. But you are very fond of Gertler – aren't you? Is he better to talk painting with than Guevara?[5] Who do you really talk to? My cold hand won't write. I must go in. But these last moments are best moments. Now a whole troupe of little cattle, goats, black sheep, brown lambs has rushed down the forest path with a wild girl & a boy behind them. They have come down from the high pastures.

I fully expected Charlie to be at Garsington. He sounded awfully nice. His Cousin Aubrey filled us with horror. We don't see the Mirror but the Daily News feeds one. This picture of him is extremely good.[6] Its the look *behind* the look which is wonderful.

I am so sorry your parcil never came. Thats the point about Switzerland. The post offices are models. People post everything to one another. One sees the poor postman delivering double beds & cannon balls and kittens. All just with a label. Its very useful though, & letters from anywhere never take more than two days. Im tempted to send you a mushroom or a squirrel for your new house.

Ive started & torn up two bad stories & now Im in the middle of the third. Its about a hypocrite. My flesh creeps as I write about him and my eyes pop at his iniquities.[7]

Heres a new "press" photo. Is it any good? Its like me, so M. says. "The spit of you". Do you think it would go all right on a cover?

Why don't you send me a picture of yourself. Id LIKE one! And my room here is so nice. Its like a wild west cabin – all wood and furs & silky stripes. I should very much like to have you on a wall.

Dont get caught in the cold blasts, little artist. Wrap yourself up. Make the charlady feed you on bakin. In my infancy I used to cry myself to bed with the tragic lines

> I bought a poun of ba-kin
> An fried it in a *pan*
> But nobody came to e-eat it
> But me-e and *my* young man!

Forgive a silly but grateful & loving

Tig.

MS Newberry. *LKM* II. 139–41.

1 Brett's letters with these details do not survive.
2 Elizabeth's new novel, *Vera*, drew heavily on her relationship with her estranged husband.
3 The rumour about Carrington's pregnancy was ill-founded.
4 Mark Gertler had been deeply in love with Carrington for several years.
5 Brett's friend, the Chilean painter Alvaro Guevara (1894–1951).
6 Charlie Chaplin, after ten years' absence in Hollywood, had recently returned to London to vast public acclaim.
7 This would seem to apply only to the incomplete 'A Married Man's Story', which she was working on in late August (see *Stories*, 571–2), and may now have come back to.

To Michael Sadler, 3 October 1921

Chalet des Sapins | Montana-s-Sierre | Valais
Switzerland
3 X 1921

Dear Michael Sadleir,

I have waited to write to you until I had heard from Pinker. On receipt of your letter I wrote to him saying I should like v. much to accept your offer. Now, today, he has sent me the agreement to sign . . . I am delighted that you care to publish the book. I hope it will be successful for 'my publisher's sake' as well as mine – –

Yours very sincerely
Katherine Mansfield.

MS Targ.

To J. B. Pinker, 3 October 1921

Chalet des Sapins | Montana-sur-Sierre | (Valais)
Switzerland.
3 X 1921

Dear Mr Pinker,

I am greatly obliged to your for arranging with Constables in the terms of this contract for the publication of my book of short stories. I return the agreement duly signed.

With many thanks
Yours sincerely
Katherine Mansfield

P.S. I note that in this agreement I receive only 3d per copy of the
Colonial edition, whereas, by the agreement for Bliss I received
6d. Is there a good reason for this?

K.M.

MS Newberry.

To Richard Murry, [4 October 1921]

[Chalet des Sapins, Montana-sur-Sierre]

Dear Richard

Drawing came today & is pinned up provisional on my nut brown
walls. Thanks most awfully. I like it Richard, very much indeed. There
seems to me such feeling for a back in it, if you know what I mean . . .
The roundness, the suppleness, the muskels. I don't forget the legs which
are beautifully drawn but its the back which holds my eye.

I regard this drawing as a birfday present. For I am 33 on Friday
week. So its doubly à propos . . . Shouldn't I have it framed in rather a
long narrow frame? Narrow white border? Thanks again, my artist
brother.

Ive sold my book to Constable who are publishing it this autumn. Id
like to heave out more than half the stories. But its no good. We've just
got to go on producing & know for ourselves where we are wrong and
how to improve. We've got to risk our failures as well as our more or
less successes. Good for ones pride, I suppose.

There's a superb sunset here while I am writing. The flocks & herds
have just raced down the hill. The trees are as still as still.

My boy, there is a village not far from here called *Lens* which you must
see, thats all. Jack & I bounded there the other day in another cart. Its
a fearful road, all water courses and upside down mountains. But the
view all the way there is the best thing Jack says he has ever *imagined*
even. On the way home we stop at the Wolf's Paw & have tea and honey
and cream & bread. I always think of you when I see anything really
'fine', as you'd say.

With my love

Katherine.

You know, Riccardo, it was fearfully nice of you to have sent me the
drawing . . .

MS R. Murry. *Adam* 370–5, 29.

To J. B. Pinker, 5 October 1921.

Chalet des Sapins | Montana-sur-Sierre | (Valais)
Switzerland.
5 X 1921

Dear Mr Pinker,

Many thanks for your letter. I returned the agreement yesterday. But of course I quite see the point about the date of publication being post-poned. Can you agree to that for me?

About the other clause – I am willing to do whatever you think best in the matter. It is always pleasanter not to be bound . . . Thank you for reassuring me about the typist.

I hope to have four new stories ready by the end of this month.

Sincerely yours
Katherine Mansfield

MS Newberry.

To Dorothy Brett, 5 October 1921.

[Chalet des Sapins, Montana-sur-Sierre]
5 X 1921

Brett dear

I did send you one. If it hasn't turned up by now, or if Mrs. Horne has used it as a plaster for the eye 2! I'll send you another. It would be 2 awful for you to have 2! But I sent one exprès asking you if you thought it would make a good 'press' photo.

Constables have taken my book and are publishing in the New Year. I am lucky. My new agent is a good man, I think, and Constables have treated me very well. If only one didn't have to pay doctors bills with the money. I sent off another cheque to Sorapure on the spot and still I owe fifty guineas to friends here. It would have been nice to have had a small splash with ones money instead. But one day I shall. I'll fly over & alight on your lawn under your windys complete with a soft snowball ready to throw. Lets have a good time some day, shall we? On our own? Cut off somewhere really thrilling for a bit? I must make enough money to bring this off . . .

Oh Brett, Ive got another old chill. Im lying on the balcony in JMMs Jaegar cardigan with a jaegar blanket up to my chest and fever. The best part of a chill is fever. Then the world has just that something added which makes it almost unbearably beautiful. It is worth it.

I am so glad you are hearing some music.' I don't think music ever makes me feel like Mozart does you, for instance. Its like being gloriously dead – if you know what I mean. One *is* not any more – one is wafted away, and yet there's a feeling of rejoicing and a kind of regret – Ah, such regret – mixed together that I feel disembodied spirits must know. But to tell you the absolute truth, though Beethoven does that for me so does Caruso[2] on a really good gramophone . . .

JMM and I, before this chill seized me have been taking some more driving *exercise*. Even the horse was amazed last time & stopped every three minutes & turned round and ogled us. I am going to wear riding breeches next time & JMM pink coat & stock made of a dinner napkin. We leapt up into the air, bounded from side to side, shook, fell forward, were tossed back. The road was an ancient water course with upside down mountains in it. But the view! The beauty of everything! The gold green pastures with herds of tiny rams & cattle & white goats. We arrived finally in a valley where the trees were turning – cherry trees a bright crimson, yellow maples, and apple trees *flashing* with apples. Little herd girls & boys with switches of mountain ash ran by. There was a very old saw mill that had turned too – a deep golden red. There cant be any place in the world more wonderful than the road to Lens. It is near there we mean to pitch our ultimate tent.

I hope Lady Ian Hamilton[3] buys a big picture. I think your idea of a show is *excellent*. Where would you have it? I do hope you carry this idea out & advertise it as much as possible. Dont you think an artist ought to have a show at least once a year? It seems to me almost as necessary as for a writer to produce a book. That sort of contact with the public – even the feeling of being at the mercy of the public is somehow *right*. After all, we express these things because we want a bigger audience than ourselves – We want to reveal what we have seen. I wish I could think I shall see your show . . .

Must stop. I only meant to write a note. If you can – send me a letter to get here on the 14th will you? Its such a thrill to get a letter on birthdays.

Dont wash up!!

I press your hand. I hope you are happy. Goodbye for now. Yours for ever

Katherine

MS Newberry. *LKM* II. 141–2.

[1] Brett was afflicted with severe deafness, and even in conversation frequently used an ear-trumpet, called 'Toby'.

[2] Enrico Caruso (1873–1921), the celebrated Italian tenor.

[3] Jean Hamilton (d. 1941) and her husband Sir Ian Hamilton (1853–1947), commanding general in the disastrous Dardanelles campaign in 1915, were patrons of the arts.

To J. B. Pinker, 10 October 1921.

Chalet des Sapins | Montana-s-Sierre | (Valais)
Switzerland.
10 X 1921

Dear Mr Pinker,

Thank you very much for letter me know about the story; I am glad the Mercury have taken it. It would be nice if we hear from America before December, so that it can be 'out' for Xmas. But perhaps that's a little too much to expect.

Would you mind – would it be a trouble – if I were to change the title of my new book of stories. What I want very much to do, if its possible, is to add a story Im finishing called *The Garden-Party* & to have the book called by that rather than At The Bay. I feel the book needs one more substantial story & a title that is *solid*. At The Bay now seems to me flimsy and vague. One forgets it – it doesn't carry and the other is a more 'compelling' (horrid word) title on a bookstall.

But this change may not be possible. I hope it is. I wrote Michael Sadleir a note to the same effect. Will you let me have your opinion, at your convenience?

Yours sincerely
Katherine Mansfield

MS Newberry.

To Michael Sadleir, 10 October 1921

Chalet des Sapins | Montana-sur-Sierre | (Valais)
Switzerland.
10 X 1921

Dear Michael Sadleir,

I have just written to Pinker saying that (if agreeable to you) I'd v. much like to *add* one story to my new book. In that case, would you mind if I changed the title of the book for the name of the new story which is *The Garden-Party*. It seems to me a much better title than the other. Also, I received yesterday two letters about the story *At the Bay* & in both cases the title was wrong: i.e. *In the Bay* & *On the Bay*. That seemed to me a bad lookout. The other name is – am I right? – more solid. Its harder to forget & would look more attractive in the bookshops. Or so I imagine. I hope you won't object . . . I'll let you have the new story at the end of next week – without fail.

My cheque for 'Bliss' made me feel an awful rich woman. For the first time in my life I *could* have bought a motorcar − a German one, at any rate.

    With best wishes
    Yours ever

                                      Katherine Mansfield.
Squire has just accepted At the Bay for The Mercury.[1]

MS Targ.

   [1] See letter to Squire, p. 250, n. 1.

To *Jeanne Renshaw, 14 October 1921*

Chalet des Sapins | Montana sur Sierre | Valais | Switzerland
                                         14 X 1921
My little sister,

    Your handkerchief is such a very gay one − it looks as though it had dropped off the handky tree. Thank you for it, darling. I remember the birthday when you bit me! It was the same one when I got a dolls pram & in a rage let it go hurling by itself down the grassy slope outside the conversatory. Father was *awfully* angry & said no one was to speak to me. Also, the white azalea bush was out. *And* Aunt Belle[1] had brought from Sydney a new receipt for icing. It was tried on my cake & wasn't a great success because it was much too brittle. I can see & feel its smoothness now. You make me long to have a talk with you, in some place like the corner of the lily lawn. Ah, Jeanne, anyone who says to me "do you remember" simply has my heart . . . I remember everything, and perhaps the great joy of Life to me is in playing just that game, going back with someone into the past − going back to the dining room at 75[2] to the proud and rather angry looking selzogene on the sideboard, with the little *bucket* under the spout. Do you remember that hiss it gave & sometimes a kind of groan? And the smell inside the sideboard of worcester sauce and corks from old claret bottles?

    But I must not begin such things. If we are ever together down the Kenepuru Sounds[3] come off with me for a whole day − will you? And lets just remember. How Chummie loved it, too. Can't you hear his soft boyish laugh and the way he said "oh − abso*lutely*!"

    Im sending you a copy of The Mercury in case you didn't see this story. Tell me if you like it. Just for once − will you? Im also slipping inside it my new press photograph in case you'd care for it. Haven't you got a photograph for me? I have such a lovely one of Marie. Its excellent. But the last was you & uncle Sid![4]

    Ever your sister

                                              K.

MS ATL. *LKM* II. 142−3.

To Dorothy Brett, 15 October 1921.

[Chalet des Sapins, Montana-sur-Sierre]
15 X 1921

Dearest Brett,

I have 2 letters to thank you for. Forgive me that I haven't written sooner, but all this week I have been most fearfully busy with a long story which was only finished late last night. Finished it is, however. Thanks be to God. Its called *The Garden Party* & I have decided to call my new book by that title instead of the other. Constable is producing it at the New Year. I told you that – didn't I? In the meantime the Mercury is bringing out that very long seaweedy story of mine At The Bay. I feel inclined to suggest to them to give away a spade an' bucket with each copy . . . The amount of work to do is awful, though.

Are you busy? Lets sit down on your couch for a talk. The light in your room is lovely today. I like to look out of the window at that long garden – – I seem to know it so well. How are you Brettushka? You know your hair grows so awfully prettily off your forehead. Sheer gold. Little bright gold feathers. I often think of them . . . There is a mass of things to say!

I was fearfully glad to hear of your success with Lady Ian Hamilton. Her house sounds lovely, too. I hope you get yours. It sounds so untroubled and hazy with gold light – like only Sussex is. I heard about Mrs Ferdy (marvellous name) from Sylvia Lynd. I dont remember her. But it all sounds rather horrid. Poor woman!

Oh, how I saw that awful party at the Wells. Beginning with Ottoline on the stairs in that mood! What a nightmare. I have a perfect horror of such affairs! They are always the same. One has to be encased in vanity like a beetle to escape being hurt. And the ghastly thing is they are so hard to forget; one lives them over and over. Dont go to them, my dear. You are too delicate. But whats the use of saying that; there are times when one has to go. Its difficult to see what compensations there are in city life. I think the best plan is to live away from them and then, when one has done a good deal of work and wants a holiday – take a real holiday in a place like Paris or Madrid or even London (but not for me London). It is nice sometimes to be with many people & to hear

---

1 Aunt Belle, KM's mother's younger sister Isobel Dyer, now Mrs Harry Trinder, wife of a wealthy English shipowner. She was the original for Beryl in both *Prelude* and 'At the Bay'.
2 75 Tinakori Road, close to the centre of Wellington, where KM lived between the ages of 10 and 14.
3 Kenepuru Sound, a long walking distance from Anikiwa in Queen Charlotte Sound, where the Beauchamp girls spent holidays with relatives.
4 Sydney Dyer, her mother's brother.

music and to be 'overcome' by a play & to watch dancing. Walking in streets is nice, too. But one always wants to have an avenue of escape. One wants to feel a stranger for these things to have their charm, and – most important of all – one wants to have a solid body of work behind one. The longer I live the more I realise that in work only lies ones strength and ones salvation. And such *supreme joy* that one gives thanks for life with every breath.

Midday. Ah, why can't you hear that darling little bell in the valley. Its misty today, but the sun shines and the mist is silver. Its still. And somewhere there rings over and over that little chime, so forgetful, so easy, so gay. Its like a gay little pattern, gold & butterflies and cherubs with trumpets in the very middle of the page – so that one pauses before one begins the afternoon chapter. We are going for a picnic. We take the jaegar rug & a bastick. And then we lie under a tree, stir our tea with a twig, look up, look down, wonder why. But it begins to get dark earlier. At seven oclock the moon is in full feather on my balcony.

I want to talk about your cats. Do you like them very much? The black one is good but I don't see it related to the other. And perhaps it is the photograph. The other looks as though it were painted *differently*. Its big, heavy, broad. Its got no muscles. Its not *nervous*, not *warm*. I don't see them as a design. The coloured balls aren't enough to bring them together. You could cut that painting in half without changing it or so it looks to me. That makes me wonder about the difference of seeing-and-feeling and *grasping*. I know that when I write stories if I write at the seeing-and-feeling stage they are no good & have to be scrapped. I have to *go on* almost squeezing them in my hands if you know what I mean until I KNOW them in every corner and part. Sometimes, in your work, it seems to me you have the idea, the feeling, the 'overwhelming emotion' right enough and then, instead of holding on you lose hold, and something shaky happens – something is not *realised fully*. So that it might be the result of an accident that the picture looked as it does at the finish. You don't do the squeezing process long enough or hard enough. Take for instance, The Mannequin. The middle figure is beautifully painted but it fails as a whole, I feel. The corner drops out. I know it wasn't finished when I saw it but then it seems to me it ought not to have been finished *all over*. It ought to have been all at a certain stage – not one figure beautifully finished. That is so devilishly dangerous. One spends oneself on the detail before the time has come for that. To put it absolutely brutally – *just where you go soft you ought to be hard*, it seems to me. Dear Brett, I know how difficult this is, and I know I am horribly outspoken. Tell me how wrong I am! I remember often a still life of yours – Asters – I think that was *most lovely*. I think you have exquisite feeling and sensibility. But you know this . . . There it is.

Dont send me any 'present'. It was a letter I wanted – and I got a lovely one – a real gift. Thank you dearest. I will remember yours on November 15th and send you an envelope & trimmings.

Write again! About Christmas. Wouldn't it be much too cold? Do you realise *how* snowed up we shall be? The height & the cold would be too much to bear so suddenly. Besides summer is so divine here. Long days, pic-nics, long drives, we might even go off on a small tour. Let it is be summer. And then there are all the flowers – Oh yes, you *must* come in the warm weather.

Goodbye for now, dear little artist. Keep warm. Be happy. I'd like to give you a small hug. If you knew how much I like your purple writing on an envelope!

Yours ever
Katherine

MS Newberry. *LKM* II. 143–4.

To Elizabeth, Countess Russell, 16 October 1921

[Chalet des Sapins, Montana-sur-Sierre]
Oct. 16. 21.

Dear Elizabeth,

I must, even though it is not my turn, send you a note in John's letter . . .

We – I – miss you, lovely little neighbour. I think of you often. Especially in the evenings, when I am on the balcony and it's too dark to write or to do anything but wait for the stars. A time I love. One feels half disembodied, sitting like a shadow at the door of one's being while the dark tide*¹ rises. Then comes the moon,* marvellously serene, and small stars, very merry for some reason of their own. It is so easy to for-get, in a *worldly* life, to attend to these miracles. But no matter. They are there waiting, when one returns. Dawn is another. The incomparable beauty of very early morning, before human beings are awake! But it all comes back to the same thing, Elizabeth. There's* no escaping the glory of Life. Let us engage to live for ever. For ever is not half long enough for me . . .

London feels far away from here. We thrill, we are round-eyed at the slightest piece of news. You cannot imagine how your letter was taken in – absorbed. I see you stepping* into carriages driving to the play, dining among mirrors and branched candlesticks and faraway sweet sounds. Disguised in 'kepanapron'! I open your door to illustrious strangers, Mighty Ones, who take off their coats in the large hall and are conducted into your special room where the books are . . . Do not forget us.

John has been so deep in Flaubert[2] this week that his voice has only sounded from under the water, as it were. He has emerged at tea time and together we have examined the – very large, solid pearls . . . I must say I do like a man to my tea.

And here are your petunias, lovely as ever, reminding me always of your garden and the grass with those flat dark rosettes where the daisy plants had been.

But this isn't a letter. Farewell. May Good Fortune fall ever more deeply in love with thee.

Katherine.

TC Huntington. *LKM* II. 144–5.

[1] See Textual Note, p. xvi.
[2] Murry's article 'Gustave Flaubert' was published in the *Times Literary Supplement* on 15 Dec. 1921.

To J. B. Pinker, 18 October 1921.

Chalet des Sapins | Montana-sur-Sierre | Valais | Switzerland.

18 X 1921

Dear Mr Pinker,

I send you the new story *The Garden-Party*.[1] By the same post I am sending a copy to Constables. Will you try & dispose of the story for me?[2] And in that case would you kindly have another copy typed, as one of these will be needed for the MS which has gone to America. I feel reasonably certain The Mercury would print this story, but its doubtful whether they will have time to use both before the book is out. And perhaps I may mention that The Dial gave me a long and pretty favourable review recently.[3] I think they are *disposed* to take my stories.

Yours sincerely
Katherine Mansfield

MS Newberry.

[1] KM noted at the end of the manuscript, 'This is a moderately successful story, and that's all. It's somehow, in the episode in the lane, scamped' (Newberry).
[2] A poorly edited version was published in the *Westminster Gazette* in Feb. 1922, the same month as the collection *The Garden Party*.
[3] Malcolm Cowley warmly reviewed *Bliss* in the *Dial*, Sept. 1921.

To S. S. Koteliansky, [18 October 1921]

Chalet des Sapins | Montana sur Sierre | (Valais) | Switzerland

Dear Koteliansky, my enemy,

Can you tell me anything about that Russian doctor[1]? If there was a
chance of seeing him and if he was not too expensive I would go to Paris
in the Spring and ask him to treat me . . .

Not a day passes but I think of you. It is sad that we are enemies.[2] If
only you would accept my love. It is *good* love – not the erotic bag kind.
But no. You wont answer my letters. When my name is mentioned you
cross yourself and touch wood.

It is sad for me

Katherine.

Dont return the postcard. If you hate me too much – burn it in a candle.[3]

MS BL. *LKM* II. 145.

[1] KM had heard from Koteliansky of the Russian doctor Ivan Manoukhin and his revolutionary method for treating tuberculosis.

[2] Virginia Woolf recorded on 13 Mar. 1921 that Koteliansky 'let out by chance that Katherine
lost 3 ms books he [word missing] of Tchehov's letters' (*Diary of Virginia Woolf*, II. 99).

[3] KM enclosed a photograph with the inscription 'With love from Katherine'. It was similar to,
and taken in the same period, as the one on the dust-jacket of *Bliss*.

To William Gerhardi, 21 October 1921

Chalet des Sapins | Montana-sur-Sierre | (Valais) | Switzerland.
21.x.1921

Dear Mr Gerhardi,

I am very honoured by your request.[1] The *trouble* is I live so far away.
Would you dare to send a new-born child all this distance? I would read
it with pleasure, and tell you just what I think. Thats what you want,
isn't it? But I think the distance will frighten you & I shall *perfectly* understand if it does. Swiss postmen are honest creatures, once it gets to
Switzerland – that's true. Do what you think best.

Yours sincerely
Katherine Mansfield.

MS ATL.

[1] Gerhardi had heard Murry deliver his lectures on style at Oxford in May, and as he recalls in
his *Memoirs of a Polyglot* (1931), 172: 'He . . . made some shy allusion to the work of his wife,
Katherine Mansfield, and when I read a story of hers I was so pleased with it that I wrote her a
letter [see p. 249, n. 2] . . . Many months later, ignored by Walpole and Bennett it occurred to me
that Katherine Mansfield might like my "Futility," and if so, find a publisher.'

To Elizabeth, Countess Russell [23 October 1921]

Chalet des Sapins | Montana/s/Sierre.
Sunday.

Dearest Elizabeth,

I actually had the strength of mind to keep your letter unopened until John came back from his wood-gathering. Then spying him from my balcony while he was yet afar off, I cried in a loud voice. And he came up and we read it together and thanked God for you . . . You do such divine things! Your visit to Stratford, Hamlet in the churchyard, the snap-dragons, the gate of Anne's cottage, King Lear on* the river[1] – it all sounded perfect. In fact, one felt that if the truth were known William had gathered you the snap-dragons and you had leaned over the gate together.

We were *very* interested in your news of Vera.[2] My heart warms to Sydney.[3] Of course one knew he would appreciate it but I'd like to talk it over with him, and agree and exclaim and admire. That is such a rare joy. I wish he had seen more reviews. My little sisters have just send a copy to my Father. Which makes me gasp. But I expect he will admire Wemyss* tremendously and agree with every thought and every feeling and shut the book with an extraordinary sense of satisfaction before climbing the stairs to my stepmother . . . The Wells party[4] sounded one of those disturbing festas where people, like plates, are no sooner set before one than they are snatched away. But I am very glad you secured Koteliansky.*[5] He would be very impervious to snatching. That is one of his charms. But he has many. I wish I could have kept him in my life.

What are you reading, Elizabeth? Is there something new which is very good. I have* turned to Milton all last week. There are times when Milton seems the only food to me. He is a most blessèd man.

> ". . . Yet not the more
> cease I to wander where the Muses haunt
> Clear* Spring, or Shadie Grove, or Sunnie Hill
> Smit with the love of sacred song;"[6]

But the more poetry one reads the more one longs to read! This afternoon John, lying on my furry rug, has been reading aloud Swinburne's Ave Atque Vale, which did not sound fearfully good. I suspect those green buds of sin and those gray fruits of shame. And try as one may, one can't see Beaudelaire.[7] Swinburne sits so very tight on the tomb. Then we read Hardy's poem to Swinburne, which John adored. I, being an inferior being, was a little troubled by the picture of Sappho and Algernon* meeting en pleine* mer[8] (if one can say such a thing) and he begging her to tell him where her manuscript was. It seemed such a watery rendezvous. But we went on reading Hardy. How exquisite – how marvellous some of those poems are! They are almost intolerably near to one. I mean I always long to weep . . . That love and regret touched so lightly – that *autumn* tone – that feeling that "Beauty passes though rare, rare it* be . . ."[9]

But speaking of autumn, it is here. Yesterday, soft, silky, sweet-smelling summer kissed the geraniums and, waving the loveliest hand, *went*. To-day it is cold, solemn, with the first snow falling. Oh, Elizabeth, how I longed for you this morning on my balcony! The sun came through, a silver star. In the folds of the mountains little clouds glittered like Dorothy Wordsworth's sheep.[10] And all that paysage across the valley was a new land. The colour is changed since you were here. The green is gold – a very deep gold like *amber*. On the higher peaks snow was falling and the wind walking among the trees had a new voice. It was like land seen from a ship. It was like arriving in the harbour, and wondering, half frightened and yet longing, whether one would go ashore. But no – I can't describe it. Soon after all was grey and down came the white bees. The feeling in the house changed immediately. Ernestine became mysterious and blithe. The Faithful One ran up and down as though with cans of hot water . . . One felt the whisper had gone round that the pains had begun and the doctor had been sent for. Those geraniums I mention so lightly are *yours*. I am taking care of them. They are full of buds. I dream of returning you seven postful from my bud in *Janvier* (Janvier is – "The month when Elizabeth returns.")

Have you begun your play? Are you working? My book is to lie in Constable's bosom[11] until after the New Year. I have changed the name to *The Garden-Party*. I am just at the beginning of a new story, which I may turn into a serial. Clement Shorter[12] wants one.* But he stipulates for thirteen 'curtains,' and an adventure note! Thirteen curtains! And my stories haven't even a wisp of blind cord as a rule. I have never been able to manage curtains. I don't think I shall be able to see such a whole-sale *hanging* through.

John decked the week with a song. He wrote a lovely poem – moon – still . . . But I must bring this letter to an end. Is it too long? It's much too long. Forgive it this once.

Farewell, lovely little artist. Don't let them hurt you.

With my love,   May you be happy!

                                                    Katherine.

The knitting becomes almost frenzied at times. We may be sober in our lives – but we shall be garish in our shrouds and flamboyant in our coffins if this goes on. John now *mixes* his wools* thereby gaining what *he* calls a "*superb* astrachan effect." Chi lo sa! I softly murmur over my needles – I find knitting turns me into an imbecile. It is the female tra-dition, I suppose.

TC Huntington. *LKM* II. 145–7.

¹ Elizabeth had written of her recent holiday at Stratford, where she read Shakespeare and visited Ann Hathaway's cottage.
² Elizabeth's estranged husband, Francis, Earl Russell, had threatened a lawsuit against her recent novel *Vera*. The story, about a thoroughly distasteful man, Wemyss, and his second wife, was evidently based on her own second marriage.
³ Elizabeth's brother Sir Sydney Beauchamp (1861–1921), an eminent physician knighted for his medical services to the Conference of Versailles, following the Great War.
⁴ On 6 Oct. Elizabeth had attended a dinner and party at the home of the novelist H. G. Wells, with whom she conducted a long affair.
⁵ Elizabeth had also met KM's old but touchy friend S. S. Koteliansky.
⁶ John Milton, *Paradise Lost*, iii. 26–9.
⁷ Taking his title from the concluding line of the Roman poet Catullus's elegy to his brother, Algernon Charles Swinburne's 'Ave atque Vale', published in *Poems and Ballads*, 2nd ser. (1878), addressed Charles Baudelaire as 'the gardener of strange flowers', speaking in sec. 17 of 'Green buds of sorrow and sin, and remnants grey'.
⁸ Thomas Hardy's elegy on the death of Swinburne in 1909, 'A Singer Asleep', the seventh stanza of which proposes the poet meeting Sappho:

> And one can hold in thought that nightly here
> His phantom may draw down to the water's brim,
> And her's come up to meet it, as a dim
> Love shine upon the heaving hydrosphere.

⁹ From Walter de la Mare's 'An Epitaph'.
¹⁰ Writing in the *Alfoxden Journal*, 26 Jan. 1798, Dorothy Wordsworth noted 'the sheep glittering in the sunshine'.
¹¹ Thomas Moult, *TP's Weekly*, 1 Dec. 1928, quotes from an undated, otherwise lost letter from KM: 'My "Garden Party" is to be in Constable's bosom until after the New Year. I'm frightened when I think of it. It's a terrifying business to write books – but how much more terrifying not to write them.'
¹² Clement Shorter, editor of the *Sphere*.

To Violet Schiff, [24 October 1921]

Chalet des Sapins | Montana-sur-Sierre | (Valais)
Switzerland.

Dearest Violet

If I were to begin apologising I should have to fill the letter with protestations. Even then . . . I have been working fearfully hard to get my new book finished. That wraps one away. One leads a double life & the half that is *this* life grows almost shadowy.

All the same, equally with Murry I have devoured Sydneys letters. Oh, how delightful his letters are! We long to see his new book.

Its horrible to know you have both been ill. Are you really better? These chills, Violet – how they persist. I wonder if you expose yourself to the direct rays of the sun? Here in Switzerland that is considered simply the cause of feverish chills. And all my South of France recurrent ones are put down to that. It seems that not to be au bord de la mer and never to sit in the sun are the only rules if you are liable to fever. Thats why the Riviera is such a fatal climate except for those who seek fever . . .

I am *sure* Switzerland is the place for health and for work – I mean especially and above all for nerves. There is an extraordinary feeling of ease here. It seems it is easy to live; one feels remote and undisturbed. Ive never known anything like the feeling of peace and when one isn't working the *freshness* – the air, the smell of pines, the taste of snow in ones teeth – – Thats exaggeration – its only the spiritual flavour. I hope you and Sydney come here. I feel sure you would like it. I think I really judge a place by how vividly I can recall the past. One lives in the Past – or I do. And here it is living. Does Sydney know what I mean?

My book is to lie in Constables bosom until after the new year. Its called, after all, *The Garden-Party.* I hope you like the title. The Mercury is publishing one of the stories in a month or two – terribly long. Too long for the Mercury. But that's enough & too much about me. And now I have forgotten my health. Thank you, dearest Violet. I think my lungs are quiescent – rather the disease is. My heart is the same at present. But I feel much better – a different person altogether on the whole. No longer an invalid, even tho' I still can't walk & still cough and so on.

Its interesting what you say about Sheila Kaye-Smith.[1] Ill try & get her book. Murry is rereading Proust[2] – all from the beginning. So far he likes it infinitely more than the first time. Ive been reading the book of Job! There are times when I turn to the bible. It is marvellous! As for papers – I wonder what you read? The Dial? It is improved, I think. Its a mixed lot but on the whole there is always something in it. I thought Lawrence was good this month[3] – so warm – so living. In spite of everything Lawrence's feeling for life is there.

Poor Eliot sounds tired to death. His London letter[4] is all a maze of words. One feels the awful effort behind it – as though he were being tortured. But perhaps thats all wrong and he enjoys writing it. I don't think people ought to be as tired as that, though. It is wrong.

It is sad to hear of the tree being attacked by its cruelle maladie. I shall see that tree for ever.

We live here in an ugly but *snug* chalet with a stalwart servant called the gentle Ernestine. Jones is, as usual, the official wife of both of us. I have a most divine balcony room to work in. Its perfect up there. Would that you & Sydney could come & take tea with us while this summer weather is still as fine as ever.

I don't know why I can so imagine you here in Switzerland. I feel it is your place.

Dearest Violet – Im writing late at night. Murry is asleep. He looks about 16. I must turn out the light. My fondest love to you and to Sydney.

Always
Your

K.M.

MS BL. *LKM* II. 137.

¹ KM had reviewed, without enthusiasm, Sheila Kaye-Smith's *Green Apple Harvest* in the *Athenaeum*, 3 Sept. 1920.
² Murry reviewed Marcel Proust, *À la recherche du temps perdu*, III: *Du côte de Guermantes*; IV: *Sodome et Gomorrhe* i, in the *Nation and the Athenaeum*, 12 Nov. 1921.
³ The first instalment of D. H. Lawrence's 'Sea and Sardinia', *Dial*, Oct. 1921.
⁴ Also in the Oct. *Dial* was T. S. Eliot's 'London Letter', discussing Igor Stravinsky's reception in London and George Bernard Shaw's *Back to Methuselah*.

To Conrad Aiken,¹ 24 October 1921

Permanent address:
c/o The Nation & The Athenaeum | 10 Adelphi Terrace | London
W.C.2
24.x.1921

Dear 'Conrad Aitken'

I want to thank you for your review of my little book in *The Freeman*.² You are too kind to me, but I shall try & deserve some of your praise, but what I want to thank you for *particularly* is for pointing out so justly where I have failed. Yes, you are quite right, I ought not to have published some of those 'stories'; Ill publish no more like them.

Queer – isn't it – how helpful it is to know that someone else sees what is wrong in ones work. At least I find it so, & Im very grateful to you.

I nearly sent you a copy of Bliss. Then I decided Id wait & send you my next one instead . . . I hope you are well & working. I always think of you as the man who loves rain.³

Yours sincerely
Katherine Mansfield.

MS Huntington.

¹ Conrad Aiken (1889–1973) was born in Savannah, Georgia, and educated at Harvard. He contributed to the *Athenaeum*, and later wrote many volumes of poetry as well as short stories and novels.
² In 'The Short Story as Poetry', his review of *Bliss* in the *Freeman*, 11 May 1921, Aiken wrote: 'Miss Mansfield is brilliant – she has, more conspicuously than any contemporary writer of fiction one calls to mind, a fine, an infinitely inquisitive sensibility; a sensibility indefatigably young which finds itself in the service of a mind often cynical, sometimes cruel, and always sophisticated.' He also remarked that when her 'hallucinated vividness' failed her, she at times resorted to 'cleverness, esurient humour, or even, at the termination of "Bliss", to the trickery of surprise'.
³ KM had read Aiken's poem 'Meretrix: Ironic', in *Others, A Magazine of the New Verse*, May–June 1916, with its lines

> . . . Rain, rain, rain. All night the rain.
> The roofs are wet, the eaves drip.
>
> .   .   .   .
>
> Something about your skin is like soft rain –
> Cool and clear. . . .

Also in *Others*, July 1916, his poem 'Illusions' repeated the line 'We hear the rain'.

To John Galsworthy,[1] *25 October 1921*

Chalet des Sapins | Montana sur Sierre | Valais | Switzerland
25 X 1921

Dear Mr Galsworthy

By an unfortunate mischance your letter only reached me today. My silence must have seemed very ungracious. Though, even now, I scarcely know how to thank you. Your noble generous praise is such precious encouragement that all I can do is try to deserve it. I want to promise you that I will never do less than my best, that I will try not to fail you. But this sounds superficial and far from my *feeling*. There the letters are, tied up in the silk handkerchief with my treasures. I shall never forget them.[2] I wish, someday, I might press your hand for them. Thank you 'for ever'.

I ought to tell you – for after all, you have the key – I have been haunting the little house in the Bayswater Road last week – looking at the place where the humming birds stood, and standing where Soames stood in the hall by the hatstand. How I can hear Smithers word "Bobbish". But one must not begin. One would go on for ever. All the life of that house flickers up, trembles, glows again, is rich again in these last moments. And then there is Soames with Fleur running out of his bosom, so swift, so careless – leaving him bare[3] . . . Thank you for these wonderful books . . .

You ask me about my work. I have just finished a new book which is to be published at the New Year. And now I am 'thinking out' a long story about a woman which has been in my mind for years. But it is difficult. I want her whole life to be in it – a sense of time – and the feeling of 'farewell'. For by the time the story is told her life is over. One tells it in taking leave of her . . . Not one of these modern women but one of those old fashioned kind who seemed to have such a rich being, to live in such a living world. Is it fancy? Is it just that the harvest of the past is gathered? Who shall say!

In November or December the London Mercury is publishing a day in the life of the little family in Prelude. If I may, I should very much like to send you a copy. The mountains here are good to live with, but it doesn't do to look

---

Aiken clearly remembered this remark of KM's when he wrote 'Your Obituary, Well Written', the opening story in *Costumes by Eros* (1928). 'There are apparent similarities between KM and Reine Wilson, a gifted and ailing writer.' There was something gingerly about her self-control; and also something profoundly terrifying. It seemed to me that I had never met anyone whose hold on life was so terribly *conscious*. . . . And to sit with her, to watch the intense restraint of all her gestures and expressions, and above all to listen to the feverish connoisseurship with which she spoke, was at once to share in this curious attitude towards life' (*The Short Stories of Conrad Aiken* (1960), 403–4).

lower. The Swiss are a *poor lot*. Honesty and Sparsam Keit – in themselves – don't warm one's heart.

But I must detain you no longer.

Fare well! May all good things attend you!

Katherine Mansfield.

MS Birmingham. *LKM* II. 147–8.

[1] John Galsworthy (1867–1933), a prolific and, commercially, vastly successful playwright and novelist, who received the Nobel Prize for Literature in 1932.

[2] KM did not, in fact, keep his letters among the comparatively few (apart from Murry's) that she particularly valued.

[3] KM is complimenting Galsworthy on episodes in *The Forsyte Saga* series of novels, the most recent of which, *In Chancery*, she discussed in her last review in the *Athenaeum*, 10 Dec. 1920, and *To Let* in the *Daily News*, 5 Nov. 1921.

To Harold Beauchamp, 1 November 1921

Confidential.[1]
Chalet des Sapins | Montana-sur-Sierre | (Valais)
Switzerland.
1 XI 1921

Father darling,

I must get over this fear of writing to you because I have not written for so long. I am ashamed to ask for your forgiveness and yet how can I approach you without it? Every single day I think and wonder how I can explain my silence. I cannot tell you how often I dream of you. Sometimes night after night I dream that I am back in New Zealand and sometimes you are angry with me and at other times this horrible behaviour of mine has not happened and all is well between us. It is simply agony *not* to write to you. My heart is full of you. But the past rises before me, when I have promised not to do this very thing that I have done and its like a wall that I cant see over.

The whole reason for my silence has been that, in the first weeks I was ill and waited until I was better. And then events conspired to throw me into a horrible depression that I could not shake off. Connie and Jinnie made me understand how very much you considered you were doing for me. They made me realise that for you to give me £300 a year was an extreme concession and that as a matter of fact my husband was the one who ought to provide for me. Of course I appreciate your great generosity in allowing me so much money. And I know it is only because I am ill in the way I am that you are doing so. But it is highly unlikely that I shall live very long and consumption is a terribly expensive illness. I thought that you did not mind looking after me to this extent. And to feel that you did – was like a blow to me – I couldn't get over it. I feel as though I didn't belong to you, really. If Chaddie or Jeanne had developed consumption husbands or no husbands they would surely have appealed to you. One does turn to ones father however old one is. Had I forfeited the right to do so? Perhaps . . . There is no reason, Father dear, that you should go on loving me through thick and thin. I see that. And I have been an extraordinarily unsatisfactory and disappointing child.

But in spite of everything, one gets shot in the wing and one believes that 'home' will receive one and cherish one. When we were together in France I was happy with you as I had always longed to be but when I knew that you grudged me the money it was simply torture. I did not know what to say about it. I waited until I saw if I could earn more myself at that time. But it was not possible. Then I had waited so long that it seemed impossible to write. Then I was so seriously ill that I was not in a state to write to anybody. And by the time that crisis was over it seemed to me my sin of silence was too great to beg forgiveness, and so it has gone on.

But I cannot bear it any longer. I must come to you and at least acknowledge my fault. I must at least tell you, even though the time has passed when you wish to listen, that never for a moment, in my folly and my fear, have I ceased to love you and to honour you. I have punished myself so cruelly that I couldn't suffer more.

Father don't turn away from me, darling. If you cannot take me back into your heart believe me when I say I am

Your devoted deeply sorrowing child

Kass

MS ATL. Alpers 1980, 348–50.

¹ Beauchamp has written across the top of the letter: 'R. 7/1/22. A. Idem. I can emphatically say that in *thought, word & deed* I have never begrudged any of my children the amounts I have paid them by way of allowances. On the contrary, I have always considered it a *pleasure* and a *privilege* to do everything possible for their comfort, happiness & worldly advancement. HB. 9/1/22.'
He underlined the letter from 'Connie and Jinnie' in the second paragraph down to 'simply torture' in the middle of p. 2. In the margin beside the first few of these lines he wrote "Quite untrue. HB." and beside the sentence ending in 'simply torture' he wrote "Quite untrue – I never made such a statement at any rate. HB."

To Richard Murry, 1 November 1921

CHALET DES SAPINS | MONTANA SUR SIERRE | VALAIS
1 XI 1921

Dear Richard

I feel a bit overwhelmed by this present. It came this morning. It is exquisite. I've never seen letter paper I like so well. But its not only the sight its the feel of it under your hand. I suppose other people do enjoy these things, are as conscious of them as I am. But I feel they can hardly be. I don't get used to things. It will be a fresh delight to me each time I use this. Thank you my generous little painter brother – *most awfully*.

Jack and I have such a thrill over presents here that we devour them, skin and bone. He immediately appropriated the two neat little wooden boards, which are to 'come in for something' – Wingley's sleigh, I think. We also read portion of magazine enclosed. It was full of meat.

By the way, from a practical point of view this paper is nothing less than a godsend. It will prevent people from sending us letters to Chalet des Lapins or Chalet des Savants or once Chalet des Serpents. Jack, observing the amount said firmly "this makes it out of the question to move for at least two years from now."

I am ignoring that card I sent you as you see. For I have to risk your still being in the mood of your letter. Well, I risk it to the extent of sending you my love, too.

Goodbye for now

Katherine.

MS R. Murry. *Adam* 370–5, 29–30.

To Vera McIntosh Bell, [early November 1921]

CHALET DES SAPINS | MONTANA-SUR-SIERRE | VALAIS
November.

Dearest Vera,

Its very late in the day to answer your birthday letter.[1] I dont know what happens to Time now-a-days. The weeks dont only seem to fly; they seem to become all tail – all Saturday to Monday. That broad middle of the week when so much is going to be accomplished is telescoped away. Do you know – with *increasing* years, my dear, this speeding up? I wish it were not so.

It was a delight to hear from you. Your handwriting always brings you back to me – the very sight of it and I see you and the way you hold the pen & I hear that pen flying. I had begun to feel we had gone into the silence, as we used to say. Marie and dear little J. give me news of you and send me snaps. (I had those summer ones from Almonte) but that is not the same. Shall I see you when you are in Europe, I wonder?[2] It would be very nice to think so. I cant imagine you won't visit France & France is only at the bottom of the road or round the corner from Switzerland. But I know no more about your 'visit' except the bare fact of it. I have asked Marie for some flesh and feathers . . .

Well, darling – how are you? I would like to sit down beside you and ask you that and have the feeling neither of us was to whirl away before the full, free, confidential, sister-to-sister answer. Do I ask too much? Are such terms over between us? Do you feel I am a little bit of a stranger & not a *real* sister like the others? I believe you do. But there was a time when we were awfully near each other's heart. Don't lets forget it.

Jack and I are fixed here for the next year and a half. We have a furnished chalet, very snug in every way, rather ugly, but with views that are really superb. We are on the threshold of our first northern winter. I wish you could give me some hints in the management of snow! Its very strange to us. Ida is 'attached'. She has a room out but comes here by the day and keeps interruptions away and acts in fact as a house-keeper and 'official wife' to both of us. She is very good at the job. I could not possibly do without her. I am no good at buttons and puddings. It is a business arrangement tinged with sincere friendship. We get on very well. But there is no "minding the invalid" included, my dear. I hope, at the end of two years here to be able to resume a normal life. That is if everything goes on well. This is the first time I have really been able to take care of myself at all as I have to, and that horrible anxiety of separation is over. Jack loves this place and the life here. He works very hard, and so do I. We have done more work here than ever before. Even if it wasn't our 'way of living' we should be compelled to, for Switzerland is quite the most expensive place I have ever known at any time. It is double the South of France and of course the exchange is against us. But there you are – I cant even keep alive at present any-where else so here we must stay. What a bother! as Pa would say. Its no hardship as regards lovely Montana. And isn't it strange that 'Elizabeth' would be our neighbour. Her chalet is at the bottom of the hill. We saw a great deal of one another all summer and we are very close friends. She is a rare lovely little being, I think and I do so admire and respect her for the way she works. Her chalet is quite magnificent . . . She looks about 35 – not a day more, runs up the hills, climbs, laughs, just like a girl. I don't think she will ever be older. Have you read her new book 'Vera'?[2] It has had rather a mixed reception, but I think its by far the most brilliant book she has ever written. I can quite understand people turning against it, though. There are few men who have not a touch of Weymss . . .

Well, darling, I must bring this letter to a close. Give my love to my nephews; Im afraid I am a shadowy figure to them. And please give Mack my kindest remembrances.[3] To you I send, as ever, my warmest love and a big sisterly hug. May we meet again!

Your own sister

K.

¹ KM's birthday was on 14 Oct.
² Vera was living in Toronto at the time.
³ Vera had married the Canadian James Mackintosh Bell in Wellington in 1909, when he was director of the geological survey of New Zealand. Their sons Andrew and John were now 9 and 7.

To Andrew Bell,¹ [early November 1921]

[Chalet de Sapins, Montana sur Sierre]

Dear Andrew,

I was so touched to hear from your mother today that you still talk sometimes of your Aunt Katherine. Dear little boy! It is very sweet of you. Now I know I shall listen very carefully when the wind from Canada is blowing this way.

Do you remember sending me a pot of wild strawberry jam? I've never forgotten that, not the jam, I mean, but the fact that you sent it to me. Ever since when people talk about wild strawberries I think of you. Give my love to John please. Je vous embrasse tous les deux de tout coeur. Ta Tante dévoue Katherine

MSC Bell.

¹ Andrew Bell (b. 1912), elder son of KM's sister Vera.

To J. B. Pinker, 2 November 1921

Chalet des Sapins | Montana-sur-Sierre | (Valais)
Switzerland.
2.XI.1921

(2 copies enclosed)

Dear Mr Pinker,

I enclose herewith a story called *The Doll's house*. It is very short. I think it is probable that The Nation would print it. . . . But I leave the disposal of it in your hands.¹

Yours sincerely
Katherine Mansfield

MS Newberry.

¹ Published in the *Nation and the Athenaeum*, 4 Feb. 1922.

To Dorothy Brett, 2 November 1921.

CHALET DES SAPINS | MONTANA-SUR-SIERRE | VALAIS
ii XI 1921

Dearest Brett,

Just as I had sent my letter away your new letter came with the bills. What a dove you were to go wool gathering so far an wide! I saw you winding your way from shop to shop. As to the dogs in Heads you should have told them to stop pulling out each other's wool. This Fearful Feebleness is because its very late night and I ate such a stupid man with my tea – I cant digest him. He is bringing out a book of Georgian Stories & he said the more 'plotty' a story I could give him the better. What about that for a word? It made my hair stand up in prongs. A nice 'plotty' story, please. People *are* funny.

The Fat Cat Sits on my Feet. Fat is not enough to describe him by now. He must weigh pounds & pounds. And his lovely black coat is turning white. I suppose its to prevent the mountains from seeing him. He sleeps here & occasionally creeps up to my chest & pads softly with his paws, singing the while. I suppose he wants to see if I have the same face all night. I long to surprise him with terrific disguises. M. calls him "my *Breakfast* cat", because they share that meal – two boys – alone together. M. *at* the table and Wingley *on.* Its awful the love one can lavish on an animal. In his Memoirs which he dictates to me M.'s name is always MastermanMan[1] – one word, my name is Grandma Jaegar, the Mountain he always calls "Fostermonger" & for some reason our servant he refers to as The Swede. He has rather a contempt for her.

Goodnight. Thank you again. We shall burn to see the wool now. *We are making a huge quilt* – it will be like lying under rainbows. With warm love

Tig

Cheque enclosed

MS Newberry. *LKM* II. 152–3.

1 Tolstoy's *Master and Man* (1895), a story of conversion in the face of death.

To William Gerhardi, 4 November 1921

[Chalet des Sapins | Montana-sur-Sierre]
4.xi.1921
Your novel arrived safely today. I am going to read it this weekend. V. many thanks for the impressive coupons.

K.M.

Postcard ATL.

To S. S. Koteliansky, 4 November 1921

Chalet des Sapins | Montana-sur-Sierre | Valais
Switzerland
4 XI 1921

Thank you for your letter, dear Koteliansky. As I cannot go to Paris until the spring I shall not write to the doctor until then. But I am very glad to have his address.

I am glad that you criticised me. It is right that you should have hated much in me. I was false in many things and *careless* – untrue in many ways. But I would like you to know that I recognise this and for a long time I have been trying "to squeeze the slave out of my soul".[1] You will understand that I dont tell you this to prove I am an angel now! No. But I need not go into the reasons; you know them.

Its marvellous here just now, my dear. The first snow has fallen on the lower peaks, and everything is crystal clear. The sky is that marvellous transparent blue one only sees in early spring and autumn. It looks so high and even joyful – tender . . . And an exciting thing has happened today. My ancient geranium which is called Sarah has been visited by the angel at last.[2] This geranium has *real personality*. It is so fearfully proud of this new bud that every leaf is curling.

Farewell.

I press your hand

Katherine.[3]

MS BL. *LKM*. II. 148–9.

[1] Between 4 Apr. and 31 Oct. 1919 the *Athenaeum* ran thirteen instalments of 'Letters of Anton Tchehov', first translated by Koteliansky, the English then polished by KM, and published under both their names. In the ninth of these selections, 25 July, was an extract from Chekhov's letter to A. S. Souvorin, 7 Jan. 1889:

Do write a story about a young man, the son of a serf, errand boy, chorister, high-school pupil, student, brought up to venerate his superiors, kiss the hands of the priests, worship borrowed ideas, who is grateful for each bit of bread, flogged often, who runs in the cold and wind without galoshes to give lessons, fights, tortures animals, loves to dine at the table of rich relatives, is insincere to God and man without meaning to be, only out of consciousness of his own nullity – do write how that young man, drop by drop, squeezes the slave out of himself, until, waking one fine morning, he feels that in his veins there runs no longer the blood of a slave, but real human blood.

[2] See Gen. 18: 1–15.
[3] A draft of part of this letter is in ATL:
Don't reply to this.
Dear *Friend*
I like your criticism. It is right you should have hated those things in me. For I was careless and false. I was not *true* in those days. But I have been trying for a long time now to "squeeze the slave out of my soul" . . . I just want to let you know.
Oh, Koteliansky, I am in the middle of a nice story.* I wish you would like it. I am writing it in this exercise book & just broke off for a minute to talk to you.
Thank you for the address. I cannot go to Paris before the Spring, so I think it would be better if I did not write until then. I feel this light treatment is the right one. Not that I am ill at present. I am not in the least an invalid, in any way.

To Sydney Waterlow, 4 November 1921

Chalet des Sapins | Montana-sur-Sierre | (Valais)
Switzerland
4 XI 1921

Dear Sydney,

Your holiday sounded very delightful. I have often wanted to visit Perpignan. Do you know a little book 'La Fortune de Becot' by Louis Codet.[1] Its about that part of the country – awfully worth reading for its first 18 chapters.

Yes, we are very happy here. Switzerland has its disadvantages, the chief being the Swiss but its an amazing spot for work. Or so I find. I love this place; I love mountains and big skies and forests. And the weather is still supremely beautiful even though the lower peaks are powdered with fresh snow. But Heavens! What sun. It never has an ending. I am basking at this minute – half past four – too hot without a hat, & the sky is that transparent blue only to be seen in autumn – the forest trees steeped in light.

Please don't think of me as 'ill'. I am not ill any longer, and never mean to be ill again – thats over.

But the prime 'reason' for your leap in the dark was the Murry & Sullivan affair wasn't it? I mustn't fly off upon the beauties of squirrels & the smell of quinces – & all those things which make Life Ah! how thrilling.

Sullivan v. Murry . . . But my dear Sydney I know no more than you. All I know is that they are not writing to each other at present. Is there really anything more definite? Cross my heart it is not known to me. I thought they had both, for the time being, come to a pause – and that was all. As to the 'Dodger', M. denies that ever was his 'mot', I think, indeed I am sure he appreciates Sullivan. I gave him your letter to read, I questioned him about it and he laughed at me. Rien de rien – so there you are. Does that seem to you highly unsatisfactory?

I am going to Italy in the spring – to Assisi to see the wild cyclamen

Its a sunny, windy day – beautiful. There is a soft roaring in the trees and little birds fly up into the air just for the fun of being tossed about.

Goodbye. I press your hand. But do you dislike the idea we should write to each other from time to time?

Katherine.

Journal 1954, 266.

* KM had just finished 'The Doll's House'.

in its glory. That is one tremendous advantage of being across the Channel – theres no Channel to cross.

But no – it won't do. I can't write to you Sydney. Its hollow – don't you feel? I can only write letters when I feel a warm living sympathy exists between me & the person who replies. And for some cursed reason you are 'suspicious' of me. Farewell. I hope you are happy.

Katherine.

MS ATL.

[1] Published in 1914.

To Michael Sadleir, [7 November 1921]

[Chalet des Sapins] | Montana [sur Sierre]

Dear Michael Sadleir,

Thank you very much for sending the books to Paris on my behalf. But I shall not get the prize.[1] Prizes *always* pass me by. Which is sad. For they are nice things.

Yours ever

K.M.

Postcard Targ.

[1] Sadleir entered *Bliss* for the Femina-Vie Heureuse prize, awarded each year to a book written in English.

To J. B. Pinker, 9 November, 1921

Chalet des Sapins | Montana-sur-Sierre | (Valais)
Switzerland.
9.XI.1921

Dear Mr Pinker

Do you think it might be as well to let the London Mercury publish At the Bay without waiting for America? I don't fancy America wants that story. Perhaps they will feel more warmly disposed when my next book is out. I am quite willing to let the story appear if the suggestion is agreeable to you. It is, of course, only a suggestion.

Yours sincerely,
Katherine Mansfield

MS Newberry.

To Michael Sadleir, 11 November 1921

CHALET DES SAPINS | MONTANA-SUR-SIERRE | VALAIS
11 XI 1921

Dear Michael Sadleir,

If anyone should want a photograph of mine before my new book appears it occurs to me that these would reproduce better than the other. They are 'sharper'. So I send them along just in case . . .

Yours ever
Katherine Mansfield.

MS Targ.

To Dorothy Brett, 11 November 1921

CHALET DES SAPINS | MONTANA-SUR-SIERRE | VALAIS
11. XI. 1921.

Dearest Brett,

Forgive my silence lately. I have been wrestling with work which wouldn't be done and had to be done *in time*. I did, in fact, write you a letter. But then I tore it up. It seemed to me not worth sending, and it wasn't. I have *thought* of you often and wished that I could whip up my pen. But it was a dry pen, a cold pen, the kind I do dislike getting.

Now I must begin a Service of Thanks. First for your letter & then for the little photograph which is the spit of you, and then for t'other photograph in the cape and cap. How well I remember those caps, especially pinned down at the back on to ones wad of hair. I had a pale blue one for one of my journeys to New Zealand and draped with a pale blue gossamer veil I felt – fearfully chic and dashing. Human flesh & blood doesn't dare to think what it really looked like . . . My sister Chaddie has an immense book full of photographs from the age of 6 months. It is the most chastening book I know. Really, ones hats, ones *waists* and a small black round cap with wings I used to affect which I called always my wooza. It was rather a good name for it. But worn in conjunction with a linen collar and large tie . . . I have *never* let M. see that book. It is too shattering.

Thanks again, dearest Brett, for the Mercury which arrived gummed to its eyebrows. I tore my way into it, at last. But a harder roll has never entered Switzerland. That blue paper of yours for one thing is a kind of very superior rag book paper. If you drew a crocodile on a piece & gave it to an infant the crocodile would live for ever. I have preserved a small portion to be used as a patch when M. starts learning to ski. I wish people would not write those kind of articles[1] for another five years at least. Though I was very glad the man liked my Daughters of the Late Colonel. For I put my all into that story & hardly anyone saw what I was getting at. Even dear old Hardy told me to write more about those sisters.[2] As if there was any more to say! But speaking dead seriously, I could do with a great deal less praise than I get. Its . . . frightening, and I feel with all my heart I want to have another two years work done at least before Im worth *talking about.* However, I am certain my new book will be a failure., There will be a reaction against it. I count on that, so I mean to make the *next* one really as good as I can.

Do send along the photograph as soon as you have one of your next picture. Is it harder to work in winter than in summer? I should think it would be, but then theres a kind of thrilling quality in the air in winter which one doesn't get at any other time. I remember it even in Hampstead − cold, bright mornings on the heath with the pond frozen & the sky so high so transparent. London, according to the papers seems to be positively hung with pictures, and no Great House but has a Guevara.[3] The Lavery ménage is rather awful isn't it. Sir John & Lady both at it. M. pines for one of *her* catalogues, written by Winston Churchill.[4] If you go to the Exhibition will you send him yours. He wants it for a *weapon.* The attitude to Art − all Art − of the rich an great in London is odious − isn't it. It always reminds me of the story by Tchekhov where the man wants to say, longs to say, "Paws off" to the plebian.[5] Id like to say it to not only Lady Cunard[6] & Cie.

Words cant describe the cold here. We have central heating which never goes out, but even then on my balcony I freeze absolutely hard. The Mountain sends up all the food buttoned into tight little suet jackets and we both wear red indian boots, fur lined. They are so nice. Ones feet feel like small animals; you discover them playing together all on their own. But what shall we do if it gets colder? At present the Big Snow has not fallen. All is frozen hard and each tree has a little mat of white before it. Oh dear, it is so beautiful. The mountains are so noble & this snowy cover makes one see their shapes − every hollow, every peak is modelled. But all agree the snow is not serious yet. It falls, small and light like confetti, or it swarms like white bees. M. comes back from his walks hung with real icicles. He has bought boots with felt tops and a leather jacket.

I had to break off there for I was being absolutely *pursued* by birds. They were flying right inside the balcony, the loveliest creatures, a bright salmon pink with silvery heads & beaks. I am afraid they must have been left behind. So now I have begged a great slice of bread from Ernestine & my balcony rail is a very nice restaurant. If only theyd come and eat. Precious little creatures − how I love them. Have I told you about my balcony? It is as big as a small room, the sides are enclosed & big double doors lead from it to my workroom. Three superb geraniums still stand on the ledge when its fine, and their rosy masses of flowers against *blue space* are wonderful. Its so high up here that one only sees the tops & halfway down of the enormous mountains opposite, and theres a great sweep of sky as one only gets at sea. In fact I always feel I am at sea – on a ship – anchored before a new, undiscovered country. At sunset, when the clouds are really too much to bear alone I call out "mountains on your right a deep blue" and M. shouts from below "Right" & I hear him go out to *his* balcony to observe. But its most beautiful at night. Last night for instance, at about 10 oclock, I wound myself up in wool & came out here & sat watching. The world was like a huge ball of ice. There wasn't a sound. It might have been ages before man.

Your Thursdays sound very fierce occasions. I expect they are fun – aren't they? Tchekhov *said* over and over again, he protested, he begged, that he had no problem. In fact you know he thought it was his weakness as an artist. It worried him but he always said the same. No problem. And, when you come to think of it what was Chaucer's problem or Shakespeare's? The 'problem' is the invention of the 19th century. The artist takes a *long look* at Life. He says softly, "So this is what Life is, is it?" And he proceeds to express that. All the rest he leaves. Tolstoi even had no problem. What he had was a propaganda & he is a great artist in spite of it. I think its a good thing I don't come to your Thursdays. I would introduce a non serious atmosphere. I'd feel inclined to suggest a game of Swarzer Peter or Hunt the Thimble. Sullivan might be extremely good at Hunt the Thimble!

But Brett dearest, forgive me, I don't think of people as "little" people. Never! And I simply cant say you-and-I. I never feel you and I with my friends. There is something forever separate in me which makes it impossible. If this is a bad limitation – I am very sorry. But I cant help it. Oh, I have just remembered. If you should see Edmund Dulac's show would you tell me about his portrait of Mrs. Wellington Koo.[1] She is a woman whose appearance I admire *tremendously*. Ive only seen bad news-paper photographs of her but she looks exquisite, even then. I should imagine it would be perfect joy to paint her as she should be painted. Couldn't you get to know her? I am sure she is as rare a little being as one can find. But its true Ive only seen her on the back page of the Daily Mail! Her babies are the greatest loves possible. M. & I nearly swooned over *their* picture. Goodbye for now. I press your hand warmly.

I am yours ever
Tig.

MS Newberry. *LKM* II. 150–2.

[1] The novelist G. B. Street, in 'Nos et Mutamur', the *London Mercury*, Nov. 1921, 54–6, expanded on why he had misunderstood KM's early work, but after reading 'The Daughters of the Late Colonel' and returning to *Bliss*, had realized 'that the expression of a phase of life, the conveying

of an atmosphere, was the first purpose of this writer. There was no intention of telling a story, the artistic intention was achieved in every instance; there was no room for anything more.'

   [2] Either a message that came through Murry or in the letter from Hardy's wife which does not survive. See p. 244, n. 1.

   [3] Brett's close friend 'Chili' Guevara was enjoying considerable social success.

   [4] Sir John Lavery (1856–1941) was born in Belfast, and trained in Glasgow, London, and Paris, before gaining enormous success as a painter of statesmen, public figures, and ceremonial occasions. Lavery spent much of his time in Tangier, and in 1921 exhibited pictures of Morocco and the Riviera, together with child studies by his wife Hazel (d. 1935) at the Alpine Club Gallery, London. The forward to the exhibition's catalogue was written by their friend Winston Churchill (1874–1965), who later painted a portrait of the artist reproduced in Lavery's biography, *The Life of a Painter* (1940).

   [5] A reference to Chekov's story 'At a Country House', translated by Constance Garnett in *The Chorus Girl and Other Stories* (1920), in which the tactless and argumentative Rashevitch declares: 'Let us give up sloppy sentimentality; enough of it! Let us all make a compact, that as soon as a plebeian comes near us we fling some careless phrase straight in his ugly face: "Paws off! Go back to your kennel, you cur!" '

   [6] Born in California, Maud Alice Burke (1872–1948) married the wealthy Sir Bache Cunard, heir to the Cunard shipping empire. Known as 'Emerald', she became a generous patron of the arts.

   [7] The wife of Wellington Koo, the recently appointed Chinese Minister to Great Britain. The French artist Edmond Dulac (1882–1953), best known for his book design and illustrations, included a portrait of her in the exhibition of the National Portrait Society at the Grafton Galleries.

To William Gerhardi, 12 November 1921

CHALET DES SAPINS | MONTANA-SUR-SIERRE | VALAIS

xii.xi.1921

Dear Mr Gerhardi,

   First of all, immediately, I think your novel is awfully good. I congratulate you. It is a living book. What I mean by that is, it is warm; one can put it down and it goes on breathing. I think it has defects. But before we speak of them Id like to tell you the things I chiefly admire. I think, perhaps, the best *moment* is at the end; the scene of your hero's return and his walk with Nina. There you really are discovered – a *real* writer. There is such feeling, such warmth, in those chapters.[1] Nina's 'whimsical' voice, those kittens, the sofa with broken springs, the "speck of soot on your nose"[2] – and then, at the very end the steamer that would not go. I am not quoting these things at random, for their charm. But because, taken altogether, they seem to convey to the reader just the 'mood' you wished to convey. I think at the very beginning the tone is just a trifle tragic as it ought not to be. But once you are launched its remarkable how quickly and easily you take the reader into that family; and how *real* you make the life, the ways, the surroundings. Fanny Ivanovna[3] is *very* good. I *see* her. But if you were here I would go into details in a way I cant in a letter. And another thing that is good is the play of humour over it all. That makes it flexible, warm, easy, as it should be. Only in Chapter XI, in your description of the 'sisters' I think you falsify the tone, it seems to me. You begin to tell us what we must feel about them, what the sight of them perched on the chairs and sofa really meant, and thats not necessary. One feels they are being 'shown off', rather than seen. And you seem in that chapter to be hinting at something, even a state of mind of your hero's, which puts the reader off the scent, a little. But thats just my feeling, of course.

Now we come to your second 'plot', as it were, the Admiral, Sir Hugh & the Russian General. What opportunities you must have had, what excellent use you made of those opportunities. This part of your book is interesting for several reasons. I mean the 'situation' quâ situation is immensely attractive, and your principal characters are painted to the Life – – They are almost too good to be true. Your Russian General is a *rare* find. I have known just such another, though he wasn't a General. But the beating in the face, in my friends case was "beaten to death, simply", and the reason was "to use the English formula the man was a blighter."[4]

I think the only thing that does not convince me is Nina's novel – that feels 'strained'. It seems to stand out too clearly, to be out of focus, even. Its such a remarkable thing to have done that instead of wondering *why* she did it, one stops short at *how*. It gives the reader the wrong *kind* of shock.[5]

Two things more I want to say. One is there are so many unexpected awfully good things that one comes upon as one reads, with a small shock of delight. Its as though, being taken by the author through his garden you suddenly discover, half tucked away, another flowery tree. "So you have these in your garden, too . . ." Thats the feeling. It makes one want to see more of your work.

The other is – I don't think this book really holds together enough, even allowing for the title. It ought to be more squeezed and pressed and moulded into shape and wrung out – if you know what I mean. And sometimes the writing is careless. All the same, if I were you, I would publish it more or less as it stands. I would let it go. You will have to take out a good many of the Russian expressions and single words. I expect you hear them so distinctly in your brain that you feel they must be there. But they will put people off.

At that moment I lit a cigarette & reread what I have written, with dismay. In trying to be honest I sound carping and cold. Not a bit what I feel. Let me end where I began by warmly, sincerely congratulating you. Thats the most important thing of all. And when I say I don't think your novel "holds together enough" please remember I'm speaking "ide-ally".

I hope you will write to me. If you feel offended please tell me. Its not easy to talk man to man at a distance. And heres your book back again.

The Swiss who can let nothing in or out of their country without taking a share, have, I am afraid, nibbled the edges of the cover.

I press your hand warmly

Yours sincerely

Katherine Mansfield.

P.S. The rain *thumped*. Dont you mean the rain *drummed*?

MS ATL. *LKM* II. 154–6.

[1] After the narrator Andrei Andreiech (whose wartime experience is very like that of the young Gerhardi) returns to England from Russia, becomes restless at Oxford, and goes back to Vladivostok to the young woman he loves. She does not reciprocate, and the novel concludes with his standing on the wharf as she and her sisters sail for Shanghai.

[2] A remark made by Nina to Andrei Andreiech as they take a walk.

[3] The German woman who lives with, but never marries, as she hopes, the father of the three Vasilievich sisters.

[4] KM is noting the similarity between her friend Koteliansky and a minor character in the novel, the kind-hearted, ineffectual disciplinarian, General Bologoevski.

[5] In the published text, Nina does not write a novel, although *Futility* begins: 'And then it struck me that the only thing to do was to fit all this into a book', so that the narrator is also writer. Gerhardi wrote on the letter '*Note*. "Futility" was then overhauled, thanks to K.M.'s helpful advice.'

To J. B. Pinker, 12 November 1921

CHALET DES SAPINS | MONTANA-SUR-SIERRE | VALAIS

12.11.1921

Dear Mr Pinker,

I return herewith the corrected proofs of the story.

I am greatly troubled to find that the typist has made mistakes which make nonsense of the text.[1] She (or he) has also left out words and substituted *bath* for *basin*, *sole* for *sour* and so on. I do not like to think the other uncorrected copy has gone to America. And I tremble to think of my poor *Garden-Party*. I suppose I can't hope to have proofs of the American copies (just supposing they ever should reach the proof stage.[2])

I trust this does not sound ungracious to you, for your kindness in arranging for them to be typed. I appreciate the fact that I *had* a risk to run.

I am sorry to make a mountain out of what must seem to anyone but an agonised parent such a very small molehill.

Yours sincerely

Katherine Mansfield

MS Newberry.

[1] A poorly edited version of 'At the Bay' appeared in the *London Mercury*, Jan. 1922.

[2] The first American edition of *The Garden Party* was published in New York by Alfred A. Knopf in 1922.

To Dorothy Brett, [*14 November 1921*]

CHALET DES SAPINS | MONTANA-SUR-SIERRE | VALAIS

1 purl *1* plain wool in front of needle knit two together *slip* one cross stitch for 94 lines *purl* again decrease to form spiral effect up leg leg *now* use the needle as for purl casting on first and so continue until length can be divided by three. Care should be taken to keep *all flat.* Press with warm iron and serve . . .
Just a little home recipe, ma chère, for a *wet* evening.

Monday

Brett dearest,

The Wools came today. They are quite lovely & I feel inclined to carry them about, just as they are, like fat dolls. J.M. was deeply moved by their beauty; he is an expert with the needles – – – But we found, by piercing the postage signs that you had paid vast sums to have them sent over. So here is another cheque – and I hope you hear our grateful thankful thanks all standing in a row & singing your praises.

Isnt lemming yellow a *fascinating* colour. There is a very pink pink here too – aster pink, which is heavenly fair. I could get a wool complex very easily . . . These are *simply perfect* in every way.

This is not a letter. Now you owe me one – pleasant thought.

The day is simply divine – so hot that my pink perishall won't keep out the sun enough. Blazing! With that ones very soul comes up to breathe, rising like a fish out of the dark water.

You were not serious about the sweater: were you? But can you make *sleeves?* I cant turn corners for nuts.

Tig.

P.S. No, what you ought to have said to the Fighting Dogs was: Will you go in or stay out? Which will you have *Heads* or *Tails?*

P.P.S. What a duck Marie Loo must be.

P.P.P.S. No, I dont like mousey colours. We began to wind after lunch today and now a miniature Garsington sits on the carpet. The cat almost had delirium tremens. We thought we should have to chloroform him finally. He sat up & began to wind his own tail.

P.P.P.P.S. M. is at this moment sliding on the ice.

P.P.P.P.P.S. I sent you those postcards just to show you how innocent a corner we keep. Now I shall get you some others to show you what it is really like.

MS Newberry, *LKM* II. 153–4.

To Elizabeth, Countess Russell, [19 November 1921]

Chalet des Sapins | Montana-sur-Sierre | Valais.

Dear Elizabeth,

It is John's turn but I can't refrain from slipping a Bon Jour into the envelope. It's such a marvellously bon jour, too; I wish I could send it you intact. Blazing hot, with a light wind singing in the trees and an exquisite transparent sky with just two little silver clouds lying on their back like cherubs basking.

We don't only read Shakespeare and the poets. I have* re-read *Queechy** lately, "fresh bursts of tears" and all. I loved it.

"Mr Carleton, who made *that*," said the child, pointing to the slowly sinking orb on* the horizon with streaming eyes.

The young English peer had no answer ready. His own eyes filled. "Will you lend me your little Bible," he said gently.

"*Oh*, Mr. C!" Sobs were her only answer, but happy sobs, grateful sobs. She could not see to hand it to him, nor he to see it offered.'[1]

I have also been reading modern novels, Stephen McKenna and W. L. George & Co for the Daily News.[2] They are a vulgar, dreary lot. Why all this pretence? When we have not said a quarter of what there is to say. Why can't writers be warm, living, simple, merry or sad as it pleases them? All this falsity is so *boring*.

I hope Rose Macaulay gets that prize rather than Brett Young; his Black Diamond had not enough spirit.[3]

It will be a happy relief to see Bertie's articles in the Nation.[4] I hope his baby is laughing at the light by now. It's nice to know they are enjoying life.

We have received a very breathed-on letter from poor old Mrs. M.[5] The blow has fallen, the axe descended. There will be a Divorce, after all. Doctor Hudson has said nothing about it but he is twice the man already and has flowered into eligible waistcoats and ties spotted like the tails of deep sea fishes.

But oh, this perfect weather! Big Snow has not come yet but the footprints of Little Snow are everywhere. John is sliding on the ice with the [word missing] of Montana each day and my faithful one sends up all the food buttoned into tight little suet jackets. Suet is a very awful invention . . .

But I must not write any more. You have had enough of us for now. We shall rejoice to see you again.

I wish my new book were better. There are holes in it, Elizabeth, black ones. I know they are there. But I shall have to trust people not losing all patience, and make my *next* one better.

The Lord be with us all,

With *love*,
Katherine.

To William Gerhardi, 21 November 1921

CHALET DES SAPINS | MONTANA-SUR-SIERRE | VALAIS
21.xi.1921

Dear Mr Gerhardi,

Your fearfully nice letter makes me wish that instead of upsetting your table you would sit down at mine & drink tea and talk. But I hasten to answer it for this reason. Have you found a publisher for your novel? I know Cobden-Sanderson very well. I should be delighted to write to him about it if you would care for me to do so. He is a publisher who has only been going for a couple of years or so but he has a very good name already. He produces his books excellently; he takes an interest in them . . . If you care to send him yours I shall ask Middleton Murry to write as well. For I confess, I let him see your novel. Was that a bad breach of confidence? I hope not. He agreed, enthusiastically that it ought to be published . . . Yes, he did remember you at that lecture; as soon as I mentioned your name he recalled the occasion.

You know – if I may speak in confidence – I shall not be 'fashionable' long. They will find me out; they will be disgusted; they will shiver in dismay. I like such awfully unfashionable things – and people – I like sitting on doorsteps, & talking to the old woman who brings quinces, & going for picnics in a jolting little waggon, and listening to the kind of music they play in public gardens on warm evenings, and talking to captains of shabby little steamers, and in fact, to all kinds of people in all kinds of places. But what a fatal sentence to begin. It goes on for ever. In fact one could spend a whole life finishing it.

But you see I am not a high brow. Sunday lunches and very intricate conversations on Sex and that 'fatigue' which is so essential and that awful 'brightness' which is even more essential – these things I flee from.

TC Huntington. *LKM* II. 149–50.

1 *Queechy* (1852) was an extremely popular novel by Elizabeth Wetherell, the pseudonym of the American novelist and children's writer Susan Warner (1819–85). The story reflects the author's own devout Christianity, as the young heroine Fleda Ringgan, given to both weeping and philosophizing, gradually draws the rich Englishman, Mr Carleton, into faith and matrimony. KM catches the tone of the narrative, and conflates two separate incidents: one when the couple watches a sunset at the end of ch. II, the other as Fleda gives her Bible to Mr Carleton.

2 KM reviewed only Stephen McKenna's *The Secret Victory* in the *Daily News*, 28 Nov. 1921, although Murry discussed both W. L. George's *The Confession of Ursula Trent* and McKenna's novel in the *Nation and the Athenaeum*, 17 Dec. 1921.

3 The Femina-Vie Heureuse prize was awarded to Rose Macaulay's *Dangerous Ages*; F. Brett Young's *The Black Diamond* was placed second; KM's *Bliss* was third.

4 His articles on his visit to China, discussed on p. 344. Bertrand Russell's son John Conrad was born on 16 Nov. 1921.

5 Mrs Maxwell, landlady of the Chalet des Sapins and mother of Dr Hudson.

I'm in love with life – terribly. Such a confession is enough to waft Bliss out of the Union[1] . . .

I am sending you a postcard of myself & the two knobs of the electric light. The photographer insisted they should be there as well.

Yes I live in Switzerland because I have consumption. But I am not an invalid. Consumption doesn't belong to me. Its only a horrid stray dog who has persisted in following me for four years, so I am trying to lose him among these mountains. But "permanently compelled" oh – no!

If you are ever in the mood to talk about writing I hope you will believe me when I say how happy I shall be – as a 'fellow worker' – to listen. I am glad you enjoyed Bertie Russell. 'Nimble' is just the word for him.

Goodbye. I hope you will write wonderful stories; numbers of them. One could not wish anyone greater happiness than that.

Yours sincerely,
Katherine Mansfield.

MS ATL. *LKM* II. 156–7.

[1] The library of the Oxford Union.

To Mr Lynd, 23 November 1921

CHALET DES SAPINS | MONTANA-SUR-SIERRE | VALAIS

23 XI 1921

Dear Mr Lynd,[1]

Your letter was rather a relief. I thought my reviews had displeased you or that they were illegible.[2] Very many thanks for your note. I shall type the next ones I do for you.

Yes, I gathered from your pickpocket adventure that you had been in Italy. I hope you both enjoyed it.

How *excellentissimo* Sylvia was on W.L. George's novel![3]

Yours sincerely

Katherine Middleton Murry.

Will you give her my love?

PC ATL.

[1] Robert Lynd (1879–1949) was born in Belfast, and after graduating from Queen's University embarked on a career in journalism in London. He published many collections of essays on a wide range of topics, from sport to politics, contributed to the *Athenaeum*, and from 1912 was literary editor of the *Daily News*. He was married to KM's friend, the novelist Sylvia Lynd.

[2] KM's review of John Galsworthy's *To Let* appeared in the *Daily News*, 5 Nov., and of *The Secret Victory* by Stephen McKenna and *The Red Knight* by F. Brett Young on 28 Nov.

[3] Sylvia Lynd reviewed W. L. George's *The Confession of Ursula Trent* in the *Daily News*, 28 Oct. 1921.

To Richard Murry, 27 November 1921

CHALET DES SAPINS | MONTANA-SUR-SIERRE | VALAIS
27 XI 1921

Dear Richard,

I have been on the point of writing to you all this week. But the week seems to have walked away with us as usual. Here it is – Sunday – Im alone in the house. Jack has gone off as usual to the big lake where he skates every afternoon. I went to see him one day. He's like a very alert careless bird swinging up and down. The lake is beautiful, with lawny slopes on the sides and clumps of dark firs. Snow lies on the grass but thin, in patches, like linen drying. And in the distance there are these huge, high peaks. I like awfully to see these little figures sliding on the ice, it reminds me of very ancient pictures. 14th century in a Munich gallery which I saw one year.[1]

We are still waiting for Big Snow who tarries out of sight. Its fine every single day. The sun burns in a brilliant, transparent sky. In the shade there is a film of frost over everything and all pools and streams are ice. But from 8.30 until 3.30 you can bask as if it were summer. Pretty good for a climate – dont you think?

I suppose one would say our Life goes on much the same. We work and want to work more; we read aloud, we *both* knit. While Jack skates I sit on my balcony & go for my walk through a pair of field glasses. There is only one real trouble & that is – never enough time. Is there any remedy for that? Its awful!

How are things looking, Richard? All kinds of things? The world in general? I am afraid that in spite of everything I care for Life so profoundly that I am one of these optimists. The wife of Jack Spratt, in fact. Though in sober fact I hate FAT. But there it is. We dont quarrel about it – which is queer. We are inclined to laugh at each other!

Theres a queer small tapping noise going on while I write, made by the birds hanging upside down eating the fir cones. Now & then a fir cone drops off & I feel another bird who sees this accident happen gives a squeak of joy.

Wing is white as snow. His name for Jack is "masteraman",[2] his name for me is Gran'ma Jaegar; he calls Ida B. the Fostermonger; and for some reason calls the servant our *Swede*. Muddled it with Swiss, I suppose. We found out these names in his memoirs.

Heres Jack and the tea tray is following him up the stairs. This is a dull letter, little brother.

I send my *love*

Katherine.

MS R. Murry. *Adam* 370-5, 30-1.

[1] The Dutch painter Hendrick Avercamp (1585–1634) made his reputation with lively outdoor winter scenes, many with figures on ice. KM would have seen examples of these in the Alte Pinakothek, Munich, when she spent time in Bavaria in 1909.

[2] See p. 311, n. 1.

To Elizabeth, Countess Russell, [29 November 1921]

Chalet des Sapins | Montana-sur-Sierre | Valais
Tuesday.

Dear Elizabeth,

I have only just read in the newspapers of [Sydney's] death.[1] I am so very deeply sorry for you. Cruel, terrible Death!

There is nothing more to say. Forgive me if this note intrudes on your sorrow, and please do not answer it.

Dear precious Elizabeth, would that this had not happened to you!

Katherine.

TC Huntington.

[1] The death a few days before of Elizabeth's brother, Sydney. (See p. 302, n. 3.)

To S. S. Koteliansky, [29 November 1921]

CHALET DES SAPINS | MONTANA-SUR-SIERRE | VALAIS

My dear Koteliansky

If I trouble you with this request please simply tell me so.

Do you know where I can obtain any information about Doctor Manoukhine's treatment? I mean – has it appeared in any possible papers or journals that I can get hold of?[1] I ask for this reason. I cannot possibly go to Paris at present. I have no one to send. In fact I have not mentioned this idea to *anyone* except my doctor here. Such things I prefer to do alone. It is not just a whim. My doctor here says he will very gladly consider any information I can get him about this treatment and as he has a very good X-ray apparatus it could, if it is not the 'professional patent' of Doctor Manoukhine, be tried here, immediately.

What should you advise me to do? My difficulty about writing direct is the language. It is one thing to explain ones case by speech, it is another to write it in a foreign tongue. I should simply antagonise him . . . But the doctor here is quite intelligent and very honest. He is interested sincerely. And I have such faith in this 'unknown' treatment. I feel it is the right thing.

And I want to stop this illness, as soon as possible.

Dear precious friend, forgive me for worrying you.

It is a beautiful, still winter day. There is the sound of a sawmill. The sun shines like a big star through the dark fir trees. How are you?

Katherine.

MS BL. LKM II. 157–8.

[1] Kot may have sent on to her Ivan Manoukhin's paper 'The Treatment of Infectious Diseases by Leucocytolysis Produced by Rontgenisation of the Spleen', *Lancet*, 2 Apr. 1921, 685–7, in which Manoukhin claimed to have cured 8,000 tubercular patients by X-rays directed to the spleen.

To Michael Sadleir, [29 November 1921]

CHALET DES SAPINS | MONTANA-SUR-SIERRE | VALAIS

Dear Michael Sadleir,

Forgive a troublesome author. But if there is still time, if the printers have not got so far would you – could you extract a story called *Sixpence* from near the end of my book & throw it away?[1] I have not a copy by me but I have a horrible feeling it is sentimental & should not be there. I may be asking something impossible. If I am Im very sorry to have worried you.

Yours very sincerely

Katherine Mansfield.

MS Targ.

[1] The story, which had appeared in the *Sphere* on 13 Aug. 1921, was dropped from *The Garden Party*.

To William Gerhardi, [30] November 1921

[Chalet des Sapins] | Montana [sur-Sierre]
November.

Dear Mr Gerhardi,

I wrote to Mr Cobden-Sanderson on the 28th of this month. I do hope you will arrive at some satisfactory arrangement with him.[1] Many thanks for your letter. Dont think Im kind. I feel so strongly that writers ought to have a real claim on each other.

K.M.

Postcard ATL.

[1] Cobden-Sanderson published *Futility* in 1922.

To J. B. Pinker, 2 December 1921

CHALET DES SAPINS | MONTANA-SUR-SIERRE | VALAIS
ii XII 1921

Dear Mr Pinker,

If you have not sent The Dolls House to the Nation and The Athenaeum – would you kindly let them see it? It does not look as though anybody is eager to print it. And I am a little discouraged that neither this story nor The Garden-Party has been accepted.[1]

Yours sincerely

Katherine Mansfield.

MS Newberry.

---

[1] 'The Doll's House' was published in the *Nation and the Athenaeum*, 4 Feb. 1922, 'The Garden Party' in the *Westminster Gazette*, 18 Feb. 1922.

To Sydney Waterlow, [3 December 1921]

CHALET DES SAPINS | MONTANA-SUR-SIERRE | VALAIS

My dear Sidney

How are you? What is happening? What are you thinking? Are you in the mood for a talk. If you are . . .

Tell me, Sidney, why are people clothed in this awful armour? Why is it shameful to feel warm hearted? Why must one go on and on pretending, "carrying it off". I remember my immense surprise when my first husband[1] sent me letters with *without prejudice* at the top. But all the letters one gets are without prejudice. Its very odd. Dont other people want real friendship as I do? Are they all content with a kind of game? But that is so boring, it is so barren, so cold. I suppose the truth is people prefer to be alone. There you are! They have not this cursed desire to share things, to understand and appreciate one another. Well, its very sad, Sidney, if that is so. In fact its insufferable. And the only way to bear it is by living in the past. But that is cold comfort. I want to live in the past, present and future all at one and the same time – dont you?

You *do* feel that, in spite of everything, there is nothing wrong with Life? And this business of accepting, submitting, giving, taking, is deeply, deeply worth while. But wouldn't it be wonderful if that was taken for granted once and for all so that we went on from that point. Ah me! Forgive me if I have bored you. Dont be bored, please.

. . . I have just finished the proofs of my new book. Its been like getting back into the skin one had sloughed off. Not at all the skin I thought it, either. But it cant be helped. I think one must risk being seen not at one's best. Its no good hiding the unfavourable photographs, though pride wants to. All the same I must take a deeper breath next time.

There is a loud fierce wind blowing tonight from God knows where. It sounds very awful.

Farewell
Yours ever
Katherine.

MS ATL.

1 George Bowden (1877–1975), a singing teacher when KM married him in London on 2 Mar. 1909. They separated the next day, but did not divorce until May 1918.

To Sydney Schiff 3 December 1921

CHALET DES SAPINS | MONTANA-SUR-SIERRE | VALAIS
3 XII 1921.

Dear dear Sydney

I do beg you to send me a copy of Elinor Colhouse[1] *as soon as possible.* You do understand how I want one? Pity me! Feel for me up here in these heaven-kissing mountains. One thing I promise you, you will not have a more ardent reader – no, not one. I wish there were some other means of communication except this cursed one of letters. It is not enough. I want to be with you – to listen, talk, look, observe, absorb, remember, rejoice in. It is so awfully nice to laugh at the same things – and then your voice – Violet's voice – her smile, your way of sitting on the arm of a chair, a black tie that Violet wears sometimes (*very* important) the lunch table at Big Tree Villa – your cigarettes. But so one could go on for ever, and its all a kind of *code*, immensely boundlessly significant for those who understand it. I miss you. And the worst of it is I feel you are not coming to Switzerland – that for the time at least Switzerland is over. I am still here to all appearance. But the 'essential moi' as Daudet would say[2] is in Paris sitting in a small darkish room opposite a man called Manoukhine. Whether I shall follow this me I don't know yet. When does one *really begin* a journey – or a friendship – or a love affair. It is those beginnings which are so fascinating and so misunderstood. There comes a moment when we realise we are already well on our way – déjà.

I wish you had J.M.'s *real* article on Proust.[3] It seems to me not only by far the best thing he has ever done – but really first-chop. We lived Proust, breathed him, talked and thought of little else for two weeks – two solid uninterrupted Swiss weeks. I confess I did not know how important he is until then – I did not *feel* his importance as I do now, and the marvel is that those books go on breathing after you have put them away; one is never at an end with them. But they spoil one – they spoil one fearfully for other things. I have begun a certain amount of novel reviewing again[4] and oh – the awful rubbish, the shameful stuff they send across! I read it; it seems too bad to blame even – and then I read the reviews and find Shaw Desmond[5] is "capable of a masterpiece, and well on the way of writing one". It is profoundly disquieting to be so out of tune with ones times. I mean that very seriously. The only way to bear the horrid truth is by writing oneself – going on . . .

I dont intend to live in Switzerland. In spite of the beautiful aspects one cant tolerate the peasants. They are so ugly, such boors, so heavy. Never have I imagined such ankles. It has always been a faint surprise to me the passion of men for ankles – their desire to kiss them – and so on. But now! Oh Heavens! I could go down on my knees to a lovely pair. The ankles of my Ernestine are an anguish to me. They haunt me. Physical beauty – how I love it! How I hate *grossness*. Here is poor good Jones with her passion for buttoning the food into little tight suet jackets. Suet is an abomination!

Let us drink champagne when we meet again. Where will that be. When? That glimpse of London in your letters – just that lift of the curtain showing lights, big gay rooms, Dorothy Ireland's mouth, the Ballet, a strain heard from afar, and people round the table and the sound of the bell . . . You took me there for the moment and I turned away from my mountains.

I see from Eliots grave letter in the Lit. Sup. that he is in Lausanne.[6] It seemed to me very fitting that Lausanne should be his address. What did you think of Lawrence in The Dial? This last month isn't anything like so good; in fact when he gets on to the subject of *maleness* I lose all patience.[7] What nonsense it all is – and he must know it is. His style changes; he can no longer write. He *begs the question*. I cant forgive him for that – its a sin. Santyana on Dickens was a revelation to me – of Santyana.[8] It showed how little he is really attached to Life. He has the ideas of a child of ten. Its absurd to pretend at this time of day that we do not know more than children. Anatole France doesn't tell half enough either in his Vie en Fleur.[9] Oh, how I hate *Pound* – Ezra Pound. I always did and always shall – with his new "lumps" or "chunks" of Proust and all his chinese tub thumping.[10] He is a vulgar fellow. All the same I do think The Dial is by far the most interesting magazine going today.

I must stop this letter. Theres my lunch – but no grilled haddock alas! In the afternoon here I go for long solitary drives. It is happiness. Sometimes I pass the lake and hail J.M. who turns, glides, whirls on the ice like an alert and careless bird. But winter in the forests is very wonderful – the streams silent –

Farewell. I press your hand warmly. My love to you both.

Ever & ever

K.M.

MS BL, *LKM* II. 159–60.

1 Schiff's new novel, published under his *nom de plume* Stephen Hudson.

2 Considering KM's tendency to speak of secret selves and concealed lives, she may have had in mind the lines in Alphonse Daudet's *Notes sur la vie* (1899), xvi, I: 'Oh, ce terrible second moi, toujours assis pendant que l'autre est debout, agit, vit, souffre, se démène. Ce second MOI que j'ai jamais pu ni griser, ni faire pleurer, ni endormir!'

3 See p. 304, n. 2.

4 KM reviewed *The Secret Victory* by Stephen McKenna and *The Red Knight* by F. Brett Young in the *Daily News*, 28 Nov. 1921.

5 Shaw Desmond (b. 1877) had variously written a guide to sex and marriage, travel books, books on politics and spiritualism, and fiction. His novel *Gods* was published in 1921, his autobiography *Pilgrim to Paradise* in 1951.

6 Writing from Lausanne, T. S. Eliot's letter on 'Poets and Anthologies', *Times Literary Supplement*, 24 Nov. 1921, objected to his inclusion, without permission, in a recent anthology *Modern American Poetry*, arguing that 'the work of any poet who has already published a book of verse is likely to be more damaged than aided by anthologies'.

7 In 'Sea and Sardinia', pt. 2, *Dial*, Nov. 1921, D. H. Lawrence gave his impressions of Cagliari, and enthused over a young peasant 'with a swift eye and hard check and hard dangerous thighs. . . How fascinating it is, after the soft Italians, to see these limbs in their close knee-breeches, so definite, so manly, with the old fierceness in them still. One realises, with horror, that the race of men is almost extinct in Europe. Only Christ-like heroes and women-worshipping Don Juans, and rabid equality-mongrels. The old, hardy, indomitable male is gone.'

8 In the same issue, George Santayana's 'Dickens' claimed: 'It is remarkable, in spite of his ardent singularity and openness of heart, how irresistible Dickens is to the greater themes of the human imagination – religion, science, politics, art.' Thomas Moult, 'Katherine Mansfield as I Knew Her', *TP's Weekly*, 1 Dec. 1928, quoted from an undated letter of KM which does not survive: 'Doesn't Charley Dickens make our little men smaller than ever – and such pencil sharpeners?'

9 The Nov. issue of the *Dial* also carried Anatole France's autobiographical 'La Vie en Fleur', pt. 2, which discussed 'Thoughts about Happiness' and 'Choice of a Career.'

10 Ezra Pound's 'Paris Letter', *Dial*, Oct. 1921, spoke of 'The new Proust, or the new lump of Proust, being the tail end of one book and the beginning of another'. Writing to Lady Ottoline Morrell in July 1919 (*CLKM* II. 343), KM referred to 'that unspeakable Ezra Pound', and to Murry, 4 July 1919 (*CLKM* III. 70), 'that arch-snorter' . . . 'that ludicrous old sea-lion', explaining that she detested him because of an offensive letter he had written to a friend.

*To Ivan Manoukhine,*¹ *4 December 1921*

CHALET DES SAPINS | MONTANA-SUR-SIERRE | VALAIS
4 xii 1921

Cher Docteur Manoukhine,

Suivant le conseil de mon ami, M.Koteliansky, de Londres, je vous écris pour vous demander si vous voulez bien m'accepter comme sujet de votre traitement de tuberculose aux rayons X. Je suis malade depuis quatre ans. Les deux poumons sont attaqués et le coeur en est embarrassé. Tout de même je ne suis pas une grande malade. Je sens qu'il y a toujours de la santé en moi et j'ai le désir le plus vif d'avoir assez de

forces pour accomplir le travail – je suis écrivain – que j'ai encore à faire.
Je serai heureux de vous envoyer tous les renseignements dant vous
aurez besoin.

Si vous préferez que je vienne à Paris pour vous voir, je m'y rendrai.

Je vous prie de me pardonner de vous approcher si brusquement –
que je fais sur l'avis exprès de M. Koteliansky – et me croire votre
sincèrement dévouée

Katherine Mansfield Murry.

MSC² ATL.

---

¹ Ivan Manoukhin, who was in charge of a Red Cross hospital in Kiev during the First World
War, had worked in Paris at the Pasteur Institute in 1913, and was now established in Paris with
his revolutionary, but medically useless, treatment of tuberculosis.
² This letter survives only in a transcription by Ruth Elvish Mantz, who with Murry wrote the
first biographical study of KM, *The Life of Katherine Mansfield* (1933).

To S. S. Koteliansky, [4 December 1921]

CHALET DES SAPINS | MONTANA-SUR-SIERRE | VALAIS

Dear Koteliansky

Thank you. I have written to M. today. Whatever he advises that will
I do. It is strange – I have faith in him. I am sure he will not have the
kind of face one walks away from. Besides – think of being "*well*". Health
is as precious as life – no less. Do you know I have not walked since
November 1920? Not more than to a carriage and back. Both my lungs
are affected, there is a cavity in one and the other is affected through.
My heart is weak, too. Can all this be cured. Ah, Koteliansky – wish for
me! But I am selfish, dear friend. No, I should not ask even a wish. Yet
to be uprooted is terrible.

Why are things so bad with you? It is a mystery why this must be so.
I press your hand.

Katherine.

MS BL. *LKM* II. 161.

To Dorothy Brett, [5 December 1921]

CHALET DES SAPINS | MONTANA-SUR-SIERRE | VALAIS

Dearest Brett,

Forgive my delay in answering. I wanted to answer bang off, but these
last few days have been rather bad ones – tired ones. I haven't been able
to do anything but read. Its on these occasions that one begins to wish

for queer things like gramophones. It wouldn't matter if one could just walk away. But thats out of the question at present. But no more of it.

If possible I will certainly meet you in Paris in the Spring near the Luxembourg Gardens. Lovely idea! It shall be done. I hope to have enough money by then to spend a month in Paris. Wouldn't it be thrilling for you to arrive? I love Paris at that time of year.

Wasn't that Van Gogh shown at the Goupil ten years ago?¹ Yellow flowers – brimming with sun in a pot? I wonder if it is the same. That picture seemed to reveal something that I hadn't realised before I saw it. It lived with me afterwards. It still does – that & another of a sea captain in a flat cap. They taught me something about writing, which was queer – a kind of freedom – or rather, a shaking free. When one has been working for a long stretch one begins to narrow ones vision a bit, to fine things down too much. And its only when something else breaks through, a picture, or something seen out of doors that one realises it. It is – literally – years since I have been to a picture show. I can *smell* them as I write.

I am writing to you before breakfast. Its just sunrise and the sky is a hedge sparrow egg blue, the fir trees are quivering with light. This is simply a marvellous climate for sun. We have far more sun than at the South of France, and while it shines it is warmer. On the other hand – out of it – one might be in the Arctic Zone – and it freezes so hard at night that one dare not let the chauffage down, even. It is queer to be in the sun and to look *down* at the clouds. We are above them here. But yesterday for instance it was like the old original flood. Just Montana bobbed above the huge lakes of pale water. There wasn't a thing to be seen but cloud below. When are the photographs of your paintings to come? Send them soon! Are you working? Or resting after your last. Are people gay in London this winter? These awful fogs – I feel I should have to fly to something to get over them, and yet – if one is well – perhaps they dont matter so much and even have their beauty, too.

Oh dear! I am sure by now you are gasping at the dullness of this letter. To tell you the truth – I am terribly unsettled for the moment. It will pass. But while it is here I seem to have no mind except for what is worrying me. I am making another effort to throw off my chains – i.e. to be well. And I am waiting for the answer to a letter – I'm half here – half away – its a bad business. But you see I have made up my mind to try the Russian doctor's treatment. I have played my card. Will he answer? Will anything come of it? One dares not speak of these things. It is so boring for it is all speculation, and yet one *cannot* stop thinking . . . thinking . . . imagining what it would be like to run again or take a little jump.

Forgive me, dear Brett. In my next letter I shall be over this. Do please write if you can. It would be fearfully nice to get a long letter, especially as I don't deserve one. And tell me please what size you take in shoes. Don't forget! It will be too late if you do, and be sure to let me know where you will be at Christmas Time. I want (as I daresay you have guessed) to send you a small present.

Goodbye for now. My *love* to you

Ever
Tig

MS Newberry. *LKM* II. 160–1.

[1] KM had seen Van Gogh's *Sunflowers* at the first post-impressionist exhibition at the Grafton Galleries (not the Goupil) in 1912.

To Sydney Schiff, 8 December 1921

[Chalet des Sapins, Montana-sur-Sierre]
December 8, 1921

I have read your *Elinor Colhouse* more than twice, and I shall read it again. I do congratulate you sincerely from my heart. It's amazingly good! So good one simply can't imagine it better. One pushes into deep water easily, beautifully, from the first sentence, and there's that feeling – so rare – of ease, of safety, of wishing only to be borne along wherever the author chooses to take one.

But how you have *conveyed* the contrast between Elinor and Richard![1] Am I fantastic in dating it from the moment when Richard leaves her after their first meeting, when he opens the door on to the brilliant light one feels the appeal of his *fairness* and her *darkness* in an astonishing way. That moment remains with me throughout the book. Let me dare to say it's almost a mystical interpretation of their relations.

Why aren't you here – that we might talk it over and over. I'd like to recall so much – scene after scene rises in my mind. But although it is Elinor's book and a triumph for Elinor it's your presentation of Richard which I admire so tremendously. I don't mean only his boyish charm – though Heaven knows that is potent enough – or even his naturalness – which at times takes my breath away. But it's Richard's innocence of the wiles and arts of Life! It's the sight of him, in the midst of all that scheming and plotting and his horror, finally, that this should happen to him.
. . .

Of course, all the detail, so fastidious, so satisfying, is beyond praise.

Elinor *lives*. I see her, hear her, recognise those fingers with the long pointed brilliant nails, look into that little brain.

Yes, I honour you for it. It's an achievement. I rejoice in your success.

MS lacking. *LKM* II. 161–2.

¹ Schiff's new novel *Elinor Colhouse* continued the story of *Richard Kurt* (1919), Elinor being the wife of Richard.

To Dorothy Brett, [11 December 1921]

CHALET DES SAPINS | MONTANA-SUR-SIERRE | VALAIS

Dearest Brett,

Your photographs have come. I am embarrassed by them and for this reason. I don't feel its quite fair to give you my opinion unless you are certain – unless you remember – its no more than the opinion of one of the public. All I know about painting is that I like certain things – they seem to me to have 'come off', or the artist has 'brought it across'. Strangeness doesn't matter as long as one feels that. Its the only crite-rion I have to go by. But you see its not much of a one. I *like* your flow-ers best. Best of all the *White Gloxinias*. No. I should like the *Asters* equally. I feel the colour is very lovely in them. Your painting – as I know it – depends very much on *colour*. Thats what makes it so hard to really judge by photographs. I don't really like *Ottoline*. You seem to have tried for subtlety in the face but there is not enough and so its weak. And the expanse of chest is ugly to me. It doesn't look living. The head doesn't look as though it belongs to it. Its not really Ottoline or a pretty lady; its a kind of giantess. That may be an 'aspect' of Ottoline but I don't think it is what you aimed at conveying. *The Dolls* depend so greatly on colour for their decorative effect that its fearfully hard to know what to say. I like the way you have painted the little dish and the bowl. Theres a feel-ing for dolls in it, a naivete – awfully nice – and the head of the black doll seems to me very solid. But the off arm worries me. But without colour it is impossible to really see this picture. Its true I think the other doll's face is not quite right. It looks flabby. But isn't that the photo-graph? And the painting of the dress doesn't look intentional enough; it looks too not considered enough.

Now we come to *Marie Loo*. I have read and reread the description so that I see it as near as I can. It sounds wonderfully attractive. The truth is I really don't know quite what you are after. I don't understand. There is Marie Loo in her own little world under her own parasol. Thats your idea – isn't it? But the painting of the figure worries me – especially the legs. Shes too much like a flat cardboard figure. I have looked at her legs and I cant see her naked. Perhaps you will say – what on earth has this to do with it? Let her legs be flat. But there's the head. You have painted the head as though it were a round object i.e. to me – the head is in one style and the rest of the body (except the hand holding the doll) in another. It seems to me your whole difficulty is technique. The feeling is there, the imagination & the colour but you cant yet express what you feel and see. Your tools are not good enough – your hands. And I also think you are a bit over anxious; you are trying too hard. What I mean is you are attempting in Marie Loo something that for the moment is beyond you. Its no good doing anything that is not just a little too diffi-cult for us – thats a most profound truth, I think – but on the other hand we have to judge the degree of difficulty. And thats not easy.

Forgive me if I hurt you. Please don't *mind* what I say. It all comes to this: I feel there is a weakness in your more ambitious painting and the cause of it is that you haven't worked long enough to overcome it yet. Dont imagine I do not realise how much work has gone into these pic-tures. Dear dear Brett – I *do* with all my heart & I respect you for it. But its useless to take that into consideration when one is considering the result – isn't it? Ill write a *letter* later. This is to catch the outgoing post. Yours ever with love

Tig

MS Newberry.

To Dorothy Brett, [13 December 1921]

CHALET DES SAPINS | MONTANA-SUR-SIERRE | VALAIS
Tuesday

Dearest Brett,

Now Ill answer your letter. I have been, am so beastly ill; its because of the weather. The cold is terrifying. I don't know how to meet it. Perhaps once the real big snow has fallen it will be better. But at pre-sent I feel like a slate pencil living on a slate and my heart does such horrid things that – – – Well, we shall see. It is very bad, though. The pictures of London reminded me of Dostoievsky. The likeness was aston-ishing. *You* meant Lytton – didn't you? The one where the head is raised & the nose like a beak & pits beneath the eyes – where he says "And since when has smoke become suspicious – may I ask?" was a very *fas-cinating* photograph. But Dostoievsky – the spit of Dostoievsky to my mind. I like very much your *habit* of sending bits in your letters. Winston Churchills article[1] – I suppose it wasnt so really offensive. I disliked it though. Under the humility I smelt insolence. But perhaps that is because I always intensely dislike that man. Dont you think *his* likeness to Clive Bell is remarkable? (Why do *all* my fountain pens die? I care for them as if they were babies and they absolutely refuse to live. Is there such a thing as a real pen?)

Do you ever see all those people who used to go [to] Garsington? It seems like fifteen years ago – a Christmas morning when I came in & you were sitting up in bed covered with bright beads, little gay silk handkerchiefs, ribbons, cards, dividing your presents. You were so very sumptuous. I must say Garsington is my beau ideal of a house. Ottoline did bring it off amazingly. The appearance of the table was perfect always – and the very scent was right. I shall always admire her for that. It was a triumph. Because she consulted nobody. It was all her own, and she took it so lightly – as a matter of course. I think of her breakfast cups now & her spoons with the tenderness of a burglar. I must say I do love civilized ways. At the same time driving out to Garsington in an open cart on a snowy night was rather a price to pay . . . and hard to forget – equally hard . . .

So you have seen little Mamselle Sullivan. Isn't S. a very proud parent? I am sure he will be absorbed in his baby. Where do they live now? What a pity it is you cant get a house in St John's Wood. I think it is the *one* darling part of London. And I am always seeing such houses advertised on the back pages of the Sunday Times and the Observer. They sound ideal. Don't you prefer it to Hampstead? It has a *charm*. But perhaps that is because I lived there in Carlton Hill for a long time when I was young and very very happy.[2] I used to walk about there at nights – late – walking and talking on nights in spring with two brothers. Our house had a real garden, too, with trees and all the rooms were good – the top rooms lovely. But its all the musical people who make St Johns Wood so delightful – those grunting cellos, those flying fiddles and the wakeful pianos. Its like a certain part of Brussels. And then the house at 5 Acacia Road. It has memories – but its not only precious because of them. It was a charming house.[3]

Oh, this cold! I feel like an explorer sending you these last lines before the snow kills him. Its fearful! One cant work; ones brain is frozen hard & I cant breathe better than a fish in an empty tank. There is no air, its a kind of ice. I would leave here tomorrow but where can one go? One begins the wandering of a consumptive – fatal! Everybody does it and dies. However I have decided to leave this particular house in June for another, more remote. I passed it one day lately when I was out driving. Its in the most superb spot. The forests are on both sides but in front there are huge meadows with clumps of fir trees dotted over them – a kind of 18th century landscape. Beyond the meadows tower the gaunt snow mountains, and behind there is a big lake. It is to let in June. We shall take it for a year. My chief reason is for the hay making. One will be in the very midst of it all through August. To watch – to hear – mowing, to see the carts, to take part in the harvest is to share the summer in a way I *love*. You will really swoon at the view – or at least I shall expect you to!! And we shall eat out of doors – eat the hay with trimmings, and get a little boat & float on the lake and put up hammocks & swing on the pines, and paddle in the little stream. Dont you love to paddle?

I must end this letter. Its so dull. Forgive it. Now a pale sun like a half sucked peppermint is melting in the sky. The cat has come in. Even his poor little paws are cold – they feel like rubber. He is sitting on my feet singing his song. Wingley does not only purr; there is a light soprano note in his voice as well. He is very nearly human because of the love that is lavished on him. And now that his new coat is grown he is like a cat in a bastick tied with ribbons. He has an immense ruff and long curly new fur. Cats are far nicer than dogs. I shall write a cat story one day. But I shall give the cat to Carrington's dressmakers the Misses Read. What appaling dressmakers they were. They seemed to fit all their patterns on to cottage loaves – life size ones – or on to ham sandwiches with heads and feet. But it was worth it – to have got into their house and heard them as one did.

Goodbye for now. Please keep a small warm place for me beside you 'ever radiant' –. But not next to Peter . . . And give my love to Gertler – will you?

Ever yours

Tig.

P.S. DEAREST Brett

Your letter has just come

Stop!

You are not to send a gramophone.

Please stop *at once*.

None of us can possibly afford such a thing. You will be bankrup after it. My dear generous Brettushka – don't do anything of the kind! Only millionaires can buy them. I know. I scan the papers! But for the really frightfully dear thought – a thousand thanks.

Yes, I will go to Paris if Manoukhin answers. But I can get no reply – which is very disappointing. I like exceedingly the sound of your new friend. Do tell me more about him. And oh! how lovely the lights sound – the bottil & glass & the motor car! Greet them for me.

If I go to Paris I will keep you to your word. I shall expect you. But today makes me feel let it be *in*doors, somewhere warm where there is music & coffee that bubbles in the cup. Heat! Heat!! This is just a note – the envelope broken to put it in to stop your extravagance. Dont do it, my dear little artist. I 'note' the size of your tootsies. *Now* send your address for Christmas.

Tig

MS Newberry. *LKM* II. 163–5.

[1] Winston Churchill, 'Painting as a Pastime', *Strand*, Dec. 1921–Jan. 1922.
[2] When KM first returned to London in 1908, and was in love with Garnet Trowell, she frequently stayed at his parents' home at 52 Carlton Hill, St John's Wood. (See *CLKM* I. 57–89.)
[3] Where KM and Murry lived after her return from Paris in June 1915, until they left for Bandol in November of the same year.

To S. S. Koteliansky, [13 December 1921]

CHALET DES SAPINS | MONTANA-SUR-SIERRE | VALAIS

Dear Koteliansky –

All I meant by a 'mystery' was that one so good and so precious as
you should have sorrows . . .

I have written a second time to Paris. If I do not hear from this letter
I will try the secretary of the *institut*. There is nothing else to be done.

Katherine.

MS BL. Dickinson, 89.

To Elizabeth, Countess Russell, [c.15 December 1921]

Chalet des Sapins, [Montana sur Sierre]
Tuesday.

Dear Elizabeth,

Forgive this paper but I am out of reach of handmaidens. So awful is
the weather that I have retired under the edredon until it changes. There
is no snow. But there is a cold sheet of icy mist, like a slate pressing
against the windows and we feel like slate pencils inside. Nothing warms
one. The chauffage goes night and day but one shivers night and day as
well. If this is the between season people are wise to avoid it. The worst
of it is our brains are frozen, too. We live for the postman and he brings
us bills. We long for letters – the kind of letters exiles are supposed to
receive, and a copy of The Nation comes instead. In fact, all is very devilish and if it weren't for Jane Austen in the evenings we should be in
despair . . . We are reading her through. She is one of those writers who
seem to not only improve by keeping but to develop entirely new
adorable qualities. 'Emma' was our first. John sighed over Jane Fairfax
– I felt that Mr. Knightley in the shrubbery would be happiness.¹ But
her management of her plot – the way, just for the exquisite fun of the
thing, she adds a new complication – *that* one can't admire too greatly.
She makes modern episodic people like me – as far as I go – look very
incompetent ninnies. In fact she is altogether a chastening influence –
But, ah, what a rare creature!

Have you seen any of the reviews of John's Poems?² Most of the
reviewers seized the book only to whack him on the head with it. But he
is the most modest soul and takes it all nobly. I should be a seething kettle of spite and venom by this time. And his calmness is not because he
does not care. He has felt it more than I like to consider. But he goes
on. I should like something excessively pleasant to happen to him now.
It is the moment.

Our quilt is done. We think it very handsome. Will Elizabeth admire it. John is very dubious, so am I. It is a kind of conjuror's blanket. One expects to lift it and see the pitch black little babies underneath. Which reminds me of Bertie's white one – Conrad the Small.[3] What happiness for him. I am always half expecting a woollen boot or a powder puff to appear in the very middle of his 'Modern China'[4] . . .

I fear I am dull; I am boring you. But I wanted so much to write just for the sake of sending you our love; of saying how often you are in our thoughts and how we long to see you. The petunias, asters, nasturtiums, sweet peas – oh, how glorious they were! – flash upon my inward eye[5] very often. But only to mention them is to remember how one loves flowers and longs for them. Even a florist's shop. I can smell one now and even the paper the roses were wrapped in has its smell.

But here is the gentle Ernestine with the supper tray, so one's nose goes into le potage instead – or rather, hovers over.

Farewell, dear Elizabeth,

Do not quite forget us,
Katherine.

TC Huntington. *LKM* II. 162–3.

[1] Jane Fairfax, a beautiful, gifted orphan, and George Knightly, a landowner 16 years Emma Woodhouse's senior, whom she eventually marries in *Emma* (1816).
[2] *Poems 1916–20*, published by Cobden-Sanderson in Sept.
[3] Bertrand Russell's son, John Conrad.
[4] See p. 345, n. 1.
[5]
> For oft, when on my couch I lie
> In vacant or in pensive mood
> They flash upon that inward eye
> Which is the bliss of solitude.

> (final stanza of Wordsworth's 'I wandered lonely as a cloud'.)

To Dorothy Brett, [19 December 1921]

[Chalet des Sapins, Montana sur Sierre]

Dearest Brett

I must write you a small Christmas letter. I do not yet know whether the furry boots I have ordered for you will arrive in time. If not I shall send you my new milanese petticoat, for there is nothing here that I can buy for you, my dear, & remembered you *shall* be. Dont be too hard on me. The shops that there are – I cannot get at even if they were to hold anything that I could send you. So wear my pink petty with my warm warm love & if its too big – I am sure it is far too big for you or for me *puff* it out with love. Since I wrote to you I have been in my familiar land of counterpane. The cold got through as I knew it would and one wing only wags. As to Doctor Manoukhin I got the Mountain to phone Paris yesterday & found he was absent & only there from time to time, très rarement. It was impossible for the secretary to say when. So that doesnt sound very hopeful. I am disappointed. I had made him my 'miracle'. One must have a miracle. Now Im without one & looking round for another . . . Have you any suggestions?

It has been a fine day. The sun came into this room all the afternoon but at dusk an old ancient wind sprang up and it is shaking now and complaining. A terrible wind – a wind that one always mercifully forgets until it blows again. Do you know the kind I mean? It brings nothing but memories – and by memories I mean those that one cannot without pain remember. It always carries my brother to me. Ah Brett, I hope with all my heart you have not known anyone who has died young, long before their time. It is bitterness. But what am I thinking of? I wanted to write you a Christmas letter. I wanted to wish you joy.

I *can* – in spite of everything in life – I *can*, and by that I dont mean that its any desperate difficulty. No, let us rejoice – that we are alive and know each other & walk the earth at the same time. Let us make plans, and fulfil them, and be happy when we meet, and laugh a great deal this year and never cry. Above all – lets be friends. There was that in your last letter which made you dearer to me than than ever before. I dont know what it was. It was as though you came out of the letter & touched me & smiled and I understood your *goodness*.

Blessings on you, dear little artist. I put my arms round you – I give you a warm embrace. Be happy!

I am your loving

Tig

MS Newberry. *LKM* II. 165–6.

To J. B. Pinker, 20 December, 1921

CHALET DES SAPINS | MONTANA-SUR-SIERRE | VALAIS
20 xii 1921

Dear Mr Pinker,

I return herewith the agreement duly signed. It seems quite satisfactory. Thank you for your letter respecting the other stories. Yes, I quite understand why *The Garden Party* cannot be placed. I am hoping to send you some more stories in the course of the next few weeks.

Yours sincerely
Katherine Mansfield

P.S. Would you please ask Mr Knopf if I may *have proofs*.

MS Newberry.

To Thomas and Bessie Moult,[1] 20 December 1921

[Chalet des Sapins, Montana-sur-Sierre]
20 December 1921

I cannot let Christmas come without sending you both my love and greetings. I love Christmas . . . In that other world where wishes are laws, there would be a great shining wreath of holly on the door knocker, lights at all the windows, and a real party going on inside. We meet in the hall and warmly re-clasp hands. Good Heavens! *I'm* not above a tree, coloured candles and crackers – are you? Wait. We shall have it all – or something better! I will never despair of a real gay meeting, one of these days, for us all. It's always only an accident that the day is not fine, that one happens for the moment to be under an umbrella. It will all flash and sparkle, I truly *believe* that, sooner than we expect. – The very fact that we rebel at our little terms of imprisonment is proof that freedom is our real element.

MS lacking, *LKM* II. 166.

---

[1] Thomas Moult (d. 1974). From a humble background in Manchester, he was involved in social work with boys' clubs and prison work as well as being a minor poet and novelist, sports journalist, lecturer, biographer, critic, and anthologist. He and KM had corresponded since 1912, but had not met until 1918. With his wife Bessie he has stayed for a few days at Portland Villas in August 1920. In 'Katherine Mansfield as I Knew Her', *TP's Weekly*, 1 Dec. 1928, reviewing *LKM*, Moult noted: 'I have many letters of hers that have not been published, and in one she spoke of living as though every day were her last day':

My gesture of love is always a gesture of farewell. The beauty of the world is a kind of anguish; it is almost too much to bear. It is such a strange way to live; it is like being a child again – but all glorified. The light shakes through the grass, and the wind whispers over, and one's heart trembles. A new flower appears in my garden. How has it come there, so silently? But when we have looked at each other I feel we understand.

But it is the silence which is so different. It's as though the silence became your old nurse who said: 'Very well, you may play a little longer if you are so happy and not tired (tired!), but *remember I have called you.*' But the sun goes down so fast, so terribly fast. Now it is shining through the topmost branches of the thinning tree – now there is only a rim of gold to the hill.

Moult quotes an extract from another letter which he does not date (neither letter seems to have survived):

Why don't we live nearer one another? I should like to feel that you two walked into my house very often – that if I made one kind of jam and you another we exchanged as a matter of course. And not only jam., but all kinds of good things, good news and dear people and poems and stories. I wish – do you? – there was more direct life flowing through a few of us – there is too much clasping of hands across a void. But after all, that is better than nothing. And when I have my small house in Sussex you will both have to come for a long holiday. . . . If Bessie were here now she should have my jar of marigolds as a tribute to her dusky hair.

Moult's article concluded: 'But the small house in Sussex and the holiday were never to come. Soon she wrote that she was no better. On the contrary, she confided (for the first time) "the barriers are down." '

To S. S. Koteliansky, [c.20 December 1921]

CHALET DES SAPINS | MONTANA SUR SIERRE | VALAIS

Koteliansky,

I want to write to you at this time in memory of that other Christmas when Lawrence gave his party in the top room of Elsie Murray's cottage.[1] Thank you again for the Vienna Café chocolates and the cigarettes. I see the boxes now. But far more plainly I see *you*, as if I could put out my hand and touch your breast.

Wasn't Lawrence awfully nice that night. Ah, one must always *love* Lawrence for his 'being'. I could love Frieda too, tonight, in her Bavarian dress, with her face flushed as though she had been crying about the 'children'.[2] It is a pity that all things must pass. And how strange it is, how in spite of everything, there are certain people, like Lawrence, who remain in one's life for ever, and others who are forever shadowy.

You, for instance, are part of my life like that. One might say 'immortal'. I mean, just supposing there were immortality it would not be at all strange if suddenly a door opened and we met and sat down to drink tea. Thus it will always be with me. It is no idle pretence. If it is in the least atom a comfort to you to know there is one who loves you and thinks of you (without a shadow of responsibility involved or of anything that is not perfectly 'simple') please remember you have

For ever
                Katherine.

And no answer is required, dear friend. I *mean* that.

MS BL. Dickinson, 89–90.

1 When KM and Murry lived at Rose Tree Cottage, Great Missenden, at the end of 1914, and the Lawrences a few miles away at Chesham.

2 When KM first knew the Lawrences in 1913, Frieda was given to lamenting her separation from her children by Ernest Weekley, professor of French at Nottingham University, after she eloped with Lawrence in May 1912.

To Ottoline Morrell, [c.20 December 1921]

CHALET DES SAPINS | MONTANA-SUR-SIERRE | VALAIS

Dearest Ottoline,

I have just found the letter I wrote you on the first of November. I would send it you as a proof of good faith but I reread it. Grim thing to do – isn't it? There is a kind of fixed smile on old letters which reminds one of the bridling look of old photographs. So its torn up and I begin again.

I don't know what happens to Time here. It seems to become shorter and shorter; to whisk round the corners, to become all tail, all Saturday to Monday. This must sound absurd coming from so remote a spot as our mountain peaks. But there it is. We write, we read, M. goes off with his skates, I go for a walk through my field glasses and another day is over. This place makes one work. Perhaps its the result of living among mountains; one must bring forth a mouse or be overwhelmed.

If climate were everything, then Montana must be very near Heaven. The sun shines and shines. Its cold in the shade, but out of it it is hot enough for a hat and a parasol – far and away hotter than the S. of France, and windless. All the streams are solid little streams of ice, there are thin patches of snow, like linen drying, on the fields. The sky is high, transparent, with marvellous sunsets. And when the moon rises & I look out of my window down into the valley full of clouds its like looking out of the Ark while it bobbed above the flood.

But all the same I shall never get over my first hatred of the *Swiss*. They are the same everywhere. Ugly, dull, solid lumps, with a passion divided between pigs and foreigners. Foreigners are what they prefer to gorge themselves with but pigs will serve. As to their ankles – they fill me with a kind of anguish. I should have an ankle complex if I lived in Switzerland long. But one never lives anywhere *long* . . .

I wonder if you are going to spend the winter in England? Everybody that one used to know seems to have disappeared. But I suppose they are really all there just as of yore. It is nice to know B. R. is so happy – with an infant Conrad, too! How amazing. I so looked forward to his Chinese sketches in the Nation, but I wish he told one more of the lakes and mountains. I could dispense with Mrs Dewey altogether if I knew the trees were shaped like umbrellas. I was thankful and fell greedily upon the little bonfires he *did* mention[1] But oh, when people have seen marvels, I wish they would tell of them!

M. and I are reading Jane Austen in the evenings. With delight. 'Emma' is really a perfect book – don't you feel? I enjoy every page. I cant have enough of Miss Bates or Mr Woodhouse's gruel[2] or that charming Mr Knightley. Its such an exquisite comfort to escape from the modern novels I have been forcibly reading. Wretched affairs! I do ask for something that I can't hand on to my dog to be read by him with relish and much tail thumping. This fascinated pursuit of the sex adventure is beyond words boring! I am so bored by sex quâ sex, by the gay dog sniffing round the prostitutes bedroom or by the ultra modern snigger – worse still – that I could die – at least.

It has turned me to Proust however at last. I have been pretending to have read Proust for years but this autumn M. and I both took the plunge. I certainly think he is by far the most interesting living writer. He is fascinating! Its a comfort to have someone whom one can so tremendously admire. It is horrible to feel so out of touch with one's time as I do nowadays – almost frightening.

Have you read Aldous' novel?[3] I have seen it reviewed but that is all. Is it very good? And did you see "Vera" by my cousin Elizabeth. I thought it far and away her best book (though I never said so to Sidney Waterlow. What he meant by saying he had seen me I cant imagine. It is years since I set eyes on him.)

Oh, how nice it would be to talk – really at one's ease – have a long talk with you in your little room. There are so many things I should love to hear. One begins to feel *too* much of an exile.

I am so glad you liked M's poems. They were very heavily sat on. But he is bursting into new books, all the same. His novel is to be published in the spring and two other tomes as well. My infant is to lie in Constable's bosom until after the New Year. I have been longing all this last week to snatch it away and bury it. Its not half good enough! I can't bear to think about it.

But this letter must end. Dearest Ottoline, if you would write to us, your letter would be read so ardently. Please don't punish me for not having written for so long. There are other reasons, too, for my silence – but they are the ancient eternal reasons – fatigue beyond words – *ill health*. One hardly dares mention it again.

I think of you more often than I can say. I wish – how I wish – but thats useless. I am always your warmly loving

Katherine.

MS Texas *LKM* II. 158–9. Cited *Exhibition*, 48.

¹ Bertrand Russell wrote three articles on 'Modern China' for the *Nation and the Athenaeum*: 'The Feast and the Eclipse', published on 14 Dec.; 'Chinese Ethics', on 21 Dec.; 'Chinese Amusements', on 28 Dec. In the first essay he spoke of Mrs Alice Dewey, the wife of the American philosopher John Dewey, both of whom accompanied him on the trip, advising the Chinese on education. Russell also related how 'When I left the banquet to go on board the boat on which I was leaving Changsha, it happened that an eclipse of the moon was in progress. As in the earliest annals of Chinese history, the streets were full of people beating gongs to frighten away the Heavenly Dog who was supposed to be trying to eat up the moon; little bonfires were being lit everywhere to rekindle the moon's light by sympathetic magic.'

² Miss Bates is a worthy but tiresome woman in Jane Austen's *Emma* (1816). Emma Woodhouse's father is a kindly hypochondriac.

³ KM was unaware that Aldous Huxley's *Crome Yellow* (1921) satirized Lady Ottoline herself, as well as Garsington Manor, where he had frequently been a guest.

To Dorothy Brett, [22 December 1921]

[Chalet des Sapins, Montana-sur-Sierre]

Brett dearest

I reply immediately. Yes I feel certain that Marie Loo had brilliancy. And don't think I am a stickler for the old laws of technique, as such. I am not. But I still cant see how you simplify a figure and leave the face out of the simplification. Its not that the face is "literary", it doesn't "tell a story" (anymore than a face justifiably in painting *does*) but that is the effect it gives when joined on to the stiff little body. It seems to float in the air, not to belong. And the trees in the background – of course one sees practically nothing of them in a photograph. They look weak stemmed, somehow. I don't know *why* I look at them. If I didn't know they had meant much to you I shouldn't see them but I cant see their part in the design.

I sympathise beyond words with your desire to discover, to explore, with your impatience at last with flower pieces. I am sure you are absolutely right and that its the only way one can ever be satisfied completely with what one is doing. I mean your whole mind, all your sensibility and intelligence must be at work and a little bit over. It seems to me the only way I can express that sympathy for you is by being as dead honest as I can be; risking your being offended or hurt. You know my opinion is only a personal opinion. But I give it to you – not quite easily – because for all we may think or believe – it is terribly hard to be honest where our hearts are involved!

But listen – Brett! This is very serious. You may depend on my *sympathy*. You may say whatever you like to me – and its safe. I mean that. But don't for Heavens sake paint something for me to show you can do it, ma chère. What earthly use would it be if you don't care to do it? Ill send you a story called 'A Tear in the Eye of a Violet' by Katherine Florence Barclay[1] Mansfield as a small return if you do.

Im very interested by what you say about 'Vera'. Wasn't the *end* extraordinarily good. It would have been so easy to miss it; she carried it right through. I admired the end most, I think. Have you ever known a Wemyss? Oh my dear, they are *very* plentiful! Few men are without a touch. And I certainly believe that husbands & wives talk like that. Lord yes. You are so very superior, Miss, in saying half an hour would be sufficient. But how is one to escape? And also, though it may be "drivel" in cold blood, it IS incredible the follies and foolishness we can bear if we think we are in love. Not that I can stand the Wemyss 'brand'. No. But I can perfectly comprehend Lucy standing it.[2] I dont think I agree about Lucy, either. She could not understand her father's *intellect* but she had a sense of humour (except where her beloved was concerned). She certainly had her own opinions and the aunt was very sodden at the funeral because of the *ghastly* effect of funerals! They make the hardest of us melt and gush. But all the same I think your criticism is awfully good of the Aunt, of the whole book in fact. Only one thing, my hand on my heart, I would swear to. Never *could* Elizabeth be influenced by me. If you knew how she would scorn the notion, how impossible it would be for her. There is a kind of turn in our sentences which is alike but that is because we are worms of the same family. But that is all.

— — About Paris. I have now received the doctor's address from the secretary of the Institute & have written him again today. If I hear I will let you know. It seems more hopeful now that I send direct. I am still in bed and dear knows when I shall be out. A reply from Manoukhin would be the only thing, I think. (I am a bit disheartened to be *back here* again with all the old paraphernalia of trays and hot bottils. Accursèd disease!) I am so glad to know what you are doing at Christmas. I hope you will be happy. I shall see you all in my mind's eye & wish I were there. Good Heavens! Is it really warm? Why is it my fate to always find the cold corner. If I go to a hot climate it freezes, if to a cold it becomes an arctic zone. I read of primroses in the paper. Primroses! Oh, what wouldn't I give for some flowers. Oh Brett – this longing for flowers. I *crave* them. I think of them – of the feeling of tulips stems and petals, of the touch of violets and the light on marigolds & the smell of wall flowers. No, it does not bear writing about. I could kiss the earth that bears flowers. Alas, I love them far TOO much!

It is ages since I have heard of Virginia. I thought she would have a new book out this winter. Perhaps it will come in the spring.[3] I can see her in that dress. She is a lovely creature in her way.

I had a laugh over Sullivan's Canadian. Did he stipulate she must be a "fighting" woman – guaranteed to have fought Red Indians? I am sure she will expect Sullivan to provide her with a Red Indian or two from time to time. But perhaps it won't be too difficult. But its very funny.

Goodbye for now. I send my loves to all who are at your hearth.

Ever
Tig.

MS Newberry. *LKM* II. 166-7.

[1] Florence L. Barclay wrote several religious novels, including *The Rosary* (1909) and *The Golden Censer* (1914), whose Preface declared: 'This little book has been written . . . as the result of much personal experience of the necessity for a careful study of Holy Scriptures, on the important matter of intercessory prayer.'

[2] Ernest Wemyss, a public figure of some eminence, meets his new young wife, Lucy, the day of her father's funeral and a fortnight after the suicide of his former wife, Vera. Lucy's maiden aunt is the only woman who stands up to Wemyss, whose treatment of his wife alternates between bullying and affectionate condescension.

[3] Virginia Woolf's *Jacob's Room* was published in 1922.

To S. S. Koteliansky, [23 December 1921]

[Chalet des Sapins, Montana-sur-Sierre]

I heard from M. today. A good letter – *very*. As soon as I am well enough to get up I shall go to Paris. He says the treatment takes 15 weeks if one is not much advanced. But no matter. It is fearfully exciting to have heard!

K.

Picture postcard BL. *LKM* II. 167–8.

To Anne Drey, 24 December 1921

CHALET DES SAPINS | MONTANA-SUR-SIERRE | VALAIS

Christmas Eve.

Darling precious Anne,

Suddenly, this afternoon, as I was thinking of you there flashed across my inward eye a beautiful poppy that we stood looking at in the garden of the Headland Hotel, Looe.[1] Do you remember that marvellous black sheen at the base of the petal and the big purplish centre? Then that took me back to our improvised café – just the same table with a bottle on it and ourselves out of space and time . . . for the moment! And from that I began to think of your très blue eyes that I love so and your neck, and the comb you wore in your hair the last time you dined with us and a pink pinny you had on the first time I ever saw you in the studio in Paris. These things are not the whole of my Anne, but they are signs and tokens of her and for them and for a thousand others what wouldn't I give at this moment to put my arms round her and give her a small squeeze!

Well, darling woman, even at this distance its a joy to know that you are you, and I am thankful that we are walking the earth at the same time. I never turn in your direction without giving you an invisible hail. You are one of those rare beings my dear that one praises Life for. Bless you and David this Christmas and a Merry Merry Nouvelle Année to you both. Please give him a butterfly kiss from me and blow softly down his neck. Why cant I come and see! I am certain there is not one of your friends who would appreciate him more than I could. But I still pin my faith on to a star (I expect David thinks that quite an ordinary feat) and believe that we shall all sit down together under a flowery tree somewhere and laugh.

How did you spend the summer? Did you get much work done? But I musn't begin asking questions. Its a bother having to answer them. But *chère* I shall be in Paris, I hope, from May on this year. Will you by any chance be there? I am going on a preliminary visit almost at once to see a specialist there – a *Russian* & to have some teeth pulled out and pulled in again. Then I come back here to save pennies for my flight in May.

I believe this Russian cures people with my complaint. He sounds wonderful.

Its so long since I have heard of any of the *old set*. Where are they? New friends are not – never can be the same, and all mine seem to be people I know as a writer not as a common garden human being. Whether they care passionately for the smell of tangerines or not I haven't the least idea. I cant really care for people who are cut off at the head. I like them to exist as far as their hearts *au moins!* Dont ever come to Switzerland Anne. Its all *scenery*. One [can] get the same in a Mountain Railway at 6d a go and get off after the last bumping. But the Swiss! The size of their ankles! Their passion for pigs and for cutting down trees. They are always cutting down trees and as the tree falls the house frau rushes out of the kitchen to see waving a pig knife and shouting a joyful *voilà!* I believe they are full of virtue, but virtue is a bad boisson to be *full* of.

This is serious, though. I wanted to send you a Christmas present. I cant. In the first place I am au lit with an attack of congestion and Murry swerves past *all* shops even if there were shops to swerve by here. So I must put it off & content myself with a cuckoo bird for David. It *is* only postponed. And will you give my love to Drey. It is so long since I heard from him that he may have forgotten me. Recall me — will you, Anne! "Cette petite personne avec les yeux comme les boutons de bottines . . . tu sais" – "That will bring me back. Id awfully like to see Drey again. Je lui serre la main bien cordialement.

For the rest – when you have the time can I have un mot to know you are well and that all goes?

Oh, Anne, do you see Horace Holley's great Tome on Bahaism is produced.[2] I expect it is very powerful! I note that Bertha sells slips, tuniques and cossaques at a li'l shop in New York. It being the pantomime season I shall make the joke . . . I expect they are *all slips*.

Have you heard how brulee Lascelles was to the Queen? Pinched her little Mary.[3] Perhaps that joke is très vieux in London. Ones sense of humour gets very keen on mountain tops –

Fare well, dear precious Anne. May good fortune fall ever deeper in love with thee.

I am always your devoted

Katherine.

MS ATL, *LKM* II. 168–9.

1 Where KM stayed July–Aug. 1918.
2 Horace Holley, *Bahai: The Spirit of the Age* (1921).
3 Henry George Lascelles, 6th Earl of Harewood (1882–1947), after a brief political career and distinguished war service, married in Feb. 1922 Princess Mary, only daughter of King George V and Queen Mary.

To Elizabeth, Countess Russell, [c.24 December 1921]

Chalet des Sapins | Montana-sur-Sierre | Valais.

Dear Elizabeth,

I must catch at the flying heels of this old year and wish you a Happy New One. I do, with all my heart. May it be rich in Blessings. Do you *like* to know you are loved, Elizabeth. If you do, think of me as a small fire, glowing, at a distance. But a self-feeding fire that needs no attention, even though it does leap for joy when you stretch forth your small, supple hand.

Your letter came this afternoon. There is something wrong with life that a man like Sydney should die and others be left to go their useless ways. If only one could believe in a kind God who moved in a mysterious way – on purpose! It does not bear writing about . . . But one *thinks* and *feels*, all the same.

It is no longer so dreadfully cold. Snow has fallen to-day, but only a sprinkle. We are longing for it to really begin. The F.O., [Faithful One] is positive all will be white for Christmas. But she has of course, a Christmas complex. She is a living tree already and never comes into my room without another candle or coloured ball or glass bird to show me. She still believes in Santa Claus *firmly* and the whole house rustles with tissue paper and I suspect even the gentle Ernestine of gambolling on the ground floor. It's awfully difficult to be adequate; my sentimental part is for her. I know she will have crackers for John to pull with her at dinner. They will dine tête-à-tête for I am cast away again, prone in my cursed bed with a touch of congestion. I don't mind for myself as much as I do for John. I am no sort of a woman for a young man of 33 to be tied to. It is devilish luck for him.

Oh, we had *such* a Christmas letter from Ma Maxwell. Except for the Divorce things have turned out "very nicely." Her dear son Jack's wife is expecting her first little one any moment now and she is there to catch it. She is "helping the young folk" prepare the nest for "the advent." I am very grateful for Mrs. Maxwell.

We are still reading Jane. Let us talk about her when you come. I believe John enjoys her more than I do. The engagements put him in a positive flutter. Innocent male! They come as a *surprise* to him. Farewell. When I think of the Chalet Soleil now there is a difference. There is a *stirring* now that January is near.

Yours ever,
Katherine.

We simply *adored* the joke about little Mary. Jokes at [words missing] go on and on resounding. John immediately walked out to find Doctor H. [Hudson] to impart it. Doctor H. will *never* get over it.

TC Huntington.

To Michael Sadler, 25 December 1921

CHALET DES SAPINS | MONTANA-SUR-SIERRE | VALAIS
25 XII 1921

Dear Michael Sadler,

If you think a small limited edition of the Garden Party would sell – then I think the idea an excellent one. My only doubt is whether the small public who read my last book wouldn't buy the limited edition and there'd be no one left to buy the other!

Should you decide, however, to print one I imagine the Oxford book-sellers might dispose of some copies.

I hope you are having a Happy Christmas & that you are going to have a Happy New Year.

Yours ever
Katherine Mansfield.

MS Targ.

To Sydney Schiff, 25 December 1921

CHALET DES SAPINS | MONTANA-SUR-SIERRE | VALAIS
25 XII 1921

Sydney

This is just a note – not a letter. My letters to you – the ones that remain unwritten – would fill volumes. But I feel you know that.

I want to tell you something. It is important. It is about your letter to Murry. I don't, personally, believe in *chance*. God knows I dont *see* the plan; I dont see what the 'authors' are driving at. But it does seem to me always more and more positive that a design there *is*. And there is a moment which is the perfect moment. But so often, until it has passed by we dont see it. We only see what we have missed. All is in retrospect. What this all leads up to is one of those moments marvellously realised, marvellously fulfilled was when you wrote to Murry. He *needed* your letter and you gave it to him. *You know* how Murry craves friends. But the men whom he knows are too . . . frightened . . . to ever show him more than a kind of head sympathy, which is very little use to him at all. But that precious sense of security that real friendship gives he has asked for in vain until unasked, you gave it him. I believe that you and I think alike about Murry, deep down, deep down. He was in a mood of awful depression just then. I could not help him. He wanted someone who was not K.M. . . . And I am sure men need men in a way few women understand . . . Well, the simple truth is Sydney, that your comprehension and your gen-erosity are beautiful. One loves you for your gifts.

I have chosen today to write because Manoukhine has come a great deal nearer. He has told me that if I go to Paris he will treat me by his new method and there is the word *guerison* shining in his letter. I believe every word of it; I believe in him implicitly. As soon as I am out of bed (the cold has been *too* cold) Jones will pack the boxes and I shall go to see him and arrange to return to him in May. I want to spend the winter here. But in May I shall go to Paris for the course of treatment which takes 15 weeks. (Manoukhine is not only a doctor. He is a whole new stage on the journey. I hardly know why.) His treatment consists of applications of the Rayons X.

One word I must say about Joyce. Having reread the Portrait it seems to me on the whole awfully *good*. We are going to buy 'Ulysses'. But Joyce is (if only Pound didn't think so, too) immensely important. Some time ago I found something so repellant in his work that it was difficult to read it. It shocks me to come upon words, expressions and so on that Id shrink from in life. But now it seems to me the *new novel*, the seeking after Truth is so by far and away the most important thing that one must conquer all minor aversions. They are unworthy.

Christmas – in cold blood – is not an attractive fête. And the English papers bulging with turkeys are disgusting. Its an awful offence to our intelligence to be served with these pages and pages about Father Christmas and "Pulling a Cracker with my Kind Daddy".

Dear Jones, of course, *revels* in it all. The whole house rustles with tissue paper. As to the gentle Ernestine she is quite overcome and there sounds a kind of elephantine gambolling from the kitchen.

But I do wish you and dearest Violet a Happy New Year. *That* is different.

With love from us both
Ever

K.M.

Forgive this disjointed letter. It is written in bed – prone.

MS BL. *LKM* II. 171.

To Anne Drey, [26 December 1921]

CHALET DES SAPINS | MONTANA-SUR-SIERRE | VALAIS
Well
Darling Anne
    Words fail me. The parcil came today. It had been detained by the Customs, but it arrived 'intacte comme un bébé' & really when I took

out that exquisite garment I felt that wherever you were, you wonderful woman, you must have felt my thrill. It is all, colour, shape, design, per-fume, perfect. Anne, will you please realise how I appreciate *every stitch.* I have looked and looked, really fed on those colours. I felt that in two minutes, so radiant was the little garment it would flap its sleeves and begin to sing. The yellow, ma chère, the blue, ma chère, the beads, the ribbon – the lining – oh dear, I could say a separate prayer to you for each separate piece.

But nothing has escaped my eye, Anne. I feel that this little coat like everything that your hands touch has a life of its own and its precious to me.

Please let me put my arms round you & give you the biggest hug for it. "David, isn't she a wonder! Dont we agree about her! What other human being would send such a present?"

In fact, Ive got it on this minute and I feel transported.

Bless you, precious woman –

Katherine.

I wrote to you in Paris. But Im not sure whether I put the right address – *rue Odessa.*

MS ATL.

To Dorothy Brett, 26 December 1921

[Chalet des Sapins | Montana-sur-Sierre]
Boxing Day

Dearest Brett,

Your parcils and your letters came today and my bed turned into a corner of Marshalls[1] – such a lovely one. Little O-T-Kosey-San sat against the lilac wall and the hankies and ribbons lay on a very gay wooly quilt. Thank you over and over. I feel I want to wave each of the hankies separately in silent greeting and to send this letter by a carrier pigeon with the three ribbons dangling from its little red feet. Please feel how I appreciate ribbon, too, how they all added to the festa. There was one the green which is really such a heavenly colour that one can hardly believe in it, but all are delicious . . . But what a terrific pace our parcels seem to have come flying at. I had barely sent my petty over the net when back came the letter. O-T-Kosey-San will be in daily use. She is very decorative.

Brett I must speak of this new photograph at once. It is extraordinary *how* different it is to the other. In fact it is almost frightening to know what a photograph can do. Now I do see a design that I simply did not see before. I mean I see a *movement* which starts at the tip of the parasol, touches the tip of Marie Loos head, goes round the doll and ends by almost touching with a light brush tip the dog & the black babby, before it "disappears" (if you know what I mean) behind that dark tree. One sees too, for the first time, the importance of the pyramidal shadow below the parasol and a kind of *fluid* beauty – *flowing* beauty in the grass. I seem to see what you are getting at – the sudden arrest, poise, *moment captured* of the figure in a flowing shade and sunlight world. To put it in another way, the décor was there and you have superimposed Marie Loo on it, or she has superimposed herself *for* you. Id give a great deal to see this picture in the flesh. The legs do still worry me. But the other photograph didn't do it anything like justice, my dear; it is *intensely* interesting, and the doll an echo of the Marie Loo design – M.L. in very little – completing her like a small shadow, is *excellent*. Yes, its easy to see why you are not content with flowers . . . I hope all this means something. Isn't it a curse one cant speak instead of write.

Yesterday I heard from Manouhkine. As soon as I am up again and can get into a train into a train I go. After that all is uncertain. Most likely I shall come back here having seen him until May and then strike camp seriously and make for Paris for the treatment. It takes at least four months. But first I must see him and also go to a dentist in Paris & get my teeth pulled out and in. The treatment is very expensive – thats another reason why I want to wait until May. I must make money to pay for it. It is 300 francs a *time*! And I shall need about 30 times – not to mention hotel bills and very good food which one has to eat all the time one is being treated. And I have to take the Mountain with me – so its always two to be paid for. This means work with a vengeance. I shall manage it, though, and if I emerge with *nothing* and health I shall be so rich, so awfully rich that I will treat everybody I meet to beaming smiles, at any rate.

The snow is here at last and still falling. It is deathly cold. But I never have a closed window, dearest. I lived out of doors on my balcony when I was up.

I must work. Goodbye for now. My mind is dressed like a ship at a regatta with little coloured hanky flags. Thanks – thanks again dearest for being who you are.

Ever
Tig

MS Newberry.

[1] Marshall & Snelgrove, a department store on Oxford Street.

To Richard Murry, [c.26 December 1921]

[Chalet des Sapins, Montana-sur-Sierre]

Richard

This letter is a very late lark indeed. It is meant to be for Christmas. Please read it before the New Year, and forgive your erring sister. Thanks most awfully for mine. The size of the pudding put heart into us. Heaven forbid Wingley should eat any for he is enormous already. We weighed him the other day. He was over 12 lbs. You should have seen him sitting in the scales, with a very smug cat -in-a-bastick expres-sion . . .

Well, Richard, how are you, I wonder? How is the world? Space? Universe? It begins to seem long since I was in England. Perhaps you are quite changed, with moustaches and a collar I have never seen before. *We* are the same except that our heads are always in the air – little Johnnies head in air – looking for the snow. Which won't fall and won't fall. Ice – we can 'do' you as much ice as you like – thick *and clear*, Sir. But ice is only half the fun. However, everybody says it must fall soon so I suppose we haven't long to wait.

It has been shockingly cold here. There are days when one is in the clouds for hours and that damp, heavy strange cold is like nothing on earth. Then just Montana clears at night and looking out of my window on to the milk white valley is like looking out of the Ark when it rested on Mount Lebanon[1] (wasn't it?) I feel like a daughter of Noah, but not one of the Daily News ones.

You know Richard I feel this next year 1922 is going to be a good one. Better than the ones that went before. There is a kind of stirring when one thinks of it, the feeling that one has on a late March night when the wind is west. Does that seem nonsense to you? I want it to be good for all of us, of course, so that this time next year here we are – rich in happiness, fat in blessings. Jack shall have a crown, you a small sceptre. Whats left for me? There is sure to be something small going. Happy Xmas, dear old Boy. A Happy New Year. With much love from Katherine.

MS R. Murry. *Adam* 370-5, 30.

[1] The Ark came to rest on the mountains of Ararat (see Gen. 8: 4).

To Ottoline Morrell, 27 December 1921

CHALET DES SAPINS | MONTANA-SUR-SIERRE | VALAIS
27 XII 1921

Dearest Ottoline,

Isn't it astonishing how a scent can carry one back – – – When I opened your envelope the delicious strange perfume quite overwhelmed me – and the queer thing was what it took me to was walking out into the air after having heard the Balalaika orchestra.[1] It was a night in spring – wasn't it? I know I felt that we had shared something wonderful, and that just for that moment we were walking the earth together and it was *happiness*.

How lovely the little handkerchiefs are with the swans sailing round them. They arrived on Christmas Day its very self too. You know how one watches for that Christmas post at this distance. I was in bed too which made my longing even more fearful. I had to wait until someone crept up the stairs instead of lurking at the door. I really feel I could write an entire book with each chapter beginning "The post did not come that day" *or* "That morning the post was late". And I at least would thrill and shiver with the horror of it. Its awful to spend *such* emotions on postmen! But there it is.

We had a 'proper' Christmas – even to a Tree, thanks to the Mountain who revels in such things and would like all the year to be December. The house whispered with tissue paper for days, a pudding appeared out of the bosom of the air and the sight of *that* fired even my gentle Ernestine who began, from the sounds, to gambol on the ground floor and toss the iron rings of the stove on to the floor. The crackers however would not pull which cast a little gloom over M. who relishes crackers and the mottoes which were German were very depressing: "Mädchen moch ich Frau dir sehn." I am glad it is all over – but the traces, the signs remain for a long time . . .

Dearest Ottoline, I think of you in your little room. How well I know that rapture that comes sometimes when one is alone. I think perhaps it is the greatest joy of all. If only it would stay – if only one might live like that, always. I sometimes think that if one were well there is no reason why it should ever go. But that is nonsense. The feeling I mean is . . . its as though the barriers were down and you stepped into another world where even the silence *lives* and you are accepted, you are received as part of everything. Nothing is hidden. And there is that precious sense of awareness . . . But speaking of this reminds me instantly of DeLaMare, who understands it so perfectly. Have you see his new book of poems *The Veil?*[2] I have just ordered it. I do hope you will see it. Do you know him? He is one of the people whom I have most enjoyed meeting in Life. There is *no one* like him.

The snow has fallen at last, here. It looks beautiful. It feels desperately cold. I have been in bed . . . lately . . . and only see the world from my window. As soon as I can get up I am going to Paris to see a new man there – a Russian who claims to completely cure this disease with applications of X rays. I believe him, absolutely, (as one does, you know) and I dream at night that I am climbing hills covered with little rose bushes and jumping across streams. Will it all come true, I wonder?

Do tell me how you are – when you have time. I wish I knew that you were really better. Do you believe at all in people like Coué,[3] the auto-suggestion man? If my Russian fails me I shall try him. It becomes really *comic* like something out of Rabelais – there ought to be pages & pages beginning "And *then* she tried . . ."

We are still reading Jane Austen. M. falls in love with all the heroines, even with Fanny Price[4] but I should be content to walk in the shrubbery with Mr Knightley. I remain faithful to him. Its greater fun for M. than for me, for all the engagements come as a *complete surprise* to him. He almost swoons with anxiety when Mr D. follows Eliza's father into the library and demands her hand, and once it is all happily settled and a fortune of ten thousand a year bestowed upon them his relief is extreme.[5] Poor M! If I were really a generous creature I would make him a widow so that he could have all this himself from the very beginning.

A Happy New Year, a New Year of lovely weather, dearest Ottoline. With warm love from

Katherine.

MS Texas. *LKM* II. 169.

[1] In her memoir 'K. M.' Lady Ottoline recalled their attending 'at a time when the War was a black unhappy cloud over life . . . a Rusian "Balaika" [sic] concert at the Grafton Gallery' *Exhibition*, 12.

[2] Published in 1921.

[3] Emile Coué (1857–1926) wrote several works, and took well-known courses on self-mastery through auto-suggestion, including, in 1921, *La maîtrise de soi même par l'autosuggestion consciente*.

[4] Fanny Price, the timid and impecunious heroine of *Mansfield Park* (1814).

[5] Fitzwilliam Darcy, the aristocratic landowner who overcomes Elizabeth Bennet's 'prejudice' and succeeds in winning her affection, in Jane Austen's *Pride and Prejudice* (1813).

To Raymond Drey,[1] 27 December 1921

CHALET DES SAPINS | MONTANA-SUR-SIERRE | VALAIS

27 xii 1921

My dear Drey,

I cant say what a pleasure it was to receive on Xmas day its very self a letter from you with the perfectly delightful enclosures. I had written to Anne just the day before; it seemed as though my letter had got there by carrier pigeon and brought the answer back. The little case is most precious for what it contained – the picture of David. My dear Drey what a shockingly proud man you must be! I should do no more work. I should just look at him, puff out my ches' and say to the passers by "il est à nous."

The butler impressed me terribly. At this height and among these mountains one scarcely dare think of butlers. My one domestic, the gentle Ernestine, who weighs about 14 stone, bounds up and down the stairs like a playful heifer and bursts into a strange terrible singing whenever she hears a pig being killed, is civilizations away from butlers. When I come to see you I expect the second footman to take my umbrella and I shall curtsy to Anne and present a bouquet. You are very grand *but* not as grand as Willy.² His party must have been a very powerful affair, Drey. Talk about numbered cloakroom tickets. Willy will have to have them for his wives, next time. He will be a terribly busy man in Heaven. I am sure the restitution of conjugal rights is a spécialité de la maison, there.

My cat has just leapt on to my bed and begun to clean his face and his two little chimneys. Its a queer thing. He started life in a humble way like One greater than he – he was born in a stable and was just an ordinary little black & white kitten. But since he came here he has turned into a real Persian with an enormous ruff and feathers on his legs. I suppose it is the cold. The Swiss of course, dont keep cats. They are frightened a cat might eat the old cabbage stalk they are saving up for the baby to cut its teeth on. They are a thrifty race.

By the way I suppose you do not know the address of a first chop dentist in Paris? I have to go to Paris very soon and while I am there I want to put my head into the jaws of a really good painless modern man. Is there such an one? If you could send me a card with his name and address I would be awfully grateful. Are you wondering why I ask you? I have a feeling you know all these things . . . I am going as soon as my feet are on the earth again, for my teeth are falling like autumn leaves. They have very large wooden buns here for tea with nails in them and powdered glass on exprès pour les anglais. I defy anyone to grind them to powder without an 'accident'.

A Happy New Year to you – you do know how I 'appreciated' your letter? Thanks again dear Drey.

With love from
K.M.

MS ATL. *LKM* II. 169–70.

¹ Raymond Drey (1885–1976) had married KM's close friend Anne Rice in 1913. A theatre and art critic, he had written for the *Athenaeum*.
² Possibly the novelist W. L. George, known to his friends as 'Willy', who had introduced KM to Murry in late 1911. (See *CLKM*, I, 109, 178.)

To Sydney Schiff [31 December 1921]
[Chalet des Sapins | Montana-sur-Sierre]
The same evening.

My dear Sydney

I answer your letter, as you suggest, immediately. Yes, I used the word friendship too lightly. I hang my head. It was *badly* done and you were right to rebuke me – I do understand. I wince, yes I confess its painful to me to read what you write at the bottom of the second page "I have not got any friends at all", and the sentences that follow. At the same time I value the remark immensely. There is a deep separateness in me which responds to it, even though I am for ever without a complete complement. But its a strange truth that the fact of you and Violet is not only a joy, its an extraordinary consolation to believe in you and in her as one does. (Violet dearest, speak to me just one moment, will you? I feel sometimes diffident of speaking to you directly. I feel there are so many others near you who claim your attention. I count on Sydney telling you whatever there is to tell. No, the truth is nearer. I write to you and to him. But you know that.) I agree absolutely with what you say when you define the forces that go to make friendship and the part played by knowledge. The more one thinks of the image of knowledge as clothing the more valuable it becomes. It is one of the images that delight the mind so much that almost apart from one's *self* one's mind goes on receiving it, turning it to the light, trying it, experimenting with it. Or that is what my mind has been doing . . . proving the truth of it mathematically speaking.

I should like to have friends, I confess. I do not suppose I ever shall. But there have been moments when I have realised what friendship might be. Rare moments, but never forgotten. I remember once talking it over with Lawrence and he said "We must swear a solemn pact of friendship. Friendship is as binding, as solemn as marriage. We take each other for life, through everything – for ever. But it is not enough to say we will do it. We must *swear*." At the time I was impatient with him. I thought it extravagant – fanatic. But when one considers what this world is like I understand perfectly why L. (especially being L.) made such claims . . . I think, myself, it is Pride which makes friendship most diffi-cult. To submit, to bow down to the other is not easy, but it must be done if one is to really understand the being of the other. Friendship isn't *merging*. One doesn't thereupon become a shadow & one remain a sub-stance. Yes, it is terribly solemn – frightening, even.

Please do not think I am all for Joyce. I am *not*. In the past I was unfair to him and to atone for my stupidity I want to be fairer now than I really feel . . . I agree that it is not all art. I would go further. Little , to me, is art at all. Its a kind of stage on the way to being art. But the act of pro-jection has not been made. Joyce remains entangled in it, in a bad sense, except at rare moments. There is, to me, the great distinction between him and Proust. (Take Swann with Odette[1] for instance). Or take Richard[2] in Elinor Colhouse . . .

Jones is waiting for this letter. I want it to catch the post. I have only begun to say what I want to say. About Paris. I cannot go just at pre-sent. Im still in bed & likely to remain there for a time. Congestion is a slow affair, especially at this height. The doctor, like all doctors, is a complete fool. I shall try & put off Paris until May. To meet there in May & to stay there (J. & I will be there four months) would be nothing short of wonderful. I hardly dare think of it. Now I know Manoukhine is there I can bear to wait. I think I shall try. Hotels & journeys are a dread prospect in any weather – in this, even more.

Forgive this haste and inadequacy. Read much more in my letter than is there, dear Sydney. With my warm love to you both

Katherine.

MS BL, *LKM,* 174–5.

1 Odette de Crécy, the beautiful but unintelligent courtesan who marries the wealthy banker Swann in Marcel Proust's *À la recherche du temps perdu.*
2 The husband of Elinor, in Schiff's recent novel.

APPENDIX

Dr Bouchage's medical report on KM at the end of April 1921.[1]

Mrs Middleton Murry came to Menton in Spt 1920 and stayed on here till the end of April 1921.

When I first saw her, Oct 15 1920, she had been suffering from lung troubles for three years, and was at the time complaining of bad attacks of coughing, especially morning and evening (in spite of codeine taken 6 times a day for the last two years), of much stiffness and pain in the right hip joint and muscles round and also in the spine, of palpitations in the heart on the least provocation. (Digitalis mixture taken for 6 months previously).

Previous history. Age 32. Excellent health till 20. Married for the 1st time at 18. Had 2 years after an attack of peritonitis (very likely from gonococcal origin) white discharge for 4 months. Left salpinx was removed then. Since that time she has never been quite well. A short time after began to suffer from rheumatism, in various muscles of the body, hip joints and small joints in feet, and has been more or less troubled with it since.

During the war, exertions and worries. In autumn 1917 actual disease began and since then has been more or less an invalid with lungs and heart and rheumatic troubles. No T.B. in family history.

In 1919 Dr Sorapure in London found "practically the whole left lung and the right apex full of large and moist rales". That condition got much better and in Sep 1920 Dr Sorapure could describe the lesion as follows. "The only lesion at present showing any sign of activity in the lung is an area of about 10 cm in diameter between the 4th and 8th ribs in the middle line of the left chest posteriorly".

Since I have attended Mrs Murry I have never found the lesion so limited. There have been variations in the condition. At first I found the area described in the left lung posteriorly with moist rales and also rales of a finer character in left apex front and back and a few dry noises at right apex posteriorly. In November this condition was improving very satisfactorily. In December condition gradually got worse after mental exertion and worries, and the heart, which had only been showing signs of tachycardia, began to be very troublesome, and a reduplication of 2nd sound has since been, more or less, heard; a gland on the right side of the neck grew at this time, and had to be punctured twice lately, in March. The cough has been very distressing at times. Expectoration has increased in quantity, and examination (microscopical: guinea-pig inoculation) has shown tubercular bacillus.

In London in 1920 3 pathologists agreed in saying that the bacillus found was not tubercular, since it took acid stain without retaining it, and since there was no giant cell formation in the lesions produced in guinea-pigs after inoculation.

The rheumatic condition has been very much improved during the last 6 months by injections of Iodeol; but lately some stiffness has been felt again.

Methodical sun-cure has been very beneficial at the beginning of the winter; later the patient was not well enough to continue it.

In April 6 injections of Angiolymphe du Dr Rous did not improve the condition much, except that gland in neck became smaller and harder and after a few days signs in left lung seemed to be not so numerous as before. But a reaction was troublesome (nausea,

---

[1] This copy of the report survives among the Ruth E. Mantz Papers in the Humanities Research Centre, University of Texas at Austin. Presumably it was translated from the original by either Mantz or Murry while they were preparing *The Life of Katherine Mansfield* (1933).

loss of appetite, a few streaks of blood in expectoration for a few days after) and no more of the treatment was given.

TC Texas.

INDEX OF RECIPIENTS

GENERAL INDEX

Notes: 1, page numbers with n refer to notes, which are generally biographical or explanatory; 2, the following abbreviations are used: DB-Dorothy Brett; JMM-John Middleton Murry; KM-Katherine Mansfield; LM-Ida Baker; RM-Richard Murry